Why Do You Need This  W9-ATN-410

If you're wondering why you should buy this new edition of *A Sequence for Academic Writing,* here are 9 good reasons!

❶ The Fourth Edition represents a major revision with freshened examples that clarify and expand instruction, and generally make the text more adaptable and accessible to help students create source-based writing in a variety of academic settings.

❷ Chapter 8 (Practicing Academic Writing) has a new focus, "The Changing Landscape of Work in the Twenty-first Century," that explores developments that economists, educators, policy analysts, and investigative reporters believe will affect the workplace students will enter in the coming decades.

❸ Chapter 1 (Summary) has a section on summarizing figures and tables that has been entirely rewritten to focus on the world's dwindling supply of oil. Chapter 1 also features a new model summary on the future of work.

❹ Chapter 2 (Critique) includes a new assignment for critique based on an article by a student columnist for NYU's *Washington Square News*, titled "The Common Application Fallacy."

❺ Chapter 3 (Explanatory Synthesis) includes a model paper focusing on the advantage of hydrogen fuel cell vehicles, with updated sources.

❻ Chapter 4 (Argument Synthesis) features a new model synthesis on balancing the claims of student privacy and public safety in the wake of the Virginia Tech shootings. The chapter also includes a new section on "The Limits of Argument," which discusses the kinds of topics that are not well suited for argument syntheses in first-year writing courses.

❼ Chapter 5 (Analysis) includes a new section, "When Your Perspective Guides the Analysis," highlighting an alternative, more personal approach to analysis than the type based on the use of formal principles and definitions.

❽ Chapter 6 (Writing as a Process) includes new examples of introductions and conclusions.

❾ Chapter 7 (Locating, Mining, and Citing Sources) now includes new MLA formats (2008) for the Works Cited listing, with guidance on citing online databases, podcasts, blogs, and wikis. The chapter also includes APA's updated (2007) guidelines for citing electronic sources.

PEARSON

A Sequence for Academic Writing

FOURTH EDITION

Laurence Behrens
University of California, Santa Barbara

Leonard J. Rosen
Bentley University

Longman

New York   San Francisco   Boston
London   Toronto   Sydney   Tokyo   Singapore   Madrid
Mexico City   Munich   Paris   Cape Town   Hong Kong   Montreal

Executive Editor: Suzanne Phelps Chambers
Editorial Assistant: Erica Schweitzer
Senior Supplements Editor: Donna Campion
Senior Marketing Manager: Sandra McGuire
Production Manager: Eric Jorgensen
Project Coordination and Text Design: Elm Street Publishing Services
Electronic Page Makeup: Integra Software Services, Pvt. Ltd.
Cover Design Manager: Wendy Ann Fredericks
Cover Designer: Nancy Sacks
Cover Photo: © Catherine Hazard/SuperStock
Visual Research Manager: Rona Tuccillo
Senior Manufacturing Buyer: Alfred C. Dorsey
Printer and Binder: RR Donnelley & Sons Company/Crawfordsville
Cover Printer: Phoenix Color Corporation

For permission to use copyrighted material, grateful acknowledgment is made to
the copyright holders on pp. 344–347, which are hereby made part of this
copyright page.

Library of Congress Cataloging-in-Publication Data
Behrens, Laurence.
  A sequence for academic writing/Laurence Behrens.—4th ed.
    p. cm.
  Includes bibliographical references and indexes.
  ISBN 978-0-205-67437-4
    1. English language—Rhetoric. 2. Academic writing.   I. Rosen, Leonard J.
  II. Title.
  PE1408.B46926 2010
  808'.042—dc22

                                                                    2008036900

1 2 3 4 5 6 7 8 9 10—DOC—12 11 10 09

Longman
is an imprint of

www.pearsonhighered.com   ISBN-13: 978-0-205-67437-4
                           ISBN-10:   0-205-67437-2

DETAILED CONTENTS

Chapter 2—Critical Reading and Critique

Chapter 7—Locating, Mining, and Citing Sources 261

PREFACE FOR INSTRUCTORS

A Sequence for Academic Writing evolved out of another of our texts, *Writing and Reading Across the Curriculum (WRAC).* Through ten editions over the last 28 years, *WRAC* has helped more than a million students prepare for the writing to be done well beyond the freshman composition course. *WRAC* features a rhetoric in which students are introduced to the core skills of summary, critique, synthesis, and analysis, and a reader that presents readings in the disciplines to which students can apply the skills learned in the earlier chapters. Because the skills of summary, critique, synthesis, and analysis are so central to academic thinking and writing, many instructors—both those teaching writing across the curriculum and those using other approaches to composition instruction—have found *WRAC* a highly useful introduction to college-level writing. We therefore adapted the rhetoric portion of *WRAC*, creating a separate book that instructors can use, apart from any additional reading content they choose to incorporate in their writing courses. *A Sequence for Academic Writing* is both an adaptation of *WRAC* and an expansion: It includes chapters, sections, and additional writing assignments not found in the parent text.

We proceed through a sequence from Summary, Paraphrase, and Quotation to Critical Reading and Critique, to Explanatory Synthesis and Argument Synthesis to Analysis. Students will find in Chapter 6 a discussion of the writing process that is reinforced throughout the text. Locating, Mining, and Citing Sources introduces students to the tools and techniques they will need to apply skills learned earlier to sources they gather themselves when conducting research. The book ends with a controlled research assignment, in Practicing Academic Writing (see A Note on the Fourth Edition). We make a special effort in all chapters to address the issue of plagiarism: We offer techniques for steering well clear of the problem, at the same time encouraging students to live up to the highest ethical standards.

Key features in *A Sequence for Academic Writing* include *boxes*, which sum up important concepts in each chapter; brief writing *exercises*, which prompt individual and group activities; *writing assignments*, which encourage students to practice the skills they learn in each chapter; and *model papers*, which provide example responses to writing assignments discussed in the text. An Instructor's Manual provides further resources for teaching with this text.

While we are keenly aware of the overlapping nature of the skills on which we focus, and while we could endlessly debate an appropriate order in which to cover these skills, a book is necessarily linear. We have chosen the sequence that makes the most sense to us, though individual instructors may choose to cover these skills in their own sequence. Teachers should feel free to use these chapters in whatever order they decide is most useful to their individual aims and philosophies. Understanding the material in a later chapter does not, in most cases, depend on students' having read material in the earlier chapters.

A NOTE ON THE FOURTH EDITION

The fourth edition of *A Sequence for Academic Writing* represents a significant revision of the previous edition. The model student summary and model argument synthesis in Chapters 1 and 4, respectively, have been replaced with papers on new subjects. The new example summary is based on "Will Your Job Be Exported?"—an article about the surge in the "offshoring" of American jobs by Princeton economist and former presidential advisor Alan Blinder. This article anticipates the new topic for Chapter 8 (Practicing Academic Writing). The new model argument synthesis in Chapter 4 focuses on the debate between student privacy rights and campus safety that was generated by the Virginia Tech shootings in April 2007. The synthesis builds on several articles and editorials on the subject, the report of the panel that investigated the shootings, and applicable federal law on student privacy.

Chapter 8 (Practicing Academic Writing) has a new focus, "The Changing Landscape of Work in the Twenty-first Century," that explores developments that economists, educators, policy analysts, and investigative reporters believe will affect the workplace that students will enter in the coming decades. In this chapter, students will practice the skills learned in Part I of the text first by reading ten selections on a tightly focused topic and then by working through carefully sequenced assignments. Students will write summaries, explanations, and a critique in preparation for writing an ambitious source-based argument.

Beyond the changes just noted, almost all the chapters in the current edition have been revised, some significantly. The "Summarizing Figures and Tables" section of Chapter 1 (Summary, Paraphrase, and Quotation) has been entirely rewritten and focuses now on the world's dwindling supply of oil. Later in the chapter, we provide several new examples of summary, quotation, and paraphrase. The model critique in Chapter 2 (Critical Reading and Critique) has been revised to show how an evaluation can be sensitive to rhetorical concerns. The article that students are to critique in the chapter's main exercise has been replaced with "The Common App[lication] Fallacy," by a student columnist for NYU's *Washington Square News*. The model paper in Chapter 3 (Explanatory Synthesis), focusing on the advantages of the hydrogen fuel-cell vehicle, has been updated with more recent sources. Chapter 4 (Argument Synthesis) features a new section, "The Limits of Argument," dealing with the kinds of topics that are not well suited for argument syntheses in freshman writing courses. Chapter 5 (Analysis) includes a new section, "When *Your* Perspective Guides the Analysis," highlighting an alternative, more personal approach to analysis than the type that is based on the use of formal principles and definitions and that continues to underlie the greater part of this chapter. Chapter 6 (Writing as a Process) includes new examples of introductions and conclusions. Chapter 7 (Locating, Mining, and Citing Sources) now includes the 2009 Modern Language Association updated formats for citing online databases, podcasts, blogs, and wikis—with an expanded discussion of (and warning about using) wikis. As well, Chapter 7 includes the American Psychological Association's updated

(June 2007) format for citing electronic sources. Instruction on proper citation styles reflects the latest editions of the MLA and APA manuals.

Thus the fourth edition of *A Sequence for Academic Writing* represents a major revision that freshens examples, clarifies and expands instruction, and generally makes more adaptable and accessible a text that, we are told, has helped introduce students to source-based writing in a variety of academic settings. As ever, we rely on the criticism of colleagues to improve our work, and we invite you to contact the publisher with suggested revisions.

SUPPLEMENTS

Instructor's Manual

The *Instructor's Manual* provides sample syllabi and assignment ideas for traditional and Web-based courses. Each IM chapter opens with summaries of each chapter in the student text, followed by bulleted highlights that outline each chapter. Writing/Critical Thinking Activities offer additional exercises that make use of Internet sources, and Revision Activities are also provided for Chapters 1–5. Each IM chapter provides extensive lists of Web source material for both students and instructors.

MyCompLab

 *MyCompLab* provides multimedia resources for students and teachers on one easy-to-use site. In this site, students will find guided assistance through each step of the writing process; interactive tutorials and videos that illustrate key concepts; over 30 model documents from across the curriculum; *Exchange,* Longman's online peer-review program; the "Avoiding Plagiarism" tutorial; diagnostic grammar tests and thousands of practice questions; and *Research Navigator*™, a database with thousands of magazines and academic journals, the subject-search archive of *The New York Times,* "Link Library," library guides, and more. Learn more about MyCompLab at **http://www.mycomplab.com**.

ACKNOWLEDGMENTS

We would like to thank the following reviewers for their help in the preparation of this text: Elizabeth Baines, Truckee Meadows Community College; Patricia Baldwin, Pitt Community College; Sherri Brouillette, Millersville University; Bryce Campbell, Victor Valley College; Margaret L. Clark, Florida Community College at Jacksonville; Diane Z. De Bella, University of Colorado; Grey Glau, Arizona State University; Pat Hartman, Cleveland State University; Wendy Hayden, University of Maryland; Randall McClure, Minnesota State University–Mankato; Jamil Mustafa, Lewis University; Deborah Richey, Owens Community College. We would also like to thank reviewers of previous editions of this text: Cora Agatucci, Central Oregon Community College; Bruce Closser,

Andrews University; Clinton R. Gardner, Salt Lake Community College; Margaret Graham, Iowa State University; Susanmarie Harrington, Indiana University and Purdue University Indianapolis; Georgina Hill, Western Michigan University; Jane M. Kinney, Valdosta State University; Susan E. Knutson, University of Minnesota–Twin Cities; Cathy Leaker, North Carolina State University; Kate Miller, Central Michigan University; Lyle W. Morgan, Pittsburg State University; Joan Perkins, University of Hawaii; Catherine Quick, Stephen F. Austin State University; Emily Rogers, University of Illinois–Urbana Champaign; William Scott Simkins, University of Southern Mississippi; Doug Swartz, Indiana University Northwest; Marcy Taylor, Central Michigan University; Zach Waggoner, Western Illinois University; Heidemarie Z. Weidner, Tennessee Technological University; Betty R. Youngkin, The University of Dayton; and Terry Meyers Zawacki, George Mason University. And we are grateful to UCSB librarian Lucia Snowhill for helping us update the reference sources in Chapter 7.

Thanks to Lynn Huddon, the editor who first suggested that we undertake *A Sequence for Academic Writing*, and who has now moved on to other projects. Suzanne Phelps Chambers, our current editor, has been a wellspring of energy and good ideas, and we thank her for ongoing contributions to the book. Thanks also to editorial assistant Erica Schweitzer for her many kindnesses during manuscript preparation and to Martha Beyerlein, whose meticulous coordination of the production process saved our sanity. We are also grateful to our copyeditor, Jo Ann Learman, our proofreader, Vernon Nahrgang, and to Eric Jorgensen, production manager, for careful and attentive handling of the production process. Each has contributed mightily to this project, and we extend our warmest appreciation.

LAURENCE BEHRENS
LEONARD J. ROSEN

NOTE TO THE STUDENT

In your sociology class, you are assigned to write a paper on the role of peer groups in influencing attitudes toward smoking. Your professor expects you to read some of the literature on the subject as well as to conduct interviews with members of such groups. For an environmental studies course, you must write a paper on how one or more industrial plants in a particular area have been affecting the local ecosystem. In your film studies class, you must select a contemporary filmmaker—you are trying to decide between Oliver Stone and Spike Lee—and examine how at least three of his films demonstrate a distinctive point of view.

These writing assignments are typical of those you will undertake during your college years. In fact, such assignments are also common for those in professional life: for instance, scientists writing environmental impact statements, social scientists writing accounts of their research for professional journals, and film critics showing how the latest effort by a filmmaker fits into the general body of his or her work.

Core Skills

To succeed in such assignments, you will need to develop and hone particular skills in critical reading, thinking, and writing. You must develop—not necessarily in this order—the ability to

- read and accurately *summarize* a selection of material on your subject;
- determine the quality and relevance of your sources through a process of *critical reading* and assessment;
- *synthesize* different sources by discovering the relationships among them and showing how these relationships produce insights about the subject under discussion;
- *analyze* objects or phenomena by applying particular perspectives and theories;
- develop effective techniques for (1) discovering and using pertinent, authoritative information and ideas and (2) presenting the results of your work in generally accepted disciplinary formats.

A Sequence for Academic Writing will help you to meet these goals. In conversations with faculty across the curriculum, time and again we have been struck by a shared desire to see students thinking and writing in subject-appropriate ways. Psychology, biology, and engineering teachers want you to think, talk, and write like psychologists, biologists, and engineers. We set out, therefore, to learn the strategies writers use to enter conversations in their respective disciplines. We discovered that four readily learned strategies—summary, critique, synthesis, and analysis—provided the basis for the great majority of writing in freshman- through senior-level courses, and in courses across disciplines. We therefore made these skills the centerpiece of instruction for this book.

Applications Beyond College

While summary, critique, synthesis, and analysis are primary critical thinking and writing skills practiced throughout the university, these skills are also crucial to the work you will do in your life outside the university. In the professional world, people write letters, memos, and reports in which they must summarize procedures, activities, and the like. Critical reading and critique are important skills for writing legal briefs, business plans, and policy briefs. In addition, these same types of documents—common in the legal, business, and political worlds, respectively—involve synthesis. A business plan, for example, will often include a synthesis of ideas and proposals in one coherent plan. Finally, the ability to analyze complex data, processes, or ideas, to apply theories or perspectives to particular subjects, and then to effectively convey the results of analysis in writing is integral to writing in medicine, law, politics, business—in short, just about any career you might pursue.

Part One ■ *Structures*

Summary, Paraphrase, and Quotation

1

◼ WHAT IS A SUMMARY?

The best way to demonstrate that you understand the information and the ideas in any piece of writing is to compose an accurate and clearly written summary of that piece. By a *summary* we mean a *brief restatement, in your own words, of the content of a passage* (a group of paragraphs, a chapter, an article, a book). This restatement should focus on the *central idea* of the passage. The briefest of summaries (one or two sentences) will do no more than this. A longer, more complete summary will indicate, in condensed form, the main points in the passage that support or explain the central idea. It will reflect the order in which these points are presented and the emphasis given to them. It may even include some important examples from the passage. But it will not include minor details. It will not repeat points simply for the purpose of emphasis. And it will not contain any of your own opinions or conclusions. A good summary, therefore, has three central qualities: *brevity, completeness,* and *objectivity.*

◼ CAN A SUMMARY BE OBJECTIVE?

Objectivity could be difficult to achieve in a summary. By definition, writing a summary requires you to select some aspects of the original and leave out others. Since deciding what to select and what to leave out calls for your personal judgment, your summary really is a work of interpretation. And, certainly, your interpretation of a passage may differ from another person's.

One factor affecting the nature and quality of your interpretation is your *prior knowledge* of the subject. For example, if you're attempting to summarize an anthropological article and you're a novice in that field, then your summary of the article will likely differ from that of your professor, who has spent twenty years studying this particular area and whose judgment about what is more or less significant is undoubtedly more reliable than your own. By the same token, your personal or professional *frame of reference* may also affect your interpretation. A union representative and a management representative attempting to summarize the latest management offer would probably come up with two very different accounts. Still, we believe that in most cases it's possible to produce a reasonably objective summary of a passage if you make a conscious, good-faith effort to be unbiased and to prevent your own feelings on the subject from coloring your account of the author's text.

■ USING THE SUMMARY

In some quarters, the summary has a bad reputation—and with reason. Summaries are often provided by writers as substitutes for analyses. As students, many of us have summarized books that we were supposed to *review critically.* All the same, the summary does have a place in respectable college work. First, writing a summary is an excellent way to understand what you read. This in itself is an important goal of academic study. If you don't understand your source material, chances are you won't be able to refer to it usefully in a paper. Summaries help you understand what you read because they force you to put the text into your own words. Practice with writing summaries also develops your general writing habits, because a good summary, like any other piece of good writing, is clear, coherent, and accurate.

Where Do We Find Written Summaries?

Here are just a few of the types of writing that involve summary:

ACADEMIC WRITING

- **Critique papers** summarize material in order to critique it.
- **Synthesis papers** summarize to show relationships between sources.
- **Analysis papers** summarize theoretical perspectives before applying them.
- **Research papers:** note-taking and reporting research require summary.
- **Literature reviews:** overviews of work are presented in brief summaries.
- **Argument papers** summarize evidence and opposing arguments.
- **Essay exams** demonstrate understanding of course materials through summary.

WORKPLACE WRITING

- **Policy briefs** condense complex public policy.
- **Business plans** summarize costs, relevant environmental impacts, and other important matters.
- **Memos, letters, and reports** summarize procedures, meetings, product assessments, expenditures, and more.
- **Medical charts** record patient data in summarized form.
- **Legal briefs** summarize relevant facts and arguments of cases.

Second, summaries are useful to your readers. Let's say you're writing a paper about the McCarthy era in the United States, and in part of that paper you want to discuss Arthur Miller's *The Crucible* as a dramatic treatment of the subject. A summary of the plot would be helpful to a reader who hasn't seen or read—or who doesn't remember—the play. Or perhaps you're writing a paper about the politics of recent American military interventions. If your reader isn't likely to be familiar with American actions in Kosovo and Afghanistan, it would be a good idea to summarize these events at some early point in the paper. In many cases (an exam, for instance), you can use a summary to demonstrate your knowledge of what your professor already knows; when writing a paper, you can use a summary to inform your professor about some relatively unfamiliar source.

Third, summaries are required frequently in college-level writing. For example, on a psychology midterm, you may be asked to explain Carl Jung's theory of the collective unconscious and to show how it differs from Sigmund Freud's theory of the personal unconscious. You may have read about Jung's theory in your textbook or in a supplementary article, or your instructor may have outlined it in her lecture. You can best demonstrate your understanding of it by summarizing it. Then you'll proceed to contrast it with Freud's theory—which, of course, you must also summarize.

■ THE READING PROCESS

It may seem to you that being able to tell (or retell) in summary form exactly what a passage says is a skill that ought to be taken for granted in anyone who can read at high school level. Unfortunately, this is not so: For all kinds of reasons, people don't always read carefully. In fact, it's probably safe to say that usually they don't. Either they read so inattentively that they skip over words, phrases, or even whole sentences, or, if they do see the words in front of them, they see them without registering their significance.

When a reader fails to pick up the meaning and implications of a sentence or two, usually there's no real harm done. (An exception: You could lose credit on an exam or paper because you failed to read or to realize the significance of a crucial direction by your instructor.) But over longer stretches—the paragraph, the section, the article, or the chapter—inattentive or haphazard reading interferes with your goals as a reader: to perceive the shape of the argument, to grasp the central idea, to determine the main points that compose it, to relate the parts of the whole, and to note key examples. This kind of reading takes a lot more energy and determination than casual reading. But in the long run it's an energy-saving method because it enables you to retain the content of the material and to draw upon that content in your own responses. In other words, it allows you to develop an accurate and coherent written discussion that goes beyond summary.

Critical Reading for Summary

- *Examine the context.* Note the credentials, occupation, and publications of the author. Identify the source in which the piece originally appeared. This information helps illuminate the author's perspective on the topic he or she is addressing.

- *Note the title and subtitle.* Some titles are straightforward; the meanings of others become clearer as you read. In either case, titles typically identify the topic being addressed and often reveal the author's attitude toward that topic.

- *Identify the main point.* Whether a piece of writing contains a thesis statement in the first few paragraphs or builds its main point without stating it up front, look at the entire piece to arrive at an understanding of the overall point being made.

- *Identify the subordinate points.* Notice the smaller subpoints that make up the main point, and make sure you understand how they relate to the main point. If a particular subpoint doesn't clearly relate to the main point you've identified, you may need to modify your understanding of the main point.

- *Break the reading into sections.* Notice which paragraphs make up a piece's introduction, body, and conclusion. Break up the body paragraphs into sections that address the writer's various subpoints.

- *Distinguish between points, examples, and counterarguments.* Critical reading requires careful attention to what a writer is *doing* as well as what he or she is *saying.* When a writer quotes someone else, or relays an example of something, ask yourself why this is being done. What point is the example supporting? Is another source being quoted as support for a point or as a counterargument that the writer sets out to address?

- *Watch for transitions within and between paragraphs.* In order to follow the logic of a piece of writing, as well as to distinguish between points, examples, and counterarguments, pay attention to the transitional words and phrases writers use. Transitions function like road signs, preparing the reader for what's next.

- *Read actively and recursively.* Don't treat reading as a passive, linear progression through a text. Instead, read as though you are engaged in a dialogue with the writer: Ask questions of the text as you read, make notes in the margin, underline key ideas in pencil, put question or exclamation marks next to passages that confuse or excite you. Go back to earlier points once you finish a reading, stop during your reading to recap what's come so far, and move back and forth through a text.

■ HOW TO WRITE SUMMARIES

Every article you read will present its own challenge as you work to summarize it. As you'll discover, saying in a few words what has taken someone else a great many can be difficult. But like any other skill, the ability to summarize improves with practice. Here are a few pointers to get you started. They represent possible stages, or steps, in the process of writing a summary. These pointers are not meant to be ironclad rules; rather, they are designed to encourage habits of thinking that will allow you to vary your technique as the situation demands.

Guidelines for Writing Summaries

- *Read the passage carefully.* Determine its structure. Identify the author's purpose in writing. (This will help you distinguish between more important and less important information.) Make a note in the margin when you get confused or when you think something is important; highlight or underline points sparingly, if at all.

- *Reread.* This time divide the passage into sections or stages of thought. The author's use of paragraphing will often be a useful guide. *Label,* on the passage itself, each section or stage of thought. *Underline* key ideas and terms. Write notes in the margin.

- *Write one-sentence summaries,* on a separate sheet of paper, of each stage of thought.

- *Write a thesis—a one- or two-sentence summary of the entire passage.* The thesis should express the central idea of the passage, as you have determined it from the preceding steps. You may find it useful to follow the approach of most newspaper stories—naming the *what, who, why, where, when,* and *how* of the matter. For persuasive passages, summarize in a sentence the author's conclusion. For descriptive passages, indicate the subject of the description and its key feature(s). Note: In some cases, *a suitable thesis statement may already be in the original passage.* If so, you may want to quote it directly in your summary.

- *Write the first draft of your summary* by (1) combining the thesis with your list of one-sentence summaries or (2) combining the thesis with one-sentence summaries *plus* significant details from the passage. In either case, eliminate repetition and less important information. Disregard minor details or generalize them (e.g., Bill Clinton and George W. Bush might be generalized as "recent presidents"). Use as few words as possible to convey the main ideas.

(continues)

> - *Check your summary against the original passage* and make what-
>   ever adjustments are necessary for accuracy and completeness.
> - *Revise your summary,* inserting transitional words and phrases where
>   necessary to ensure coherence. Check for style. *Avoid a series of short,
>   choppy sentences.* Combine sentences for a smooth, logical flow of
>   ideas. Check for grammatical correctness, punctuation, and spelling.

■ DEMONSTRATION: SUMMARY

To demonstrate these points at work, let's go through the process of summarizing a passage of expository material—that is, writing that is meant to inform
and/or persuade. Read the following selection carefully. Try to identify its
parts and understand how they work together to create an overall statement.

WILL YOUR JOB BE EXPORTED?

Alan S. Blinder

*Alan S. Blinder is the Gordon S. Rentschler Memorial Professor of Economics at Princeton
University. He has served as vice chairman of the Federal Reserve Board and was a member
of President Clinton's original Council of Economic Advisers.*

The great conservative political philosopher Edmund Burke, who probably would not
have been a reader of *The American Prospect,* once observed, "You can never plan
the future by the past."* But when it comes to preparing the American workforce for
the jobs of the future, we may be doing just that.

    For about a quarter-century, demand for labor appears to have shifted toward
the college-educated and away from high school graduates and dropouts. This shift,
most economists believe, is the primary (though not the sole) reason for rising
income inequality, and there is no end in sight. Economists refer to this phenomenon
by an antiseptic name: skill-biased technical progress. In plain English, it means that
the labor market has turned ferociously against the low skilled and the uneducated.

    In a progressive society, such a worrisome social phenomenon might elicit
some strong policy responses, such as more compensatory education, stepped-up
efforts at retraining, reinforcement (rather than shredding) of the social safety net,
and so on. You don't fight the market's valuation of skills; you try to mitigate its more
deleterious effects. We did a bit of this in the United States in the 1990s, by raising the
minimum wage and expanding the Earned Income Tax Credit.† Combined with tight

---

*Edmund Burke (1729–1797) was a conservative British statesman, philosopher, and author.
The American Prospect, in which "Will Your Job Be Exported?" first appeared in the November
2006 issue, describes itself as "an authoritative magazine of liberal ideas."
†The Earned Income Tax Credit, an anti-poverty measure enacted by Congress in 1975 and
revised in the 1980s and 1990s, provides a credit against federal income taxes for any filer who
claims a dependent child.

labor markets, these measures improved things for the average worker. But in this decade, little or no mitigation has been attempted. Social Darwinism has come roaring back.*

With one big exception: We have expended considerable efforts to keep more young people in school longer (e.g., reducing high-school dropouts and sending more kids to college) and to improve the quality of schooling (e.g., via charter schools and No Child Left Behind†). Success in these domains may have been modest, but not for lack of trying. You don't have to remind Americans that education is important; the need for educational reform is etched into the public consciousness. Indeed, many people view education as the silver bullet. On hearing the question "How do we best prepare the American workforce of the future?" many Americans react reflexively with: "Get more kids to study science and math, and send more of them to college."

5   Which brings me to the future. As I argued in a recent article in *Foreign Affairs* magazine, the greatest problem for the next generation of American workers may not be lack of education, but rather "offshoring"—the movement of jobs overseas, especially to countries with much lower wages, such as India and China. Manufacturing jobs have been migrating overseas for decades. But the new wave of offshoring, of *service* jobs, is something different.

Traditionally, we think of service jobs as being largely immune to foreign competition. After all, you can't get your hair cut by a barber or your broken arm set by a doctor in a distant land. But stunning advances in communication technology, plus the emergence of a vast new labor pool in Asia and Eastern Europe, are changing that picture radically, subjecting millions of presumed-safe domestic service jobs to foreign competition. And it is not necessary actually to move jobs to low-wage countries in order to restrain wage increases; the mere threat of offshoring can put a damper on wages.

Service-sector offshoring is a minor phenomenon so far, Lou Dobbs notwithstanding; probably well under 1 percent of U.S. service jobs have been outsourced.** But I believe that service-sector offshoring will eventually exceed manufacturing-sector offshoring by a hefty margin—for three main reasons. The first is simple arithmetic: There are vastly more service jobs than manufacturing jobs in the United States (and in other rich countries). Second, the technological advances that have made service-sector offshoring possible will continue and accelerate, so the range of services that can be moved offshore will increase ineluctably. Third, the number of (e.g., Indian and

---

*Social Darwinism, a largely discredited philosophy dating from the Victorian era and espoused by Herbert Spenser, asserts that Charles Darwin's observations on natural selection apply to human societies. Social Darwinists argue that the poor are less fit to survive than the wealthy and should, through a natural process of adaptation, be allowed to die out.

†Charter schools are public schools with specialized missions to operate outside of regulations that some feel restrict creativity and performance in traditional school settings. The No Child Left Behind Act of 2001 (NCLB) mandates standards-based education for all schools receiving federal funding. Both the charter schools movement and NCLB can be understood as efforts to improve public education.

**Lou Dobbs, a conservative columnist and political commentator for CNN, is well known for his anti-immigration views.

Chinese) workers capable of performing service jobs offshore seems certain to grow, perhaps exponentially.

I do not mean to paint a bleak picture here. Ever since Adam Smith and David Ricardo, economists have explained and extolled the gains in living standards that derive from international trade.* Those arguments are just as valid for trade in services as for trade in goods. There really *are* net gains to the United States from expanding service-sector trade with India, China, and the rest. The offshoring problem is not about the adverse nature of what economists call the economy's eventual equilibrium. Rather, it is about the so-called transition—the ride from here to there. That ride, which could take a generation or more, may be bumpy. And during the long adjustment period, many U.S. wages could face downward pressure.

Thus far, only American manufacturing workers and a few low-end service workers (e.g., call-center operators) have been competing, at least potentially, with millions of people in faraway lands eager to work for what seems a pittance by U.S. standards. But offshoring is no longer limited to low-end service jobs. Computer code can be written overseas and e-mailed back to the United States. So can your tax return and lots of legal work, provided you do not insist on face-to-face contact with the accountant or lawyer. In writing and editing this article, I communicated with the editors and staff of *The American Prospect* only by telephone and e-mail. Why couldn't they (or I, for that matter) have been in India? The possibilities are, if not endless, at least vast.

10   What distinguishes the jobs that cannot be offshored from the ones that can? The crucial distinction is not—and this is the central point of this essay—the required levels of skill and education. These attributes have been critical to labor-market success in the past, but may be less so in the future. Instead, the new critical distinction may be that some services either require personal delivery (e.g., driving a taxi and brain surgery) or are seriously degraded when delivered electronically (e.g., college teaching—at least, I hope!), while other jobs (e.g., call centers and keyboard data entry) are not. Call the first category personal services and the second category impersonal services. With this terminology, I have three main points to make about preparing our workforce for the brave, new world of the future.

First, we need to think about, plan, and redesign our educational system with the crucial distinction between personal service jobs and impersonal service jobs in mind. Many of the impersonal service jobs will migrate offshore, but the personal service jobs will stay here.

Second, the line that divides personal services from impersonal services will move in only one direction over time, as technological progress makes it possible to deliver an ever-increasing array of services electronically.

Third, the novel distinction between personal and impersonal jobs is quite different from, and appears essentially unrelated to, the traditional distinction between jobs that do and do not require high levels of education.

---

*Adam Smith (1723–1790), Scottish author of *An Inquiry into the Nature and Causes of the Wealth of Nations* (1776), established the foundations of modern economics. David Ricardo (1772–1823) was a British businessman, statesman, and economist who founded the classical school of economics and is best known for his studies of monetary policy.

For example, it is easy to offshore working in a call center, typing transcripts, writing computer code, and reading X-rays. The first two require little education; the last two require quite a lot. On the other hand, it is either impossible or very difficult to offshore janitorial services, fast-food restaurant service, college teaching, and open-heart surgery. Again, the first two occupations require little or no education, while the last two require a great deal. There seems to be little or no correlation between educational requirements (the old concern) and how "offshorable" jobs are (the new one).

15   If so, the implications could be startling. A generation from now, civil engineers (who must be physically present) may be in greater demand in the United States than computer engineers (who don't). Similarly, there might be more divorce lawyers (not offshorable) than tax lawyers (partly offshorable). More imaginatively, electricians might earn more than computer programmers. I am not predicting any of this; lots of things influence relative demands and supplies for different types of labor. But it all seems within the realm of the possible as technology continues to enhance the offshorability of even highly skilled occupations. What does seem highly likely is that the relative demand for labor in the United States will shift away from impersonal services and toward personal services, and this shift will look quite different from the familiar story of skill-biased technical progress. So Burke's warning is worth heeding.

I am *not* suggesting that education will become a handicap in the job market of the future. On the contrary, to the extent that education raises productivity and that better-educated workers are more adaptable and/or more creative, a wage premium for higher education should remain. Thus, it still makes sense to send more of America's youth to college. But, over the next generation, the kind of education our young people receive may prove to be more important than how much education they receive. In that sense, a college degree may lose its exalted "silver bullet" status.

Looking back over the past 25 years, "stay in school longer" was excellent advice for success in the labor market. But looking forward over the next 25 years, more subtle occupational advice may be needed. "Prepare yourself for a high-end personal service occupation that is not offshorable" is a more nuanced message than "stay in school." But it may prove to be more useful. And many non-offshorable jobs—such as carpenters, electricians, and plumbers—do not require college education.

The hard question is how to make this more subtle advice concrete and action-able. The children entering America's educational system today, at age 5, will emerge into a very different labor market when they leave it. Given gestation periods of 13 to 17 years and more, educators and policy-makers need to be thinking now about the kinds of training and skills that will best prepare these children for their future working lives. Specifically, it is essential to educate America's youth for the jobs that will actually be available in America 20 to 30 years from now, not for the jobs that will have moved offshore.

Some of the personal service jobs that will remain in the United States will be very high-end (doctors), others will be less glamorous though well paid (plumbers), and some will be "dead end" (janitor). We need to think long and hard about the types of skills that best prepare people to deliver high-end personal services, and how to teach those skills in our elementary and high schools. I am not an education specialist, but it strikes me that, for example, the central thrust of No Child Left Behind is pushing the nation in exactly the wrong direction. I am all for accountability. But the nation's school system will not build the creative, flexible, people-oriented workforce we will need in the future by drilling kids incessantly with rote preparation for standardized tests in the vain hope that they will perform as well as memory chips.

20   Starting in the elementary schools, we need to develop our youngsters' imaginations and people skills as well as their "reading, writing, and 'rithmetic." Remember that kindergarten grade for "works and plays well with others"? It may become increasingly important in a world of personally delivered services. Such training probably needs to be continued and made more sophisticated in the secondary schools, where, for example, good communications skills need to be developed.

More vocational education is probably also in order. After all, nurses, carpenters, and plumbers are already scarce, and we'll likely need more of them in the future. Much vocational training now takes place in community colleges; and they, too, need to adapt their curricula to the job market of the future.

While it is probably still true that we should send more kids to college and increase the number who study science, math, and engineering, we need to focus on training more college students for the high-end jobs that are unlikely to move offshore, and on developing a creative workforce that will keep America incubating and developing new processes, new products, and entirely new industries. Offshoring is, after all, mostly about following and copying. America needs to lead and innovate instead, just as we have in the past.

Educational reform is not the whole story, of course. I suggested at the outset, for example, that we needed to repair our tattered social safety net and turn it into a retraining trampoline that bounces displaced workers back into productive employment. But many low-end personal service jobs cannot be turned into more attractive jobs simply by more training—think about janitors, fast-food workers, and nurse's aides, for example. Running a tight labor market would help such workers, as would a higher minimum wage, an expanded Earned Income Tax Credit, universal health insurance, and the like.

Moving up the skill ladder, employment is concentrated in the public or quasi-public sector in a number of service occupations. Teachers and health-care workers are two prominent examples. In such cases, government policy can influence wages and working conditions directly by upgrading the structure and pay of such jobs—developing more professional early-childhood teachers and fewer casual daycare workers for example—as long as the taxpayer is willing to foot the bill. Similarly, some service jobs such as registered nurses are in short supply mainly because we are not training enough qualified personnel. Here, too, public policy can help by widening the pipeline to allow more workers through. So there are a variety of policy levers that might do some good—if we are willing to pull them.

25   But all that said, education is still the right place to start. Indeed, it is much more than that because the educational system affects the entire population and

because no other institution is nearly as important when it comes to preparing our youth for the world of work. As the first industrial revolution took hold, America radically transformed (and democratized) its educational system to meet the new demands of an industrial society. We may need to do something like that again. There is a great deal at stake here. If we get this one wrong, the next generation will pay dearly. But if we get it (close to) right, the gains from trade promise coming generations a prosperous future.

The somewhat inchoate challenge posed here—preparing more young Americans for personal service jobs—brings to mind one of my favorite Churchill quotations: "You can always count on Americans to do the right thing—after they've tried everything else." It is time to start trying.

Read, Reread, Highlight

Let's consider our recommended pointers for writing a summary.

As you reread the passage, note in the margins of the essay important points, shifts in thought, and questions you may have. Consider the essay's significance as a whole and its stages of thought. What does it say? How is it organized? How does each part of the passage fit into the whole? What do all these points add up to?

Here is how several paragraphs from the middle of Blinder's article might look after you have marked the main ideas by highlighting and by marginal notations.

Offshored service jobs will eclipse lost manufacturing jobs—3 reasons

Service-sector offshoring is a minor phenomenon so far, Lou Dobbs notwithstanding; probably well under 1 percent of U.S. service jobs have been outsourced. But I believe that service-sector offshoring will eventually exceed manufacturing-sector offshoring by a hefty margin—for three main reasons. The first is simple arithmetic: There are vastly more service jobs than manufacturing jobs in the United States (and in other rich countries). Second, the technological advances that have made service-sector offshoring possible will continue and accelerate, so the range of services that can be moved offshore will increase ineluctably. Third, the number of (e.g., Indian and Chinese) workers capable of performing service jobs off-shore seems certain to grow, perhaps exponentially.

Long-term economy will be ok. Short-to-middle term will be "bumpy"

I do not mean to paint a bleak picture here. Ever since Adam Smith and David Ricardo, economists have explained and extolled the gains in living standards that derive from international trade. Those arguments are just as valid for trade in services as for trade in goods. There really *are* net gains to the United States from expanding service-sector trade with India, China, and the rest. The offshoring problem is not about the adverse nature of what economists call the economy's eventual equilibrium. Rather, it is about the so-called transition—the ride from here to there. That ride, which could take a generation or more, may be bumpy. And during the long adjustment period, many U.S. wages could face downward pressure.

Thus far, only American manufacturing workers and a few low-end service workers (e.g., call-center operators) have been competing, at least potentially, with millions of people in faraway lands eager to work for what seems a pittance by U.S. standards. But offshoring is no longer limited to low-end service jobs. Computer code can be written overseas and e-mailed back to the United States. So can your tax return and lots of legal work, provided you do not insist on face-to-face contact with the accountant or lawyer. In writing and editing this article, I communicated with the editors and staff of *The American Prospect* only by telephone and e-mail. Why couldn't they (or I, for that matter) have been in India? The possibilities are, if not endless, at least vast.

What distinguishes the jobs that cannot be offshored from the ones that can? The crucial distinction is not—and this is the central point of this essay—the required levels of skill and education. These attributes have been critical to labor-market success in the past, but may be less so in the future. Instead, the new critical distinction may be that some services either require personal delivery (e.g., driving a taxi and brain surgery) or are seriously degraded when delivered electronically (e.g., college teaching—at least, I hope!), while other jobs (e.g., call centers and keyboard data entry) are not. Call the first category personal services and the second category impersonal services. With this terminology, I have three main points to make about preparing our workforce for the brave, new world of the future.

First, we need to think about, plan, and redesign our educational system with the crucial distinction between personal service jobs and impersonal service jobs in mind. Many of the impersonal service jobs will migrate offshore, but the personal service jobs will stay here.

Second, the line that divides personal services from impersonal services will move in only one direction over time, as technological progress makes it possible to deliver an ever-increasing array of services electronically.

Third, the novel distinction between personal and impersonal jobs is quite different from, and appears essentially unrelated to, the traditional distinction between jobs that do and do not require high levels of education.

Margin annotations:
High-end jobs to be lost

B's main point: Key distinction: Personal service jobs stay; impersonal jobs go

3 points re: prep of future workforce

Movement: impersonal → personal

Level of ed. not related to future job security

Divide into Stages of Thought

When a selection doesn't contain sections with thematic headings, as is the case with "Will Your Job Be Exported?" how do you determine where one stage of thought ends and the next one begins? Assuming that what you have read is coherent and unified, this should not be difficult. (When a selection is unified, all of its parts pertain to the main subject; when a selection is coherent, the parts follow one another in logical order.) Look particularly for transitional sentences at the beginning of paragraphs. Such sentences generally work in one or both of two ways: (1) they summarize what has come before; (2) they set the stage for what is to follow.

Look at the sentences that open paragraphs 5 and 10: "Which brings me to the future" and "What distinguishes the jobs that cannot be offshored from the ones that can?" In both cases Blinder makes a clear announcement. Grammatically speaking, "Which brings me to the future" is a fragment, not a sentence. Experienced writers will use fragments on occasion to good effect, as in this case. The fragment clearly has the sense of a complete thought: the pronoun "which" refers readers to the content of the preceding paragraphs, asking readers to summarize that content and then, with the predicate "brings me to the future," to move forward into the next part of the article. Similarly, the question "What distinguishes the jobs that cannot be offshored from the ones that can?" implicitly asks readers to recall an important distinction just made (the definitions of offshorable and non-offshorable jobs) and then clearly moves readers forward to new, related content. As you can see, the openings of paragraphs 5 and 10 announce new sections in the article.

Each section of an article generally takes several paragraphs to develop. Between paragraphs, and almost certainly between sections of an article, you will usually find transitions that help you understand what you have just read and what you are about to read. For articles that have no subheadings, try writing your own section headings in the margins as you take notes. Blinder's article can be divided into five sections.

> **Section 1:** *Recent past: education of workers important*—For twenty-five years, the labor market has rewarded workers with higher levels of education (paragraphs 1–4).
>
> **Section 2:** *Future: ed level won't always matter—workers in service sector will lose jobs offshore*—Once thought immune to outsourcing, even highly trained service workers will lose jobs to overseas competition (paragraphs 5–9).
>
> **Section 3:** *Which service jobs at highest risk?*—Personal service workers are safe; impersonal service workers, both highly educated and not, will see jobs offshored (paragraphs 10–15).
>
> **Section 4:** *Educating the future workforce*—Emphasizing the kind, not amount, of education will help to prepare workers for jobs of the future (paragraphs 16–22).
>
> **Section 5:** *Needed policy reforms*—Government can improve conditions for low-end service workers and expand opportunities for higher-end service workers; start with education (paragraphs 23–26).

Write a Brief Summary of Each Stage of Thought

The purpose of this step is to wean you from the language of the original passage, so that you are not tied to it when writing the summary. Here are brief summaries, one for each stage of thought in "Will Your Job Be Exported?"

Section 1: Recent past: education of workers important (paragraphs 1–4).

> For the past twenty-five years, the greater a worker's skill or level of education, the better and more stable the job.

Section 2: Future: ed level won't always matter—workers in service sector will lose jobs offshore (paragraphs 5–9).

> Advances in technology have brought to the service sector the same pressures that forced so many manufacturing jobs offshore to China and India. The rate of offshoring in the service sector will accelerate and "eventually exceed" job losses in manufacturing, says Blinder, and jobs requiring both relatively little education (like call-center staffing) and extensive education (like software development) will be lost to workers overseas.

Section 3: Which service jobs at highest risk? (paragraphs 10–15).

> While "personal services" workers (like barbers and surgeons) will be relatively safe from offshoring because their work requires close physical proximity to customers, "impersonal services" workers (like call-center operators and radiologists), regardless of their skill or education, will be at risk because their work can be completed remotely without loss of quality and then delivered via phone or computer. Blinder believes that "the relative demand for labor in the United States will [probably] shift away from impersonal services and toward personal services."

Section 4: Educating the future workforce (paragraphs 16–22).

> Blinder advises young people to plan for "a high-end personal service occupation that is not offshorable." He also urges educators to prepare the future workforce by anticipating the needs of a personal services economy and redesigning classroom instruction and vocational training accordingly.

Section 5: Needed policy reforms (paragraphs 23–26).

> Blinder urges the government to develop policies that will improve wages and conditions for low-wage personal service workers (like janitors); to encourage more low-wage workers (like daycare providers) to retrain and take on better jobs; and to increase opportunities for professional and vocational training in high-demand areas (like nursing and carpentry).

Write a Thesis: A Brief Summary of the Entire Passage

The thesis is the most general statement of a summary (or any other type of academic writing). It is the statement that announces the paper's subject and the claim that you or—in the case of a summary—another author will be making about that subject. Every paragraph of a paper illuminates the thesis by providing supporting detail or explanation. The relationship of these paragraphs to the thesis is analogous to the relationship of the sentences within a paragraph to the topic sentence. Both the thesis and the topic sentences are general statements (the thesis being the more general) that are followed by systematically arranged details.

To ensure clarity for the reader, *the first sentence of your summary should begin with the author's thesis, regardless of where it appears in the article itself.* An author may locate her thesis at the beginning of her work, in which case the thesis operates as a general principle from which details of the presentation follow. This is called a *deductive* organization: thesis first, supporting details second. Alternatively, an author may locate his thesis at the end of the work, in which case the author begins with specific details and builds toward a more general conclusion, or thesis. This is called an *inductive* organization. And, as you might expect, an author might locate the thesis anywhere between beginning and end, at whatever point it seems best positioned.*

A thesis consists of a subject and an assertion about that subject. How can we go about fashioning an adequate thesis for a summary of Blinder's article? Probably no two versions of Blinder's thesis statement would be worded identically, but it is fair to say that any reasonable thesis will indicate that Blinder's subject is the future loss to offshoring of American jobs in the service sector—that part of the economy that delivers services to consumers, from low end (e.g., janitorial services) to high end (e.g., neuro-surgery). How does Blinder view the situation? How secure will service jobs be if Blinder's distinction between personal and impersonal services is valid? Looking back over our section summaries, we find that Blinder insists on three points: (1) that education and skill matter less than they once did in determining job quality and security; (2) that the distinction between personal and impersonal services will increasingly determine which jobs remain and which are offshored; and (3) that the distinction between personal and impersonal has implications for both the future of education and public policy.

Does Blinder make a statement anywhere in this passage that pulls all this together? Examine paragraph 10 and you will find his thesis—two sentences that answer his question about which jobs will and will not be sent offshore: "The crucial distinction is not—and this is the central point of this essay—the required levels of skill and education. . . . Instead, the new critical distinction may be that some services either require personal delivery (e.g., driving a taxi

---

*Blinder positions his thesis midway through his five-section article. He opens the selection by discussing the role of education in the labor market during the past twenty-five years (Section 1, pars. 1–4). He continues by summarizing an earlier article on the ways in which service jobs are following manufacturing jobs offshore (Section 2, pars. 5–9). He then presents a two-sentence thesis in answer to the question that opens paragraph 10: "What distinguishes the jobs that cannot be offshored from the ones that can?" The remainder of the article either develops this thesis (Section 3, pars. 10–15) or follows its implications for education (Section 4, pars. 16–22) and public policy (Section 5, pars. 23–26).

and brain surgery) or are seriously degraded when delivered electronically (e.g., college teaching—at least, I hope!), while other jobs (e.g., call centers and keyboard data entry) are not."

You may have learned that a thesis statement must be expressed in a single sentence. We would offer a slight rewording of this generally sound advice and say that a thesis statement must be *expressible* in a single sentence. For reasons of emphasis or style, a writer might choose to distribute a thesis across two or more sentences. Certainly, the sense of Blinder's thesis can take the form of a single statement: "The critical distinction is X, not Y." For reasons largely of emphasis, he divides his thesis into two sentences—in fact, separating these sentences with another sentence that explains the first part of the thesis: "These attributes [that is, skill and education] have been critical to labor-market success in the past, but may be less so in the future."

Here is a one-sentence version of Blinder's two-sentence thesis:

> The quality and security of future jobs in America's service sector will be determined by how "offshorable" those jobs are.

Notice that the statement anticipates a summary of the *entire* article: both the discussion leading up to Blinder's thesis and his discussion after. To clarify for our readers the fact that this idea is Blinder's and not ours, we might qualify the thesis as follows:

> In "Will Your Job Be Exported?" economist Alan S. Blinder argues that the quality and security of future jobs in America's service sector will be determined by how "offshorable" those jobs are.

The first sentence of a summary is crucially important, for it orients readers by letting them know what to expect in the coming paragraphs. In the example above, the first sentence refers directly to an article, its author, and the thesis for the upcoming summary. The author and title reference could also be indicated in the summary's title (if this were a free-standing summary), in which case their mention could be dropped from the thesis statement. And lest you become frustrated too quickly with how much effort it takes to come up with this crucial sentence, keep in mind that writing an acceptable thesis for a summary takes time. In this case, it took three drafts, roughly ten minutes, to compose a thesis and another few minutes of fine-tuning after a draft of the entire summary was completed. The thesis needed revision because the first draft was vague; the second draft was improved but too specific on a secondary point; the third draft was more complete but too general on a key point:

> **Draft 1:** We must begin now to train young people for high-quality personal service jobs.
> (Vague. The question of why we should begin training isn't clear, nor is the phrase "high-quality personal service jobs." Define this term or make it more general.)

Draft 2: Alan S. Blinder argues that unlike in the past, the quality and security of future American jobs will not be determined by skill level or education but rather by how "offshorable" those jobs are.

(Better, but the reference to "skill level or education" is secondary to Blinder's main point about offshorable jobs.)

Draft 3: In "Will Your Job Be Exported?" economist Alan S. Blinder argues that the quality and security of future jobs will be determined by how "offshorable" those jobs are.

(Close—but not "all" jobs. Blinder specifies which types of jobs are "offshorable.")

Final Draft: In "Will Your Job Be Exported?" economist Alan S. Blinder argues that the quality and security of future jobs in America's service sector will be determined by how "offshorable" those jobs are.

Write the First Draft of the Summary

Let's consider two possible summaries of Blinder's article: (1) a short summary, combining a thesis with brief section summaries, and (2) a longer summary, combining thesis, brief section summaries, and some carefully chosen details. Again, keep in mind that you are reading final versions; each of the following summaries is the result of at least two full drafts. Highlighting indicates transitions added to smooth the flow of the summary.

Summary 1: Combine Thesis Sentence with Brief Section Summaries

In "Will Your Job Be Exported?" economist Alan S. Blinder argues that the quality and security of future jobs in America's service sector will be determined by how "offshorable" those jobs are. For the past twenty-five years, the greater a worker's skill or level of education, the better and more stable the job. No longer. Advances in technology have brought to the service sector the same pressures that forced so many manufacturing jobs offshore to China and India. The rate of offshoring in the service sector will accelerate, and jobs requiring both relatively little education (like call-center staffing) and extensive education (like software development) will increasingly be lost to workers overseas.

These losses will "eventually exceed" losses in manufacturing, but not all services jobs are equally at risk. While "personal services" workers (like barbers and surgeons) will be relatively safe from offshoring because their work requires close physical proximity to customers, "impersonal services" workers (like call-center operators and radiologists), regardless of their skill or education, will be at risk because their work can be completed remotely without loss of quality and then delivered via phone or computer. "[T]he relative demand for labor in the United States will [probably] shift away from impersonal services and toward personal services."

Blinder recommends three courses of action: He advises young people to plan for "a high-end personal service occupation that is not offshorable." He urges educators to prepare the future workforce by anticipating the needs of a personal services economy and redesigning classroom instruction and vocational training accordingly. Finally, he urges the government to adopt policies that will improve existing personal services jobs by increasing wages for low-wage workers; retraining workers to take on better jobs; and increasing opportunities in high-demand, well-paid areas like nursing and carpentry. Ultimately, Blinder wants America to prepare a new generation to "lead and innovate" in an economy that will continue exporting jobs that require "following and copying."

The Strategy of the Shorter Summary

This short summary consists essentially of a restatement of Blinder's thesis plus the section summaries, modified or expanded a little for stylistic purposes. You'll recall that Blinder locates his thesis midway through the article, in paragraph 10. But note that this model summary *begins* with a restatement of his thesis. Notice also the relative weight given to the section summaries within the model. Blinder's main point, his "critical distinction" between personal and impersonal services jobs, is summarized in paragraph 2 of the model. The other paragraphs combine summaries of relatively less important (that is, supporting or explanatory) material. Paragraph 1 combines summaries of the article's Sections 1 and 2; paragraph 3 combines summaries of Sections 4 and 5.

Between the thesis and the section summaries, notice the insertion of three (highlighted) transitions. The first—a fragment (*No longer*)—bridges the first paragraph's summaries of Sections 1 and 2 of Blinder's article. The second transition links a point Blinder makes in his Section 2 (*Losses in the service sector will "eventually exceed" losses in manufacturing*) with an introduction to the key point he will make in Section 3 (*Not all service jobs are equally at risk*). The third transition (*Blinder recommends three courses of action*) bridges the summary of Blinder's Section 3 to summaries of Sections 4 and 5. Each transition, then, links sections of the whole: each casts the reader back to recall points just made; each casts the reader forward by announcing related points about to be made. Our model ends with a summary of Blinder's motivation for writing, the sense of which is implied by the section summaries but nowhere made explicit.

Summary 2: Combine Thesis Sentence, Section Summaries, and Carefully Chosen Details

The thesis and brief section summaries could also be used as the outline for a more detailed summary. However, most of the details in the passage won't be necessary in a summary. It isn't necessary even in a longer summary of this passage to discuss all of Blinder's examples of jobs that are more or less likely to be sent offshore. It would be appropriate, though, to mention one example of such a job; to review his reasons for thinking "that service-sector offshoring will eventually exceed manufacturing-sector offshoring by a hefty margin"; and to expand on his point that a college education in itself will no longer ensure job security.

None of these details appeared in the first summary; but in a longer summary, a few carefully selected details might be desirable for clarity. How do you decide which details to include? First, working with Blinder's point that one's job type (personal services vs. impersonal services) will matter more for future job quality and security than did the once highly regarded "silver bullet" of education, you may want to cite some of the most persuasive evidence supporting this idea. For example, you could explore why some highly paid physicians, like radiologists, might find themselves competing for jobs with lower-paid physicians overseas. Further, your expanded summary might reflect the relative weight Blinder gives to education (seven paragraphs, the longest of the article's five sections).

You won't always know which details to include and which to exclude. Developing good judgment in comprehending and summarizing texts is largely a matter of reading skill and prior knowledge (see page 3). Consider the analogy of the seasoned mechanic who can pinpoint an engine problem by simply listening to a characteristic sound that to a less-experienced person is just noise. Or consider the chess player who can plot three separate winning strategies from a board position that to a novice looks like a hopeless jumble. In the same way, the more practiced a reader you are, the more knowledgeable you become about the subject and the better able you will be to make critical distinctions between elements of greater and lesser importance. In the meantime, read as carefully as you can and use your own best judgment as to how to present your material.

Here's one version of a completed summary with carefully chosen details. Note that we have highlighted phrases and sentences added to the original, briefer summary.

> In "Will Your Job Be Exported?" economist Alan S. Blinder argues that the quality and security of future jobs in America's service sector will be determined by how "offshorable" those jobs are. For the past twenty-five years, the greater a worker's skill or level of education, the better and more stable the job. Americans have long regarded education as the "silver bullet" that could propel motivated people to better jobs and a better life. No longer. Advances in technology have brought to the service sector the same pressures that forced so many manufacturing jobs offshore to China and India. The rate of offshoring in the service sector will accelerate, says Blinder, and jobs requiring both relatively little education (like call-center staffing) and extensive education (like software development) will increasingly be lost to workers overseas.
>
> Blinder expects that job losses in the service sector will "eventually exceed" losses in manufacturing, for three reasons. Developed countries have

more service jobs than manufacturing jobs; as technology speeds communications, more service jobs will be offshorable; and the numbers of qualified offshore workers is increasing. Service jobs lost to foreign competition may cause a "bumpy" period as the global economy sorts out what work gets done where, by whom. In time, as the global economy finds its "eventual equilibrium," offshoring will benefit the United States; but the consequences in the meantime may be painful for many.

That pain will not be shared equally by all service workers, however. While "personal service" workers (like barbers and surgeons) will be relatively safe from offshoring because their work requires close physical proximity to customers, "impersonal service" workers (like audio transcribers and radiologists), regardless of their skill or education, will be at risk because their work can be completed remotely without loss of quality and then delivered via phone or computer. In the coming decades, says Blinder, "the relative demand for labor in the United States will [probably] shift away from impersonal services and toward personal services." This shift will be influenced by the desire to keep good jobs in the United States while exporting jobs that require "following and copying." Highly trained computer coders will face the same pressures of outsourcing as relatively untrained call-center attendants. A tax attorney whose work requires no face-to-face interaction with clients may see her work migrate overseas while a divorce attorney, who must interact with clients on a case-by-case basis, may face no such competition. Same educations, different outcomes: what determines their fates in a global economy is the nature of their work (that is, personal vs. impersonal), not their level of education.

Based on this analysis, Blinder recommends three courses of action: First, he advises young people to plan for "a high-end personal service occupation that is not offshorable." Many good jobs, like carpentry and plumbing, will not require a college degree. Next, Blinder urges educators to prepare the future workforce by anticipating the needs of a personal services economy and redesigning classroom instruction and vocational training accordingly. These efforts should begin in elementary school and develop imagination and interpersonal skills rather than capacities for rote memorization. Finally, Blinder urges the government to develop policies that will improve wages and conditions for low-wage personal services workers (like janitors); to encourage more low-wage workers (like daycare providers) to retrain and take on better service jobs; and to increase opportunities for professional and vocational training for workers in high-demand services areas (like nurses and electricians). Ultimately, Blinder wants America to prepare a new generation of workers who will "lead and innovate . . . just as we have in the past."

The Strategy of the Longer Summary

Compared to the first, briefer summary, this effort (seventy percent longer than the first) includes Blinder's reasons for suggesting that job losses in the services sector will exceed losses in manufacturing. It emphasizes Blinder's point that job type (personal vs. impersonal services), not a worker's education level, will ensure job security. It includes Blinder's point that offshoring in the service sector is part of a larger global economy seeking "equilibrium." And it offers more on Blinder's thoughts concerning the education of future workers.

The final two of our suggested steps for writing summaries are (1) to check your summary against the original passage, making sure that you have included all the important ideas, and (2) to revise so that the summary reads smoothly and coherently. The structure of this summary generally reflects the structure of the original article—with one significant departure, as noted earlier. Blinder uses a modified inductive approach, stating his thesis midway through the article. The summary, however, states the thesis immediately, then proceeds deductively to develop that thesis.

■ HOW LONG SHOULD A SUMMARY BE?

The length of a summary depends both on the length of the original passage and on the use to which the summary will be put. If you are summarizing an entire article, a good rule of thumb is that your summary should be no longer than one-fourth the length of the original passage. Of course, if you were summarizing an entire chapter or even an entire book, it would have to be much shorter than that. The longer summary above is one-quarter the length of Alan Blinder's original. Although it shouldn't be very much longer, you have seen (pp. 19–20) that it could be quite a bit shorter.

The length as well as the content of the summary also depends on the *purpose* to which it will be put. Let's suppose you decided to use Blinder's piece in a paper that dealt with the loss of manufacturing jobs in the United States and the rise of the service economy. In this case, in an effort to explain the complexities of the service economy to your readers, you might summarize *only* Blinder's core distinction between jobs in personal services and impersonal services, likely mentioning that jobs in the latter category are at risk of offshoring. If, instead, you were writing a paper in which you argued that the forces of globalization will eventually collapse the world's economies into a single, global economy, you would likely give less attention to Blinder's distinction between personal and impersonal services. More to the point might be his observation that highly skilled, highly educated workers in the United States are now finding themselves competing with qualified, lower-wage workers in China and India. Thus, depending on your purpose, you would summarize either selected portions of a source or an entire source. We will see this process more fully demonstrated in the upcoming chapters on syntheses.

Individual and Collaborative Summary Practice

Turn to Chapter 2 and read Damon Beres's opinion piece in the *Washington Square News* (the New York University student newspaper): "The Common App Fallacy" (pp. 84–86). Follow the steps for writing summaries outlined above—read, underline, and divide into stages of thought. Write a one- or two-sentence summary of each stage of thought in Beres's essay. Then gather in groups of three or four classmates and compare your summary sentences. Discuss the differences in your sentences, and come to some consensus about the divisions in Beres's stages of thought—and the ways in which to best sum them up.

As a group, write a one- or two-sentence thesis statement summing up the entire passage. You could go even further, and, using your individual summary sentences—or the versions of them your group revised—put together a brief summary of Beres's essay. Model your work on the brief summary of Blinder's article, on pp. 19–20.

■ SUMMARIZING A NARRATIVE OR PERSONAL ESSAY

Narratives and personal essays differ from expository essays in that they focus on personal experiences and/or views, they aren't structured around an explicitly stated thesis, and their ideas are developed more through the description of events or ideas than through factual evidence or logical explanation. A *narrative* is a story, a retelling of a person's experiences. That person and those experiences may be imaginary, as is the case with fiction, or they may be real, as in biography. In first-person narratives, you can't assume that the narrator represents the author of the piece, unless you know the narrative is a memoir or biography. In a *personal essay,* on the other hand, the narrator is the author. And while the writer of a personal essay may tell stories about his or her experiences, usually writers of such essays discuss thoughts and ideas as much as or more than they tell stories. Personal essays also tend to contain more obvious points than do narratives. Summarizing personal essays or narratives presents certain challenges—challenges that are different from those presented by summarizing expository writing.

You have seen that an author of an *expository* piece (such as Blinder's "Will Your Job Be Exported?") follows assertions with examples and statements of support. Narratives, however, are usually less direct. The author relates a story—event follows event—the point of which may never be stated directly. The charm, the force, and the very point of the narrative lie in the telling; generally, narratives do not exhibit the same logical development of expository writing. They do not, therefore, lend themselves to summary in quite the same way. Narratives do have a logic, but that logic may be emotional, imaginative, or plot-bound. The writer who summarizes a narrative is obliged to give an overview—a synopsis—of the story's events and an account of how those events affect the central character(s). The summary must explain the significance or *meaning* of the events.

Similarly, while personal essays sometimes present points more explicitly than do narratives, their focus and structure link them to narratives. Personal essays often contain inexplicit main points, or multiple points; they tend to *explore* ideas and issues, rather than make explicit *assertions* about those ideas. This exploratory character often means that personal essays exhibit a loose structure, and they often contain stories or narratives within them. While summarizing a personal essay may not involve a synopsis of events, an account of the progression of thoughts and ideas is necessary and, as with a narrative, summaries of personal essays must explain the significance of what goes on in the piece being summarized.

The following is the first chapter of Bruce Chatwin's celebrated *In Patagonia* (1977), his narrative account of a journey to the remotest reaches of South America. Read the chapter, and as you do so consider how you might summarize it. Imagine that you might provide a summary of the opening to Chatwin's *In Patagonia* for a review of the book or for a paper on literature of travel.

DREAMS OF PATAGONIA
*Bruce Chatwin**

Bruce Chatwin (1940–1989) began his career as a specialist in modern art at Sotheby's auction house. He later studied archaeology and served as a journalist for the London Sunday Times Magazine, *which sent him on far-flung assignments, whetting his appetite for travel and honing his literary skills. After three years, he left the magazine to devote himself full time to travel writing, fiction, and essay writing.* In Patagonia *won the 1978 Hawthornden Prize and the 1979 E. M. Forster Award of the American Academy of Arts and Letters. Chatwin is equally well known for his second literary travelogue,* The Songlines *(1987), an account of aboriginal "walkabouts" in Australia.*

In my grandmother's dining-room there was a glass-fronted cabinet and in the cabinet a piece of skin. It was a small piece only, but thick and leathery, with strands of coarse, reddish hair. It was stuck to a card with a rusty pin. On the card was some writing in faded black ink, but I was too young then to read.

"What's that?"

"A piece of brontosaurus."

My mother knew the names of two prehistoric animals, the brontosaurus and the mammoth. She knew it was not a mammoth. Mammoths came from Siberia.

5   The brontosaurus, I learned, was an animal that had drowned in the Flood, being too big for Noah to ship aboard the Ark. I pictured a shaggy lumbering creature with claws and fangs and a malicious green light in its eyes. Sometimes the brontosaurus would crash through the bedroom wall and wake me from my sleep.

---

*Bruce Chatwin, *In Patagonia* (New York: Penguin, 1977) 1–3.

This particular brontosaurus had lived in Patagonia, a country in South America, at the far end of the world. Thousands of years before, it had fallen into a glacier, travelled down a mountain in a prison of blue ice, and arrived in perfect condition at the bottom. Here my grandmother's cousin, Charley Milward the Sailor, found it.

Charley Milward was captain of a merchant ship that sank at the entrance to the Strait of Magellan. He survived the wreck and settled nearby, at Punta Arenas, where he ran a ship-repairing yard. The Charley Milward of my imagination was a god among men—tall, silent and strong, with black mutton-chop whiskers and fierce blue eyes. He wore his sailor's cap at an angle and the tops of his sea-boots turned down.

Directly he saw the brontosaurus poking out of the ice, he knew what to do. He had it jointed, salted, packed in barrels, and shipped to the Natural History Museum in South Kensington. I pictured blood and ice, flesh and salt, gangs of Indian workmen and lines of barrels along a shore—a work of giants and all to no purpose; the brontosaurus went rotten on its voyage through the tropics and arrived in London a putrefied mess; which was why you saw brontosaurus bones in the museum, but no skin.

Fortunately cousin Charley had posted a scrap to my grandmother.

10   My grandmother lived in a red-brick house set behind a screen of yellow-spattered laurels. It had tall chimneys, pointed gables and a garden of blood-coloured roses. Inside it smelled of church.

I do not remember much about my grandmother except her size. I would clamber over her wide bosom or watch, slyly, to see if she'd be able to rise from her chair. Above her hung paintings of Dutch burghers, their fat buttery faces nesting in white ruffs. On the mantelpiece were two Japanese homunculi with red and white ivory eyes that popped out on stalks. I would play with these, or with a German articulated monkey, but always I pestered her: "Please can I have the piece of brontosaurus."

Never in my life have I wanted anything as I wanted that piece of skin. My grandmother said I should have it one day, perhaps. And when she died I said: "Now I *can* have the piece of brontosaurus," but my mother said: "Oh, that thing! I'm afraid we threw it away."

At school they laughed at the story of the brontosaurus. The science master said I'd mixed it up with the Siberian mammoth. He told the class how Russian scientists had dined off deep-frozen mammoth and told me not to tell lies. Besides, he said, brontosauruses were reptiles. They had no hair, but scaly armoured hide. And he showed us an artist's impression of the beast—so different from that of my imagination—grey-green, with a tiny head and gigantic switchback of vertebrae, placidly eating weed in a lake. I was ashamed of my hairy brontosaurus, but I knew it was not a mammoth.

It took some years to sort the story out. Charley Milward's animal was not a brontosaurus, but the mylodon or Giant Sloth. He never found a whole specimen, or even a whole skeleton, but some skin and bones, preserved by the cold, dryness and salt, in a cave on Last Hope Sound in Chilean Patagonia. He sent the collection to England and sold it to the British Museum. This version was less romantic but had the merit of being true.

15   My interest in Patagonia survived the loss of the skin; for the Cold War woke in me a passion for geography. In the late 1940s the Cannibal of the Kremlin shadowed our lives; you could mistake his moustaches for teeth. We listened to lectures about the war he was planning. We watched the civil defence lecturer ring the cities of Europe to show the zones of total and partial destruction. We saw the zones bump one against the other leaving no space in between. The instructor wore khaki shorts. His knees were white and knobbly, and we saw it was hopeless. The war was coming and there was nothing we could do.

Next, we read about the cobalt bomb, which was worse than the hydrogen bomb and could smother the planet in an endless chain reaction.

I knew the colour cobalt from my great-aunt's paintbox. She had lived on Capri at the time of Maxim Gorky and painted Capriot boys naked. Later her art became almost entirely religious. She did lots of St Sebastians, always against a cobalt-blue background, always the same beautiful young man, stuck through and through with arrows and still on his feet.

So I pictured the cobalt bomb as a dense blue cloudbank, spitting tongues of flame at the edges. And I saw myself, out alone on a green headland, scanning the horizon for the advance of the cloud.

And yet we hoped to survive the blast. We started an Emigration Committee and made plans to settle in some far corner of the earth. We pored over atlases. We learned the direction of prevailing winds and the likely patterns of fall-out. The war would come in the Northern Hemisphere, so we looked to the Southern. We ruled out Pacific Islands for islands are traps. We ruled out Australia and New Zealand, and we fixed on Patagonia as the safest place on earth.

20   I pictured a low timber house with a shingled roof, caulked against storms, with blazing log fires inside and the walls lined with the best books, somewhere to live when the rest of the world blew up.

Then Stalin died and we sang hymns of praise in chapel, but I continued to hold Patagonia in reserve.

How to Summarize Personal Essays and Narratives

- Your summary will *not* be a narrative, but rather the synopsis of a narrative or personal account. Your summary will likely be a paragraph at most.
- You will want to name and describe the principal character(s) of the narrative and describe the narrative's main actions or events; or, in the case of the personal essay, identify the narrator and his or her relationship to the discussion.
- You should seek to connect the narrative's character(s) and events: describe the significance of events for (or the impact of events on) the character(s) and/or the narrator.

If you have read the book *In Patagonia,* you may have done so because you were interested in the subject or because someone recommended it to you. Or you may have encountered this passage during the process of research or as an assigned reading for a course on the literature of travel, the culture and geography of South America, or social anthropology. In any case, you could draw on this passage for a number of purposes: to demonstrate the interplay of imagination and memory in motivating travel writers to set off on their journeys; to study narrative technique; to understand how an accomplished writer can, within a few pages—even within a few paragraphs—establish a voice; or to investigate how, in storytelling, facts can sometimes conflict with emotional truth. Having established your purpose, you decide to use the events recounted in this passage to support one or more points you intend to make.

When you summarize a narrative or personal essay, bear in mind the principles that follow, as well as those listed in the box on p. 27.

To summarize events, reread the narrative and make a marginal note each time you see that an action advances the story from one moment to the next. (In Chatwin, the "actions" are two memories, separate but linked to the same remote, fascinating place: Patagonia.) The key here is to recall that narratives take place *in time.* In your summary, be sure to re-create for your reader a sense of time flowing. Name and describe the character(s) as well. (For our purposes, *character* refers to the person, real or fictional, about whom the narrative is written.) The trickiest part of the summary will be describing the connection between events and characters. Earlier (p. 3) we made the point that summarizing any selection involves a degree of interpretation, and this is especially true of summarizing narratives and personal essays. What, in the case of Chatwin, is the significance of his narrative—or of any particular event he recounts? For example, what is the significance of the fact that the brontosaurus that figured so prominently in his childhood imagination turned out to be a remnant of a Giant Sloth? Or of his equally vivid, but mistaken, conviction that the world was going to end in a nuclear catastrophe and that he had better find the remotest region on earth if he hoped to survive? Such narrative moments—in Chatwin's case, recollections—may be used to illustrate a particular point. The events on which you choose to focus while summarizing a narrative will depend entirely on your purpose in using the narrative in the first place.

The general principles of summarizing narratives are similar to those of summarizing expository or persuasive passages. Make sure that you cover the major events, in the order in which they occurred (in line with your overall purpose, of course). Bring in details only to the extent that they support your purpose.

Here is a three-paragraph summary of the first chapter of Bruce Chatwin's *In Patagonia.* (The draft is the result of two prior drafts.)

> In the first chapter of *In Patagonia,* Bruce Chatwin recounts two childhood memories, one based on a misunderstanding and the other on an unrealized fear, that sparked his desire "to hold Patagonia in reserve" and

one day travel there. First, Chatwin recalls a patch of brontosaurus skin (supposedly from Patagonia); later, he recalls the fear of a Soviet-inspired nuclear holocaust and the realization that to survive he would need to travel to a safe, remote location (such as Patagonia).

Growing up, Chatwin coveted a flap of weathered skin his grandmother kept in a glass case and which he understood to be the partial remains of a brontosaurus. To account for the specimen, he constructed an elaborate story centered on an actual but mythologized distant relation, "Charley Milward the Sailor." When Captain Milward's ship sank at the tip of South America and he settled in Patagonia, he discovered, preserved, and shipped back to England a dinosaur that emerged whole from a glacier. The scrap of dinosaur skin found a place of honor in Grandmother's home, alongside "paintings of Dutch burghers . . . and Japanese homunculi." Patagonia later figured into young Chatwin's imagination when, growing up in England at the start of the Cold War, he feared an imminent nuclear holocaust. It was the Stalin era in the Soviet Union, and English school children like Chatwin believed that inhabitants of the Northern Hemisphere would soon be incinerated or die of radiation sickness. Chatwin and others therefore formed "an Emigration Committee [that] made plans to settle in some far corner of the earth" and survive the destruction. That "far corner" was Patagonia.

Both memories were proved unfounded. The brontosaurus skin that prompted in young Chatwin visions of "a shaggy lumbering creature with claws and fangs and a malicious green light in its eyes" turned out to be the remains of a Giant Sloth, part of which (not the whole animal) had been preserved in the dry, cold environment of Patagonia. Nor did Stalin launch the much-feared nuclear war that had prompted Chatwin to investigate a place so remote that the "likely patterns of fallout" would not reach him. Both memories nonetheless prompted in young Chatwin a fascination with one of the most remote and, to his mind, one of the most exotic places on earth. His fascination would last into adulthood, eventually prompting the trip that would lead to his award-winning travelogue, *In Patagonia*.

Depending upon how you use Chatwin's passage, you may not need as many details as are provided in the preceding summary. A briefer version would treat only the major events—the two childhood memories, one based on a misunderstanding and the other on a fear, but both contributing to a lifelong fascination. You might in this case preserve only a sentence or two of each of the original summary's three paragraphs, omitting such details as the description of the brontosaurus or of Grandmother's house. (The description of his grandmother and her home that "smelled of church" would be more relevant if you were writing a paper on the economy with which Chatwin describes people. The details you choose for a summary depend on the purpose to which you put the summary.)

Here is a briefer summary of the passage:

> In the first chapter of *In Patagonia*, Bruce Chatwin recounts two childhood memories, one based on a misunderstanding and the other on an unrealized fear, that sparked his interest in one day traveling to Patagonia. As a child, Chatwin was fascinated by a patch of what he thought was brontosaurus skin on display in his grandmother's home. That specimen was sent by distant relation "Charley Milward the Sailor" from Patagonia. Patagonia again figured into young Chatwin's imagination when, growing up in England at the start of the Cold War, he feared an imminent nuclear disaster and, in response, formed "an Emigration Committee" to scout remote locations that would escape nuclear destruction. Events later blurred these two memories. The brontosaurus skin turned out to be the remains of a Giant Sloth, and the much-feared war never materialized. Still, Chatwin's memories prompted in him a lifelong fascination with one of the most remote and, to his mind, one of the most exotic places on earth. As an adult, he would eventually make the trip that would end in his award-winning travelogue, *In Patagonia*.

The passage could be made briefer still: Your purpose in your paper might be served by a one-sentence reference to Chatwin's narrative:

> In the first chapter of his award-winning travelogue, Bruce Chatwin recounts two childhood memories that prompted his lifelong fascination with Patagonia.

Here, only the major purpose of Chatwin's opening chapter is treated, with no details offered about the two memories that prompted his later fascination with Patagonia. Brief as it is, this summary conveys how Chatwin traces his motivation to travel in and write about Patagonia to events in his childhood.

■ SUMMARIZING FIGURES AND TABLES

In your reading in the sciences and social sciences, you will often find data and concepts presented in nontext forms—as figures and tables. Such visual devices offer a snapshot, a pictorial overview of material that is more quickly and clearly communicated in graphic form than as a series of (often complicated) sentences. Note that in essence, figures and tables are themselves summaries. The writer uses a graph, which in an article or book is labeled as a numbered "figure," and presents the quantitative results of research as points on a line or a bar or as sections ("slices") of a pie. Pie charts show relative proportions, or percentages. Graphs, especially effective in showing patterns, relate one variable to another: for instance, income to years of education, or sales figures of a product over a period of three years.

Writers regularly draw on graphs, charts, and tables to provide information or to offer evidence for points they are arguing. Consider the following passage from an op-ed article by Michael Klare arguing that the United States and China should cooperate, rather than compete, in order to supply their future energy needs:

> In 2007, according to Energy Department figures, the United States consumed about 21 million barrels of oil a day, nearly three times as much as China. Even more significant, we imported 13 million barrels every day, a vastly greater amount than China's import tally. So, although it is indeed true that Chinese and American consumers are competing for access to overseas supplies, thereby edging up prices, American consumption still sets the pace in international oil markets.
>
> The reality is that as far as the current run-up in gasoline prices is concerned, other factors are more to blame: shrinking oil output from such key producers as Mexico, Russia and Venezuela; internal violence in Iraq and Nigeria; refinery inadequacies in the U.S. and elsewhere; speculative stockpiling by global oil brokers, and so on. These conditions are likely to persist for the foreseeable future, so prices will remain high.
>
> Peer into the future, however, and the China factor starts looming much larger.
>
> With its roaring economy and millions of newly affluent consumers—many of whom are now buying their first automobiles—China is rapidly catching up with the United States in its net oil intake. According to the most recent projections, Chinese petroleum consumption is expected to jump from 8 million barrels a day in 2008 to an estimated 12 million in 2020 and to 16 million in 2030. American consumption will also climb, but not as much, reaching an estimated 27 million barrels a day in 2030. In terms of oil imports, moreover, the gap will grow even smaller. Chinese imports are projected to hit 10.8 million barrels a day in 2030, compared with 16.4 million for the United States. Clearly, the Sino-American competition for foreign oil supplies will grow ever more intense with every passing year.*

A good deal of the data Klare provides in this passage likely came from graphs, charts, and tables.

In the following pages, we present four figures and a table from various sources, all related to the world's rising oil consumption and its dwindling supply. (Some promising alternative sources of energy for automobiles and other vehicles are discussed in our model explanatory synthesis, "The Car of the Future?" in Chapter 3, pp. 123–132.)

---

*Michael T. Klare, "The U.S. and China are over a Barrel," *Los Angeles Times* 28 Apr. 2008: 17. Klare is professor of peace and world security studies at Hampshire College and the author of *Rising Powers, Shrinking Planet: The New Geopolitics of Energy.*

Bar Graphs

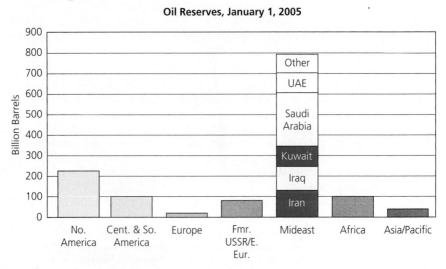

■ Figure 1.1   World Oil Reserves by Region, January 1, 2005*

Figure 1.1 is a bar graph indicating the world's known oil reserves as of January 2005. The vertical axis of this graph indicates the number of barrels, in billions, estimated to be available. The horizontal axis indicates various regions of the world. The vertical bar above each region indicates the number of billions of barrels. Note that the bar indicating the largest available supplies, the Mideast, is subdivided into the nations of that region in control of the largest oil reserves.

Here is a summary of the information presented in Figure 1.1:

> As of January 1, 2005, the Middle East had by far the largest quantities of oil reserves in the world, almost 800 billion barrels. North America, the region with the next highest oil reserves, has slightly more than a quarter of this quantity, just over 200 billion barrels. Central and South America and Africa come next, each with about 100 billion barrels. Russia and Eastern Europe have slightly less than this quantity. Compared to these oil-rich regions, Asia and the Pacific region and Europe have relatively minimal amounts. Within the Middle East region, Saudi Arabia has the largest oil reserves, about 250 billion barrels. This one country therefore has more oil than any other entire region in the world. Iran, Iraq, and Kuwait each have at least 100 million barrels of

Oil and Gas Journal 1 Jan. 2005. <http://www.eia.doe.gov/pub/oil_gas/petroleum/analysis_publications/oil_market_basics/sup_image_reserves.htm>.

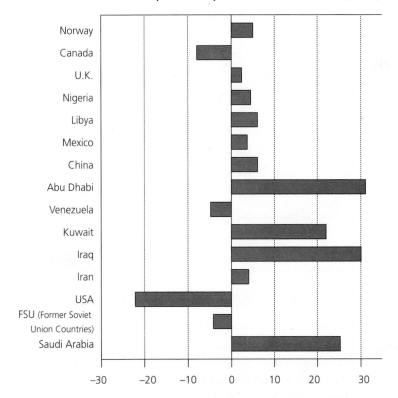

Time to Depletion Midpoint of Oil Reserves, 2003 (Years)

Figure 1.2   This graph illustrates the number of years to the midpoint of the depletion of oil reserves for various major oil-producing nations in 2003. A negative value means that the midpoint was in the past. The only countries a significant distance from their midpoints are the major Middle East producers.*

oil. Each of these countries, therefore, has at least as much in oil reserves as all of the African countries or all of the Central and South American countries combined.

Figure 1.2, another bar graph, indicates the number of years (from 2003— the "zero" point on the horizontal axis) until the midpoint of depletion of national oil reserves for fifteen countries. Note that this graph features bars stretching in opposite directions: The bars to the left indicate negative values; the bars to the right indicate positive values. Thus, Norway will have used up half of its total oil reserves by 2008, five years after the date the chart was prepared. Canada, by contrast, reached the midpoint of its depletion about eight years *before* 2003.

---

*The Hubbert Peak for World Oil. Chart updated 2003. <http://www.oilcrisis.com/ summary.htm>.

Pie Charts

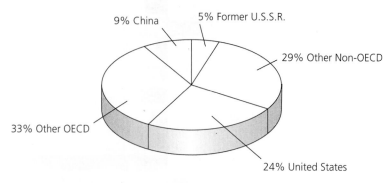

The Oil Consumption Pie, 2007

9% China

5% Former U.S.S.R.

29% Other Non-OECD

33% Other OECD

24% United States

■ Figure 1.3   The Oil Consumption Pie*

Bar graphs are useful for visually comparing numerical quantities. Pie charts, on the other hand, are useful for visually comparing percentages of a whole. The pie represents the whole; the individual slices represent the relative sizes of the parts. Figure 1.3 is a pie chart indicating the relative oil consumption of various regions of the world in 2007. Each slice represents a percentage of the world's total oil consumption.

In this chart, OECD stands for the Organization for Economic Cooperation and Development.[†] Note that only two of the five pie slices represent individual countries: the United States (an OECD country) and China. Two additional slices represent "other OECD countries" and "other Non–OECD countries" (i.e., countries other than China and the former USSR, which are separately represented in the chart). Finally, note that the "former USSR" slice indicates Russia and Eastern European countries—such as Bulgaria, Romania, and Estonia—that are not presently members of the OECD (as are Hungary and Poland).

---

*Association for the Study of Peak Oil and Gas—U.S.A. <http://www.aspo-usa.com/index.php?option=com_content&task=view&id=298&Itemid=91>.

[†]The OECD is a Paris-based international group, founded in 1961, that collects and analyzes economic data. According to its Web site <http://www.oecd.org>, "[I]ts mission [is] to help . . . member countries to achieve sustainable economic growth and employment and to raise the standard of living in member countries while maintaining financial stability . . . [and contributing] to the development of the world economy." OECD countries, democracies with market economies, include Australia, Austria, Belgium, Canada, the Czech Republic, Denmark, Finland, France, Germany, Greece, Hungary, Iceland, Ireland, Italy, Japan, Korea, Luxembourg, Mexico, Netherlands, New Zealand, Norway, Poland, the Slovak Republic, Spain, Switzerland, Sweden, Turkey, the United Kingdom, and the United States.

Exercise 1.3

Summarizing Pie Charts

Write a brief summary of the data in Figure 1.3. Use our summary of Figure 1.1 (or your summary of Figure 1.2) as a model.

Line Graphs

Line graphs are useful for showing trends over a period of time. Usually, the horizontal axis indicates years, months, or shorter periods, and the vertical axis indicates a quantity: dollars, barrels, personnel, sales, anything that can be counted. The line running from left to right indicates the changing values, over a given period, of the object of measurement. Frequently, a line graph will feature multiple lines (perhaps in different colors, perhaps some solid, others dotted, etc.), each indicating a separate variable to be measured. Thus, a line graph could show the changing approval ratings of several presidential candidates over the course of a campaign season. Or it could indicate the number of iPhones vs. Blackberries sold in a given year.

The line graph shown in Figure 1.4 indicates the changes in several U.S. oil consumption variables, over time: (1) total oil demand (in millions of

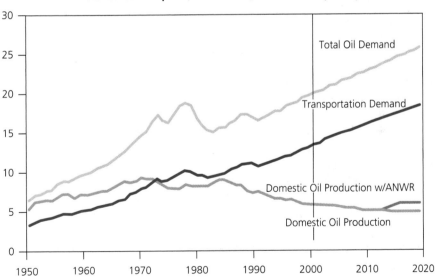

■ Figure 1.4   U.S. Oil Consumption, 1950–2020*

---

*Energy Information Administration (EIA), Annual Energy Outlook, 2001: "Potential Oil Production from the Coastal Plain of ANWR [Arctic National Wildlife Refuge [ANWR]," EIR Reserves and Production Division. <http://energy.senate.gov/legislation/energybill/charts/chart8.pdf>.

barrels per day), (2) oil consumption demand for transportation alone, and (3) domestic oil production. Note that because the graph was produced in 2001, the fifty-year period before that indicates historical data; the twenty-year period following is a projection based on estimates. Note also that somewhere around 2015, the domestic oil production line splits in two: The upper range indicates the level of oil production if Alaskan oil reserves were included; the lower range indicates domestic production without this particular resource.

Exercise 1.4

Summarizing Line Graphs

Write a brief summary of the key data in Figure 1.4. Use our summary of Figure 1.1 (or your summary of Figure 1.2) as a model.

Tables

A table presents numerical data in rows and columns for quick reference. If the writer chooses, tabular information can be converted to graphic information. Charts and graphs are preferable when the writer wants to emphasize a pattern or relationship; tables are preferable when the writer wants to emphasize numbers. While the previous charts and graphs represented a relatively small number of factors (regions or countries, quantities of oil produced or consumed in a given year or over a period of time), Table 1.1 breaks down oil production into numerous countries, organized by region.* Note that since production is represented in thousands of barrels daily, each number should be multiplied by 1000. The number at the upper left corner of page 37, 8295, therefore represents the 8,295,000 barrels a day produced by the USA in 1996. "Total World" production that year (p. 39, lower left) was 69,931,000 barrels per day.

A table may contain so much data that you would not want to summarize *all* of it for a particular paper. In this case, you would summarize the *part* of a table that you find useful. Here is a summary drawn from the information from Table 1.1 focusing just on the North American and Middle Eastern sections. Notice that the summary requires the writer to read closely and discern which information is significant. The table reports raw data and does not speak for itself. At the end of the summary the writer, using information not only from this table but also from Figure 1.4, "U.S. Oil Consumption, 1950–2020," draws her own conclusions:

> In 1996, the United States produced 8.3 million barrels of oil daily,
> or 89% of Saudia Arabia's production of 9.3 million barrels. By 2006,

---

*"British Petroleum Statistical Review of World Energy 2006: Oil Production." British Petroleum, 2007. <http://www.bp.com/liveassets/bp_internet/globalbp/globalbp_uk_english/reports_and_publications/statistical_energy_review_2007/STAGING/local_assets/downloads/pdf/table_of_world_oil_production_2007.pdf>.

Table 1.1 Oil Production by Country, 1996–2006*

Producer	Thousands of barrels daily											Change: 2006 over 2005	2006 share of total
	1996	1997	1998	1999	2000	2001	2002	2003	2004	2005	2006		
USA	8295	8269	8011	7731	7733	7669	7626	7400	7228	6895	6871	−0.5%	8.0%
Canada	2480	2588	2672	2604	2721	2677	2858	3004	3085	3041	3147	4.4%	3.9%
Mexico	3277	3410	3499	3343	3450	3560	3585	3789	3824	3760	3683	−2.1%	4.7%
Total North America	**14,052**	**14,267**	**14,182**	**13,678**	**13,904**	**13,906**	**14,069**	**14,193**	**14,137**	**13,695**	**13,700**	**0.1%**	**16.5%**
Argentina	823	877	890	847	819	830	818	806	754	725	716	−1.3%	0.9%
Brazil	807	868	1003	1133	1268	1337	1499	1555	1542	1715	1809	5.5%	2.3%
Colombia	635	667	775	838	711	627	601	564	551	554	558	0.7%	0.7%
Ecuador	393	397	385	383	409	416	401	427	535	541	545	0.7%	0.7%
Peru	121	120	116	107	100	98	98	92	94	111	116	3.5%	0.1%
Trinidad & Tobago	141	135	134	141	138	135	155	164	152	171	174	1.5%	0.2%
Venezuela	3137	3321	3480	3126	3239	3142	2895	2554	2907	2937	2824	−3.9%	3.7%
Other S. & Cent. America	102	108	125	124	130	137	152	153	144	142	140	−1.7%	0.2%
Total S. & Cent. America	**6159**	**6493**	**6908**	**6699**	**6813**	**6722**	**6619**	**6314**	**6680**	**6897**	**6881**	**−0.4%**	**8.8%**
Azerbaijan	183	182	231	279	282	301	311	313	315	452	654	44.9%	0.8%
Denmark	208	230	238	299	363	348	371	368	390	377	342	−9.3%	0.4%
Italy	104	114	108	96	88	79	106	107	105	117	111	−5.6%	0.1%
Kazakhstan	474	536	537	631	744	836	1018	1111	1297	1356	1426	5.6%	1.7%
Norway	3232	3280	3138	3139	3346	3418	3333	3264	3188	2969	2778	−6.9%	3.3%
Romania	142	141	137	133	131	130	127	123	119	114	105	−8.0%	0.1%
Russian Federation	6114	6227	6169	6178	6536	7056	7698	8544	9287	9552	9769	2.2%	12.3%
Turkmenistan	90	108	129	143	144	162	182	202	193	192	163	−15.2%	0.2%
United Kingdom	2735	2702	2807	2909	2667	2476	2463	2257	2028	1809	1636	−9.6%	2.0%
Uzbekistan	174	182	191	191	177	171	171	166	152	126	125	−0.7%	0.1%
Other Europe & Eurasia	546	524	506	474	465	465	501	509	496	469	454	−2.9%	0.5%
Total Europe & Eurasia	**14,003**	**14,226**	**14,190**	**14,473**	**14,943**	**15,444**	**16,281**	**16,965**	**17,570**	**17,533**	**17,563**	**0.2%**	**21.6%**

(continued)

37

Table 1.1 (continued)

Thousands of barrels daily

Producer	1996	1997	1998	1999	2000	2001	2002	2003	2004	2005	2006	Change: 2006 over 2005	2006 share of total
Iran	3759	3776	3855	3603	3818	3794	3543	4183	4248	4268	4343	1.2%	5.4%
Iraq	580	1166	2121	2610	2614	2523	2116	1344	2030	1833	1999	9.0%	2.5%
Kuwait	2129	2137	2232	2085	2206	2148	1995	2329	2482	2643	2704	2.4%	3.4%
Oman	897	909	905	911	959	961	900	824	756	779	743	−4.6%	0.9%
Qatar	568	719	747	797	855	854	783	917	990	1045	1133	8.1%	1.3%
Saudi Arabia	9299	9482	9502	8853	9491	9209	8928	10,164	10,638	11,114	10,859	−2.3%	13.1%
Syria	586	577	576	579	548	581	548	527	495	458	417	−8.9%	0.5%
United Arab Emirates	2438	2567	2643	2511	2626	2534	2324	2611	2656	2751	2969	7.3%	3.5%
Yemen	357	375	380	405	450	455	457	448	420	426	390	−8.7%	0.5%
Other Middle East	50	50	49	48	48	47	48	48	48	34	32	−7.7%	**
Total Middle East	**20,662**	**21,758**	**23,010**	**22,402**	**23,614**	**23,107**	**21,642**	**23,395**	**24,764**	**25,352**	**25,589**	**0.7%**	**31.2%**
Algeria	1386	1421	1461	1515	1578	1562	1680	1852	1946	2016	2005	−0.3%	2.2%
Angola	716	741	731	745	746	742	905	862	976	1233	1409	14.3%	1.8%
Cameroon	110	124	105	95	88	81	75	68	62	58	63	8.6%	0.1%
Chad	–	–	–	–	–	–	–	24	168	173	153	−11.7%	0.2%
Rep. of Congo (Brazzaville)	200	225	264	266	254	234	231	215	216	246	262	6.7%	0.3%
Egypt	894	873	857	827	781	758	751	749	721	696	678	−2.5%	0.8%
Equatorial Guinea	17	62	85	96	117	173	215	247	343	356	358	0.6%	0.5%
Gabon	365	364	337	340	327	301	295	240	235	234	232	−0.9%	0.3%
Libya	1452	1491	1480	1425	1475	1427	1375	1485	1624	1751	1835	4.2%	2.2%
Nigeria	2145	2316	2167	2066	2155	2274	2103	2263	2502	2580	2460	−4.9%	3.0%
Sudan	5	9	12	63	174	211	233	255	325	355	397	11.8%	0.5%
Tunisia	89	81	83	84	78	71	75	68	72	74	69	−7.1%	0.1%

Table 1.1 (continued)

Producer	Thousands of barrels daily											Change: 2006 over 2005	2006 share of total
	1996	1997	1998	1999	2000	2001	2002	2003	2004	2005	2006		
Other Africa	62	64	63	56	56	53	63	71	75	72	68	-5.3%	0.1%
Total Africa	**7441**	**7770**	**7644**	**7579**	**7830**	**7887**	**8001**	**8398**	**9263**	**9846**	**9990**	**1.4%**	**12.1%**
Australia	619	669	644	625	809	733	731	624	541	554	544	-2.1%	0.6%
Brunei	165	163	157	182	193	203	210	214	210	206	221	7.1%	0.3%
China	3170	3211	3212	3213	3252	3306	3346	3401	3481	3627	3684	1.6%	4.7%
India	778	800	787	788	780	780	801	798	816	784	807	3.1%	1.0%
Indonesia	1680	1557	1520	1408	1456	1389	1288	1183	1152	1129	1071	-5.3%	1.3%
Malaysia	773	777	779	737	735	719	757	776	793	767	747	-3.1%	0.9%
Thailand	105	126	130	140	176	191	204	236	223	265	286	8.7%	0.3%
Vietnam	179	205	245	296	328	350	354	364	427	398	367	-8.0%	0.5%
Other Asia Pacific	245	229	217	218	200	195	193	195	186	197	215	8.0%	0.3%
Total Asia Pacific	**7615**	**7737**	**7692**	**7608**	**7928**	**7866**	**7884**	**7791**	**7829**	**7926**	**7941**	**0.1%**	**9.7%**
TOTAL WORLD	**69,931**	**72,251**	**73,626**	**72,439**	**75,033**	**74,932**	**74,496**	**77,056**	**80,244**	**81,250**	**81,663**	**0.4%**	**100.0%**
of which:													
European Union 25	3325	3304	3407	3542	3355	3147	3203	2995	2774	2535	2306	-9.0%	2.8%
OECD	21,355	21,660	21,492	21,095	21,514	21,297	21,422	21,156	20,716	19,825	19,398	-2.2%	23.3%
OPEC	28,472	29,953	31,207	29,999	31,512	30,857	29,031	30,884	33,175	34,068	34,202	0.2%	41.7%
Non-OPEC‡	**34,288**	**34,925**	**35,028**	**34,887**	**35,507**	**35,415**	**35,933**	**35,673**	**35,661**	**35,343**	**35,162**	**-0.5%**	**43.0%**
Former Soviet Union	7171	7374	7391	7552	8014	8660	9533	10,499	11,407	11,840	12,299	3.9%	15.3%

*Includes crude oil, shale oil, oil sands and NGLs (the liquid content of natural gas where this is recovered separately). Excludes liquid fuels from other sources such as biomass and coal derivatives.
‡Excludes Former Soviet Union.
**Less than 0.05%

Note: Annual changes and shares of total are calculated using million tons per annum figures.

the United States was producing less than 7 million barrels, or 62% of Saudi Arabia's 11 million barrels. If we compare by region, the figures are only marginally more favorable to Americans. In 1996, the countries of North America produced 68% of the oil produced by the countries of the Middle East. Ten years later, that 68% had declined to 54%. Though the years between 1996 and 2006 have seen ups and downs in oil production by both regions, the overall trend is clear: North American production is falling and Middle East production is rising. Further, North American production is falling primarily because of declines in U.S. production; generally, Canadian and Mexican production have seen small but steady rises. Canada, for example, was producing about 2.5 million barrels of oil in 1996 and just over 3 million barrels in 2006. But this half-million-barrel rise was dwarfed by the 1.5-million-barrel rise in production by Saudi Arabia during that same period. The implications are clear: far from being self-sufficient in oil production, the United States is becoming less self-sufficient every year and is becoming ever more dependent for its petroleum supplies on a region whose political stability and reliability as a petroleum source are in serious question.

Exercise 1.5

Summarizing Tables

Focus on other data in Table 1.1 and write a brief summary of your own. Or locate another table on the general topic of oil production or consumption and summarize part or all of its data. Suggestion: "Oil Production and Consumption Country Comparison Table" from the World Factbook <http://education.yahoo.com/reference/factbook/countrycompare/oil/1a.html>.

■ PARAPHRASE

In certain cases, you may want to *paraphrase* rather than summarize material. Writing a paraphrase is similar to writing a summary: It involves recasting a passage into your own words, so it requires your complete understanding of the material. The difference is that while a summary is a shortened version of the original, the paraphrase is approximately the same length as the original.

Why write a paraphrase when you can quote the original? You may decide to offer a paraphrase of material written in language that is dense, abstract, archaic, or possibly confusing.

Let's consider some examples. If you were investigating the ethical concerns relating to the practice of in vitro fertilization, you might conclude that you should read some medical literature. You might reasonably want to hear from the doctors who are themselves developing, performing, and questioning the procedures that you are researching. In professional journals and bulletins, physicians write to one another, not to the general public. They use specialized language. If you wanted to refer to the following technically complex selection, you might need to write a paraphrase.

> [I]t is not only an improvement in the success-rate that participating research scientists hope for but, rather, developments in new fields of research in in-vitro gene diagnosis and in certain circumstances gene therapy. In view of this, the French expert J. F. Mattei has asked the following question: "Are we forced to accept that in vitro fertilization will become one of the most compelling methods of genetic diagnosis?" Evidently, by the introduction of a new law in France and Sweden (1994), this acceptance (albeit with certain restrictions) has already occurred prior to the application of in vitro fertilization reaching a technically mature and clinically applicable phase. This may seem astonishing in view of the question placed by the above-quoted French expert: the idea of embryo production so as to withhold one or two embryos before implantation presupposes a definite "attitude towards eugenics." And to destroy an embryo merely because of its genetic characteristics could signify the reduction of a human life to the sum of its genes. Mattei asks: "In face of a molecular judgment on our lives, is there no possibility for appeal? Will the diagnosis of inherited monogenetic illnesses soon be extended to genetic predisposition for multi-factorial illnesses?"*

Like most literature intended for physicians, the language of this selection is somewhat forbidding to nonspecialists, who will have trouble with phrases such as "predisposition for multi-factorial illnesses." As a courtesy to your readers and in an effort to maintain a consistent tone and level in your essay, you could paraphrase this paragraph from a medical newsletter. First, of course, you must understand the meaning of the passage, perhaps no small task. But, having read the material carefully (and consulted a dictionary), you might prepare a paraphrase like this one:

> Writing in *Biomedical Ethics,* Dietmar Mieth reports that fertility specialists today want not only to improve the success rates of their procedures but also to diagnose and repair genetic problems before they implant fertilized eggs. Because the result of the in vitro process is often more fertilized eggs than can be used in a procedure, doctors may examine test-tube embryos for genetic defects and "withhold one or two" before implanting them. The practice of selectively implanting embryos raises concerns about eugenics and the rights of rejected embryos. On what genetic grounds will specialists distinguish flawed from healthy embryos

---

*Dietmar Mieth, "In Vitro Fertilization: From Medical Reproduction to Genetic Diagnosis," *Biomedical Ethics: Newsletter of the European Network for Biomedical Ethics* 1.1 (1996): 45.

and make a decision whether or not to implant? The appearance of single genes linked directly to specific, or "monogenetic," illnesses could be grounds for destroying an embryo. More complicated would be genes that predispose people to an illness but in no way guarantee the onset of that illness. Would these genes, which are only one factor in "multi-factorial illnesses" also be labeled undesirable and lead to embryo destruction? Advances in fertility science raise difficult questions. Already, even before techniques of genetic diagnosis are fully developed, legislatures are writing laws governing the practices of fertility clinics.

We begin our paraphrase with the same "not only/but also" logic of the original's first sentence, introducing the concepts of genetic diagnosis and therapy. The next four sentences in the original introduce concerns of a "French expert." Rather than quote Mieth quoting the expert, and immediately mentioning new laws in France and Sweden, we decided (first) to explain that in vitro fertilization procedures can give rise to more embryos than needed. We reasoned that nonmedical readers would appreciate our making explicit the background knowledge that the author assumes other physicians possess. Then we quote Mieth briefly ("withhold one or two" embryos) to provide some flavor of the original. We maintain focus on the ethical questions and wait until the end of the paraphrase before mentioning the laws to which Mieth refers. Our paraphrase is roughly the same length as the original, and it conveys the author's concerns about eugenics. As you can see, the paraphrase requires a writer to make decisions about the presentation of material. In many, if not most, cases, you will need to do more than simply "translate" from the original, sentence by sentence, to write your paraphrase.

When you come across a passage that you don't understand, the temptation is to skip over it. Resist this temptation! Use a paraphrase as a tool for explaining to yourself the main ideas of a difficult passage. By translating another writer's language into your own, you clarify what you understand and pinpoint what you don't. The paraphrase therefore becomes a tool for learning the subject.

The following pointers will help you write paraphrases.

How to Write Paraphrases

- Make sure that you understand the source passage.
- Substitute your own words for those of the source passage; look for synonyms that carry the same meaning as the original words.

(continues)

> • Rearrange your own sentences so that they read smoothly. Sentence structure, even sentence order, in the paraphrase need not be based on that of the original. A good paraphrase, like a good summary, should stand by itself.

Paraphrases are generally about the same length as (and sometimes shorter than) the passages on which they are based. But sometimes clarity requires that a paraphrase be longer than a tightly compacted source passage. For example, suppose you wanted to paraphrase this statement by Sigmund Freud:

> We have found out that the distortion in dreams which hinders our understanding of them is due to the activities of a censorship, directed against the unacceptable, unconscious wish-impulses.

If you were to paraphrase this statement (the first sentence in the Tenth Lecture of his *General Introduction to Psychoanalysis*), you might come up with something like this:

> It is difficult to understand dreams because they contain distortions. Freud believed that these distortions arise from our internal censor, which attempts to suppress unconscious and forbidden desires.

Essentially, this paraphrase does little more than break up one sentence into two and somewhat rearrange the sentence structure for clarity.

Like summaries, then, paraphrases are useful devices, both in helping you to understand source material and in enabling you to convey the essence of this source material to your readers. When would you choose to write a summary instead of a paraphrase (or vice versa)? The answer depends on your purpose in presenting the source material. As we've said, summaries are generally based on articles (or sections of articles) or books. Paraphrases are generally based on particularly difficult (or important) paragraphs or sentences. You would seldom paraphrase a long passage, or summarize a short one, unless there were particularly good reasons for doing so. (A lawyer might want to paraphrase several pages of legal language so that his or her client, who is not a lawyer, could understand it.) The purpose of a summary is generally to save your reader time by presenting him or her with a brief version of a lengthy source. The purpose of a paraphrase is generally to clarify a short passage that might otherwise be unclear. Whether you summarize or paraphrase may also depend on the importance of your source. A particularly important source—if it is not too long—may rate a paraphrase. If it is less important, or peripheral to your central argument, you may write a summary instead. And, of course, you may choose to summarize only part of your source—the part that is most relevant to the point you are making.

Exercise 1.6

Paraphrasing

Locate and photocopy three relatively complex, but brief, passages from readings currently assigned in your other courses. Paraphrase these passages, making the language more readable and understandable. Attach the photocopies to the paraphrases.

■ QUOTATIONS

A *quotation* records the exact language used by someone in speech or writing. A *summary*, in contrast, is a brief restatement in your own words of what someone else has said or written. And a *paraphrase* is also a restatement, although one that is often as long as the original source. Any paper in which you draw upon sources will rely heavily on quotation, summary, and paraphrase. How do you choose among the three?

Remember that the papers you write should be your own—for the most part: your own language and certainly your own thesis, your own inferences, and your own conclusion. It follows that references to your source materials should be written primarily as summaries and paraphrases, both of which are built on restatement, not quotation. You will use summaries when you need a *brief* restatement, and paraphrases, which provide more explicit detail than summaries, when you need to follow the development of a source closely. When you quote too much, you risk losing ownership of your work: More easily than you might think, your voice can be drowned out by the voices of those you've quoted. So *use quotation sparingly*, as you would a pungent spice.

Nevertheless, quoting just the right source at the right time can significantly improve your papers. The trick is to know when and how to use quotations.

Quotations can be direct or indirect. A *direct* quotation is one in which you record precisely the language of another. An *indirect* quotation is one in which you report what someone has said without repeating the words exactly as spoken (or written):

Direct quotation: Franklin D. Roosevelt said, "The only thing we have to fear is fear itself."

Indirect quotation: Franklin D. Roosevelt said that we have nothing to fear but fear itself.

The language in a direct quotation, which is indicated by a pair of quotation marks (" "), must be faithful to the language of the original passage. When using an indirect quotation, you have the liberty of changing words (although not changing meaning). For both direct and indirect quotations, *you must credit your sources*, naming them either in (or close to) the sentence that includes the quotation or in a parenthetical citation. (See Chapter 7, pp. 288–307, for specific rules on citing sources properly.)

Choosing Quotations

You'll find that using quotations can be particularly helpful in several situations.

Quoting Memorable Language

You should quote when the source material is worded so eloquently or powerfully that to summarize or paraphrase it would be to sacrifice much of the impact and significance of the meaning. Here, for example, is the historian John Keegan describing how France, Germany, Austria, and Russia slid inexorably in 1914 into the cataclysm of World War I:

> In the event, the states of Europe proceeded, as if in a dead march and a dialogue of the deaf, to the destruction of their continent and its civilization.

No paraphrase could do justice to the power of Keegan's words, as they appear in his book *The First World War* (1998). You would certainly want to quote them in any paper dealing with the origins of this conflict.

When to Quote

- Use quotations when another writer's language is particularly memorable and will add interest and liveliness to your paper.
- Use quotations when another writer's language is so clear and economical that to make the same point in your own words would, by comparison, be ineffective.
- Use quotations when you want the solid reputation of a source to lend authority and credibility to your own writing.

Quoting Clear and Concise Language

You should quote a source when its language is particularly clear and economical—when your language, by contrast, would be wordy. Read this passage from a biology text by Patricia Curtis:

> The honeybee colony, which usually has a population of 30,000 to 40,000 workers, differs from that of the bumblebee and many other social bees or wasps in that it survives the winter. This means that the bees must stay warm despite the cold. Like other bees, the isolated honeybee cannot fly if the temperature falls below 10°C (50°F) and cannot walk if

the temperature is below 7°C (45°F). Within the wintering hive, bees maintain their temperature by clustering together in a dense ball; the lower the temperature, the denser the cluster. The clustered bees produce heat by constant muscular movements of their wings, legs, and abdomens. In very cold weather, the bees on the outside of the cluster keep moving toward the center, while those in the core of the cluster move to the colder outside periphery. The entire cluster moves slowly about on the combs, eating the stored honey from the combs as it moves.*

A summary of this paragraph might read:

Honeybees, unlike many other varieties of bee, are able to live through the winter by "clustering together in a dense ball" for body warmth.

A paraphrase of the same passage would be considerably more detailed:

Honeybees, unlike many other varieties of bee (such as bumblebees), are able to live through the winter. The 30,000 to 40,000 bees within a honeybee hive could not, individually, move about in cold winter temperatures. But when "clustering together in a dense ball," the bees generate heat by constantly moving their body parts. The cluster also moves slowly about the hive, those on the periphery of the cluster moving into the center, those in the center moving to the periphery, and all eating honey stored in the combs. This nutrition, in addition to the heat generated by the cluster, enables the honeybee to survive the cold winter months.

In both the summary and the paraphrase we've quoted Curtis's "clustering together in a dense ball," a phrase that lies at the heart of her description of wintering honeybees. For us to describe this clustering in any language other than Curtis's would be pointless when her description is admirably brief and precise.

Quoting Authoritative Language

You should use quotations that lend authority to your work. When quoting an expert or a prominent political, artistic, or historical figure, you elevate your own work by placing it in esteemed company. Quote respected figures to establish background information in a paper, and your readers will tend to perceive that information as reliable. Quote the opinions of respected figures to endorse a statement that you've made, and your statement becomes more credible to your readers. Here, in a discussion of space flight, the writer David Chandler refers to a physicist and a physicist-astronaut:

A few scientists—notably James Van Allen, discoverer of the Earth's radiation belts—have decried the expense of the manned space program

---

*Patricia Curtis, "Winter Organization," *Biology*, 2nd ed. (New York: Worth, 1976) 822–23.

and called for an almost exclusive concentration on unmanned scientific exploration instead, saying this would be far more cost-effective.

Other space scientists dispute that idea. Joseph Allen, physicist and former shuttle astronaut, says, "It seems to be argued that one takes away from the other. But before there was a manned space program, the funding on space science was zero. Now it's about $500 million a year."

In the first paragraph Chandler has either summarized or used an indirect quotation to incorporate remarks made by James Van Allen into the discussion on space flight. In the second paragraph, Chandler directly quotes Joseph Allen. Both quotations, indirect and direct, lend authority and legitimacy to the article, for both James Van Allen and Joseph Allen are experts on the subject of space flight. Note that Chandler provides brief but effective biographies of his sources, identifying each one, so that their qualifications to speak on the subject are known to all:

James Van Allen, *discoverer of the Earth's radiation belts* . . .

Joseph Allen, *physicist and former shuttle astronaut* . . .

The phrases in italics are *appositives*. Their function is to rename the nouns they follow by providing explicit, identifying detail. Any information about a person that can be expressed in the following sentence pattern can be made into an appositive phrase:

James Van Allen is the *discoverer of the Earth's radiation belts*.

He has decried the expense of the manned space program.   .

Sentence with an appositive:

James Van Allen, *discoverer of the Earth's radiation belts*, has decried the expense of the manned space program.

Appositives (in the example above, "discoverer of the Earth's radiation belts") efficiently incorporate identifying information about the authors you quote, while adding variety to the structure of your sentences.

Incorporating Quotations into Your Sentences

Quoting Only the Part of a Sentence or Paragraph That You Need

We've said that a writer selects passages for quotation that are especially vivid, memorable, concise, or authoritative. Now put these principles into practice. Suppose that while conducting research on college sports, you've come across the following, written by Robert Hutchins, former president of the University of Chicago:

If athleticism is bad for students, players, alumni, and the public, it is even worse for the colleges and universities themselves. They want to be educational institutions, but they can't. The story of the famous halfback whose only regret, when he bade his coach farewell, was that he hadn't learned to read and write is probably exaggerated. But we must admit that pressure from trustees, graduates, "friends," presidents, and even professors has tended to relax academic standards. These gentry often overlook the fact that a college should not be interested in a fullback who is a half-wit. Recruiting, subsidizing and the double educational standard cannot exist without the knowledge and the tacit approval, at least, of the colleges and universities themselves. Certain institutions encourage susceptible professors to be nice to athletes now admitted by paying them for serving as "faculty representatives" on the college athletic board.*

Suppose that in this paragraph you find a gem, a sentence with striking language that will enliven your discussion:

These gentry often overlook the fact that a college should not be interested in a fullback who is a half-wit.

Incorporating the Quotation into the Flow of Your Own Sentence

Once you've selected the passage you want to quote, you need to work the material into your paper in as natural and fluid a manner as possible. Here's how we would quote Hutchins:

Robert Hutchins, former president of the University of Chicago, asserts that "a college should not be interested in a fullback who is a half-wit."

Note that we've used an appositive to identify Hutchins. And we've used only the part of the paragraph—a single clause—that we thought memorable enough to quote directly.

Avoiding Freestanding Quotations

A quoted sentence should never stand by itself, as in the following example:

Various people associated with the university admit that the pressures of athleticism have caused a relaxation of standards. "These gentry often overlook the fact that a college should not be interested in a fullback who is a half-wit." But this kind of thinking is bad for the university and even worse for the athletes.

Even if it were followed by a parenthetical citation, a freestanding quotation would be jarring to the reader. You need to introduce the quotation with a *signal phrase* that attributes the source, not in a parenthetical citation but in

---

*Robert Hutchins, "Gate Receipts and Glory," *Saturday Evening Post* 3 Dec. 1983: 38.

some other part of the sentence—beginning, middle, or end. Thus, you could write:

> As Robert Hutchins notes, "These gentry often overlook the fact that a college should not be interested in a fullback who is a half-wit."

Here's a variation with the signal phrase in the middle:

> "These gentry," asserts Robert Hutchins, "often overlook the fact that a college should not be interested in a fullback who is a half-wit."

Another alternative is to introduce a sentence-long quotation with a colon:

> But Robert Hutchins disagrees: "These gentry often overlook the fact that a college should not be interested in a fullback who is a half-wit."

Use colons also to introduce indented quotations (as when we introduce long quotations in this chapter).

When attributing sources in signal phrases, try to vary the standard *states, writes, says,* and so on. Stronger verbs you might consider are: *asserts, argues, maintains, insists, asks,* and even *wonders.*

Exercise 1.7

Incorporating Quotations

Return to the article (pp. 8–13) by Alan S. Blinder, "Will Your Job Be Exported?" Find sentences that you think make interesting points. Imagine you want to use these points in a paper you're writing on job prospects in the twenty-first century. Write five different sentences that use a variety of the techniques discussed thus far to incorporate whole sentences as well as phrases from Blinder's article.

Using Ellipses

Using quotations becomes somewhat complicated when you want to quote the beginning and end of a passage but not its middle. Here's part of a paragraph from Thoreau's *Walden*:

> To read well, that is to read true books in a true spirit, is a noble exercise, and one that will task the reader more than any exercise which the customs of the day esteem. It requires a training such as the athletes underwent, the steady intention almost of the whole life to this object. Books must be read as deliberately and reservedly as they were written.*

---

*Henry David Thoreau, *Walden* (New York: Signet Classic, 1960) 72.

And here is how we can use this material in a quotation:

> Reading well is hard work, writes Henry David Thoreau in <u>Walden,</u> "that will task the reader more than any exercise which the customs of the day esteem. . . . Books must be read as deliberately and reservedly as they were written."

Whenever you quote a sentence but delete words from it, as we have done, indicate this deletion to the reader with three spaced periods—called an "ellipsis"—in the sentence at the point of deletion. The rationale for using an ellipsis mark is that a direct quotation must be reproduced *exactly* as it was written or spoken. When writers delete or change any part of the quoted material, readers must be alerted so they don't think the changes were part of the original. When deleting an entire sentence or sentences from a quoted paragraph, as in the example above, end the sentence you have quoted with a period, place the ellipsis, and continue the quotation.

If you are deleting the middle of a single sentence, use an ellipsis in place of the deleted words:

> "To read well . . . is a noble exercise, and one that will task the reader more than any exercise which the customs of the day esteem."

If you are deleting material from the end of one sentence through to the beginning of another sentence, add a sentence period before the ellipsis:

> "It requires a training such as the athletes underwent. . . . Books must be read as deliberately and reservedly as they were written."

If you begin your quotation of an author in the middle of his or her sentence, you need not indicate deleted words with an ellipsis. Be sure, however, that the syntax of the quotation fits smoothly with the syntax of your sentence:

> Reading "is a noble exercise," writes Henry David Thoreau.

Using Brackets to Add or Substitute Words

Use brackets whenever you need to add or substitute words in a quoted sentence. The brackets indicate to the reader a word or phrase that does not appear in the original passage but that you have inserted to avoid confusion. For example, when a pronoun's antecedent would be unclear to readers, delete the pronoun from the sentence and substitute an identifying word or phrase in brackets. When you make such a substitution, no ellipsis mark is needed. Assume that you wish to quote either of the underlined sentences in the following passage by Jane Yolen:

> Golden Press's *Walt Disney's Cinderella* set the new pattern for America's Cinderella. This book's text is coy and condescending. (Sample: "And her best friends of all were—guess who—the mice!") The illustrations are poor cartoons. And Cinderella herself is a disaster. She cowers as her

sisters rip her homemade ball gown to shreds. (Not even homemade by Cinderella, but by the mice and birds.) <u>She answers her stepmother with whines and pleadings. She is a sorry excuse for a heroine, pitiable and useless.</u> She cannot perform even a simple action to save herself, though she is warned by her friends, the mice. She does not hear them because she is "off in a world of dreams." Cinderella begs, she whimpers, and at last has to be rescued by—guess who—the mice!*

In quoting one of these sentences, you would need to identify to whom the pronoun *she* refers. You can do this inside the quotation by using brackets:

> Jane Yolen believes that "[Cinderella] is a sorry excuse for a heroine, pitiable and useless."

When the pronoun begins the sentence to be quoted, you can identify the pronoun outside the quotation and begin quoting your source one word later:

> Jane Yolen believes that in the Golden Press version, Cinderella "is a sorry excuse for a heroine, pitiable and useless."

Here's another example of a case where the pronoun needing identification occurs in the middle of the sentence to be quoted. Newspaper reporters must use brackets when quoting a source, who in an interview might say this:

> After the fire they did not return to the station house for three hours.

When to Summarize, Paraphrase, and Quote

SUMMARIZE:

- To present main points of a lengthy passage (article or book)
- To condense peripheral points necessary to discussion

PARAPHRASE:

- To clarify a short passage
- To emphasize main points

QUOTE:

- To capture another writer's particularly memorable language
- To capture another writer's clearly and economically stated language
- To lend authority and credibility to your own writing

---

*Jane Yolen, "America's 'Cinderella,'" *Children's Literature in Education* 8 (1977): 22.

If the reporter wants to use this sentence in an article, he or she needs to identify the pronoun:

> An official from City Hall, speaking on the condition that he not be identified, said, "After the fire [the officers] did not return to the station house for three hours."

You will also need to add bracketed information to a quoted sentence when a reference essential to the sentence's meaning is implied but not stated directly. Read the following paragraph from Walter Isaacson's recent biography of Albert Einstein, *Einstein: His Life and Universe:*

> Newton had bequeathed to Einstein a universe in which time had an absolute existence that tick-tocked along independent of objects and observers, and in which space likewise had an absolute existence. Gravity was thought to be a force that masses exerted on one another rather mysteriously across empty space. Within this framework, objects obeyed mechanical laws that had proved remarkably accurate—almost perfect—in explaining everything from the orbits of the planets, to the diffusion of gases, to the jiggling of molecules, to the propagation of sound (though not light) waves.

If you wanted to quote only the underlined sentence above, you would need to provide readers with a bracketed explanation; otherwise, the phrase "this framework" would be unclear. Here is how you would manage the quotation:

> According to Walter Isaacson, Newton's universe was extremely regular and predictable:
>
> > Within this framework [that time and space exist independently of their observation and that gravity results from masses exerting a remote attraction on one another], objects obeyed mechanical laws that had proved remarkably accurate—almost perfect—in explaining everything from the orbits of the planets, to the diffusion of gases, to the jiggling of molecules, to the propagation of sound (though not light) waves. (223)

■ Incorporating Quotations into Your Sentences

- **Quote only the part of a sentence or paragraph that you need**. Use no more of the writer's language than necessary to make or reinforce your point.
- **Incorporate the quotation into the flow of your own sentence**. The quotation must fit, both syntactically and stylistically, into your surrounding language.

(continues)

- **Avoid freestanding quotations**. A quoted sentence should never stand by itself. Use a *signal phrase*—at the beginning, the middle, or the end of the sentence—to attribute the source of the quotation.
- **Use ellipsis marks**. Indicate deleted language in the middle of a quoted sentence with ellipsis marks. Deleted language at the beginning or end of a sentence generally does not require ellipsis marks.
- **Use brackets to add or substitute words**. Use brackets to add or substitute words in a quoted sentence when the meaning of the quotation would otherwise be unclear—for example, when the antecedent of a quoted pronoun is ambiguous.

Exercise 1.8

Using Brackets

Write your own sentences incorporating the following quotations. Use brackets to clarify information that isn't clear outside its original context—and refer to the original sources to remind yourself of this context.

From the David Chandler paragraph on James Van Allen (pp. 46–47):

    a.   Other space scientists *dispute that idea*.
    b.   Now *it's about $500 million a year*.

From the Jane Yolen excerpt on Cinderella (pp. 50–51):

    a.   *This book's* text is coy and condescending.
    b.   *She* cannot perform even a simple action to save herself, though she is warned by her friends, the mice.
    c.   She does not hear *them* because she is "off in a world of dreams."

Remember that when you quote the work of another, you are obligated to credit—or cite—the author's work properly; otherwise, you may be guilty of plagiarism. See pp. 288–308 for guidance on citing sources.

■ AVOIDING PLAGIARISM

Plagiarism is generally defined as the attempt to pass off the work of another as one's own. Whether born out of calculation or desperation, plagiarism is the least tolerated offense in the academic world. The fact that most plagiarism is unintentional—arising from an ignorance of the conventions rather than deceitfulness—makes no difference to many professors.

The ease of cutting and pasting whole blocks of text from Web sources into one's own paper makes it tempting for some to take the easy way out and avoid doing their own research and writing. But, apart from the serious ethical issues involved, the same technology that makes such acts possible also makes it possible for instructors to detect them. Software marketed to instructors allows them to conduct Web searches, using suspicious phrases as keywords. The results often provide irrefutable evidence of plagiarism.

Of course, plagiarism is not confined to students. Recent years have seen a number of high-profile cases—some of them reaching the front pages of newspapers—of well-known scholars who were shown to have copied passages from sources into their own book manuscripts, without proper attribution. In some cases, the scholars maintained that these appropriations were simply a matter of carelessness, that in the press and volume of work they had lost track of which words were theirs and which were the words of their sources. But such excuses sounded hollow: These careless acts inevitably embarrassed the scholars professionally, tarnished their otherwise fine work and reputations, and disappointed their many admirers.

You can avoid plagiarism and charges of plagiarism by following the basic rules provided on page 55.

Following is a passage from an article by Richard Rovere on Senator Joseph P. McCarthy, along with several student versions of the ideas represented.

> McCarthy never seemed to believe in himself or in anything he had said. He knew that Communists were not in charge of American foreign policy. He knew that they weren't running the United States Army. He knew that he had spent five years looking for Communists in the government and that—although some must certainly have been there, since Communists had turned up in practically every other major government in the world—he hadn't come up with even one.*

One student version of this passage reads:

> McCarthy never believed in himself or in anything he had said. He knew that Communists were not in charge of American foreign policy and weren't running the United States Army. He knew that he had spent five years looking for Communists in the government, and although there must certainly have been some there, since Communists were in practically every other major government in the world, he hadn't come up with even one.

Clearly, this is intentional plagiarism. The student has copied the original passage almost word for word.

Here is another version of the same passage:

> McCarthy knew that Communists were not running foreign policy or the Army. He also knew that although there must have been some

---

*Richard Rovere, "The Most Gifted and Successful Demagogue This Country Has Ever Known," *New York Times Magazine*, 30 Apr. 1967.

> Communists in the government, he hadn't found a single one, even
> though he had spent five years looking.

This student has attempted to put the ideas into her own words, but both
the wording and the sentence structure are so heavily dependent on the
original passage that even if it *were* cited, most professors would consider it
plagiarism.

In the following version, the student has sufficiently changed the wording and sentence structure, and she uses a *signal phrase* (a phrase used to
introduce a quotation or paraphrase, signaling to the reader that the words
to follow come from someone else) to properly credit the information to
Rovere, so that there is no question of plagiarism:

> According to Richard Rovere, McCarthy was fully aware that
> Communists were running neither the government nor the Army. He
> also knew that he hadn't found a single Communist in government,
> even after a lengthy search (192).

And although this is not a matter of plagiarism, as noted above, it's
essential to quote accurately. You are not permitted to change any part of a
quotation or to omit any part of it without using brackets or ellipses.

Rules for Avoiding Plagiarism

- Cite *all* quoted material and *all* summarized and paraphrased material,
  unless the information is common knowledge (e.g.: the Civil War was
  fought from 1861 to 1865).
- Make sure that both the *wording* and the *sentence structure* of your
  summaries and paraphrases are substantially your own.

 # WRITING ASSIGNMENT: SUMMARY

Read "The Political Genius of Abraham Lincoln" by Doris Kearns Goodwin.
(This selection by the Pulitzer Prize–winning historian is from her 2005 book
Team of Rivals: The Political Genius of Abraham Lincoln.) Write a summary of the
passage, following the directions in this chapter for dividing the article into
sections, for writing a one-sentence summary of each section, and then for
joining section summaries with a thesis. Prepare for the summary by making
notes in the margins. You may find it useful to recall that well-written pieces,
like Goodwin's, often telegraph clues to their own structure as a device for
assisting readers. Such clues can be helpful when preparing a summary. Your
finished product should be the result of two or more drafts.

Note: Additional summary assignments will be found in Chapter 8, "Practicing Academic Writing," focusing on the changing landscape of jobs in a
global economy.

THE POLITICAL GENIUS OF ABRAHAM LINCOLN

*Doris Kearns Goodwin**

Doris Kearns Goodwin won the Pulitzer Prize in history for No Ordinary Time. *She is the author of* Wait Till Next Year, The Fitzgeralds and the Kennedys, *and* Lyndon Johnson and the American Dream.

In 1876, the celebrated orator Frederick Douglass dedicated a monument in Washington, D.C., erected by black Americans to honor Abraham Lincoln. The former slave told his audience that "there is little necessity on this occasion to speak at length and critically of this great and good man, and of his high mission in the world. That ground has been fully occupied. . . . The whole field of fact and fancy has been gleaned and garnered. Any man can say things that are true of Abraham Lincoln, but no man can say anything that is new of Abraham Lincoln."

Speaking only eleven years after Lincoln's death, Douglass was too close to assess the fascination that this plain and complex, shrewd and transparent, tender and iron-willed leader would hold for generations of Americans. In the nearly two hundred years since his birth, countless historians and writers have uncovered new documents, provided fresh insights, and developed an ever-deepening understanding of our sixteenth president.

In my own effort to illuminate the character and career of Abraham Lincoln, I have coupled the account of his life with the stories of the remarkable men who were his rivals for the 1860 Republican presidential nomination—New York senator William H. Seward, Ohio governor Salmon P. Chase, and Missouri's distinguished elder statesman Edward Bates.

Taken together, the lives of these four men give us a picture of the path taken by ambitious young men in the North who came of age in the early decades of the nineteenth century. All four studied law, became distinguished orators, entered politics, and opposed the spread of slavery. Their upward climb was one followed by many thousands who left the small towns of their birth to seek opportunity and adventure in the rapidly growing cities of a dynamic, expanding America.

5   Just as a hologram is created through the interference of light from separate sources, so the lives and impressions of those who companioned Lincoln give us a clearer and more dimensional picture of the president himself. Lincoln's barren childhood, his lack of schooling, his relationships with male friends, his complicated marriage, the nature of his ambition, and his ruminations about death can be analyzed more clearly when he is placed side by side with his three contemporaries.

When Lincoln won the nomination, each of his celebrated rivals believed the wrong man had been chosen. Ralph Waldo Emerson recalled his first reception of the news that the "comparatively unknown name of Lincoln" had been selected: "we heard the result coldly and sadly. It seemed too rash, on a purely local reputation, to build so grave a trust in such anxious times."

Lincoln seemed to have come from nowhere—a backwoods lawyer who had served one undistinguished term in the House of Representatives and had lost

---

*Doris Kearns Goodwin, *Team of Rivals: The Political Genius of Abraham Lincoln,* (New York: Simon and Schuster, 2005) v–viii.

two consecutive contests for the U.S. Senate. Contemporaries and historians alike have attributed his surprising nomination to chance—the fact that he came from the battleground state of Illinois and stood in the center of his party. The comparative perspective suggests a different interpretation. When viewed against the failed efforts of his rivals, it is clear that Lincoln won the nomination because he was shrewdest and canniest of them all. More accustomed to relying upon himself to shape events, he took the greatest control of the process leading up to the nomination, displaying a fierce ambition, an exceptional political acumen, and a wide range of emotional strengths, forged in the crucible of personal hardship, that took his unsuspecting rivals by surprise.

That Lincoln, after winning the presidency, made the unprecedented decision to incorporate his eminent rivals into his political family, the cabinet, was evidence of a profound self-confidence and a first indication of what would prove to others a most unexpected greatness. Seward became secretary of state, Chase secretary of the treasury, and Bates attorney general. The remaining top posts Lincoln offered to three former Democrats whose stories also inhabit these pages—Gideon Welles, Lincoln's "Neptune," was made secretary of the navy, Montgomery Blair became post-master general, and Edwin M. Stanton, Lincoln's "Mars," eventually became secretary of war. Every member of this administration was better known, better educated, and more experienced in public life than Lincoln. Their presence in the cabinet might have threatened to eclipse the obscure prairie lawyer from Springfield.

It soon became clear, however, that Abraham Lincoln would emerge the undisputed captain of this most unusual cabinet, truly a team of rivals. The powerful competitors who had originally disdained Lincoln became colleagues who helped him steer the country through its darkest days. Seward was the first to appreciate Lincoln's remarkable talents, quickly realizing the futility of his plan to relegate the president to a figurehead role. In the months that followed, Seward would become Lincoln's closest friend and advisor in the administration. Though Bates initially viewed Lincoln as a well-meaning but incompetent administrator, he eventually concluded that the president was an unmatched leader, "very near being a perfect man." Edwin Stanton, who had treated Lincoln with contempt at their initial acquaintance, developed a great respect for the commander in chief and was unable to control his tears for weeks after the president's death. Even Chase, whose restless ambition for the presidency was never realized, at last acknowledged that Lincoln had outmaneuvered him.

10   This, then, is a story of Lincoln's political genius revealed through his extraordinary array of personal qualities that enabled him to form friendships with men who had previously opposed him; to repair injured feelings that, left untended, might have escalated into permanent hostility; to assume responsibility for the failures of subordinates; to share credit with ease; and to learn from mistakes. He possessed an acute understanding of the sources of power inherent in the presidency, an unparalleled ability to keep his governing coalition intact, a tough-minded appreciation of the need to protect his presidential prerogatives, and a masterful sense of timing. His success in dealing with the strong egos of the men in his cabinet suggests that in the hands of a truly great politician the qualities we generally associate with decency and morality—kindness, sensitivity, compassion, honesty, and empathy—can also be impressive political resources.

2 Critical Reading and Critique

■ CRITICAL READING

When writing papers in college, you are often called on to respond critically to source materials. Critical reading requires the abilities to both summarize and evaluate a presentation. As you have seen in Chapter 1, a *summary* is a brief restatement in your own words of the content of a passage. An *evaluation*, however, is a more ambitious undertaking. In your college work, you read to gain and *use* new information; but because sources are not equally valid or equally useful, you must learn to distinguish critically among them by evaluating them.

There is no ready-made formula for determining validity. Critical reading and its written equivalent—the *critique*—require discernment, sensitivity, imagination, knowledge of the subject, and above all, willingness to become involved in what you read. These skills are developed only through repeated practice. You must begin somewhere, though, and we recommend that you start by posing two broad questions about passages, articles, and books that you read: (1) To what extent does the author succeed in his or her purpose? (2) To what extent do you agree with the author?

Question 1: To What Extent Does the Author Succeed in His or Her Purpose?

All critical reading *begins with an accurate summary.* Thus, before attempting an evaluation, you must be able to locate an author's thesis and identify the selection's content and structure. You must understand the author's *purpose.* Authors write to inform, to persuade, and to entertain. A given piece may be primarily *informative* (a summary of the research on cloning), primarily *persuasive* (an argument on why the government must do something to alleviate homelessness), or primarily *entertaining* (a play about the frustrations of young lovers). Or it may be all three (as in John Steinbeck's novel *The Grapes of Wrath,* about migrant workers during the Great Depression). Sometimes authors are not fully conscious of their purpose. Sometimes their purpose changes as they write. Also, multiple purposes can overlap: An essay may need to inform the reader about an issue in order to make a persuasive point. But if the finished piece is coherent, it will have a primary reason for having been written, and it should be apparent that the author is attempting primarily to inform, persuade, or entertain a particular audience. To identify this primary reason—this purpose—is your first job as a critical reader. Your next job is to determine how successful the author has been.

Where Do We Find Written Critiques?

Here are just a few of the types of writing that involve critique:

ACADEMIC WRITING

- **Research papers** critique sources in order to establish their usefulness.
- **Position papers** stake out a position by critiquing other positions.
- **Book reviews** combine summary with critique.
- **Essay exams** demonstrate understanding of course material by critiquing it.

WORKPLACE WRITING

- **Legal briefs and legal arguments** critique previous arguments made by opposing counsel.
- **Business plans and proposals** critique other less cost-effective, efficient, or reasonable approaches.
- **Policy briefs** communicate failings of policies and legislation through critique.

As a critical reader, you bring various criteria, or standards of judgment, to bear when you read pieces intended to inform, persuade, or entertain.

Writing to Inform

A piece intended to inform will provide definitions, describe or report on a process, recount a story, give historical background, and/or provide facts and figures. An informational piece responds to questions such as:

What (or who) is _____?

How does _____ work?

What is the controversy or problem about?

What happened?

How and why did it happen?

What were the results?

What are the arguments for and against _____?

To the extent that an author answers these and related questions and the answers are a matter of verifiable record (you could check for accuracy if you had the time and inclination), the selection is intended to inform. Having determined this, you can organize your response by considering three other criteria: accuracy, significance, and fair interpretation of information.

Evaluating Informative Writing

Accuracy of Information   If you are going to use any of the information presented, you must be satisfied that it is trustworthy. One of your responsibilities as a critical reader, then, is to find out if it is accurate. This means you should check facts against other sources. Government publications are often good resources for verifying facts about political legislation, population data, crime statistics, and the like. You can also search key terms in library databases and on the Web. Since material on the Web is essentially self-published, however, you must be especially vigilant in assessing its legitimacy. A wealth of useful information is now available on the Internet—but there is also a tremendous amount of misinformation, distorted "facts," and unsupported opinion.

Significance of Information   One useful question that you can put to a reading is "So what?" In the case of selections that attempt to inform, you may reasonably wonder whether the information makes a difference. What can the reader gain from this information? How is knowledge advanced by the publication of this material? Is the information of importance to you or to others in a particular audience? Why or why not?

Fair Interpretation of Information   At times you will read reports, the sole purpose of which is to relate raw data or information. In these cases, you will build your response on Question 1, introduced on page 58: To what extent does the author succeed in his or her purpose? More frequently, once an author has presented information, he or she will attempt to evaluate or interpret it—which is only reasonable, since information that has not been evaluated or interpreted is of little use. One of your tasks as a critical reader is to make a distinction between the author's presentation of facts and figures and his or her attempts to evaluate them. Watch for shifts from straightforward descriptions of factual information ("20 percent of the population") to assertions about what this information means ("a *mere* 20 percent of the population"), what its implications are, and so on. Pay attention to whether the logic with which the author connects interpretation with facts is sound. You may find that the information is valuable but the interpretation is not. Perhaps the author's conclusions are not justified. Could you offer a contrary explanation for the same facts? Does more information need to be gathered before firm conclusions can be drawn? Why?

Writing to Persuade

Writing is frequently intended to persuade—that is, to influence the reader's thinking. To make a persuasive case, the writer must begin with an assertion that is arguable, some statement about which reasonable people could disagree. Such an assertion, when it serves as the essential organizing principle of the article or book, is called a *thesis*. Here are two examples:

> Because they do not speak English, many children in this affluent land are being denied their fundamental right to equal educational opportunity.

> Bilingual education, which has been stridently promoted by a small group of activists with their own agenda, is detrimental to the very students it is supposed to serve.

Thesis statements such as these—and the subsequent assertions used to help support them—represent conclusions that authors have drawn as a result of researching and thinking about an issue. You go through the same process yourself when you write persuasive papers or critiques. And just as you are entitled to evaluate critically the assertions of authors you read, so your professors—and other students—are entitled to evaluate *your* assertions, whether they be written arguments or comments made in class discussion.

Keep in mind that writers organize arguments by arranging evidence to support one conclusion and oppose (or dismiss) another. You can assess the validity of an argument and its conclusion by determining whether the author has (1) clearly defined key terms, (2) used information fairly, and (3) argued logically and not fallaciously (see pages 65–69).

Exercise 2.1

Informative and Persuasive Thesis Statements

With a partner from your class, identify at least one informative and one persuasive thesis statement from two passages of your own choosing. Photocopy these passages and highlight the statements you have selected.

As an alternative, and also working with a partner, write one informative and one persuasive thesis statement for *three* of the topics listed in the last paragraph of this exercise. For example, for the topic of prayer in schools, your informative thesis statement could read:

> Both advocates and opponents of school prayer frame their position as a matter of freedom.

Your persuasive thesis statement might be worded:

> As long as schools don't dictate what kinds of prayers students should say, then school prayer should be allowed and even encouraged.

Don't worry about taking a position that you agree with or feel you could support; this exercise doesn't require that you write an essay. The topics:

school prayer

gun control

stem cell research

grammar instruction in English class

    violent lyrics in music

    teaching computer skills in primary schools

    curfews in college dormitories

    course registration procedures

Evaluating Persuasive Writing

Read the argument that follows on the nation's troubled "star" system for producing elite athletes and dancers. We will illustrate our discussion on defining terms, using information fairly, and arguing logically by referring to Joan Ryan's argument. The model critique that follows these illustrations will be based on this same argument.

WE ARE NOT CREATED EQUAL IN EVERY WAY

Joan Ryan

In an opinion piece for the San Francisco Chronicle *(December 12, 2000), columnist and reporter Joan Ryan takes a stand on whether the San Francisco Ballet School did or did not discriminate against 8-year-old Fredrika Keefer when it declined to admit her on the grounds that she had the wrong body type to be a successful ballerina. Keefer's mother subsequently sued the ballet school for discrimination, claiming that the rejection had caused her daughter confusion and humiliation. Ryan examines the question of setting admissions standards and also the problems some parents create by pushing their young children to meet these standards.*

Fredrika Keefer is an 8-year-old girl who likes to dance, just like her mother and grandmother before her. She relishes playing the lead role of Clara in the Pacific Dance Theater's "Petite Nutcracker." So perhaps she is not as shy as many fourth-graders. But I wonder how she feels about her body being a topic of public discussion.

Fredrika and her mother filed suit because, as her mother puts it, she "did not have the right body type to be accepted" by the San Francisco Ballet School. "My daughter is very sophisticated, so she understands why we're doing this," Krissy Keefer said. "And the other kids think she's a celebrity."

There is no question Keefer raises a powerful point in her complaint. The values placed on an unnaturally thin body for female performers drives some dancers to potentially fatal eating disorders. But that isn't exactly the issue here. This is: Does the San Francisco Ballet School have the right to give preference to leaner body types in selecting 300 students from this year's 1,400 applicants?

Yes, for the same reason UC Berkeley can reject students based on mental prowess and a fashion modeling school can reject students based on comeliness. Every institution has standards that weed out those who are less likely to succeed. I know this flies in the face of American ideals. But the reality is that all men and women are not created equal.

5   Like it or not, the ethereal, elongated body that can float on air is part of the look and feel of classical ballet. You and I might think ballet would be just as pleasing

with larger bodies. But most of those who practice the art disagree, which is their right. This doesn't mean that women with different body types cannot become professional dancers. They just have to find a different type of dance—jazz, tap, modern—just as athletes have to find sports that fit certain body types. A tall, blocky man, for example, could not be a jockey but he could play baseball.

Having written extensively about the damaging pressures on young female gymnasts and figure skaters, I understand Keefer's concerns about body type. But for me, the more disturbing issue in this story isn't about weight but age.

The San Francisco Ballet School is very clear and open about the fact it is strictly a training ground for professional dancers. "We are not a recreation department," said a ballet spokeswoman.

In other words, children at age 8 are already training for adult careers. By age 12 or 13, the children are training so much that they either begin homeschooling or attend a school that accommodates the training schedule. The child has thrown all her eggs into this one little basket at an age when most kids can barely decide what to wear to school in the morning. And the child knows the parents are paying lots of money for this great opportunity.

The ballet school usually has a psychologist to counsel the students, but at the moment there is not one on staff. And the parents are given no training by the school on the pitfalls their daughters might encounter as they climb the ballet ladder: weight issues, physical ailments, social isolation, psychological pressure.

10   Just as in elite gymnastics and figure skating, these children are in the netherland of the law. They are neither hobbyists nor professionals. There is no safety net for them, no arm of government that makes sure that the adults in their lives watch out for their best interests.

Keefer said she would drop her lawsuit if the school accepted her daughter. The San Francisco Ballet School offers the best training in the Bay Area, she said. Fredrika, however, has said she is quite happy dancing where she is. Still, the mother gets to decide what's best for her daughter's dancing career. The child is clearly too young to make such a decision. Yet, in the skewed logic of elite athletics and dancing, she is not too young to pay the price for it.

Exercise 2.2

Critical Reading Practice

Look back at the Critical Reading for Summary box on p. 6 of Chapter 1. Use each of the guidelines listed there to examine the essay by Joan Ryan. Note in the margins of the selection, or on a separate sheet of paper, the essay's main point, subpoints, and use of examples.

Persuasive Strategies

Clearly Defined Terms   The validity of an argument depends to some degree on how carefully an author has defined key terms. Take the assertion, for example, that American society must be grounded in "family values." Just what do people who use this phrase mean by it? The validity of their argument depends on whether they and their readers agree on a definition of "family values"—as well as what it means to be "grounded in" family values. If an author writes that in the recent past "America's elites accepted as a matter of course that a free society can sustain itself only through virtue and temperance in the people" (Charles Murray, "The Coming White Underclass," *Wall Street Journal,* October 20, 1993), readers need to know what exactly the author means by "elites" and by "virtue and temperance" before they can assess the validity of the argument. In such cases, the success of the argument—its ability to persuade—hinges on the definition of a term. So, in responding to an argument, be sure you (and the author) are clear on what exactly is being argued. Unless you are, no informed response is possible.

Ryan uses several terms important for understanding her argument. The primary one is the "body type" that the San Francisco Ballet School uses as an application standard. Ryan defines this type (paragraph 5) as the "elongated body that can float on air." Leaving other terms undefined, she writes that the ballet school's use of body type as a standard "flies in the face of American ideals" (paragraph 4). Exactly *which* ideals she leaves for the reader to define: They might include fair play, equality of access, or the belief that decisions ought to be based on talent, not appearance. The reader cannot be sure. When she reports that a spokeswoman for the school stated that "We are not a recreation department," Ryan assumes the reader will understand the reference. The mission of a recreation department is to give *all* participants equal access. In a youth recreation league, children of all abilities would get to play in a baseball game. In a league for elite athletes, in which winning was a priority, coaches would permit only the most talented children to play.

When writing a paper, you will need to decide, like Ryan, which terms to define and which you can assume the reader will define in the same way you do. As the writer of a critique, you should identify and discuss any undefined or ambiguous term that might give rise to confusion.

Fair Use of Information   Information is used as evidence in support of arguments. When you encounter such evidence, ask yourself two questions: (1) "Is the information accurate and up to date?" At least a portion of an argument becomes invalid when the information used to support it is inaccurate or out of date. (2) "Has the author cited *representative* information?" The evidence used in an argument must be presented in a spirit of fair play. An author is less than ethical when he presents only evidence favoring his own views even though he is well aware that contrary evidence exists. For instance, it would be dishonest to argue that an economic recession is imminent and to cite only indicators of economic downturn while ignoring and failing to cite contrary (positive) evidence.

As you have seen, "We Are Not Created Equal in Every Way" is not an information-heavy essay. The success of the piece turns on the author's use of logic, not facts and figures. In this case, the reader has every reason to trust that Ryan has presented the facts accurately: An 8-year-old girl has been denied admission to a prestigious ballet school. The mother of the girl has sued the school.

Logical Argumentation: Avoiding Logical Fallacies

At some point, you will need to respond to the logic of the argument itself. To be convincing, an argument should be governed by principles of *logic*— clear and orderly thinking. This does *not* mean that an argument should not be biased. A biased argument—that is, an argument weighted toward one point of view and against others, which is in fact the nature of argument— may be valid as long as it is logically sound.

Let's examine several types of faulty thinking and logical fallacies you will need to watch for.

Emotionally Loaded Terms   Writers sometimes attempt to sway readers by using emotionally charged words. Words with positive connotations (e.g., "family values") are intended to sway readers to the author's point of view; words with negative connotations (e.g., "paying the price") try to sway readers away from an opposing point of view. The fact that an author uses emotionally loaded terms does not necessarily invalidate an argument. Emotional appeals are perfectly legitimate and time-honored modes of persuasion. But in academic writing, which is grounded in logical argumentation, they should not be the *only* means of persuasion. You should be sensitive to *how* emotionally loaded terms are being used. In particular, are they being used deceptively or to hide the essential facts?

Ryan appeals to our desire to protect children in "We Are Not Created Equal in Every Way." She writes of "disturbing issue[s]," lack of a "safety net" for young people on the star track to elite performance, and an absence of adults "watch[ing] out for [the children's] best interests." Ryan understands that no reader wants to see a child abused; and while she does not use the word *abuse* in her essay, she implies that parents who push young children too hard to succeed commit abuse. That implication is enough to engage the sympathies of the reader. As someone evaluating the essay, you should be alert to this appeal to your emotions and then judge whether or not the appeal is fair and convincing. Above all, you should not let an emotional appeal blind you to shortcomings of logic, ambiguously defined terms, or a misuse of facts.

***Ad Hominem* Argument**   In an *ad hominem* argument, the writer rejects opposing views by attacking the person who holds them. By calling opponents names, an author avoids the issue. Consider this excerpt from a political speech:

> I could more easily accept my opponent's plan to increase revenues by collecting on delinquent tax bills if he had paid more than a hundred dollars in state taxes in each of the past three years. But the fact is, he's a millionaire with a millionaire's tax shelters. This man hasn't paid a wooden nickel for the state services he and his family depend on. So I ask you: Is *he* the one to be talking about taxes to *us?*

It could well be that the opponent has paid virtually no state taxes for three years; but this fact has nothing to do with, and is used as a ploy to divert attention from, the merits of a specific proposal for increasing revenues. The proposal is lost in the attack against the man himself, an attack that violates principles of logic. Writers (and speakers) should make their points by citing evidence in support of their views and by challenging contrary evidence.

Does Ryan attack Fredrika Keefer's mother in this essay? You be the judge. Here are lines referring directly or indirectly to Krissy Keefer. Is Ryan criticizing the mother, directly or indirectly? Cite specific words and phrases to support your conclusion.

> Fredrika and her mother filed suit because, as her mother puts it, she "did not have the right body type to be accepted" by the San Francisco Ballet School. "My daughter is very sophisticated, so she understands why we're doing this," Krissy Keefer said. "And the other kids think she's a celebrity."
>
> There is no question Keefer raises a powerful point in her complaint.
>
> Keefer said she would drop her lawsuit if the school accepted her daughter. The San Francisco Ballet School offers the best training in the Bay Area, she said. Fredrika, however, has said she is quite happy dancing where she is. Still, the mother gets to decide what's best for her daughter's dancing career. The child is clearly too young to make such a decision. Yet, in the skewed logic of elite athletics and dancing, she is not too young to pay the price for it.

Faulty Cause and Effect   The fact that one event precedes another in time does not mean that the first event has caused the second. An example: Fish begin dying by the thousands in a lake near your hometown. An environmental group immediately cites chemical dumping by several manufacturing plants as the cause. But other causes are possible: A disease might have affected the fish; the growth of algae might have contributed to the deaths; or acid rain might be a factor. The origins of an event are usually complex and are not always traceable to a single cause. So you must carefully examine cause-and-effect reasoning when you find a writer using it. In Latin, this fallacy is known as *post hoc, ergo propter hoc* ("after this, therefore because of this").

Tone

Tone refers to the overall emotional effect produced by a writer's choice of language. Writers might use especially emphatic words to create a tone: A film reviewer might refer to a "magnificent performance," or a columnist might criticize "sleazeball politics."

These are extreme examples of tone; but tone can be more subtle, particularly if the writer makes a special effort *not* to inject emotion into the

(continues)

writing. As we indicated in the section on emotionally loaded terms, the fact that a writer's tone is highly emotional does not necessarily mean that the writer's argument is invalid. Conversely, a neutral tone does not ensure an argument's validity.

Many instructors discourage student writing that projects a highly emotional tone, considering it inappropriate for academic or preprofessional work. (One sure sign of emotion: the exclamation mark, which should be used sparingly.)

The debate over the San Francisco Ballet School's refusal to admit Fredrika Keefer involves a question of cause and effect. Fredrika Keefer's rejection by the ballet school was caused by the school's insistence that its students have an "ethereal, elongated body." If the school changes that standard, the outcome could change: Fredrika Keefer might be admitted.

Ryan also uses cause-and-effect logic in her essay to suggest that Fredrika Keefer's mother, and by extension all parent managers, can cause their children harm by pushing them too hard in their training. At the end of the essay, Ryan writes that Fredrika is too young "to decide what's best for her... dancing career" but that "she is not too young to pay the price for" the decisions her mother makes to promote that career. The "price" Fredrika pays will be "caused" by her mother's (poor) decisions.

Either/Or Reasoning   Either/or reasoning also results from an unwillingness to recognize complexity. If in analyzing a problem an author artificially restricts the range of possible solutions by offering only two courses of action, and then rejects the one that he opposes, he cannot logically argue that the remaining course of action, which he favors, is therefore the only one that makes sense. Usually, several other options (at least) are possible. For whatever reason, the author has chosen to overlook them. As an example, suppose you are reading a selection on genetic engineering in which the author builds an argument on the basis of the following:

> Research in gene splicing is at a crossroads: Either scientists will be carefully monitored by civil authorities and their efforts limited to acceptable applications, such as disease control; or, lacking regulatory guidelines, scientists will set their own ethical standards and begin programs in embryonic manipulation that, however well intended, exceed the proper limits of human knowledge.

Certainly other possibilities for genetic engineering exist beyond the two mentioned here. But the author limits debate by establishing an either/or choice. Such a limitation is artificial and does not allow for complexity. As a critical reader, you need to be on the alert for either/or reasoning.

Hasty Generalization   Writers are guilty of hasty generalization when they draw their conclusions from too little evidence or from unrepresentative evidence. To argue that scientists should not proceed with the human genome project because a recent editorial urged that the project be abandoned is to make a hasty generalization. That lone editorial may be unrepresentative of the views of most individuals—both scientists and laypeople—who have studied and written about the matter. To argue that one should never obey authority because Stanley Milgram's Yale University experiments in the 1960s showed the dangers of obedience is to ignore the fact that Milgram's experiments were concerned primarily with obedience to *immoral* authority. Thus the experimental situation was unrepresentative of most routine demands for obedience—for example, to obey a parental rule or to comply with a summons for jury duty—and a conclusion about the malevolence of all authority would be a hasty generalization.

False Analogy   Comparing one person, event, or issue to another may be illuminating, but it can also be confusing or misleading. Differences between the two may be more significant than their similarities, and conclusions drawn from one may not necessarily apply to the other. A writer who argues that it is reasonable to quarantine people with AIDS because quarantine has been effective in preventing the spread of smallpox is assuming an analogy between AIDS and smallpox that is not valid (because of the differences in transmission between the two diseases).

Ryan compares the San Francisco Ballet School's setting an admissions standard to both a university's and a modeling school's setting standards. Are the analogies apt? Certainly one can draw a parallel between the standards used by the ballet school and those of a modeling school: Both emphasize a candidate's appearance, among other qualities. Are the admissions standards of a university based on appearance? In principle, no. At least that's not a criterion any college admissions office would post on its Web site. A critical reader might therefore want to object that one of Ryan's analogies is faulty.

Ryan attempts to advance her argument by making another comparison:

> [The rejection of a candidate because she does not have a body suited to classical ballet] doesn't mean that women with different body types cannot become professional dancers. They just have to find a different type of dance—jazz, tap, modern—just as athletes have to find sports that fit certain body types. A tall, blocky man, for example, could not be a jockey but he could play baseball.

The words "just as" signal an attempt to advance the argument by making an analogy. What do you think? Is the analogy sufficiently similar to Fredrika Keefer's situation to persuade you?

Begging the Question   To beg the question is to assume as proven fact the very thesis being argued. To assert, for example, that America is not in decline because it is as strong and prosperous as ever does not prove anything: It merely repeats the claim in different words. This fallacy is also known as *circular reasoning*.

When Ryan writes that "There is no safety net for [children placed into elite training programs], no arm of government that makes sure that the adults in their lives watch out for their best interests," she assumes that there should be such a safety net. But, as you will read in the model critique, this is a point that must be argued, not assumed. Is such intervention wise? Under what circumstances would authorities intervene in a family? Would authorities have the legal standing to get involved if there were no clear evidence of physical abuse? Ryan is not necessarily wrong in desiring "safety nets" for young, elite athletes and dancers, but she assumes a point that she should be arguing.

Non Sequitur   *Non sequitur* is Latin for "it does not follow"; the term is used to describe a conclusion that does not logically follow from a premise. "Since minorities have made such great strides in the past few decades," a writer may argue, "we no longer need affirmative action programs." Aside from the fact that the premise itself is arguable (*have* minorities made such great strides?), it does not follow that because minorities *may* have made great strides, there is no further need for affirmative action programs.

Oversimplification   Be alert for writers who offer easy solutions to complicated problems. "America's economy will be strong again if we all 'buy American,'" a politician may argue. But the problems of America's economy are complex and cannot be solved by a slogan or a simple change in buying habits. Likewise, a writer who argues that we should ban genetic engineering assumes that simple solutions ("just say no") will be sufficient to deal with the complex moral dilemmas raised by this new technology.

Exercise 2.3

Understanding Logical Fallacies

Make a list of the nine logical fallacies discussed in the preceding section. Briefly define each one in your own words. Then, in a group of three or four classmates, review your definitions and the examples we've provided for each logical fallacy. Collaborate with your group to find or invent examples for each of the fallacies. Compare your examples with those generated by the other groups in your class.

Writing to Entertain

Authors write not only to inform and persuade but also to entertain. One response to entertainment is a hearty laugh, but it is possible to entertain without encouraging laughter: A good book or play or poem may prompt you to reflect, grow wistful, become elated, get angry. Laughter is only one of many possible reactions. Like a response to an informative piece or an argument, your response to an essay, poem, story, play, novel, or film should be precisely stated and carefully developed. Ask yourself some of the following questions (you won't have space to explore all of them, but try to consider the most important): Did I care for the portrayal of a certain character? Did that character (or a group of characters united by occupation, age, ethnicity, etc.) seem overly sentimental, for example, or heroic? Did his adversaries seem too villainous or stupid? Were the situations believable? Was the action interesting or merely formulaic? Was the theme developed subtly or powerfully, or did the work come across as preachy or shrill? Did the action at the end of the work follow plausibly from what had come before? Was the language fresh and incisive or stale and predictable? Explain as specifically as possible what elements of the work seemed effective or ineffective and why. Offer an overall assessment, elaborating on your views.

Question 2: To What Extent Do You Agree with the Author?

When formulating a critical response to a source, try to distinguish your evaluation of the author's purpose and success at achieving that purpose from your own agreement or disagreement with the author's views. The distinction allows you to respond to a piece of writing on its merits. As an unbiased, even-handed critic, you evaluate an author's clarity of presentation, use of evidence, and adherence to principles of logic. To what extent has the author succeeded in achieving his or her purpose? Still withholding judgment, offer your assessment and give the author (in effect) a grade. Significantly, your assessment of the presentation may not coincide with your views of the author's conclusions: You may agree with an author entirely but feel that the presentation is superficial; you may find the author's logic and use of evidence to be rock solid but at the same time you may resist certain conclusions. A critical evaluation works well when it is conducted in two parts. After evaluating the author's purpose and design for achieving that purpose, respond to the author's main assertions. In doing so, you'll want to identify points of agreement and disagreement and also evaluate assumptions.

Identify Points of Agreement and Disagreement

Be precise in identifying where you agree and disagree with an author. You should state as clearly as possible what *you* believe, and an effective way of doing this is to define your position in relation to that presented in the piece. Whether you agree enthusiastically, agree with reservations, or disagree, you can organize your reactions in two parts: (1) summarize the author's position; and (2) state your own position and elaborate on your reasons for holding it. The elaboration, in effect, becomes an argument itself, and this is true regardless of the position you take. An opinion is effective when you support it by supplying evidence from your reading (which should be properly cited), your observation, or your personal experience. Without such evidence, opinions cannot be authoritative. "I thought the article on inflation was lousy." Or: "It was terrific." Why? "I just thought so, that's all." This opinion is worthless because the criticism is imprecise: The critic has taken neither the time to read the article carefully nor the time to explore his or her own reactions carefully.

Exercise 2.4

Exploring Your Viewpoints—in Three Paragraphs

Go to a Web site that presents short persuasive essays on current social issues, such as reason.com, opinion-pages.org, drudgereport.com, or Speakout.com. Or go to an Internet search engine and type in a social issue together with the word "articles," "editorials," or "opinion," and see what you find. Locate a selection on a topic of interest that takes a clear, argumentative position. Print out the selection on which you choose to focus. Write one paragraph summarizing the author's key argument. Write two paragraphs articulating your agreement or disagreement with the author. (Devote each paragraph to a *single* point of agreement or disagreement.) Be sure to explain why you think or feel the way you do and, wherever possible, cite relevant evidence—from your reading, experience, or observation.

Explore the Reasons for Agreement and Disagreement: Evaluate Assumptions

One way of elaborating your reactions to a reading is to explore the underlying *reasons* for agreement and disagreement. Your reactions are based largely on assumptions that you hold and how those assumptions compare with the author's. An *assumption* is a fundamental statement about the world and its operations that you take to be true. A writer's assumptions may be explicitly stated; but just as often, assumptions are implicit and you can only infer them.

Assumptions provide the foundation on which entire presentations are built. When you find an author's assumptions invalid—that is, not supported by factual evidence—or if you disagree with value-based assumptions underlying an author's position, you may well disagree with the conclusions that follow from these assumptions. Alternatively, if you find that your own assumptions are contradicted by actual experience, you may be forced to conclude that your premises were mistaken.

An interesting example of an assumption fatally colliding with reality was revealed during a recent congressional investigation into the financial meltdown of late 2008 precipitated by the collapse of the home mortgage market—itself precipitated, many believed, by an insufficiently regulated banking and financial system run amuck. During his testimony before the House Oversight Committee in October of that year, former Federal Reserve chairman Alan Greenspan was grilled by committee chairman Henry Waxman (D-CA) about his "ideology"—essentially an assumption or set of assumptions raised to the level of a governing principle.

Greenspan responded, "I do have an ideology. My judgment is that free, competitive markets are by far the unrivaled way to organize economies.

We have tried regulation; none meaningfully worked." Greenspan defined an ideology as "a conceptual framework [for] the way people deal with reality. Everyone has one. You have to. To exist, you need an ideology." And he pointed out that the assumptions on which he and the Federal Reserve operated were supported by "the best banking lawyers in the business . . . and an outside counsel of expert professionals to advise on regulatory matters."

Greenspan then admitted that in light of the economic disaster engulfing the nation, he had found a "flaw" in his ideology. The testimony continues:

> Chairman Waxman: You found a flaw?
>
> Mr. Greenspan: I found a flaw in the model that I perceived is the critical functioning structure that defines how the world works, so to speak.
>
> Chairman Waxman: In other words, you found that your view of the world, your ideology, was not right, it was not working.
>
> Mr. Greenspan: Precisely. That's precisely the reason I was shocked, because I had been going for 40 years or more with very considerable evidence that it was working exceptionally well.*

The lesson? All the research, expertise, and logical argumentation in the world will fail if the premise (assumption, ideology) on which it is based turns out to be "flawed."

How do you determine the validity of assumptions once you have identified them? In the absence of more scientific criteria, you may determine validity by how well the author's assumptions stack up against your own experience, observations, reading, and values. A caution, however: The overall value of an article or book may depend only to a small degree on the validity of the author's assumptions. For instance, a sociologist may do a fine job of gathering statistical data on the incidence of crime in urban areas along the eastern seaboard. The sociologist might also be a Marxist, and you may disagree with the subsequent analysis of the data. Yet you may still find the data extremely valuable for your own work.

Readers will want to examine two assumptions at the heart of Ryan's essay on Fredrika Keefer and the San Francisco Ballet School's refusal to admit her. First, Ryan assumes that setting a standard for admission based on a candidate's appearance is equivalent to setting a standard based on a candidate's "mental prowess," the admissions standard (presumably) used by universities. An appearance-based standard, Ryan writes, will "weed out those who are less likely to succeed" in professional ballet. The writer of the critique that follows agrees with Ryan's assumption. But you may not. You may assume, by contrast, that standards based on appearance are arbitrary while those based on intellectual ability rest on documented talent (SAT scores or high school transcripts, for instance). Ryan makes a second assumption: that there are

---

*United States. Cong. House Committee on Oversight and Government Reform. *The Financial Crisis and the Role of Federal Regulators.* 110th Cong. 2nd sess. Washington: GPO, 2008.

appropriate and inappropriate ways to raise children. She does not state the ways explicitly, but that does not keep her from using them to judge Krissy Keefer harshly. You may disagree with her and find a reason to cheer Krissy Keefer's defense of her daughter's rights. That's your decision. What you must do as a critical reader is recognize assumptions whether they are stated or not. You should spell them out and then accept or reject them. Ultimately, your agreement or disagreement with an author will rest on your agreement or disagreement with the author's assumptions.

■ CRITIQUE

In Chapter 1 we focused on summary—the condensed presentation of ideas from another source. Summary is key to much of academic writing because it relies so heavily on the works of others for the support of claims. It's not going too far to say that summarizing is the critical thinking skill from which a majority of academic writing builds. However, most academic thinking and writing do not stop at summary; usually we use summary to restate our understanding of things we see or read. Then we put that summary to use. In academic writing, one typical use of summary is as a prelude to critique.

A *critique* is a *formalized, critical reading of a passage.* It is also a personal response, but writing a critique is considerably more rigorous than saying that a movie is "great," or a book is "fascinating," or "I didn't like it." These are all responses, and, as such, they're a valid, even essential, part of your understanding of what you see and read. But such responses don't illuminate the subject — even for you—if you haven't explained how you arrived at your conclusions.

Guidelines for Writing Critiques

- *Introduce.* Introduce both the passage under analysis and the author. State the author's main argument and the point(s) you intend to make about it.

  Provide background material to help your readers understand the relevance or appeal of the passage. This background material might include one or more of the following: an explanation of why the subject is of current interest; a reference to a possible controversy surrounding the subject of the passage or the passage itself; biographical information about the author; an account of the circumstances under which the passage was written; a reference to the intended audience of the passage.

- *Summarize.* Summarize the author's main points, making sure to state the author's purpose for writing.

(continues)

- *Assess the presentation.* Evaluate the validity of the author's presentation, as distinct from your points of agreement or disagreement. Comment on the author's success in achieving his or her purpose by reviewing three or four specific points. You might base your review on one or more of the following criteria:

    Is the information accurate?

    Is the information significant?

    Has the author defined terms clearly?

    Has the author used and interpreted information fairly?

    Has the author argued logically?

- *Respond to the presentation.* Now it is your turn to respond to the author's views. With which views do you agree? With which do you disagree? Discuss your reasons for agreement and disagreement, when possible tying these reasons to assumptions—both the author's and your own. Where necessary, draw on outside sources to support your ideas.

- *Conclude.* State your conclusions about the overall validity of the piece—your assessment of the author's success at achieving his or her aims and your reactions to the author's views. Remind the reader of the weaknesses and strengths of the passage.

Your task in writing a critique is to turn your critical reading of a passage into a systematic evaluation in order to deepen your reader's (and your own) understanding of that passage. Among other things, you're interested in determining what an author says, how well the points are made, what assumptions underlie the argument, what issues are overlooked, and what implications can be drawn from such an analysis. Critiques, positive or negative, should include a fair and accurate summary of the passage; they may draw on and cite information and ideas from other sources (your reading or your personal experience and observations); and they should also include a statement of your own assumptions. It is important to remember that you bring to bear an entire set of assumptions about the world. Stated or not, these assumptions underlie every evaluative comment you make; you therefore have an obligation, both to the reader and to yourself, to clarify your standards by making your assumptions explicit. Not only do your readers stand to gain by your forthrightness, but so do you. In the process of writing a critical assessment, you are forced to examine your own knowledge, beliefs, and assumptions. Ultimately, the critique is a way of learning about yourself—yet another example of the ways in which writing is useful as a tool for critical thinking.

How to Write Critiques

You may find it useful to organize a critique into five sections: introduction, summary, assessment of the presentation (on its own terms), your response to the presentation, and conclusion.

The box on pp. 73–74 offers guidelines for writing critiques. They do not constitute a rigid formula. Thousands of authors write critiques that do not follow the structure outlined here. Until you are more confident and practiced in writing critiques, however, we suggest you follow these guidelines. They are meant not to restrict you, but rather to provide a workable sequence for writing critiques.

■ DEMONSTRATION: CRITIQUE

The critique that follows is based on Joan Ryan's op-ed piece "We Are Not Created Equal in Every Way" (pp. 62–63), which we have already begun to examine. In this formal critique, you will see that it is possible to agree with an author's main point, at least provisionally, yet disagree with other elements of the argument. Critiquing a different selection, you could just as easily accept the author's facts and figures but reject the conclusion he draws from them. As long as you carefully articulate the author's assumptions and your own, explaining in some detail your agreement and disagreement, the critique is yours to take in whatever direction you see fit.

Let's summarize the preceding sections by returning to the core questions that guide critical reading. You will see how, when applied to Joan Ryan's argument, they help to set up a critique.

To What Extent Does the Author Succeed in His or Her Purpose?

To answer this question, you will need to know the author's purpose. Joan Ryan's "We Are Not Created Equal in Every Way" is an argument—actually, *two* related arguments. She wants readers to accept her view that (1) a school of performing arts has the right to set admissions standards according to criteria it believes will ensure the professional success of its graduates; and (2) parents may damage their children by pushing them too hard to meet the standards set by these schools.

By supporting a ballet school's right to set admission standards based on appearance, Ryan supports the star system that produces our elite athletes and performers. At the same time, she disapproves of parents who risk their children's safety and welfare by pushing them through this system. Ryan both defends the system and attacks it. Her ambivalence on the issue keeps the argument from succeeding fully.

To What Extent Do You Agree with the Author? Evaluate Assumptions

Ryan's views on the debate surrounding Fredrika Keefer's rejection by the San Francisco School of Ballet rest on the assumption that the school has the right to set its own admissions standards—even if we find those standards harsh. All private institutions, she claims, have that right. The writer of the critique that follows agrees with Ryan, although we have seen how it is possible to disagree.

Ryan's second argument concerns the wisdom of subjecting an 8-year-old to the rigors of professional training. Ryan disapproves. The writer of the critique, while sympathetic to Ryan's concerns, states that as a practical and even as a legal matter it would be nearly impossible to prevent parents such as Krissy Keefer from doing exactly as they please in the name of helping their children. In our culture, parents have the right (short of outright abuse) to raise children however they see fit.

Finally, the writer of the critique notes a certain ambivalence in Ryan's essay: her support of the ballet school's admission standards on the one hand and her distaste for parent managers like Krissy Keefer on the other. The writer does not find evidence of a weak argument in Ryan's mixed message but rather a sign of confusion in the broader culture: We love our young stars, but we condemn parents for pushing children to the breaking point in the name of stardom.

The selections you are likely to critique will be those, like Ryan's, that argue a specific position. Indeed, every argument you read is an invitation to agree or disagree. It remains only for you to speak up and justify your position.

MODEL CRITIQUE

Eric Ralston

Professor Reilly

Writing 2

11 January 2008

A Critique of "We Are Not Created Equal
in Every Way" by Joan Ryan

(1)   Most freshmen know how it feels to apply to a school and be rejected. Each year, college admissions offices mail thousands of thin letters that begin: "Thank you for your application. The competition this year was unusually strong. . . ." We know that we will not get into every college on our list or pass every test or win the starring role after every audition, but we believe that we deserve the chance to try. And we can tolerate rejection if we know that we compete on a level playing field. But when that field seems to arbitrarily favor some candidates over others, we take offense. At least that's when an ambitious mother took offense, bringing to court a suit that claimed her eight-year-old daughter, Fredrika Keefer, was denied admission to the prestigious San Francisco Ballet School because she had the wrong "body type" (A29).

(2)   In an opinion piece for the *San Francisco Chronicle* (12 December 2000), Joan Ryan asks: "Does [a ballet school] have the right to give preference to leaner body types?" Her answer is a firm yes. Ryan argues that institutions have the right to set whatever standards they want to ensure that those they admit meet the physical or intellectual requirements for professional success. But she also believes that some parents push their children too hard to meet those standards. Ryan offers a questionable approach to protecting children from the possible abuses of such parents. Overall, however, she raises timely issues in discussing the star system that produces our world-class athletes

and performers. The sometimes conflicting concerns she expresses reflect contradictions and tensions in our larger culture.

③   The issue Ryan discusses is a particularly sensitive one because the child's mother charged the ballet school with discrimination. As a society we have made great strides over the past few decades in combating some of the more blatant forms of discrimination—racial, ethnic, and sexual. But is it possible, is it desirable, to eliminate *all* efforts to distinguish one person from another? When is a standard that permits some (but not all) people entry to an institution discriminatory and when is it a necessary part of doing business? Ryan believes that schools discriminate all the time, and rightly so when candidates for admission fail to meet the stated criteria for academic or professional success. That UC Berkeley does not accept every applicant is *discriminating,* not discriminatory. Ryan recognizes the difference.

④   She maintains, correctly, that the San Francisco Ballet School, like any other private institution, has the right to set standards by which it will accept or reject applicants. Rejection is a part of life, she writes, expressing the view that gives her essay its title: "We Are Not Created Equal in Every Way." And because we are not created equal, not everyone will be admitted to his or her number one school or get a turn on stage. That's the inevitable consequence of setting standards: Some people will meet them and gain admission, others won't. Ryan quotes the spokesperson who explained that the San Francisco Ballet School is "'not a recreation department'" (A29). In other words, a professional ballet school, like a university, is within its rights to reject applicants with body types unsuited to its view of success in professional ballet. The standard may be cruel and to some even arbitrary, but it is understandable. To put the matter bluntly, candidates with unsuitable body types, however talented or otherwise attractive, are less likely to succeed in professional ballet than those with "classical" proportions. Female dancers, for example, must regularly be lifted and carried, as if effortlessly, by their male counterparts—a feat that is difficult enough even with "leaner body types." Ryan points out that candidates without the ideal body type for ballet are not barred from professional dance: "[t]hey just have to find a different type of dance . . . just as athletes have to find sports that fit certain body types" (A29).

(5)   The San Francisco Ballet School is *not* saying that people of a certain skin color or religious belief are not welcome. That *would* be discriminatory and wrong. But the standard concerning body type cuts across *all* people, rich or poor, black or white, Protestant or Jew, male or female. Such a broad standard could be termed an equal opportunity standard: If it can be used to distinguish among all people equally, it is discriminating, not discriminatory.

(6)   Ryan's parallel concern in this essay is the damage done to children by parents who push them at an early age to meet the high standards set by professional training programs. Children placed onto such star tracks attend special schools (or receive home schooling) in order to accommodate intense training schedules that sometimes lead to physical or psychological injuries. In healthy families, we might expect parents to protect children from such dangers. But parents who manage what they view as their children's "careers" may be too single-minded to realize that their actions may place Johnny and Susie at risk.

(7)   Ryan disapproves of a star track system that puts children into professional training at a young age. In pursuing a career in dance, for instance, a young "child has thrown all her eggs into this one little basket at an age when most kids can barely decide what to wear to school in the morning" (A29). The law makes no provision for protecting such elite performers in training, writes Ryan: "There is no safety net for them, no arm of government that makes sure that the adults in their lives watch out for their best interests" (A29).

(8)   Like the rest of us, Ryan assumes there are appropriate and less appropriate ways to raise children. While she does not explicitly share her preferred approach, she uses language effectively (both her own and her subjects') to suggest what does not work: pushing an otherwise "quite happy" eight-year-old who "relishes" dancing into professional ballet school. Ryan is subtle enough not to attack Krissy Keefer directly, instead letting the mother undermine

herself with a comment few could take seriously: "My daughter is very sophisticated, so she understands why we're [bringing a lawsuit]." No eight-year-old could fully understand the motivations behind a lawsuit, and the statement suggests a mother pursuing her own—not her daughter's—agenda. Ryan suggests that Krissy Keefer has succumbed to "the skewed logic of elite athletics and dancing" that has damaged too many young people. When Ryan points out that "no arm of government" looks out for children like Frederika, she implies the need for a Department of Youth Services to supervise parent managers. This is not a good idea.

⑨   There is no sure way to tell when a parent's managing of a child's dance or athletic schedule is abusive or constructive. Intense dedication is necessary for would-be elite athletes and performers to succeed, and such dedication often begins in childhood. Since young children are not equipped to organize their lives in pursuit of a single goal, parents step in to help. That's what the parents of Tiger Woods did on recognizing his talents:

> [H]is father . . . [started] him very early. . . . [Tiger] was on the Mike Douglas show hitting golf balls when he was three years old. I mean, this is a prodigy type thing. This is like Mozart writing his first symphony when he was six, that sort of thing, and he did show unique ability right from the beginning. And his life has been channeled into being a pro. His father has devoted his life to bringing him to this point. His father hasn't worked full-time since 1988. That's what it's been all about. (Feinstein)

⑩   Ryan would point out, correctly, that for every Tiger Woods or Michelle Kwan there are many child-athletes and performing artists who fall short of their goals. They may later regret the single-minded focus that robbed them of their childhood, but there is no way to know before committing a child to years of dedicated practice whether he or she will become the next Tiger or an embittered also-ran. We simply do not have the wisdom to intervene in a parent manager's training program for her child. And Joan Ryan is not going to find an "arm of government" to intervene in the child rearing of Fredrika Keefer, however much she may "pay the price for" (A29) her mother's enthusiasm.

(11)   The tension in Ryan's essay over high standards and the intense preparation to meet them mirrors a tension in the larger culture. On the one hand,
Ryan argues persuasively that elite institutions like the San Francisco Ballet
School have the right to set standards for admission. At such institutions,
high standards give us high levels of achievement—dancers, for instance, who
"can float on air" (A29). We cheer brilliant performers like Tiger Woods and
Michelle Kwan who started on their roads to success while still children. The
star system produces stars. On the other hand, Ryan condemns parents who
buy into the star system by pushing their children into professional training
programs that demand a single-minded focus. We are horrified to learn that
Macaulay Culkin of the *Home Alone* movies never really had a childhood
(Peterson). Of course Culkin and others like him didn't have childhoods: They
were too busy practicing their lines or their jumps and spins. If Ryan defends
high standards in one breath and criticizes parents in the next for pushing
children to achieve these standards, she is only reflecting a confusion in the
larger culture: We love our stars, but we cannot have our stars without a star
system that demands total (and often damaging) dedication from our
youngest and most vulnerable citizens. That parents can be the agent of this
damage is especially troubling.

(12)   Joan Ryan is right to focus on the parents of would-be stars, and she is
right to remind us that young children pressured to perform at the highest levels
can suffer physically and psychologically. Perhaps it was better for Fredrika Keefer
the child (as opposed to Fredrika Keefer the future professional dancer) that she
was not admitted to the San Francisco School of Ballet. For Keefer's sake and that
of other child performers, we should pay attention to the dangers of the star
system and support these children when we can. But without clear evidence of
legally actionable neglect or abuse, we cannot interfere with parent managers,
however much we may disagree with their decisions. We may be legitimately
concerned, as is Ryan, that such a parent is driving her child to become not the
next Tiger Woods but the next admission to a psychiatric ward. In a free society,
for better or for worse, parents have the right to guide (or misguide) the lives of
their children. All the rest of us can do is watch—and hope for the best.

Ralston 6

Works Cited

Feinstein, John. "Year of the Tiger." Interview by Jim Lehrer. *Online News Hour.*
    PBS, 14 Apr. 1997. Web. 8 Jan. 2008.

Peterson, Paul. Interview by Gary James. *ClassicBands.com.* Classic Bands,
    12 Feb. 2000. Web. 8 Jan. 2008. <http://www.classicbands.com/
    PaulPetersonInterview.html>.

Ryan, Joan. "We Are Not Created Equal in Every Way." *San Francisco Chronicle*
    12 Dec. 2000: A29. Print.

Exercise 2.5

Informal Critique of the Model Critique

Before reading our analysis of this model critique, write your own informal response to the critique. What are its strengths and weaknesses? To what extent does the critique follow the general Guidelines for Writing Critiques that we outlined on pp. 73–74? To the extent it varies from the guidelines, speculate on why. Jot down ideas for a critique that takes a different approach to Ryan's essay.

Critical Reading for Critique

- *Use the tips from Critical Reading for Summary on p. 6.* Remember to examine the context; note the title and subtitle; identify the main point; identify the subpoints; break the reading into sections; distinguish between points, examples, and counterarguments; watch for transitions within and between paragraphs; and read actively.

- *Establish the writer's primary purpose in writing.* Is the piece meant primarily to inform, persuade, or entertain?

- *Evaluate informative writing. Use these criteria (among others):*
    Accuracy of information
    Significance of information
    Fair interpretation of information

- *Evaluate persuasive writing. Use these criteria (among others):*
    Clear definition of terms

(continues)

Fair use and interpretation of information

Logical reasoning

- *Evaluate writing that entertains. Use these criteria (among others):*

  Interesting characters

  Believable action, plot, and situations

  Communication of theme

  Use of language

- *Decide whether you agree or disagree with the writer's ideas, position, or message.* Once you have determined the extent to which an author has achieved his or her purpose, clarify your position in relation to the writer's.

The Strategy of the Critique

- Paragraph 1 of the model critique introduces the issue to be reviewed. It provides brief background information and sets a general context that explains why the topic of fair (and unfair) competition is important.

- Paragraph 2 introduces the author and the essay and summarizes the author's main claims. The paragraph ends (see the final three sentences) with the writer's overall assessment of the essay.

- Paragraph 3 sets a specific context for evaluating Ryan's first claim concerning admissions standards. The writer summarizes Ryan's position by making a distinction between the terms *discriminating* and *discriminatory.*

- Paragraph 4 evaluates Ryan's first claim, that the ballet school has the right to set admission standards. The writer supports Ryan's position.

- Paragraph 5 continues the evaluation of Ryan's first claim. Again, the writer of the critique supports Ryan, returning to the distinction between *discriminating* and *discriminatory.*

- Paragraphs 6–7 summarize Ryan's second claim, that parents can damage their children by pushing them too hard through professional training programs at too early an age.

- Paragraphs 8–10 evaluate Ryan's second claim. In paragraph 8 the writer states that Ryan makes a mistake in implying that a government agency should safeguard the interests of children like Fredrika Keefer. Paragraphs 9–10 present the logic for disagreeing with Ryan on this point.

- Paragraph 11 evaluates the essay as a whole. Ryan defends the right of schools in the star system to set high standards but objects when parents push young children into this system. This "tension" in the essay reflects a confusion in the larger culture.

- Paragraph 12 concludes the critique. The writer offers qualified support of Ryan's position, agreeing that children caught in the star system can suffer. The writer also states that there is not much we can do about the problem except watch and hope for the best.

 ## WRITING ASSIGNMENT: CRITIQUE

Read and write a critique of "The Common App Fallacy," in which a columnist for New York University's *Washington Square News* argues against the wisdom of using the Common Application in the college application process. You might read such an essay in your own college newspaper; here is your opportunity to respond. The piece originally appeared in the *Washington Square News* on January 22, 2008.

Before reading, review the tips presented in the Critical Reading for Critique box (pp. 82–83). When you're ready to write your critique, start by jotting down notes in response to the tips for critical reading and the earlier discussions of evaluating writing in this chapter. What assumptions does Damon Beres make? Review the logical fallacies on pp. 65–69, and identify any that appear in the essay. Work out your ideas on paper, perhaps producing an outline. Then write a rough draft of your critique. Review the reading and revise your rough draft at least once before considering it finished. You may want to look ahead to Chapter 6, Writing as a Process, to help guide you through writing your critique.

For an additional exercise in writing critiques, see Chapter 8, a practice chapter that assembles readings on the topic of the changing nature of jobs in a global economy. You will have the opportunity to write a critique that you then place into a larger argument.

THE COMMON APP FALLACY

Damon Beres

It's a small miracle that I'm able to have this column for you today. No, I'm not a victim of crippling arthritis, nor did my sticky laptop keyboard give me carpal tunnel syndrome. Rather, it dawned on me that I was one of over 11,000 chosen from a pool of nearly 34,000 students, as the Office of Undergraduate Admissions reports, to join New York University's freshman class last year. If I were a smarter man, I'd start playing the lottery.

Truth is, college applications are a crapshoot in this day and age. My friends back home, with GPAs that resemble the population of China and extracurriculars that make Jimmy Carter look like a lazy old coot, are getting shut out of the Ivies, shut out of their "targets," and, well, shut out of everywhere. At this rate, it seems the only thing most of them will be getting into is antidepressants.

Colleges nationwide, from Yale University to the University of South Carolina, have been reporting substantial increases in applications for years now. Part of that is good, as that probably means that more kids are interested in pursuing higher education. The downside, of course, is that many aren't getting into the schools they want or deserve.

In order to counter this, students apply to as many schools as they can, spitting applications out like bitter saliva. The average from people I've talked to seems to be around 10, though many that I know have applied to upward of 16. What they don't seem to realize is that hedging their bets like this is only making things worse for everyone. Schools have a larger, more competitive application pool to pick from, and kids are taking spots at universities that they may, in fact, have little to no interest in.

5   It's not their fault, though; universities, the College Board, and worst of all, the Common Application are encouraging this dance. The College Board makes it easy to blast those precious SAT scores out to every college under the sun, provided mommy and daddy's credit card isn't maxed out, while the Common Application makes shuttling apps to any number of schools a simple process of point-and-click. With such tools at their disposal, and knowing that the competition will make full use of them, how could any student resist mass applications?

As the nation's top "dream school," as reported by the *Princeton Review* (and why not? We've had Olsens, an Osment and that little girl from *Matilda*), NYU is in a prime position to affect the application process. Harvard caused quite a stir when it got rid of early admissions, so why won't NYU's admissions department do something similar and become a nationwide trendsetter?

It's simple, really: Get rid of the Common Application. Besides pulling in easy money from application fees, what benefit does it provide? New York University is already a competitive institution, a school that's more than able to play in the big leagues, so it certainly doesn't need the extra applicants that the Common App brings in. The more universities that can shake faith in the Common App, the better; it's a cheap, money-making scheme that homogenizes applicants and schools alike. A supplemental essay or two for each school—essays that can easily be adapted from essays for other schools—certainly can't make up for a personalized, unique application that shows a serious interest in the school. It's troubling that nearly 100 universities, including the likes of Dartmouth, Northwestern and Yale, are Common App–exclusive, as it indicates that the college application process has turned from an individualized search for the right place into a cold, sterile business. NYU has a reputation, so why doesn't it use it?

Maybe it has to be a joint endeavor. Maybe high school students should actually care about their applications, which might mean taking the time to search for a handful of schools that they feel are perfect fits. Maybe the College Board and Common App should go all-out with their greed and charge more to send out scores and applications to discourage students from sending them out with reckless abandon. Maybe it doesn't all have to be such a crapshoot.

For the class of 2011, Williams College accepted 1,194 students out of 6,448. Massachusetts Institute of Technology accepted 1,553 out of 12,445. Brown University accepted 2,683 out of 19,059. Princeton University accepted 1,838 out of 18,942. I have about a one-in-five chance of winning on a "Crazy Cash" scratch-off ticket. Shouldn't students have a better chance at getting into college?

Explanatory Synthesis ▪ 3

▪ WHAT IS A SYNTHESIS?

A *synthesis* is a written discussion that draws on two or more sources. It follows that your ability to write syntheses depends on your ability to infer relationships among sources—essays, articles, fiction, and also nonwritten sources such as lectures, interviews, visual media, and observations. This process is nothing new for you because you infer relationships all the time—say, between something you've read in the newspaper and something you've seen for yourself, or between the teaching styles of your favorite and least favorite instructors. In fact, if you've written research papers, you've already written syntheses. In a *synthesis,* you make explicit the relationships that you have inferred among separate sources.

The skills you've already learned and practiced in the previous two chapters will be vital in writing syntheses. Before you're in a position to draw relationships between two or more sources, you must understand what those sources say; you must be able to *summarize* those sources. Readers will frequently benefit from at least partial summaries of sources in your synthesis essays. At the same time, you must go beyond summary to make judgments—judgments based on your *critical reading* of your sources: what conclusions you've drawn about the quality and validity of these sources, whether you agree or disagree with the points made in your sources, and why you agree or disagree.

In a synthesis, you go beyond the critique of individual sources to determine the relationships among them. Is the information in source B, for example, an extended illustration of the generalizations in source A? Would it be useful to compare and contrast source C with source B? Having read and considered sources A, B, and C, can you infer something else— in other words, D (not a source, but your own idea)?

Because a synthesis is based on two or more sources, you will need to be selective when choosing information from each. It would be neither possible nor desirable, for instance, to discuss in a ten-page paper on the American Civil War every point that the authors of two books make about their subject. What you as a writer must do is select from each source the ideas and information that best allow you to achieve your purpose.

▪ PURPOSE

Your purpose in reading source materials and then drawing on them to write your own material is often reflected in the wording of an assignment. For instance, consider the following assignments on the Civil War:

American History: Evaluate the author's treatment of the origins of the Civil War.

Economics: Argue the following proposition, in light of your readings: "The Civil War was fought not for reasons of moral principle but for reasons of economic necessity."

Government: Prepare a report on the effects of the Civil War on Southern politics at the state level between 1870 and 1917.

Mass Communications: Discuss how the use of photography during the Civil War may have affected the perceptions of the war by Northerners living in industrial cities.

Literature: Select two Southern writers of the twentieth century whose work you believe was influenced by the divisive effects of the Civil War. Discuss the ways this influence is apparent in a novel or a group of short stories written by each author. The works should not be *about* the Civil War.

Applied Technology: Compare and contrast the technology of warfare available in the 1860s with the technology available a century earlier.

Where Do We Find Written Syntheses?

Here are just a few of the types of writing that involve synthesis:

ACADEMIC WRITING

- **Analysis papers** synthesize and apply several related theoretical approaches.
- **Research papers** synthesize multiple sources.
- **Argument papers** synthesize different points into a coherent claim or position.
- **Essay exams** demonstrate understanding of course material through comparing and contrasting theories, viewpoints, or approaches in a particular field.

WORKPLACE WRITING

- **Newspaper and magazine articles** synthesize primary and secondary sources.
- **Position papers and policy briefs** compare and contrast solutions for solving problems.
- **Business plans** synthesize ideas and proposals into one coherent plan.
- **Memos and letters** synthesize multiple ideas, events, and proposals into concise form.
- **Web sites** synthesize information from various sources to present in Web pages and related links.

Each of these assignments creates a particular purpose for writing. Having located sources relevant to your topic, you would select for possible use in a paper only the parts of those sources that helped you in fulfilling this purpose. And how you used those parts—how you related them to other material from other sources—would also depend on your purpose. For instance, if you were working on the government assignment, you might draw on the same source as a student working on the literature assignment by referring to Robert Penn Warren's novel *All the King's Men,* about Louisiana politics in the early part of the twentieth century. But because the purposes of the two assignments are different, you and the other student would make different uses of this source. The parts or aspects of the novel that you find worthy of detailed analysis might be mentioned only in passing—or not at all—by the other student.

■ USING YOUR SOURCES

Your purpose determines not only what parts of your sources you will use but also how you will relate them to one another. Since the very essence of synthesis is the combining of information and ideas, you must have some basis on which to combine them. *Some relationships among the material in your sources must make them worth synthesizing.* It follows that the better able you are to discover such relationships, the better able you will be to use your sources in writing syntheses. Notice that the mass communications assignment requires you to draw a *cause-and-effect* relationship between photographs of the war and Northerners' perceptions of the war. The applied technology assignment requires you to *compare and contrast* state-of-the-art weapons technology in the eighteenth and nineteenth centuries. The economics assignment requires you to *argue* a proposition. In each case, *your purpose will determine how you relate your source materials to one another.*

Consider some other examples. You may be asked on an exam question or in the instructions for a paper to *describe* two or three approaches to prison reform during the past decade. You may be asked to *compare and contrast* one country's approach to imprisonment with another's. You may be asked to *develop an argument* of your own on this subject, based on your reading. Sometimes (when you are not given a specific assignment) you determine your own purpose: You are interested in exploring a particular subject; you are interested in making a case for one approach or another. In any event, your purpose shapes your essay. Your purpose determines which sources you research, which ones you use, which parts of them you use, at which points in your paper you use them, and in what manner you relate them to one another.

■ TYPES OF SYNTHESES: EXPLANATORY AND ARGUMENT

In this and the next chapter we categorize syntheses into two main types: *explanatory* and *argument*. The easiest way to recognize the difference between the two types may be to consider the difference between a news article and an editorial on the same subject. For the most part, we'd say that the main purpose of the news article is to convey *information,* and the main purpose of the editorial is to convey *opinion* or *interpretation*. Of course, this distinction is much too simplified: News articles often convey opinion or bias, sometimes subtly, sometimes openly; and editorials often convey unbiased information along with opinion. But as a practical matter we can generally agree on the distinction between a news article that primarily conveys information and an editorial that primarily conveys opinion. You should be able to observe this distinction in the selections shown here as Explanation and Argument.

Explanation: News Article from the New York Times

PRIVATE GETS 3 YEARS FOR IRAQ PRISON ABUSE

By David S. Cloud

September 28, 2005

Pfc. Lynndie R. England, a 22-year-old clerk in the Army who was photographed with naked Iraqi detainees at Abu Ghraib prison, was sentenced on Tuesday to three years in prison and a dishonorable discharge for her role in the scandal.

After the sentence was announced, Private England hung her head and cried briefly before hugging her mother, one of the few signs of emotion she showed in the six-day trial.

She had been found guilty on Monday of one count of conspiracy to maltreat prisoners, four counts of maltreatment and one count of committing an indecent act.

She made no comment on Tuesday as she was led out of the courthouse in handcuffs and leg shackles.

5   Earlier in the day, though, she took the stand and apologized for abusing the prisoners, saying her conduct was influenced by Specialist Charles A. Graner Jr., her boyfriend at the time.

She said she was "embarrassed" when photographs showing her posing next to naked detainees became public in 2004.

"I was used by Private Graner," she said. "I didn't realize it at the time."

Specialist Graner was reduced in rank after he was convicted in January as ringleader of the abuse.

Often groping for words and staring downward, Private England directed her apology to the detainees and to any American troops and their families who might have been injured or killed as a result of the insurgency in Iraq gaining strength.

10   Prosecutors argued on Tuesday that the anti-American feeling generated in
Arab and Muslim countries by the Abu Ghraib scandal justified sentencing Private
England to four to six years in prison and dishonorably discharging her from the
Army. The charges the jury found her guilty of on Monday carried a maximum
penalty of nine years. . . .

Argument: Editorial from the Boston Globe

MILITARY ABUSE

September 28, 2005

The court-martial conviction Monday of reservist Lynndie England for her role in the
abuse of Iraqi prisoners at Abu Ghraib should fool no one that the Pentagon is taking
seriously the mistreatment of Iraqis, especially after the release last Friday of a report
on torture by members of the 82d Airborne Division stationed near Fallujah. . . .

If the [new] allegations are found credible, they further demolish the
contention by officials that the abuse first reported at Abu Ghraib in 2004 was an
isolated case of a few bad apples. Pentagon brass also tried to explain away
the activities of England's unit as the actions of relatively untrained reservists. It
is less easy to dismiss as a fluke such abuse when it occurs at the hands of the
82d Airborne, a thoroughly trained and highly decorated division.

The new charges, along with other accusations of abuse that have emerged
since Abu Ghraib, including 28 suspicious detainee deaths, provide strong
evidence that both reservist and active duty troops throughout Iraq were confused
about their responsibility to treat detainees as prisoners of war under the terms of
the Geneva Conventions. . . . Congress should have long since created a special
commission, as proposed in a bill by Senator Carl Levin of Michigan, to investigate
the issue of prisoner abuse. . . .

A truly independent inquiry, along the lines of the one done by the 9/11 commission, could trace accountability for prisoner abuse through statements and
policies by ranking civilian and military officials in the Bush administration.
Accountability for the shame of prisoner torture and abuse should not stop with
Lynndie England and her cohort.

We'll say, for the sake of convenience, that the news article provides an
explanation of England's sentence and that the editorial provides an *argument*
for investigating responsibility *beyond* England.

As a further example of the distinction between explanation and argument,
read the following paragraph:

> Researchers now use recombinant DNA technology to analyze
> genetic changes. With this technology, they cut and splice DNA from
> different species, then insert the modified molecules into bacteria or

> other types of cells that engage in rapid replication and cell division. The cells copy the foreign DNA right along with their own. In short order, huge populations produce useful quantities of recombinant DNA molecules. The new technology also is the basis of genetic engineering, by which genes are isolated, modified, and inserted back into the same organism or into a different one.*

Now read this paragraph:

> Many in the life sciences field would have us believe that the new gene splicing technologies are irrepressible and irreversible and that any attempt to oppose their introduction is both futile and retrogressive. They never stop to even consider the possibility that the new genetic science might be used in a wholly different manner than is currently being proposed. The fact is, the corporate agenda is only one of two potential paths into the Biotech Century. It is possible that the growing number of anti-eugenic activists around the world might be able to ignite a global debate around alternative uses of the new science—approaches that are less invasive, more sustainable and humane and that conserve and protect the genetic rights of future generations.†

Both of these passages deal with the topic of biotechnology, but the two take quite different approaches. The first passage comes from a biology textbook, while the second appears in a magazine article. As we might expect from a textbook on the broad subject of biology, the first passage is explanatory and informative; it defines and explains some of the key concepts of biotechnology without taking a position or providing commentary about the implications of the technology. Magazine articles often present information in the same ways; however, many magazine articles take specific positions, as we see in the second passage. This passage is argumentative or persuasive: its primary purpose is to convey a point of view regarding the topic of biotechnology.

While each of these excerpts presents a clear instance of writing that is either explanatory or argumentative, it is important to note that both the textbook chapter and the magazine article contain elements of both explanation and argument. The textbook writers, while they refrain from taking a particular position, do note the controversies surrounding biotechnology and genetic engineering. They might even subtly reveal a certain bias in favor of one side of the issue, through their word choice and tone, and perhaps through devoting more space and attention to one point of view. Explanatory and argumentative writing are not mutually exclusive. The overlap of explanation and argument is also found in the magazine article: In order to make his case

---

*Cecie Starr and Ralph Taggart, "Recombinant DNA and Genetic Engineering," *Biology: The Unity and Diversity of Life* (New York: Wadsworth, 1998).
†Jeremy Rifkin, "The Ultimate Therapy: Commercial Eugenics on the Eve of the Biotech Century," *Tikkun* May-June 1998: 35.

against genetic engineering, the writer has to explain certain elements of the issue. Yet even while these categories overlap to a certain extent, the second passage clearly has argument as its primary purpose, and the first passage is primarily explanatory.

In Chapter 2 we noted that the primary purpose in a piece of writing may be informative, persuasive, or entertaining (or some combination of the three). Some scholars of writing argue that all writing is essentially persuasive, and even without entering into that complex argument, we've just seen how the varying purposes in writing do overlap. In order to persuade others of a particular position, we typically must inform them about it; conversely, a primarily informative piece of writing must also work to persuade the reader that its claims are truthful. Both informative and persuasive writing often include entertaining elements, and writing intended primarily to entertain also typically contains information and persuasion. For practical purposes, however, it is possible—and useful—to identify the *primary* purpose in a piece of writing as informative/explanatory, persuasive/argumentative, or entertaining. Entertainment as a primary purpose is the one least often practiced in purely academic writing—perhaps to your disappointment!—but information and persuasion are ubiquitous. So, while recognizing the overlap that will occur between these categories, we distinguish in this chapter between two types of synthesis writing: explanatory (or informative) and argument (or persuasive). Just as distinguishing the primary purpose in a piece of writing helps you to critically read and evaluate it, distinguishing the primary purpose in your own writing will help you to make the appropriate choices regarding your approach.

■ HOW TO WRITE SYNTHESES

Although writing syntheses can't be reduced to a lockstep method, it should help you to follow the guidelines listed in the box below.

Guidelines for Writing Syntheses

- *Consider your purpose in writing.* What are you trying to accomplish in your paper? How will this purpose shape the way you approach your sources?
- *Select and carefully read your sources,* according to your purpose. Then reread the passages, mentally summarizing each. Identify those aspects or parts of your sources that will help you fulfill your purpose. When rereading, *label* or *underline* the sources for main ideas, key terms, and any details you want to use in the synthesis.

(continues)

- *Take notes on your reading.* In addition to labeling or underlining key points in the readings, you might write brief one- or two-sentence summaries of each source. This will help you in formulating your thesis statement and in choosing and organizing your sources later.

- *Formulate a thesis.* Your thesis is the main idea that you want to present in your synthesis. It should be expressed as a complete sentence. You might do some predrafting about the ideas discussed in the readings in order to help you work out a thesis. If you've written one-sentence summaries of the readings, looking them over will help you to brainstorm connections between readings and to devise a thesis.

  When you write your synthesis drafts, you will need to consider where your thesis fits in your paper. Sometimes the thesis is the first sentence, but more often it is *the final sentence of the first paragraph.* If you are writing an *inductively arranged* synthesis (see p. 158), the thesis sentence may not appear until the final paragraphs.

- *Decide how you will use your source material.* How will the information and the ideas in the passages help you fulfill your purpose?

- *Develop an organizational plan,* according to your thesis. How will you arrange your material? It is not necessary to prepare a formal outline. But you should have some plan that will indicate the order in which you will present your material and that will indicate the relationships among your sources.

- *Draft the topic sentences for the main sections.* This is an optional step, but you may find it a helpful transition from organizational plan to first draft.

- *Write the first draft* of your synthesis, following your organizational plan. Be flexible with your plan, however. Frequently, you will use an outline to get started. As you write, you may discover new ideas and make room for them by adjusting the outline. When this happens, reread your work frequently, making sure that your thesis still accounts for what follows and that what follows still logically supports your thesis.

- *Document your sources.* You must do this by crediting sources within the body of the synthesis—citing the author's last name and the page number from which the point was taken—and then providing full citation information in a list of "Works Cited" at the end. Don't open yourself to charges of plagiarism! (See pp. 53–55.)

- *Revise your synthesis,* inserting transitional words and phrases where necessary. Make sure that the synthesis reads smoothly, logically, and clearly from beginning to end. Check for grammatical correctness, punctuation, and spelling.

(continues)

> **Note:** *The writing of syntheses is a recursive process, and you should accept a certain amount of backtracking and reformulating as inevitable. For instance, in developing an organizational plan (Step 6 of the procedure), you may discover a gap in your presentation that will send you scrambling for another source—back to Step 2. You may find that formulating a thesis and making inferences among sources occur simultaneously; indeed, inferences are often made before a thesis is formulated. Our recommendations for writing syntheses will give you a structure that will get you started. But be flexible in your approach; expect discontinuity and, if possible, be assured that through backtracking and reformulating you will produce a coherent, well-crafted paper.*

In this chapter we'll focus on explanatory syntheses. In the next chapter, we'll discuss the argument synthesis.

■ THE EXPLANATORY SYNTHESIS

Many of the papers you write in college will be more or less explanatory in nature. An explanation helps readers understand a topic. Writers explain when they divide a subject into its component parts and present them to the reader in a clear and orderly fashion. Explanations may entail descriptions that recreate in words some object, place, emotion, event, sequence of events, or state of affairs. As a student reporter, you may need to explain an event—to relate when, where, and how it took place. In a science lab, you would observe the conditions and results of an experiment and record them for review by others. In a political science course, you might review research on a particular subject—say, the complexities underlying the debate over gay marriage—and then present the results of your research to your professor and the members of your class.

Your job in writing an explanatory paper—or in writing the explanatory portion of an argumentative paper—is not to argue a particular point, but rather *to present the facts in a reasonably objective manner.* Of course, explanatory papers, like other academic papers, should be based on a thesis (see pp. 105–106). But the purpose of a thesis in an explanatory paper is less to advance a particular opinion than to focus the various facts contained in the paper.

■ DEMONSTRATION: EXPLANATORY SYNTHESIS—THE CAR OF THE FUTURE?

To illustrate how the process of synthesis works, we'll begin with a number of short extracts from several articles on the same subject.

Suppose you were writing a paper on a matter that auto manufacturers, along with many drivers upset by escalating gasoline prices, are discussing: efficient, environmentally sound alternatives to the internal combustion engine. Some writers and thinkers are excited about the possibility that one alternative energy source in particular, hydrogen fuel cells, could both free Americans of reliance on foreign oil and slow the degradation of the earth's atmosphere. Others, recognizing the need for new ways to power automobiles, cite difficulties with the current state-of-the-art fuel cell technology and favor other approaches, including the hybrid (gasoline and electric) engine.

Exercise 3.1

Exploring the Topic

Before reading what others have written on the subject of alternative energy vehicles, write a page or so exploring what you know and what you think about this topic. You might focus your first paragraph on your own experience with alternative energy sources—for instance, water power, steam, solar, wind, or hybrid. If you have no direct experience with the topic, recall what you have read, seen, or heard about levels of petroleum consumption in the United States, the controversies surrounding the search for oil in this country, or the advertising buzz surrounding hybrid cars. What do you imagine are some concerns people have about alternative energy vehicles? What do you think would be of most interest to journalists, politicians, and businesspeople?

Because the topic of hydrogen fuel cells is a technical one and you may not have the expertise to write knowledgeably on it just yet, and also because you are aware that the hydrogen fuel cell is but one of several technologies being discussed as replacements to the internal combustion engine, you decide to investigate what has been written on the subject, in both print and electronic texts. In the following pages we present several excerpts from the kinds of articles your research might locate.

Note: To save space and for the purpose of demonstration, we offer excerpts from four sources only; a full list of sources appears in the "Works Cited" of the model synthesis on pp. 130–132. In preparing your paper, of course, you would draw on the entire articles from which these extracts were made. (The discussion of how these passages can form the basis of an explanatory synthesis resumes on p. 104.)

THE FUEL SUBSIDY WE NEED

Ricardo Bayon

A fellow at the New America Foundation, Ricardo Bayon writes on the intersection of finance, public policy, and environmental studies. The following is excerpted from an article in the Atlantic Monthly, *January/February 2003.*

The American economy is, after Canada's, the most energy-dependent in the advanced industrialized world, requiring the equivalent of a quarter ton of oil to produce $1,000 of gross domestic product. We require twice as much energy as

Germany—and three times as much as Japan—to produce the same amount of GDP. Overall the United States consumes 25 percent of the oil produced in the world each year. This binds us to the Middle East, which still holds more than 65 percent of the world's proven oil reserves. Even if we were to buy all our oil from Venezuela, Canada, and Russia, or to find more oil here in the United States (which currently holds only 2.9 percent of proven reserves), Persian Gulf producers with excess capacity, such as Saudi Arabia and the United Arab Emirates, would still largely dictate the price we paid for it.

America's economic vulnerability to oil-price fluctuations has led Washington to strike a tacit bargain with Saudi Arabia and other Persian Gulf oil producers. In return for U.S. military protection and silence about the more unsavory aspects of their societies, these countries increase production when prices get too high and cut it when they get too low. In addition, they price their oil in dollars and recycle their petro-profits through U.S. financial institutions. But this has made the United States vulnerable not only to a sustained spike in oil prices but also to the possible fall of the dollar. In part because the dollar has been strong, we have been able to consume more than we produce and then to make up the difference by borrowing from abroad. As a result, our current net international debt has risen to $2.3 trillion, or 22.6 percent of GDP. What would happen if a war in Iraq went badly or if Islamic extremists gained ground in key oil-producing states? Oil prices could rise and the dollar could fall, inflicting a double blow to the U.S. economy from which it could not easily recover.

The way to escape this abiding insecurity is to wean the U.S. economy—and the world economy, too—off oil. And the way to do that is to encourage the commercial development of a technology called the hydrogen fuel cell. Solar power and windmills will surely be important parts of our energy future, but only the fuel cell can address our oil dependency by challenging the primacy of the internal-combustion engine.

Fuel cells are actually a relatively old technology (they were invented in 1839, Jules Verne wrote about them in the 1870s, and they were used by U.S. astronauts in the 1960s), and the concept underlying them is simple: by mixing hydrogen and oxygen, fuel cells generate both water and electricity. Not only do fuel cells turn two of nature's most abundant elements into enough energy to power a car, but they create no toxic emissions (drinkable water is their only by-product). And fuel cells are completely quiet, meaning that it is now realistic to imagine living in a world of silent cars and trucks.

5   The technology is not science fiction: fuel cells are on their way toward commercial viability. Fuel-cell-powered buses are running in Vancouver, Chicago, London, and parts of Germany. BMW has a prototype car powered solely by fuel cells. Honda, Toyota, and DaimlerChrysler announced recently that they would begin shipping fuel-cell cars to retail customers around the world; General Motors and Ford are not far behind. Honda's car was shipped to its first major customer—the city of Los Angeles—at the beginning of December.

Geoffrey Ballard, the founder of the Canadian manufacturer Ballard Power Systems, has said, "The internal-combustion engine will go the way of the horse. It will be a curiosity to my grandchildren." Even large oil companies believe that they must embrace hydrogen power.

PUTTING THE HINDENBURG TO REST

Jim Motavalli

Jim Motavalli is editor of the environmentally focused E Magazine *and writes extensively on environmental matters for newspapers and magazines nationally. This article appeared in the* New York Times *on June 5, 2005.*

Some transportation experts are betting that hydrogen will eventually power most cars, while others see substantial, perhaps insurmountable, hurdles. Here is a primer on the benefits and disadvantages:

Q. *What is hydrogen, and where does it come from?*

A. *It is the lightest gas and the simplest, most abundant element in the universe. Because it is present in so many compounds, including water, supplies cannot be exhausted. But hydrogen is not actually a fuel, and can be used in a vehicle only after it is separated from other elements. This process itself consumes energy.*

Q. *How is hydrogen used to power a car? And what's a fuel cell?*

A. *A fuel cell uses a chemical process, similar to that in a battery, to produce electricity—in this case, from hydrogen that flows into the cell from a storage tank. This electricity drives the fuel-cell car's electric motor; the only byproducts are heat and water.*

Q. *What are the potential advantages?*

A. *Because hydrogen is found everywhere, supplies are not only infinite, they pose no geographic challenges. It can be produced, albeit expensively, from emission-free sources like solar panels, wind turbines or even nuclear plants. Fuel cells can be easily scaled up or down in size, so they could replace small computer batteries or large power plants. A hydrogen car emits no pollution or global warming gases, aside from what might have resulted from producing the hydrogen itself.*

Q. *If it's so great, why aren't we driving hydrogen cars right now?*

A. *Widespread use of fuel-cell cars will have to wait until the cells become cheaper and more efficient, and until storage methods have evolved to give vehicles a travel range of perhaps 300 miles. Hydrogen production will have to be scaled up and standardized, and pumping stations equipped for hydrogen refueling at an affordable price.*

Q. *I've heard about the Hindenburg—is hydrogen safe?*

A. *Hydrogen is very flammable, and poses special challenges: it burns without a visible flame, for instance. But it is arguably no more dangerous than gasoline, and fuel-cell cars are built with leak detectors and very strong crash-resistant tanks. As for the Hindenburg tragedy of 1937, a retired NASA engineer, Addison Bain, theorizes that the dirigible burned not because it contained hydrogen, but because its cloth skin was coated with highly flammable paint. Others disagree with his assessment.*

Q. *How will a car carry hydrogen?*

A. *Hydrogen can be stored as a gas, as a liquid or in metal hydrides, which are chemical sponges, but each form has advantages and disadvantages. Still, much of automakers' current research focuses on pressurized hydrogen gas.*

Q. *When will I have a hydrogen car in my driveway?*

A. *Joseph Romm, a former Department of Energy official and author of "The Hype About Hydrogen" (Island Press, 2004), says, "I doubt that in the next 20 years an affordable, durable and efficient vehicle will be delivered that will be attractive to the public." But a renewable energy advocate, Amory Lovins of the Rocky Mountain Institute, says the nation's car fleet could be converted to hydrogen in less than a decade, and a network of small hydrogen reformers (devices that produce hydrogen from natural gas or other sources) could be quickly installed in 10 to 20 percent of the nation's 180,000 gas stations for $2 billion to $4 billion.*

Q. *Is this just a lot of hype?*

A. *Some overblown claims have already been disproved. But there is also groundbreaking research backed by serious testing programs. Lawrence D. Burns, General Motors' vice president for research and planning, says G.M. aims to have a production-ready fuel-cell vehicle (built on an innovative "skateboard" platform that could support a variety of bodies) by 2010. DaimlerChrysler is running 30 fuel-cell buses in Europe and helping to seed a hydrogen infrastructure in Iceland.*

Fuel-cell Toyota Highlanders are being tested at two California universities; both the City of Los Angeles and the State of New York are using Honda FCX's. Nissan will reportedly lease a few X-Trail fuel-cell S.U.V.'s to American businesses in 2007.

Q. *Will fuel-cell cars be cheap to operate? Where will I fill up?*

A. *Hydrogen's current price is three to four times that of gasoline. The Department of Energy has issued optimistic cost estimates, but they assume widespread commercial acceptance of hydrogen fuel—which is at least a decade away. There are only a few hydrogen stations scattered around the country, though California envisions a 170-station "hydrogen highway" by 2010; Florida has announced a similar plan.*

Q. *How long will fuel cells last?*

A. *The journal of the American Institute of Chemical Engineers says the life of fuel cells may be only a fifth as long as that of a typical gasoline engine—about 30,000 miles versus 150,000. Ben Knight, vice president for automotive engineering at Honda, agrees that the durability of fuel-cell stacks is "a work in progress," but promises "a significantly longer life" from newer designs.*

Q. *Can you run a regular engine with hydrogen, without fuel cells?*

A. *Yes. A hydrogen Cadillac was featured at President Jimmy Carter's inauguration in 1977. A Mini with a hydrogen-powered internal combustion engine was displayed at the Frankfurt auto show in 2001, and Ford has*

> *shown prototypes. BMW plans to offer a "dual fuel" 7 Series sedan, which could run on either gasoline or hydrogen, by 2008. That V-12 car would have a range of 125 miles on hydrogen and 185 on gasoline.*

USING FOSSIL FUELS IN ENERGY PROCESS GETS US NOWHERE

Jeremy Rifkin

Jeremy Rifkin, a prolific writer well known for his cautionary views on technology (especially genetic technologies), is the author of The Hydrogen Economy: The Creation of the World Wide Energy Web and the Redistribution of Power on Earth *(2002). This selection is excerpted from an article in the* Los Angeles Times, *November 9, 2003.*

Hydrogen—the lightest and most abundant element of the universe—is the next great energy revolution. Scientists call it the "forever fuel" because it never runs out. And when hydrogen is used to produce power, the only byproducts are pure water and heat.

The shift to fuel cells and hydrogen energy—when it happens—will be as significant and far-reaching in its effect on the American and global economy as the steam engine and coal in the 19th century and the internal combustion engine and oil in the 20th century.

Hydrogen has the potential to end the world's reliance on oil from the Persian Gulf. It will dramatically cut down on carbon dioxide emissions and mitigate the effects of global warming. And because hydrogen is so plentiful, people who have never before had access to electricity will be able to generate it.

The environmental community is up in arms over the Bush hydrogen agenda. Why? Hydrogen has a Janus face. Though it is found everywhere on Earth, it rarely exists free-floating in nature. Hydrogen has to be extracted from fossil fuels or water or biomass.

5   In other words, there is "black" hydrogen and "green" hydrogen. And it is this critical difference that separates Bush's vision of a hydrogen future from the vision many of us hold in the environmental movement.

Bush and Secretary of Energy Spencer Abraham say hydrogen can free us from dependence on foreign oil. What they leave unsaid is that their plan calls for extracting hydrogen from all of the old energy sources—oil, natural gas and coal—and by harnessing nuclear power. Bush would like to take us into a hydrogen future without ever leaving the fossil fuels and nuclear past.

Today, most commercial hydrogen is extracted from natural gas via a steam reforming process. Although natural gas emits less carbon dioxide than other fossil fuels in producing hydrogen, it is a finite resource and in relatively short supply.

Hydrogen can also be extracted from coal, and enthusiasts point out that the U.S. enjoys ample coal reserves. The problem is that coal produces twice as much carbon dioxide as natural gas, which means a dramatic increase in global warming.

The coal industry counters that it might be possible to safely store the carbon dioxide emissions underground or in the ocean depths for thousands of years and has convinced the White House to subsidize further research into this. For many environmentalists, the issue of storing carbon dioxide seems eerily reminiscent of the arguments used by the nuclear industry about nuclear waste.

10 The nuclear industry would like to produce hydrogen, but there are still unresolved issues surrounding the safe storage of nuclear waste, the skyrocketing costs of building new reactors and the vulnerability of nuclear power plants to terrorist attacks.

There is another way to produce hydrogen—the green way—that uses no fossil fuels or nuclear power. Renewable sources of energy—wind, hydro- and geothermal power and photovoltaic cells—are increasingly being used to produce electricity. That electricity, in turn, can be used, in a process called electrolysis, to split water into hydrogen and oxygen.

Hydrogen could also be extracted from sustainable energy crops and agricultural waste in a process called gasification. There would be no increase in carbon dioxide emissions because the carbon taken from the atmosphere by the plants is released back during hydrogen production.

The White House proposal calls for large subsidies to the coal and nuclear industries to extract hydrogen. The Secretary of Energy claims that the administration is equally committed to research and development of renewable sources of energy to extract hydrogen.

However, the White House and the Republican Party have systematically blocked efforts in Congress to establish target dates for the phasing in of renewable sources of energy in the generation of electricity and for transport.

15 If the U.S. is successful in steering the International Partnership for the Hydrogen Economy toward a black hydrogen future, it could lock the global economy into the old energy regime for much of the 21st century, with dire environmental and economic consequences.

The real benefits of a hydrogen future can be realized only if renewable sources of energy are phased in and eventually become the primary source for extracting hydrogen. In the interim, the U.S. government should be supporting much tougher automobile fuel standards, hybrid cars, the overhaul of the nation's power grid with emphasis on smart technology, the Kyoto Protocol on global warming and benchmarks for renewable energy adoption.

All of these other initiatives should be carried on concurrently with an ambitious national effort to subsidize and underwrite the research and development of renewable energy technology, hydrogen and fuel cells.

The goal should be a fully integrated green hydrogen economy by the end of the first half of the 21st century.

LOTS OF HOT AIR ABOUT HYDROGEN

Joseph J. Romm

Joseph Romm is a former Acting Assistant Secretary of Energy and author of the book The Hype About Hydrogen: Fact and Fiction in the Race to Save the Climate. *The selection originally appeared in the* Los Angeles Times, *Opinion section, March 29, 2004.*

WASHINGTON—Earlier this month, the South Coast Air Quality Management District approved a $4-million program to put a mustache on the Mona Lisa—at least that's how it seems to me. What the agency actually did was approve spending millions to take 35 or so of the greenest, most energy-efficient sedans ever made—the hybrid gasoline-electric Toyota Prius—and turn them all into dirty energy guzzlers.

It is going to achieve this giant leap backward by converting the hybrids to run on hydrogen, the most overhyped alternative fuel since methyl tertiary-butyl ether, or MTBE.

Hybrids are already extremely efficient. The Prius, for example, generates only about 210 grams of carbon dioxide—the principal heat-trapping gas that causes global warming—per mile. The car is also a partial zero-emission vehicle, which means that when it uses California's low-sulfur gasoline, it produces very little of the smog-forming pollutants, like nitrogen oxides.

Hydrogen is not a primary fuel, like oil, that we can drill for. It is bound up tightly in molecules of water, or hydrocarbons like natural gas. A great deal of energy must be used to unbind it—something the AQMD plans to do by electrolyzing water into its constituents: hydrogen and oxygen. And because the resulting hydrogen is a gas, additional energy must be used to compress it to very high pressures to put it in the tank of your car.

5 With all the energy needed to create and compress that hydrogen—even with the relatively clean electric grid of California—a Prius running on hydrogen would result in twice as much greenhouse gas emissions per mile as an unmodified car. It would result in more than four times as much nitrogen oxides per mile.

I own a Prius, so that's the hybrid I am most familiar with. But Honda also makes a hybrid vehicle, and thanks to California's leadership in vehicle emissions regulations, many other car companies plan to introduce them soon. These cars will get even greener over time as technology improves.

Sadly, two of the features I love most about my car would be wiped out by the AQMD's expensive "upgrade." First, the hybrid has cut my annual fuel bill by half. Hydrogen is so expensive to make that even with California's high gasoline prices, the hydrogen hybrid will have more than four times the annual fuel bill of a gasoline hybrid. Second, my car can go twice as far on a tank of gas as my old Saturn, so I have to make those unpleasant trips to the gas station only half as often. The hydrogen hybrid would have less than half the range of my car. With hydrogen fueling stations so scarce, hydrogen hybrid drivers will constantly be scampering back to the fueling stations before the tanks get too low.

Why is the AQMD spending millions of dollars to increase pollution and destroy all the desirable features of one of the greenest, most efficient cars ever made? It has bought into the hype about hydrogen, the myth that this miracle fuel will somehow solve all of our energy and environmental problems.

When I was helping to oversee clean-energy programs at the U.S. Department of Energy in the mid-1990s, I too was intrigued by hydrogen, mainly because of recent advances in fuel cells. Fuel cells are electrochemical devices that take in hydrogen and oxygen and generate electricity and heat with high efficiency. The only "emission" is water. They have been an elusive technological goal since the first fuel cell was invented in 1839. During the 1990s, we increased funding for hydrogen tenfold and for transportation fuel cells threefold.

10   I began to change my mind about hydrogen while researching a book over the last 12 months. After speaking to dozens of experts and reviewing the extensive literature, I came to realize that hydrogen cars still needed several major breakthroughs and a clean-energy revolution to be both practical and desirable.

A recent Energy Department report noted that transportation fuel cells were 100 times more expensive than internal combustion engines. Historically, even the most aggressively promoted energy technologies, such as wind and solar power, have taken 20 years just to see a tenfold decline in prices.

The most mature onboard hydrogen storage systems—using ultrahigh pressure—contain 10 times less energy per unit volume than gasoline, in addition to requiring a significant amount of compression energy. A National Academy of Sciences panel concluded in February that such storage had "little promise of long-term practicality for light-duty vehicles" and urged the Department of Energy to halt research in this area. Yet this kind of storage is precisely what the AQMD plans to put in its hydrogen hybrids.

Another problem with hydrogen is in how it is made. Although people seem to view hydrogen as a pollution-free elixir, hydrogen is just an energy carrier, like electricity. And, like electricity, it is no cleaner than the fuels used to make it. For the next several decades, the National Academy panel concluded, "it is highly likely that fossil fuels will be the principal sources of hydrogen." Making hydrogen from fossil fuels won't solve our major environmental problems.

It's possible, of course, to make hydrogen with renewable electricity, such as solar and wind power, but that is a lousy use for renewables, since they can directly displace more than four times as much carbon dioxide from coal power compared with using that renewable power to make hydrogen for vehicles. And these savings can all be achieved without spending hundreds of billions of dollars on a new hydrogen infrastructure and hydrogen vehicles.

15   As one 2002 British study concluded, "Until there is a surplus of renewable electricity, it is not beneficial in terms of carbon reduction to use renewable electricity to produce hydrogen—for use in vehicles, or elsewhere." That surplus is, sadly, a long way off, given that Congress hasn't been willing to pass legislation requiring that even 10% of U.S. electricity in 2020 be from renewables like wind and solar.

Finally, delivering renewable hydrogen to a car in usable form is prohibitively expensive today—equal to gasoline at $7 to $10 a gallon—and likely to remain so for decades in the absence of major technology advances.

For at least several decades, hydrogen cars are exceedingly unlikely to be a cost-effective solution for global warming. Until we achieve major breakthroughs in vehicle technology, hydrogen storage, hydrogen infrastructure and renewable hydrogen production, hydrogen cars will remain inferior to the best hybrids in cost, range, annual fueling bill, convenience, roominess, safety and greenhouse gas emissions.

While we wait, California should continue to lead the way in building renewable-power generation and in advancing the most environmentally responsible cars in the world—hybrid partial zero-emission vehicles.

Consider Your Purpose

We asked a student, Janice Hunte, to read these four selections and to use them (and others) as sources in an explanatory paper on fuel cell technology. (We also asked her to write additional comments describing the process of developing her ideas into a draft.) Her paper (the final version begins on p. 123) drew on more than twenty selections on hydrogen fuel cell technology. How did she—how do you—go about synthesizing the sources?

First, remember that before considering the *how*, you must consider the *why*. In other words, what is your *purpose* in synthesizing these sources? You might use them for a paper dealing with a broader issue: "green," or environmentally friendly, technologies, for instance. If this were your purpose, these sources would be used in your sections on the problems associated with petroleum-based technologies and on the eco-neutral potential of fuel cells. Because such a broader paper would consider power sources other than fuel cells (for instance, wind, solar, and geothermal), it would also need to draw on additional sources. For a marketing course, you might consider strategies for encouraging public acceptance of fuel cells, the challenge being that at first they may be more expensive or less convenient than gasoline engines. The sources would clarify for you how fuel cells work, their potential, and the technical challenges that must be overcome in order for them to become a reasonable energy source. For a paper on the challenges of promoting acceptance of fuel cells, you would (again) need to consult more sources than we've gathered here in order to write an effective synthesis. Moving out of the academic world and into the commercial one, you might be an engineer preparing a brochure for your company's new fuel cell design. In this brochure, you might want to address the challenges of conventional designs and the advantages that your company's product offers.

But for now let's keep it simple: You want to write a paper, or a section of a paper, that simply explains the potential of fuel cell technology to alleviate our dependence on foreign oil and to provide a power source for cars that does not degrade the environment. Your job, then, is to write an *explanatory* synthesis—one that presents information but does not advance your own opinion on the subject.

Exercise 3.2

Critical Reading for Synthesis

Look over the four readings on hydrogen fuel cell technology and make a list of the ways they address the problems associated with petroleum-based technology and the potential of alternative technologies, especially fuel cells. Make your list as specific and detailed as you can. Assign a source to each item on the list.

Formulate a Thesis

The difference between a purpose and a thesis is primarily a difference of focus. Your purpose provides direction to your research and gives a focus to your paper. Your thesis sharpens this focus by narrowing it and formulating it in the words of a single declarative statement. (Chapter 6 has more on formulating thesis statements.)

Since Hunte's purpose in this case was to synthesize source material with little or no comment, her thesis would be the most obvious statement she could make about the relationship among the source readings. By "obvious" we mean a statement that is broad enough to encompass the main points of all the readings. Taken as a whole, what do they *mean?* Here Hunte describes the process she followed in coming up with a preliminary thesis for her explanatory synthesis:

> I began my writing process by looking over all the readings and noting the main point of each reading in a sentence on a piece of paper.
>
> Then I reviewed all of these points and identified the patterns in the readings. These I listed underneath my list of main points:—All the readings focus on the energy needed to power cars and, more generally, the American economy. The readings explain America's dependence on foreign oil, the wisdom of that dependence, technologies that could free us of this dependence, and the plusses and minuses of two technologies in particular, hydrogen fuel cell and gasoline/electric hybrids.
>
> Looking over these points, I drafted a preliminary thesis. This thesis summed up the different issues in the sources and stated how they were interrelated.
>
>> America's dependence on dwindling foreign oil reserves has spurred research into alternative technologies for powering cars.
>
> This was a true statement, but it sounded too vague and too obvious. I didn't feel it adequately represented the readings' points, especially since several experts hotly debate the advantages of fuel cells vs. hybrids. I wanted my thesis to more fully reflect the complexity of people's concerns regarding how these technologies are evolving as auto manufacturers search for ever more efficient designs. My next version followed:
>
>> Many people believe hybrids will solve our energy needs, but since hybrids still depend on gasoline, others insist that another technology will take its place: fuel cells.
>
> This thesis reflected the disagreement among experts concerning the two technologies, but I didn't feel I said enough about what makes fuel cells so attractive—namely, that they are powered by hydrogen, which is a clean-burning fuel with a virtually inexhaustible supply (unlike petroleum). In my next attempt, I tried to be more specific and a little more emphatic:
>
>> Although many see hybrids as merely transitional vehicles, since they require gasoline, others believe that fuel-cell vehicles powered by

hydrogen, a clean-burning and abundant energy source, will become the norm for roadway and highway travel.

Although this sentence was too long and sounded awkward to me, I thought it could be a good working thesis because it would help to define important parts of my paper: for instance, what are hybrids, why would they be transitional, what are fuel cells, what are their advantages over hybrids? Now I proceeded to the next step in writing—organizing my material.

Decide How You Will Use Your Source Material

The easiest way to deal with sources is to summarize them. But because you are synthesizing *ideas* rather than sources, you will have to be more selective than if you were writing a simple summary. You don't have to treat *all* the ideas in your sources, only the ones related to your thesis. Some sources might be summarized in their entirety; others, only in part. Look over your earlier notes or sentences discussing the topics covered in the readings, and refer back to the readings themselves. Focusing on the more subtle elements of the issues addressed by the authors, expand your earlier summary sentences. Write brief phrases in the margin of the sources, underline key phrases or sentences, or take notes on a separate sheet of paper or in a word processing file or electronic data filing program. Decide how your sources can help you achieve your purpose and support your thesis. For example, how might you use a diagram explaining the basics of fuel cell technology? How would you present disagreements over the perceived problems with and the potential of fuel cell technology? How much would you discuss gasoline/electric hybrids?

Develop an Organizational Plan

An organizational plan is your map for presenting material to the reader. What material will you present? To find out, examine your thesis. Do the content and structure of the thesis (that is, the number and order of assertions) suggest an organizational plan for the paper? Expect to devote at least one paragraph of your paper to developing each section of this plan. Having identified likely sections, think through the possibilities of arrangement. Ask yourself: What information does the reader need to understand first? How do I build on this first section—what block of information will follow? Think of each section in relation to others until you have placed them all and have worked your way through to a plan for the whole paper.

Study your thesis, and let it help suggest an organization. Bear in mind that any one paper can be written—successfully—according to a variety of plans. Your job before beginning your first draft is to explore possibilities. Sketch a series of rough outlines: Arrange and rearrange your paper's likely sections until you develop a plan that both facilitates the reader's understanding and achieves your objectives as a writer. Think carefully about the logical order of your points: Does one idea or point lead to the next? If not, can you find a more logical place for the point, or are you just not clearly articulating the connections between the ideas?

Your final paper may well deviate from your final sketch; in the act of writing you may discover the need to explore new material, to omit planned material, to refocus or to reorder your entire presentation. Just the same, a well-conceived organizational plan will encourage you to begin writing a draft.

Summary Statements

In her notes describing the process of organizing her material, Hunte refers to all the sources she used, including the four excerpted in this chapter.

> In reviewing my sources and writing summary statements, I noted the most important aspects of problems associated with reliance on petroleum and the promise and problems of fuel cells and other alternative technologies:
>
> - Saudi Arabia is running out of oil, and when it does the "Petroleum Age" will end with catastrophic results, unless economies prepare by changing their patterns of energy consumption (Sherman).
> - America is dangerously dependent on foreign oil. We can "wean" our economy off oil by developing hydrogen fuel cell technology (Bayon).
> - Hydrogen fuel cells work by combining hydrogen and oxygen. Because "free hydrogen" does not exist in nature, hydrogen must be separated from the substance to which it has bonded. This process requires energy ("Hydrogen Fuel Cell").
> - There are eco-friendly (green) ways to isolate hydrogen and unfriendly (black) ways. Unless we focus on the green approaches, the environmental costs of producing hydrogen for fuel cells will be unacceptably high (Rifkin).
> - The energy required to isolate hydrogen is "prohibitively expensive" and the much dreamed of "hydrogen economy" creates more problems than it solves (Anthrop).
> - High gasoline prices have sparked interest in gasoline/electric hybrid cars such as Toyota's Prius. Though hybrids may not be the technology that ultimately replaces the gasoline engine, hybrids are selling "briskly" today (Mackinnon and Scott).
> - Because of the energy needed to isolate hydrogen, the technical problems of storing hydrogen once it is isolated, and the cost of hydrogen to the consumer, hydrogen fuel cell technology should not replace hybrid technology (Romm).
>
> I tried to group some of these topics into categories that would have a logical order. The first thing that I wanted to communicate was the growing awareness that our dependence on petroleum is an increasing problem, both because of the dwindling reserves of the world's oil and because of the greenhouse emissions that result from burning oil.

Next, I thought I should explain what technologies are being developed to replace the gasoline engine: chiefly hybrids and fuel cells.

I also wanted to explain the problems people find with each of these technologies. Because the emphasis of my paper is on hydrogen fuel cells, this is the technology that should receive most of my attention. Still, because hybrid cars are gaining in popularity, I thought I should devote some attention to them—both to their potential and to their limitations.

Finally, I intended to present the serious doubts people have about hydrogen as the fuel of the future. With all the optimism, there are still reasons to be cautious.

I returned to my thesis, converting it to two sentences to make it less awkward and adding a phrase or two:

> Many see hybrids, which use gasoline, as merely transitional vehicles. In the future, they believe, fuel-cell vehicles powered by hydrogen, a clean-burning and abundant energy source, will become the norm for roadway and highway transportation.

Based on her thesis, Hunte developed an outline for a thirteen-paragraph paper, including introduction and conclusion:

A. Set a context. Introduce the problem of global warming.
B. Review the history of alternatives to gasoline-powered internal combustion engines, including compressed natural gas, hybrids, and flexible-fuel hybrids.
C. Present hydrogen as an alternative fuel, including its history. Explain how a hydrogen fuel cell works.
D. Explain the problems that limit widespread use of hydrogen fuel at present. Provide examples of current (limited) use.
E. Report on U.S. government backing for hydrogen fuel cell technology.
F. Conclude.

Write the Topic Sentences

Writing draft versions of topic sentences (an optional step) will get you started on each main idea of your synthesis and will help give you the sense of direction you need to proceed. Here are Hunte's draft topic sentences for sections, based on the thesis and organizational plan she developed. Note that when read in sequence following the thesis, these sentences give an idea of the logical progression of the essay as a whole.

- In recent years, the major automakers have been exploring alternatives to the gasoline-powered internal combustion engine.
- Over the years, many alternative fuel technologies have been proposed, but all have shown limited practicality or appeal.
- The most popular alternative energy vehicle in this country is

the hybrid, which combines an electric motor with a standard gasoline engine.

- Hybrids may not be a long-term solution.
- A variation on the standard hybrid is the plug-in, flexible fuel-tank hybrid.
- There are two advantages that make hydrogen stand out from other alternative energy sources.
- The fuel cell was first proposed by a British physicist.
- At present, widespread use of hydrogen technology is not practical.
- Some major automakers recognize the inevitable end of the petroleum era. They have committed themselves to developing and producing fuel-cell vehicles.
- The federal government is supporting the new technology.
- Successful development of hydrogen fuel-cell vehicles faces significant roadblocks.
- There is also the problem of hydrogen leakage from large numbers of fuel-cell vehicles.
- Hydrogen fuel cells use platinum, which is a precious and expensive metal in limited supply.
- Taking these concerns into account, many experts believe that evolving technology will eventually solve the major problems and obstacles.

Organize a Synthesis by Idea, Not by Source

A synthesis is a blending of sources organized by *ideas*. The following rough sketches suggest how to organize and how *not* to organize a synthesis. The sketches assume you have read seven sources on a topic, Sources A–G.

INCORRECT: ORGANIZING BY SOURCE + SUMMARY

Thesis

Summary of source A in support of the thesis.

Summary of source B in support of the thesis.

Summary of source C in support of the thesis.

(Etc.)

Conclusion

This is *not* a synthesis because it does not blend sources. Each source stands alone as an independent summary. No dialogue among sources is possible.

(continues)

CORRECT: ORGANIZING BY IDEA

Thesis

First idea: Refer to and discuss *parts* of sources (perhaps A, C, F) in support of the thesis.

Second idea: Refer to and discuss *parts* of sources (perhaps B, D) in support of the thesis.

Third idea: Refer to and discuss *parts* of sources (perhaps A, E, G) in support of the thesis.

(Etc.)

Conclusion

This *is* a synthesis because the writer blends and creates a dialogue among sources in support of an idea. Each organizing idea, which can be a paragraph or group of related paragraphs, in turn supports the thesis.

Write Your Synthesis

Here is the first draft of Hunte's explanatory synthesis. Thesis and topic sentences are highlighted. Modern Language Association (MLA) documentation style, explained in Chapter 7, is followed throughout.

Alongside this first draft we have included comments and suggestions for revision from Hunte's instructor. For purposes of demonstration, these comments are likely to be more comprehensive than the selective comments provided by most instructors.

■ EXPLANATORY SYNTHESIS: FIRST DRAFT

Janice Hunte

Professor Case

English 101

22 January 2009

The Hydrogen Fuel-Cell Car

One of the most serious problems facing the world today is global warming. According to Michael D. Mastrandrea and Stephen H. Schneider in their article *Global Warming,* "Global warming is an increase in the average temperature of the Earth's surface. Since the Industrial Revolution, that temperature has gone up by 0.7 to 1.4 °F." The authors point out that Americans are responsible for almost 25% of the greenhouse gas pollution that causes global warming, even though they make up only 5% of the world's population. The authors also note that global warming is caused primarily by the burning of fossil fuels, such as coal, natural gas, and oil, and that much of this burning occurs in the gasoline engines that power automobiles, as well as "in factories, and in electric power plants that provide energy for houses and office buildings (47)." It is clear, then, that gasoline-powered cars are a major cause of the greenhouse gas pollution that is responsible for global warming. In the future, some believe, this problem may be solved by vehicles powered by hydrogen, a clean-burning and abundant energy source, which will become the norm for roadway and highway transportation.

Title and Paragraph 1

Your title could be more interesting and imaginative. The first paragraph gets off on the wrong foot because it provides a misleading impression of what the synthesis is going to be about. A reader might reasonably conclude from this paragraph that the paper was going to deal with global warming, rather than with alternative energy vehicles, and particularly with the hydrogen fuel-cell car. By the end of the first paragraph you do get to a thesis that more accurately reflects the subject of the paper, but this thesis seems awkwardly tacked on to the end of a paragraph about something else.

Suggestions for Revision

Make the title more interesting. Rewrite the first paragraph so that it provides a clear indication of the subject of the synthesis as a whole. You could begin with an anecdote that illustrates the subject, a provocative quotation, a set of questions, or a historical review of attempts to develop alternatives to the internal combustion engine. Fix mechanics errors: The article title "Global Warming" should be within quotation marks, not set in italics. Later in the paragraph, the close quotation mark should *precede,* rather than follow, the parenthetical page reference.

Hunte 2

2   In recent years, the major automakers have been exploring alternatives to the gasoline-powered internal combustion engine. A few years ago, the electric car was widely seen as one viable alternative. Between 1996 and 2003, the Big Three U.S. automakers produced prototype electric vehicles, among them G.M.'s EVI, that were leased to a limited number of consumers. But these battery-powered, zero-emission cars proved problematic. Most had to be recharged every 100 miles or so, considerably limiting their range; and drivers found relatively few recharging stations. Manufacturers could never figure out how to reduce the batteries to manageable size or how to produce them at reasonable cost. In the end, the automakers reclaimed all but a few of the leased electric vehicles and destroyed them (Ortiz D1).

3   Over the years, many alternative fuel technologies have been proposed, but all have shown limited practicality or appeal. Compressed natural gas (CNG), which powers the Honda Civic GX, is a reliable, clean-burning, renewable (though fossil) fuel, in plentiful supply. But because of their limited range (about 200 miles) and the absence of a significant CNG infrastructure, natural gas vehicles are employed primarily in fleets that have relatively short routes and access to their own filling stations (Neil). A third alternative-fuel vehicle, powered by compressed air, is being developed by a French company, Moteur Developpement International. A prototype car can achieve a speed of 70 miles an hour and has a

---

Paragraph 2

This paragraph does make the transition to the true subject of the synthesis: alternative energy vehicles, particularly the hydrogen fuel-cell car. But it could be more fully developed: Consider discussing other reasons (besides the need to reduce greenhouse gas pollution) for the inevitable end of the internal combustion engine era. For example, we are rapidly exhausting our supplies of petroleum, a fact that may be more significant to automobile manufacturers—as well as to consumers—than the dangers of global warming.

Suggestions for Revision

Devise a clearer thesis and place it at the end of the first or second paragraph (depending on how you introduce the synthesis). Expand your discussion of why gasoline will soon become impractical as the primary means of powering automobiles.

Hunte 3

range of 120 miles. It takes about four hours to recharge the onboard air tanks, using a compressor that can be plugged into a wall outlet. So far, the company's U.S. representative has not sold any manufacturing franchises in this country and has had trouble attracting investment capital (Weikel B2). Another alternative energy source, biodiesel fuel, was promoted in mid-2005 by President Bush. Biodiesel fuel can be made from soybeans (which can be produced domestically). "Biodiesel burns more completely and produces less air pollution than gasoline or regular diesel," declared the president. "And every time we use homegrown diesel, we support American farmers, not foreign oil producers." Critics point out, however, that biodiesel fuel can be as much as 20 cents a gallon more expensive than gasoline (Chen 15). And diesel-powered cars have never caught on in the United States, as they have in Europe.

(4) The most popular alternative energy vehicle in this country is the hybrid, which combines an electric motor with a standard gasoline engine. The battery is used to accelerate the car from a standing position to 30 to 35 miles an hour; then the gasoline engine takes over. Unlike all-electric vehicles, hybrid cars are self-charging; they don't need to be regularly plugged in (Mackinnon and Scott D1). Priuses have been so much in demand that there is an average waiting period of 6 months for new purchasers (McDonald 1). In 2004 Toyota announced that it would step up production of the vehicles and double the number

---

Paragraph 3

Since this paper is largely about the hydrogen fuel-cell car, you devote too much space to discussing vehicles powered by other energy sources. While you could mention natural gas, compressed air, and biodiesel vehicles in passing, your extensive discussion of them here tends to blur what should be a sharp focus on hydrogen fuel cell vehicles.

Suggestions for Revision

Reduce the information in this paragraph to just two or three sentences. Consider appending these sentences to the paragraph discussing electric cars. This paragraph, then, would concern the least practical, appealing, or marketable alternative fuel technologies.

Paragraphs 4, 5, and 6

These paragraphs cover the subject of hybrids well, but this section is still too long, given that the real subject of the paper is the hydrogen fuel cell car.

Suggestions for Revision

Consider combining these three paragraphs into one shorter paragraph, cutting the discussion by at least one third. Perhaps reduce the block quotation from *Consumer Reports* to a summary sentence.

Hunte 4

for sale in the U.S. (Ohnsman E3). In 2006 the automaker plans to introduce a hybrid version of its popular Camry. Other automakers have also been getting into the act: Honda is currently producing Civic, Insight, and Accord hybrids; Ford has introduced the hybrid Mercury Mariner and the Ford Escape (Mackinnon and Scott D1). Hybrids win praise from both consumers and critics. One satisfied customer, Wendy Brown of Akron, Ohio, said that she went "from Akron to Virginia Beach on one tank of gas. It was awesome" (qtd. in Mackinnon and Scott D1). In its April 2005 Auto Issue, *Consumer Reports* had this to say about the Prius:

> Toyota's second-generation Prius is unbeatable for its economy, acceleration and interior room. It couples a 1.5 liter gasoline engine with an electric motor, and it automatically switches between them or runs on both as needed. The car shuts the engine off at idle. We got an excellent 44 mpg overall in our tests. . . . Reliability has been outstanding. (77)

(5) But hybrids may not be a long-term solution. Most Americans remain wary of the new technology, perhaps some thinking that with their gasoline engines, they may remain transitional vehicles. From 1999 to mid-2005, 340,000 hybrids have been sold worldwide. But in 2004 alone, Americans bought 900,000 gas-hungry SUVs (McDonald 1). Hybrids may use less gasoline than standard cars, but they still use gasoline, and

Hunte 5

therefore rely on a rapidly depleting resource. And
hybrids aren't cheap: consumers pay a premium of
about $3,000 over similarly sized cars: "The higher
initial purchase price, coupled with higher
insurance premiums and related expenses, offset
the gasoline savings, the recent Edmunds study
concluded. Edmunds said a typical hybrid might
actually cost its owner $5,283 more over five years
than its nonhybrid counterpart" (Mackinnon and
Scott D1).

6   A variation of the standard hybrid is the plug-in,
flexible-fuel tank hybrid. According to *Newsweek*
columnist Fareed Zakaria, a standard hybrid that gets
50 miles to the gallon could get 75 if the electric
motor could be recharged by plugging in to a
120-volt outlet. And "[r]eplace the conventional fuel
tank with a flexible-fuel tank that can run on a
combination of 15 percent petroleum and 85 percent
ethanol or methanol, and you get between 400 and
500 miles per gallon of gasoline" (Zakaria 27).
According to Max Boot, "[t]hat's not science fiction;
that's achievable right now." Other advantages of
plug-in, flexible-fuel hybrids: such technology would
reduce U.S. dependence on foreign (i.e., Middle East)
oil, reduce toxic emissions, and give a boost to U.S.
carmakers, who could manufacture such vehicles, and
sell them not only domestically, but also in Europe
and Asia (Boot B5).

7   There are two advantages that make hydrogen
stand out from other alternative energy sources.
First, it is clean burning (the only by-products from
the combining of hydrogen and oxygen are water

Hunte 6

and electricity), and secondly, it is an inexhaustible and widely available element. The principle behind the fuel-cell vehicle is simple. Essentially, an electric current is used to separate hydrogen from other elements with which it is bonded, such as oxygen. When the hydrogen is recombined with oxygen in a fuel cell, the reverse process occurs and electricity is generated. As reporter Elizabeth Kolbert notes, "[t]he elegance of hydrogen technology is hard to resist" (40). She describes a visit to the office of Bragi Aronson. Aronson is a chemistry professor whose office is in Reykjavik, Iceland, a country that relies heavily on clean energy sources:

> On the counter was a device with a
> photovoltaic cell on one end and a little
> fan on the other. In between was a
> cylinder of water, some clear plastic
> tubes, and a fuel cell, which looked like
> two sheets of cellophane stretched over
> some wire mesh. When Aronson turned
> on a desk lamp, the photovoltaic cell
> began to produce electricity, which
> electrolyzed the water. Hydrogen and
> oxygen ran through the tubes to the fuel
> cell, where they recombined to produce
> more water, in the process turning the
> fan. It was an impressive display.
> (Kolbert 40)

The fuel cell was first proposed in 1839 by a British physicist (and justice of the high court) William Grove. Jules Verne wrote about hydrogen fuel cells in his 1875 novel *The Mysterious Island*.

Paragraph 7
This paragraph provides a clear description of hydrogen fuel-cell technology, with good use of block quotation. But the transition from other alternative energy vehicles to hydrogen fuel-cell cars, by means of the topic (first) sentence, is overly abrupt. The writing is occasionally wordy and overly passive.

Suggestions for Revision
Develop an introductory sentence that more smoothly and effectively makes the transition between what has come before (a discussion of various alternative energy-source vehicles) and what is to follow (a discussion of hydrogen fuel-cell vehicles). For emphasis, consider making this paragraph a short one and leaving the discussion of the mechanics of the fuel cell to the next paragraph. Rewrite the *weak* "There are" sentence opening ("There are two advantages . . ."), making the sentence more *active* ("Two advantages combine . . ."). Fix surface problems, like the inconsistency of "First" followed by "secondly." Toward the end of the paragraph, the repetition of "Aronson" is awkward. Rewrite, perhaps converting the sentence beginning "Aronson is a chemistry professor" into an appositive phrase ("a chemistry professor") and combining this phrase with the previous sentence. You could also create a stronger transition, after the block quotation, to the historical development of the hydrogen fuel cell.

Hunte 7

And fuel cells have been used by American astronauts since the 1960s (Bayon 117). It is only in recent years that hydrogen fuel cells have been proposed and tested for use in automobiles and other vehicles. The fuel-cell vehicle operates on the same principle as the fan in Aronson's office. Pressurized or supercooled liquid hydrogen from a storage canister in the vehicle flows into a stack of fuel cells, where it is combined with oxygen. This chemical process generates electricity (and water), which impels the electric motor, which turns the vehicle's wheels (Kolbert 38; Motavalli 12.1). The process is clean, cool, and virtually silent (Kolbert 39–40).

(8) At present, widespread use of hydrogen technology (corresponding to widespread use of hybrid cars) is not practical. For one thing, fuel cells are expensive. It costs more to generate a kilowatt of electricity from a fuel cell than it does to generate a corresponding quantity of power from an internal combustion engine. Second, the nation has no hydrogen infrastructure through which hydrogen can be extracted from water or natural gas and then delivered to customers through a network of hydrogen stations (Bayon 118). But this situation is likely to change, if not over the next few years, then over the next few decades. Hydrogen fuel cells are more promising than that of other alternative fuel technologies, such as electric cars or natural gas or compressed air vehicles. This is because some of the major automakers recognize the inevitable end of the petroleum era. Accordingly, they have to a

Paragraph 8

This paragraph does a nice job of presenting some of the advantages of hydrogen fuel-cell vehicles, but it gets off on the wrong foot by focusing initially on the problems with the technology. Since you deal at some length with these problems later in the synthesis, it would be better to move the opening sentences of the paragraph to a later point. And while the examples of hydrogen prototype vehicles are fine, they may be more than you need to establish the fact that auto manufacturers are interested in developing the new technology.

Suggestions for Revision

Move the first few sentences of this paragraph to a later paragraph where you begin focusing on the problems with and drawbacks of hydrogen fuel technology. Cut some of the repetitive examples of prototype hydrogen fuel-cell vehicles in operation around the world. Fix occasionally awkward phrases ("are more promising than that of other alternative fuel technologies"), choppy sentence structure ("This is because . . ."), and illogical series.

Hunte 8

significant degree committed themselves to developing and producing fuel-cell vehicles. Some of these vehicles are now in operation. In 2003 General Motors developed an early fuel-cell prototype vehicle, the Hy-Wire, which it proudly showed off to reporters and National Highway Traffic Safety Administration officials (Kolbert 38). GM's vice president for research and planning, Lawrence D. Burns, says that the company "aims to have a production-ready fuel-cell vehicle . . . by 2010" (Motavalli 12.1). In January 2005, GM introduced its hydrogen fuel-cell prototype, the Sequel. This is the first hydrogen fuel-cell vehicle with a range of 300 miles, the minimum necessary to render it marketable. The Ford Motor Company will provide hydrogen-powered buses for passengers at Dallas–Fort Worth International Airport (Schneider A.01). BMW, Honda, Toyota, and DaimlerChrysler are all developing vehicles using the new technology. As Bayon reports, "[f]uel cell-powered buses are running in Vancouver, Chicago, London, and parts of Germany" (Bayon 117). Hydrogen fuel-cell buses are also undergoing trials in other cities, including Perth, Stockholm, Barcelona, Amsterdam, and Madrid ("Buses" 12). Nissan plans to lease fuel-cell SUVs to selected American businesses in 2007 (Motavalli 12.1). And in November 2004, "a Shell station in Washington, D.C. became the first in the nation to provide a hydrogen-fuel dispenser alongside its gasoline pumps" to service the six HydroGen3 minivans that GM uses to demonstrate hydrogen technology to members of Congress (Solheim).

Hunte 9

⑨ The federal government has also supported the new technology. In 2003 President Bush, who has long been identified with the oil industry, proposed, in his State of the Union address, a $1.2 billion research program for the development of hydrogen cars (Kolbert 36). The following year he recommended spending $227 million for fuel cell research and development in 2005. The ultimate goal is to make hydrogen fuel-cell vehicles "road ready by 2020" (Durbin).

⑩ In spite of these promising steps, successful development of hydrogen fuel-cell vehicles faces significant roadblocks. As indicated above, hydrogen fuel cells are expensive to produce and the nation has no hydrogen infrastructure. But there may be more fundamental problems. According to Peter Eisenberger, chairman of the American Physical Society, "major scientific breakthroughs are needed for the hydrogen economy to succeed" (qtd. in Durbin). Though hydrogen is the most abundant element in the universe (Motavalli 12.1), it rarely occurs in free form in nature: it is typically bound up with other elements, such as oxygen or carbon. Significant quantities of energy must be employed to unbind it. Donald F. Anthrop, who is a professor of environmental science at San Jose State University, points out that the energy required to operate fuel cells will exceed the energy that they produce. He further argues that "[t]he cost of this energy will be prohibitively expensive" (Anthrop 10). Joseph Romm, who is a former acting assistant Secretary of Energy, believes that hybrids are a

Paragraph 9
This paragraph is fine as a means of illustrating federal government support of hydrogen fuel-cell technology.

Suggestions for Revision
Only minor tinkering needed here: perhaps combine the first two and the last two sentences.

Paragraph 10
Since, in this generally well-developed paragraph, you begin discussing the drawbacks of hydrogen fuel-cell technology, you can move some of the material in the opening sentences of paragraph 8 here (as discussed in the comments above) and combine it with the opening sentences of the present paragraph. Otherwise, fix wordy sentences and awkward constructions.

Suggestions for Revision
Combine opening sentences of paragraph 8 and paragraph 10 here. Fix wordiness later in the paragraph by replacing "who is" constructions with appositive phrases. Make "a proven vehicle technology" into another appositive.

Hunte 10

proven vehicle technology, and that they are
preferable to hydrogen fuel-cell vehicles. He argues
that it is likely that fossil fuels such as coal and
natural gas are likely to be our major sources of
hydrogen, and that the process of extracting
hydrogen from these sources and then compressing
the gas for storage in tanks will not only consume
large quantities of energy, it will also generate
significant quantities of carbon dioxide. Thus,
"[m]aking hydrogen . . . won't solve our major
environmental problems" (Romm M3).

(11)   There is also the problem of hydrogen leakage
from large numbers of fuel-cell vehicles. Over time
this process could increase the level of greenhouse
gases and affect the world's climate. "Hydrogen is
not necessarily more benign," maintains Werner
Zittel, a German energy consultant. "It depends on
how you produce it" (qtd. in Ananthaswamy 6).
Jeremy Rifkin, who is a supporter of hydrogen fuel-
cell development, cautions that we should focus on
the development of "green hydrogen" rather than
"black hydrogen." The latter, extracted from such
fossil fuels as oil, coal, and natural gas, or derived
from nuclear power, generates large quantities of
carbon dioxide and other toxic emissions. "Green
hydrogen," on the other hand, derives from
renewable energy sources such as wind, water,
geothermal power, energy crops, and agricultural
waste (Rifkin M5).

(12)   Plus, hydrogen fuel cells use platinum, which
is a precious and expensive metal in limited supply.
There is not enough platinum in the world to

Paragraph 11
This paragraph works well to
establish the potential environmental drawbacks of hydrogen
fuel cell technology. It begins
awkwardly, however, with a
"There is" topic sentence.

Suggestions for Revision
Make the first sentence more
active and perhaps combine it
with the second sentence. Eliminate the "who is" construction
after "Jeremy Rifkin"; create an
appositive phrase here.

Hunte 11

replace all the existing internal combustion engines with fuel cells—at least not with fuel cells built on existing technology (Mackintosh and Morrison 22). Some people are concerned about the safety of hydrogen. These people remember the Hindenburg disaster in 1937 in which the hydrogen-filled transatlantic German airship burst into flames shortly before landing in Lakehurst, New Jersey, killing 36 persons (Motavalli 12.1). But others downplay both concerns. Alternatives to platinum may be found and future hydrogen fuel cells will use considerably less of the metal (Mackintosh and Morrison 22). Safety measures can prevent another Hindenburg-type disaster (Motavalli 12.1).

(13)   Taking these concerns into account, many experts believe that evolving technology will eventually solve the major problems and obstacles. But whether the car of the future is powered by hydrogen fuel cells or by some other form of energy, it is clear that gasoline-powered cars are going the way of the dinosaurs. We must take steps, as soon as possible, to reduce our dependence upon the internal combustion engine. Hopefully, human ingenuity will prevail in solving this critical problem.

Paragraph 12
This paragraph needs a better topic sentence to introduce a paragraph that deals both with shortage and safety issues.

Suggestions for Revision
Write a topic sentence that covers both the platinum supply and safety concerns. Eliminate the awkward repetition of "people" ("Some people . . . These people") later in the paragraph. Provide a transitional word or term before the final sentence of the paragraph.

Paragraph 13
The conclusion is overgeneralized. While the first sentence provides the beginning of an effective transition to the closing, what follows merely summarizes what has come before ("We must take steps . . . to reduce our dependence on the internal combustion engine"). The final sentence is vague and anticlimactic.

Suggestions for Revision
Develop a conclusion more rooted in specific facts and quotations by those who believe the problems described in the preceding paragraphs will be overcome. Appeal to reader interest in the subject as a way of closing strongly.

Revise Your Synthesis: Global, Local, and Surface Revisions

Many writers find it helpful to plan for three types of revision: global, local, and surface.

Global revisions affect the entire paper: the thesis, the type and pattern of evidence employed, the overall organization, the tone. A global revision may also emerge from a change in purpose. For example, the writer of this paper might decide to rewrite, focusing not on a broad introduction to and explanation of fuel-cell technology but on plans to create a national hydrogen infrastructure, similar to the existing network of gas stations, that would enable drivers to re-fuel their hydrogen-powered vehicles at their convenience.

Local revisions affect paragraphs: topic and transitional sentences; the type of evidence presented within a paragraph; evidence added, modified, or dropped within a paragraph; logical connections from one sentence or set of sentences within a paragraph to another.

Surface revisions deal with sentence style and construction, word choice, and errors of grammar, mechanics, spelling, and citation form.

Revising the First Draft: Highlights

Global

- Refocus the paper so that it emphasizes hydrogen fuel-cell vehicles and de-emphasizes (while still briefly covering) such other alternative energy vehicles as hybrids and electrics.
- Sharpen the *thesis* so that it focuses on hydrogen fuel-cell vehicles.
- In the body of the paper (e.g., paragraphs 3–6), cut back on references to alternative energy vehicles other than hydrogen fuel-cell cars.

Local

- More fully develop paragraph 2, providing additional reasons for the inevitable end of the internal combustion engine era.
- Combine information in paragraphs 4, 5, and 6 into one shorter paragraph, cutting the discussion by at least one third.
- Improve topic and transitional sentences in paragraphs 7, 8, and 12.
- Move the opening sentences of paragraph 8 to a corresponding position in paragraph 10 to improve coherence and logic.
- In paragraph 8, cut some of the repetitive examples of prototype hydrogen fuel-cell vehicles around the world.
- Improve the conclusion, making it more specific and appealing more strongly to reader interest.

Surface

- Avoid passive phrases such as "is used."
- Avoid phrases such as "there is" and "there are."
- Fix errors in mechanics: place titles of articles (like "Global Warming") within quotation marks, rather than italicizing them.
- Follow principles of parallelism for items in a series: "First" should be followed by "Second," not "Secondly."

- Reduce wordiness throughout.
- Fix awkward phrases (e.g., "are more promising than that of other alternative fuel technologies").

Exercise 3.3

Revising the Explanatory Synthesis

Try your hand at creating a final draft of the paper on pp. 111–121 by following the revision suggestions above and using your own best judgment about how to improve the first draft. Make global, local, and surface changes. After writing your own version of the paper, compare it to the revised version of our student paper below.

MODEL EXPLANATORY SYNTHESIS

Hunte 1

Janice Hunte

Professor Case

English 101

31 January 2009

The Car of the Future?

(1)　In July 2005 a California family, the Spallinos, took proud possession of a new silver and blue Honda FCX. Never heard of the FCX? That's because this particular model is not a part of Honda's standard product line. It's a prototype powered by hydrogen fuel cells. Although companies like Honda, Toyota, GM, and Chrysler have been experimenting with hydrogen-powered vehicles for some years, the Spallinos' car is the first to be placed in private hands for road testing. The family was selected by Honda because they already own a Civic powered by natural gas and so are used to the inconveniences of driving a vehicle that needs the kind of fuel available only in a limited number of commercial outlets. Mr. Spallino is excited at the prospect of test driving the FCX: "Maybe this is the technology of the future. Maybe it isn't," says Spallino, who commutes 77 miles a day. "But if I can be part of the evolution of this technology, that would be a lot of fun" (Molloy).

(2)   Are hydrogen fuel-cell cars the wave of the future? In recent years, the major automakers, with some financial incentives from the federal government, have been exploring alternatives to the gasoline-powered internal combustion engine. We've seen vehicles powered by electricity, natural gas, even compressed air. Diesel engines have been popular in Europe for decades, though they have a much smaller customer base in the United States. Currently, the most popular alternative energy vehicles are the hybrids, such as the Toyota Prius, vehicles that run on both gasoline engines and electric motors. But many see hybrids, which use gasoline, as merely transitional vehicles. In the future, they believe, fuel-cell vehicles powered by hydrogen, a clean-burning and abundant energy source, will become the norm for roadway and highway transportation.

(3)   But why not continue to rely indefinitely on gasoline? The answer is that the days of the gasoline-powered internal combustion engine are numbered. First, gasoline is an environmentally dirty fuel that, when burned, creates the toxic greenhouse gas pollution that contributes to global warming. Second, oil is a rapidly depleting resource. As energy expert Paul Roberts points out, "the more you produce, the less remains in the ground, and the harder it is to bring up that remainder." Today, we import most of our oil from Saudi Arabia, a country previously thought to have virtually inexhaustible supplies of oil. But many experts believe that the Saudi fields are in decline, or have at least "matured," with most of their easily extractable petroleum already gone (Klare A19). Such "peak oil" theorists predict that in the near future, the Saudis may no longer be able to meet world demand (Sherman 7). Roberts notes that the demand for oil today stands at 29 billion barrels of oil a year. Currently, the supply matches the demand; but by 2020, with increasing demands for oil by emerging industrial countries like India and China, the demand will far outstrip the supply. Prices, typically around $60 a barrel, may soar. (For a few months in 2008, prices rose to $140 a barrel.) If the U.S. does not reduce its demand for oil, a future shortage could mean that "the global economy is likely to slip into a recession so severe that the Great Depression will look like a dress rehearsal" (Roberts).

(4)   Over the years, many alternative fuel technologies have been proposed, but all have shown limited practicality or appeal. Fifteen to twenty years ago,

electric cars looked attractive. But those battery-powered, zero-emission cars proved problematic: most had to be recharged every 100 miles or so, considerably limiting their range. Manufacturers could never figure out how to reduce the batteries to manageable size or how to produce them at reasonable cost. Currently, not a single full-sized electric car capable of reaching highway speeds is in mass production (Ulrich A8). Other alternative fuel sources include compressed natural gas (CNG), compressed air, and biodiesel fuel. While prototype vehicles using these various technologies have been built, none appears likely to succeed in the American mass market. In fact, a recent congressional initiative to convert food stocks to biofuel may have backfired--with critics accusing such biofuel of damaging the environment and contributing to a global food shortage blamed for food riots in countries like Haiti (Brown A19).

(5) Currently, the most popular alternative energy vehicle in this country is the hybrid, which combines an electric motor with a standard gasoline engine. The battery is used to accelerate the car from a standing position to 30 to 35 miles an hour; then the gasoline engine takes over. Unlike all-electric vehicles, hybrid cars are self-charging; they don't need to be regularly plugged in (Mackinnon and Scott D1). The most popular hybrid, the Toyota Prius, is in so much demand that new purchasers must typically wait six months to get one. Other manufacturers, including Honda, Ford, and General Motors, also sell or soon plan to offer hybrid vehicles. *Consumer Reports* called the Prius "unbeatable for its economy, acceleration and interior room" and in 2005 declared the Honda Accord hybrid its highest scoring family sedan ("Best" 76–77). Despite their advantages, however, hybrids may still be transitional vehicles. They may use less gasoline than standard cars, but they still use gasoline and therefore rely on a rapidly depleting resource. And hybrids aren't cheap: consumers pay a premium of about $3,000 over similarly sized cars, an amount that could easily offset for years any savings in gasoline expenses. A variation of the standard hybrid, the plug-in, flexible-fuel tank hybrid, offers greatly improved fuel economy. In these vehicles, gasoline could be mixed with cheaper fuels like ethanol or methanol. Of course, consumers may find plugging in their cars inconvenient or (if they are on the road) impractical; and flexible-fuel hybrids would be reliant on a national ethanol/methanol infrastructure, which doesn't yet exist.

(6)   With these alternatives to the standard gasoline-powered internal combustion engine, what is the special appeal of the hydrogen fuel-cell vehicle? Two advantages combine to make hydrogen stand out from the rest: it is clean burning (the only by-products from the combining of hydrogen and oxygen are water and electricity), and it is an inexhaustible and widely available element.

(7)   The principle behind the fuel-cell vehicle is simplicity itself. Essentially, an electric current is used to separate hydrogen from other elements with which it is bonded, such as oxygen. When the hydrogen is recombined with oxygen in a fuel cell, the reverse process occurs and electricity is generated. As reporter Elizabeth Kolbert notes, "[t]he elegance of hydrogen technology is hard to resist" (40). She describes a visit to the office of Bragi Aronson, a chemistry professor, in his office in Reykjavik, Iceland, a country that relies heavily on clean energy sources:

> On the counter was a device with a photovoltaic cell on one end and a little fan on the other. In between was a cylinder of water, some clear plastic tubes, and a fuel cell, which looked like two sheets of cellophane stretched over some wire mesh. When Aronson turned on a desk lamp, the photovoltaic cell began to produce electricity, which electrolyzed the water. Hydrogen and oxygen ran through the tubes to the fuel cell, where they recombined to produce more water, in the process turning the fan. It was an impressive display. (40)

(8)   The fuel cell is not exactly cutting-edge technology: the concept itself was first proposed in 1839 by British physicist (and justice of the high court) William Grove. Jules Verne wrote about hydrogen fuel cells in his 1875 novel *The Mysterious Island*. And fuel cells have been used by American astronauts since the 1960s (Bayon 117). It is only in recent years, however, that hydrogen fuel cells have been proposed and tested for use in automobiles and other vehicles. The fuel-cell vehicle operates on the same principle as the fan in Aronson's office. Pressurized or supercooled liquid hydrogen from a storage canister in the vehicle flows into a stack of fuel cells, where it is combined with oxygen. This chemical process generates electricity (and water), which impels the electric motor,

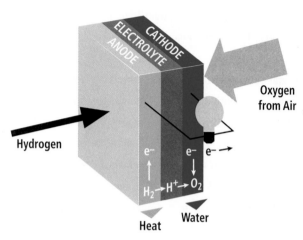

Fig. 1.　How a hydrogen fuel cell works

which turns the vehicle's wheels (Kolbert 38; Motavalli, "Putting").
(See Figure 1.) The process is clean, cool, and virtually silent (Kolbert 39–40).

What makes the successful development of hydrogen fuel cells more promising than that of other alternative fuel technologies, such as electric cars or natural gas or compressed air vehicles, is that a number of major automakers, recognizing the inevitable end of the petroleum era, have to a significant degree committed themselves to developing and producing fuel-cell vehicles. In 2003 General Motors developed an early fuel-cell prototype vehicle, the Hy-Wire (Kolbert 38). In January 2005, GM introduced the Sequel, a hydrogen vehicle with a range of 300 miles--the minimum necessary to render it marketable (Schneider A.01). The company "aims to have a production-ready fuel-cell vehicle . . . by 2010" (Motavalli, "Putting"). The Ford Motor Company produces the E-450 Shuttle, a hydrogen-powered bus now in operation around airport parking lots and hotels. Teamed with the British oil company BP, Ford has built a fleet of 30 E-450 Shuttle buses (Sherman 7). BMW, Honda, Toyota, and Chrysler are all developing vehicles using the new technology; Honda said it would begin leasing its FCX fuel cell-powered vehicles in limited quantities in 2008 (Motavalli, "Universe" 5). As Bayon reports, "[f]uel cellpowered buses are running in Vancouver, Chicago, London, and parts of

Germany" (118), and they are undergoing trials elsewhere. Nissan planned to lease fuel-cell SUVs to selected American businesses in 2007 (Motavalli, "Putting").

⑩   The federal government has also supported the new technology: in 2003 President Bush, long identified with the oil industry, proposed in his State of the Union address a $1.2 billion research program for the development of hydrogen cars (Kolbert 36). The following year he recommended spending $227 million for fuel-cell research and development in 2005, with the ultimate goal of making hydrogen fuel-cell vehicles "road ready by 2020" (Durbin).

⑪   At present, widespread use of hydrogen technology (corresponding to widespread use of hybrid cars) is not practical (Committee 116–17). For one thing, fuel cells are expensive. It costs more to generate a kilowatt of electricity from a fuel cell than it does to generate a corresponding quantity of power from an internal combustion engine. For another, the nation has no hydrogen infrastructure through which hydrogen can be extracted from water or natural gas and then delivered to customers through a network of hydrogen stations (Bayon 118). This situation is likely to change, however, if not over the next few years, then over the next few decades. But there may be more fundamental problems with hydrogen fuel cell technology. According to Peter Eisenberger, chairman of the American Physical Society, "major scientific breakthroughs are needed for the hydrogen economy to succeed" (qtd. in Durbin). Though hydrogen is the most abundant element in the universe (Motavalli, "Putting"), it rarely occurs in free form in nature: it is typically bound up with other elements, such as oxygen or carbon. Significant quantities of energy must be employed to unbind it. Donald F. Anthrop, a professor of environmental science at San Jose State University, points out that the energy required to operate fuel cells will exceed the energy that they produce. He further argues that "[t]he cost of this energy will be prohibitively expensive" (10). Joseph Romm, a former Acting Assistant Secretary of Energy, believes that hybrids, a proven vehicle technology, are preferable to hydrogen fuel-cell vehicles. He argues fossil fuels such as coal and natural gas are likely to be our major sources of hydrogen and that the process of extracting hydrogen from these sources and then compressing the gas for storage in tanks will not only consume large quantities of energy but will also generate significant quantities of carbon dioxide. Thus, "[m]aking hydrogen . . . won't solve our major environmental problems" (Romm).

(12)   Others worry about hydrogen leakage from large numbers of fuel-cell vehicles, which could, over time, increase the level of greenhouse gases and affect the world's climate. "Hydrogen is not necessarily more benign," maintains Werner Zittel, a German energy consultant. Its ecological impact "depends on how you produce it" (qtd. in Ananthaswamy 6). Jeremy Rifkin, a supporter of hydrogen fuel cell development, cautions that we should focus on the development of "green hydrogen" rather than "black hydrogen." The latter, extracted from such fossil fuels as oil, coal, and natural gas, or derived from nuclear power, generates large quantities of carbon dioxide and other toxic emissions. "Green hydrogen," on the other hand, derives from renewable energy sources such as wind, water, geothermal power, energy crops, and agricultural waste (Rifkin).

(13)   Other problems confront hydrogen advocates. Hydrogen fuel cells use platinum, a precious and expensive metal in limited supply. There is not enough platinum in the world to replace all the existing internal combustion engines with fuel cells--at least not with fuel cells built on existing technology (Mackintosh and Morrison). Some are concerned about the safety of hydrogen--mindful of the Hindenburg disaster in 1937, when the hydrogen-filled transatlantic German airship burst into flames shortly before landing in Lakehurst, New Jersey, killing 36 persons (Motavalli, "Putting"). As an extremely light gas, hydrogen is something of an "escape artist," easily able to leak out of pipelines and holding tanks. This makes it unforgiving and expensive to transport (Motavalli, "Universe" 5). But others downplay both concerns: alternatives to platinum may be found and future hydrogen fuel cells will use considerably less of the metal (Mackintosh and Morrison). And safety measures-- which in time will become more efficient--can prevent another Hindenburg-type disaster (Motavalli, "Putting").

(14)   Taking these concerns into account, many experts believe that evolving technology will eventually solve the major problems and obstacles. To critics like Max Boot, widespread use of hydrogen fuel-cell cars is "science fiction." But

Hunte 8

it's worth remembering that in 1870 the telephone was science fiction, as was the airplane in 1900, home television in 1920, the desktop computer in 1970, and the World Wide Web in 1990. In none of those years was the know-how and technology yet available for the corresponding scientific development. Such developments were made possible--and, in later years, both affordable and indispensable to modern life--because of the commitment and hard work of one or more individuals. One reader of Joseph Romm's article "Lots of Hot Air About Hydrogen" responded, "Had bureaucrats like Romm discouraged James Watt in the eighteenth century regarding the harnessing of steam energy, our economic engines would still be powered by horses" (Hoffman). It may indeed turn out that the problems of developing affordable and practical hydrogen vehicles on a large scale prove insurmountable. But many believe that the promise of hydrogen fuel cells as a provider of clean and virtually inexhaustible energy makes further research and development vital for the transportation needs of the twenty-first century. As for the internal combustion engine--according to Geoffrey Ballard, founder of Ballard Power Systems, it "will go the way of the horse. It will be a curiosity to my grandchildren" (qtd. in Bayon 118).

Hunte 9

Works Cited

Ananthaswamy, Anil. "Reality Bites for the Dream of a Hydrogen Economy." *New Scientist* 15 Nov. 2003: 6+. Print.

Anthrop, Donald F. Letter. "Renewable Energy and Fuel Cells." *Oil and Gas Journal* 10 Oct. 2004: 10. Print.

Bayon, Ricardo. "The Fuel Subsidy We Need." *Atlantic Monthly* Jan./Feb. 2003: 117-18. Print.

"Best 2005 Cars." *Consumer Reports* Apr. 2005: 76 (Toyota Prius); 77 (Honda Accord). Print.

Hunte 10

Board on Energy and Environmental Systems. Committee on Alternatives and
    Strategies for Future Hydrogen Production and Use. *The Hydrogen
    Economy: Opportunities, Costs, Barriers, and RD Needs*. Washington:
    National Academies P, 2004. Print.

Boot, Max. "The 500-Mile-Per-Gallon Solution." *Los Angeles Times*
    24 Mar. 2005: B5. *LexisNexis*. Web. 20 Jan. 2009.

Brown, Lester, and Jonathan Lewis. "Ethanol's Failed Promise." *Washington
    Post* 22 Apr. 2008: A19. *Academic Search Complete*. Web. 19 Jan. 2009.

Durbin, Dee-Ann. "Official Defends Fuel Cell Study Funds." *Los Angeles Times*
    8 Mar. 2004: B1. *ProQuest*. Web. 18 Jan. 2009.

Hoffman, Robert D. Letter. *Los Angeles Times* 3 Apr. 2004: B4. *LexisNexis*.
    Web. 20 Jan. 2009.

"How a Hydrogen Fuel Cell Works." *Creating a Sustainable Energy System for
    New Zealand*. Ministry of Economic Development, New Zealand,
    Oct. 2004. Web. 18 Jan. 2009.

Klare, Michael T. "The Vanishing Mirage of Saudi Oil: Dwindling Reserves May
    End the Petroleum Age." *Los Angeles Times* 2 June 2005: B9. *LexisNexis*.
    Web. 20 Jan. 2009.

Kolbert, Elizabeth. "The Car of Tomorrow." *New Yorker* 11 Aug. 2003: 36–40. Print.

Mackinnon, Jim, and Dave Scott. "Prices Fueling Hybrid Interest." *Akron Beacon
    Journal* 24 July 2005: D1+. *Academic Search Complete*. Web. 18 Jan. 2009.

Mackintosh, James, and Kevin Morrison. "Car Makers Gear Up for the Next
    Shortage--Platinum." *Financial Times* [London] 6 July 2005: 22.
    Academic Search Complete. Web. 19 Jan. 2009.

Molloy, Tim. "Tomorrow's Car: It's a Gas to Drive." *Courier Mail* [Queensland,
    Australia] 2 July 2005: 18. *ProQuest*. Web. 17 Jan. 2009.

Motavalli, Jim. "Putting the Hindenburg to Rest." *New York Times*
    5 June 2005: 12.1. *InfoTrac*. Web. 18 Jan. 2009.

---. "A Universe of Promise (and a Tankful of Caveats)." *New York Times*
    29 Apr. 2007: 1+. *InfoTrac*. Web. 18 Jan. 2009.

Rifkin, Jeremy. "Using Fossil Fuels in Energy Process Gets Us Nowhere."
    Los Angeles Times 9 Nov. 2003: M5. *LexisNexis*. Web. 19 Jan. 2009.

Hunte 11

Roberts, Paul. "Running Out of Oil--and Time." *Los Angeles Times*

7 Mar. 2004: M1. *Academic Search Complete*. Web. 21 Jan. 2009.

Romm, Joseph J. "Lots of Hot Air about Hydrogen." *Los Angeles Times*

28 Mar. 2004: M3. *Academic Search Complete*. Web. 21 Jan. 2009.

Schneider, Greg. "Automakers Put Hydrogen Power on the Fast Track."

Washington Post 9 Jan. 2005: A.01. *LexisNexis*. Web. 21 Jan. 2009.

Sherman, Don. "On the Road, Hope for a Zero-Pollution Car." *New York Times*

29 Apr. 2007: A1+. *InfoTrac*. Web. 19 Jan. 2009.

Ulrich, Lawrence. "They're Electric, but Can They Be Fantastic?" *New York Times*

23 Sept. 2007: A1+. *InfoTrac*. Web. 19 Jan. 2009.

Critical Reading for Synthesis

- *Use the tips from Critical Reading for Summary on p. 6.* Remember to examine the context; note the title and subtitle; identify the main point; identify the subpoints; break the reading into sections; distinguish between points, examples, and counterarguments; watch for transitions within and between paragraphs; and read actively and recursively.

- *Establish the writer's primary purpose.* Use some of the guidelines discussed in Chapter 2. Is the piece primarily informative, persuasive, or entertaining? Assess whether the piece achieves its purpose.

- *Read to identify a key idea.* If you begin reading your source materials with a key idea or topic already in mind, read to identify what your sources have to say about the idea.

- *Read to discover a key idea.* If you begin the reading process without a key idea in mind, read to discover a key idea that your sources address.

- *Read for relationships.* Regardless of whether you already have a key idea or you are attempting to discover one, your emphasis in reading should be on noting the ways in which the readings relate to each other, to a key idea, and to your purpose in writing the synthesis.

WRITING ASSIGNMENT: THE CHANGING LANDSCAPE OF WORK IN THE TWENTY-FIRST CENTURY

Now we'll give you an opportunity to practice your skills in planning and writing an explanatory synthesis. See Chapter 8 pp. 309–343, where we provide nine sources on the way that work will continue to change over the next few decades. Who will be the "winners" and "losers" among American workers? To what extent will education be a factor in your having the career of your choice? Is your job likely to be exported? What forces are changing the shape of employment in business, technology, law, and medicine? Your task in the synthesis will be to understand and present to others less knowledgeable than you the key aspects of the changing landscape of work.

Note that your instructor may want you to complete related assignments in Chapter 8, asking you to write summaries in preparation for writing a larger explanatory synthesis.

Exercise 3.4

Exploring Online Sources

The online databases available through your school's library, as well as Internet search engines such as Google.com, will yield many sources beyond the ones gathered for you on the topic of "The Changing Landscape of Work in the Twenty-first Century" in Chapter 8. Read the articles on pp. 319–343. Then use one or more of your library's databases to conduct an Internet search for additional sources on this topic. You are likely to find more recent sources than those reprinted here. If you end up using any Internet sources for the explanatory synthesis assignment, review our cautionary discussion about using Web-based sources (pp. 273–275).

---

4 Argument Synthesis

■ WHAT IS AN ARGUMENT SYNTHESIS?

An argument is an attempt to persuade a reader or listener that a particular and debatable claim is true. Writers argue in order to establish facts, to make statements of value, and to recommend policies. For instance, answering the question *Why do soldiers sometimes commit atrocities in wartime?* would involve making an argument. To develop this argument, researchers might conduct experiments, collect historical evidence, and examine and interpret data. The researchers might then present their findings at professional conferences and in journals and books. The extent to which readers (or listeners) accept these findings will depend on the quality of the supporting evidence and the care with which the researchers have argued their case. What we are calling an argument *synthesis* draws upon evidence from a variety of sources in an attempt to persuade others of the truth or validity of a debatable claim.

By contrast, the explanatory synthesis, as we have seen, is fairly modest in purpose. It emphasizes the sources themselves, not the writer's use of sources to persuade others. The writer of an explanatory synthesis aims to inform, not persuade. Here, for example, is a thesis devised for an explanatory synthesis on the ubiquity of cell phones in contemporary life:

> Cell phones make it possible for us to be always within reach, though many
> people would prefer *not* to be always within reach.

This thesis summarizes two viewpoints about the impact of cell phones on contemporary life, arguing neither for nor against either viewpoint.

An argumentative thesis, however, is *persuasive* in purpose. A writer working with the same source material might conceive and support an opposing thesis:

> Cell phones have ruined our ability to be isolated, to be willfully *out of touch*
> with the rest of the world.

So the thesis for an argument synthesis is a claim about which reasonable people could disagree. It is a claim with which—given the right arguments—your audience might be persuaded to agree. The strategy of your argument synthesis is therefore to find and use convincing *support* for your *claim*.

The Elements of Argument: Claim, Support, and Assumption

One way of looking at an argument is to see it as an interplay of three essential elements: claim, support, and assumption. A *claim* is a proposition or conclusion that you are trying to prove. You prove this claim by using *support* in the form of fact or expert opinion. Linking your supporting evidence to your claim is your *assumption* about the subject. This assumption, also called a *warrant*, is—as we've discussed in Chapter 2—an underlying belief or principle about some aspect of the world and how it operates. By nature, assumptions (which are often unstated) tend to be more general than either claims or supporting evidence.

Here are the essential elements of an argument advocating parental restriction of television viewing for high school children:

Claim

High school students should be restricted to no more than two hours of TV viewing per day.

Support

An important new study and the testimony of educational specialists reveal that students who watch more than two hours of TV a night have, on average, lower grades than those who watch less TV.

Assumption

Excessive TV viewing adversely affects academic performance.

For another example, here's an argumentative claim on the topic of what some call computer-mediated communication (CMC):

CMC threatens to undermine human intimacy, connection, and ultimately community.

Here are the other elements of this argument:

Support

- While the Internet presents us with increased opportunities to meet people, these meetings are limited by geographical distance.
- People are spending increasing amounts of time in cyberspace: In 1998, the average Internet user spent over four hours per week online, a figure that has nearly doubled recently.
- College health officials report that excessive Internet use threatens many college students' academic and psychological well-being.
- New kinds of relationships fostered on the Internet often pose challenges to pre-existing relationships.

Assumptions

- The communication skills used and the connections formed during Internet contact fundamentally differ from those used and formed during face-to-face contact.

- "Real" connection and a sense of community are sustained by face-to-face contact, not by Internet interactions.

For the most part, arguments should be constructed logically so that assumptions link evidence (supporting facts and expert opinions) to claims. As we'll see, however, logic is only one component of effective arguments.

Exercise 4.1

Practicing Claim, Support, and Assumption

Devise two sets of claims, support, and assumptions. First, in response to the example above on computer-mediated communication and relationships, write a one-sentence claim addressing the positive impact (or potentially positive impact) of CMC on relationships—whether you personally agree with the claim or not. Then list the supporting statements on which such a claim might rest, and the assumption that underlies them. Second, write a claim that states your own position on any debatable topic you choose. Again, devise statements of support and relevant assumptions.

The Three Appeals of Argument: Logos, Ethos, Pathos

Speakers and writers have never relied on logic alone in advancing and supporting their claims. More than 2000 years ago, the Athenian philosopher and rhetorician Aristotle explained how speakers attempting to persuade others to their point of view could achieve their purpose by relying on one or more *appeals*, which he called *logos*, *ethos*, and *pathos*.

Since we frequently find these three appeals employed in political argument, we'll use political examples in the following discussion. But keep in mind that these appeals are also used extensively in advertising, legal cases, business documents, and many other types of argument.

Logos

Logos is the rational appeal, the appeal to reason. If speakers expect to persuade their audiences, they must argue logically and must supply appropriate evidence to support their case. Logical arguments are commonly of two types (often combined): deductive and inductive. The *deductive* argument begins with a generalization, then cites a specific case related to that generalization, from which follows a conclusion.

An example of a deductive argument may be seen in President John F. Kennedy's address to the nation in June 1963 on the need for sweeping civil rights legislation. Kennedy begins with the generalizations that it "ought to be possible . . . for American students of any color to attend any public institution they select without having to be backed up by troops" and that "it ought to be possible for American citizens of any color to register and vote in a free election without interference or fear of reprisal."

Kennedy then provides several specific examples (primarily recent events in Birmingham, Alabama) and statistics to show that this was not the case. He concludes:

> We face, therefore, a moral crisis as a country and a people. It cannot be met by repressive police action. It cannot be left to increased demonstrations in the streets. It cannot be quieted by token moves or talk. It is time to act in the Congress, in your state and local legislative body, and, above all, in all of our daily lives.

Underlying Kennedy's argument is this reasoning:

All Americans should enjoy certain rights. (*assumption*)

Some Americans do not enjoy these rights. (*support*)

We must take action to ensure that all Americans enjoy these rights. (*claim*)

Another form of logical argumentation is *inductive* reasoning. A speaker or writer who argues inductively begins not with a generalization, but with several pieces of specific evidence. The speaker then draws a conclusion from this evidence. For example, in a 1990 debate on gun control, Senator Robert C. Byrd cited specific examples of rampant crime involving guns: "I read of young men being viciously murdered for a pair of sneakers, a leather jacket, or $20." He also offered statistical evidence of the increasing crime rate: "in 1951, there were 3.2 policemen for every felony committed in the United States; this year nearly 3.2 felonies will be committed per every police officer." He concluded, "Something has to change. We have to stop the crimes that are distorting and disrupting the way of life for so many innocent, law-respecting Americans. The bill that we are debating today attempts to do just that."

Senator Edward M. Kennedy also used statistical evidence in arguing for passage of the Racial Justice Act of 1990, which was designed to ensure that minorities were not disproportionately singled out for the death penalty. Kennedy pointed out that between 1973 and 1980, 17 defendants in Fulton County, Georgia, were charged with killing police officers, but the only defendant who received the death sentence was a black man. Kennedy also cited statistics to show that "those who killed whites were 4.3 times more likely to receive the death penalty than were killers of blacks," and that "in Georgia, blacks who killed whites received the death penalty 16.7 percent of the time, while whites who killed received the death penalty only 4.2 percent of the time."

Of course, the mere piling up of evidence does not in itself make the speaker's case. As Donna Cross explains in "Politics: The Art of Bamboozling,"* politicians are very adept at "card-stacking." And statistics can be

---

*Donna Cross, *Word Abuse: How the Words We Use Use Us* (New York: Coward, 1979).

selected and manipulated to prove anything, as demonstrated in Darrell Huff's landmark book *How to Lie with Statistics* (1954). Moreover, what appears to be a logical argument may in fact be fundamentally flawed. (See Chapter 2 for a discussion of logical fallacies and faulty reasoning strategies.) On the other hand, the fact that evidence can be distorted, statistics misused, and logic fractured does not mean that these tools of reason can be dispensed with or should be dismissed. It means only that audiences have to listen and read critically—perceptively, knowledgeably, and skeptically (though not necessarily cynically).

Sometimes in political disagreements, people can turn their opponents' faulty logic against them. For example, in the wake of the meltdown in 2008 of the mortgage loan industry, with more than 1.2 million homes in foreclosure, some argued that it would be bad policy to help homeowners who had lost their homes as a consequence of no longer being able to make mortgage payments. Their argument worked like this:

> Financially irresponsible behavior should not be rewarded with government bailouts. (*assumption*)
>
> Taking on a mortgage that one cannot afford is financially irresponsible behavior. (*support*)
>
> Taking on a mortgage that one cannot afford should not be rewarded with government bailouts. (*claim*)

But this argument was made to work for the opposite position by those who favored government assistance. Their strategy was simply to change the middle term—the *support*. In light of the almost immediate massive financial support provided by the Federal Reserve to assist the large investment banking house Bear Stearns when it was threatened with bankruptcy, the middle term was switched to:

> Large-scale investing in subprime mortgages is financially irresponsible behavior.

Thus, the inescapable conclusion—the *claim*—of this argument inevitably became:

> Banks threatened with bankruptcy as a result of having made poor investments in subprime mortgages should not be rewarded with government bailouts.

The inconsistency of helping out investment banks while not helping out homeowners was illogical enough that Congress rushed to consider legislation that would also help out homeowners. But beyond being illogical, the initial decision not to help out individual homeowners created a powerful appeal to *pathos*: Legislators did not want to be seen as unsympathetic to families who, because of large-scale economic factors beyond their control, would lose their homes and, in effect, be thrown out on the streets.

Exercise 4.2

Using Deductive and Inductive Logic

Choose an issue currently being debated at your school, or a college-related issue about which you are concerned. Write a claim about this issue. Then write two paragraphs addressing your claim—one in which you organize your points deductively, and one in which you organize them inductively. Possible issues might include college admissions policies, classroom crowding, or grade inflation. Alternatively, you could base your paragraphs on a claim generated in Exercise 4.1.

Ethos

Ethos, or the ethical appeal, is based not on the ethical rationale for the subject under discussion, but rather on the ethical status of the person making the appeal. A person making an argument must have a certain degree of credibility: That person must be of good character, have sound sense, and be qualified to hold the office or recommend policy.

For example, Elizabeth Cervantes Barrón, running for senator as the Peace and Freedom candidate, begins her statement with "I was born and raised in central Los Angeles. I grew up in a multiethnic, multicultural environment where I learned to respect those who were different from me. . . . I am a teacher and am aware of how cutbacks in education have affected our children and our communities."

On the other end of the political spectrum, the American Independent gubernatorial candidate Jerry McCready also begins with an ethical appeal: "As a self-employed businessman, I have learned firsthand what it is like to try to make ends meet in an unstable economy being manipulated by out-of-touch politicians." Both candidates are making an appeal to *ethos*, an appeal based on the strength of their personal qualities for the office they seek.

L. A. Kauffman is not running for office but writing an article arguing against socialism as a viable ideology for the future ("Socialism: No," *Progressive*, April 1, 1993). To defuse objections that he is simply a tool of capitalism, Kauffman begins with an appeal to *ethos:* "Until recently, I was executive editor of the journal *Socialist Review*. Before that I worked for the Marxist magazine, *Monthly Review*. My bookshelves are filled with books of Marxist theory, and I even have a picture of Karl Marx up on my wall." Thus, Kauffman establishes his credentials to argue knowledgeably about Marxist ideology.

The conservative commentator Rush Limbaugh frequently makes use of the ethical appeal by linking himself with the kind of Americans he assumes his audiences to be (the writer Donna Cross calls this "glory by association"):

> In their attacks [on me], my critics misjudge and insult the American people. If I were really what liberals claim—racist, hatemonger, blowhard—I would years ago have deservedly gone into oblivion.

The truth is, I provide information and analysis the media refuses to disseminate, information and analysis the public craves. People listen to me for one reason: I am effective. And my credibility is judged in the marketplace every day. . . . I represent America's rejection of liberal elites. . . . I validate the convictions of ordinary people.*

Exercise 4.3

Using Ethos

Return to the claim you used for Exercise 4.2 and write a paragraph in which you use an appeal to *ethos* to make a case for that claim.

Pathos

Finally, speakers and writers appeal to their audiences by using *pathos*, the appeal to the emotions. Nothing is inherently wrong with using an emotional appeal. Indeed, because emotions often move people far more powerfully than reason alone, speakers and writers would be foolish not to use emotion. And it would be a drab, humorless world if human beings were not subject to the sway of feeling as well as reason. The emotional appeal becomes problematic only when it is the *sole* or *primary* basis of the argument. This imbalance of emotion over logic is the kind of situation that led, for example, to the internment of Japanese Americans during World War II or that leads to periodic political spasms that call for enacting anti-flag-burning legislation.

President Ronald Reagan was a master of emotional appeal. He closed his first Inaugural Address with a reference to the view from the Capitol to the Arlington National Cemetery, where lie thousands of markers of "heroes":

> Under one such marker lies a young man, Martin Treptow, who left his job in a small-town barbershop in 1917 to go to France with the famed Rainbow Division. There, on the western front, he was killed trying to carry a message between battalions under heavy artillery fire. We're told that on his body was found a diary. On the flyleaf under the heading, "My Pledge," he had written these words: "America must win this war. Therefore, I will work, I will save, I will sacrifice, I will endure, I will fight cheerfully and do my utmost, as if the issue of the whole struggle depended on me alone." The crisis we are facing today does not require of us the kind of sacrifice that Martin Treptow and so many thousands of others were called upon to make. It does require, however, our best effort and our willingness to believe in ourselves and to believe in our capacity to perform great deeds, to believe that together with God's help we can and will resolve the problems which now confront us.

Surely, Reagan implies, if Martin Treptow can act so courageously and so selflessly, we can do the same. His logic is somewhat unclear because the connection between Martin Treptow and ordinary Americans of 1981 is rather

*Rush Limbaugh, "Why I Am a Threat to the Left," *Los Angeles Times* 9 Oct. 1994.

tenuous (as Reagan concedes); but the emotional power of Martin Treptow, whom reporters were sent scurrying to research, carries the argument.

A more recent president, Bill Clinton, also used *pathos*. Addressing an audience of the nation's governors about his welfare plan, Clinton closed his remarks by referring to a conversation he had had with a welfare mother who had gone through the kind of training program Clinton was advocating. Asked by Clinton whether she thought that such training programs should be mandatory, the mother said, "I sure do." Clinton in his remarks explained what she said when he asked her why:

> "Well, because if it wasn't, there would be a lot of people like me home watching the soaps because we don't believe we can make anything of ourselves anymore. So you've got to make it mandatory." And I said, "What's the best thing about having a job?" She said, "When my boy goes to school, and they say, 'What does your mama do for a living?' he can give an answer."

Clinton uses the emotional power he counts on in that anecdote to set up his conclusion: "We must end poverty for Americans who want to work. And we must do it on terms that dignify all of the rest of us, as well as help our country to work better. I need your help, and I think we can do it."

Exercise 4.4

Using Pathos

Return to the claim you used for Exercises 4.2 and 4.3, and write a paragraph in which you use an appeal to *pathos* to argue for that claim.

The Limits of Argument

Our discussion of *ethos* and *pathos* indicates a potentially troubling but undeniable reality: Arguments are not won on the basis of logic and evidence alone. In the real world, arguments don't operate like academic debates. If the purpose of argument is to get people to change their minds or to agree that the writer's or speaker's position on a particular topic is the best available, then the person making the argument must be aware that factors other than evidence and good reasoning come into play when readers or listeners are considering the matter.

These factors involve deep-seated cultural, religious, ethnic, racial, and gender identities, moral predilections, and the effects of personal experiences (either pleasant or unpleasant) that are generally impervious to the weight of reasoning, however well-framed. Try—using the best available arguments—to convince someone who is pro-life to agree with the pro-choice position (or vice versa). Try to persuade someone who opposes capital punishment to believe that state-endorsed executions are necessary for deterrence (or for any other reason). Marshall your evidence and logic to persuade someone whose family members have had run-ins with the law that police efforts are directed at protecting the law-abiding. On such emotionally loaded topics, it is extremely difficult, if not impossible, to get people to change their minds because they are so personally invested in their beliefs. (See the discussion of *assumptions* in Chapter 2, pp. 71–73.) It is not just a matter of their forming or choosing an opinion on a particular topic; it is a matter of an opinion's emerging naturally from an often long-established component of the person's psyche. Someone who believes that all life is sacred is not likely to be swayed by an argument that abortion or stem-cell research that involves the destruction of a fetus is acceptable. As Susan Jacoby, author of *The Age of American Unreason*, notes, "Whether watching television news, consulting political blogs, or (more rarely) reading books, Americans today have become a people in search of validation for opinions that they already hold."*

The tenacity with which people hold on to longtime beliefs does not mean, however, that they cannot change their minds or that subjects like abortion, capital punishment, gun control, and gay marriage should be off-limits to reasoned debate. It means only that you should be aware of the limits of argument. The world is not populated by Mr. and Ms. Spocks of *Star Trek* fame, whose brains function by reason alone. Even those who claim to be open-minded on a given topic are often captive to deeply held beliefs and, so, deceive themselves concerning their willingness to respond rationally to arguments. As one letter writer to the *New York Times Book Review* observed, "[P]eople often fail to identify their own biases because of a compelling human desire to believe they are fair-minded and decent."†

The most fruitful topics for argument in a freshman composition setting, therefore, tend to be those on which most people are persuadable, either because they know relatively little about the topic or because deep-rooted cultural, religious, or moral beliefs are not involved. At least initially in your career as a writer of academic papers, it's probably best to avoid "hot button" topics that are the focus of broader cultural debates, and to focus instead on topics in which *pathos* plays less of a part. Most people are not heavily invested in plug-in hybrid or hydrogen-powered vehicles, so an argument on behalf of the more promising technology for the coming decades will not be complicated by deep-seated beliefs. Similarly, most people don't know enough about the mechanics of sleep to have strong opinions on how to deal with sleep deprivation. Your arguments on such topics, therefore, will provide opportunities both to inform your readers or listeners and to persuade them that your arguments, if well reasoned and supported by sound evidence, are at least plausible if not entirely convincing.

---

*Susan Jacoby, "Talking to Ourselves: Americans Are Increasingly Close-Minded and Unwilling to Listen to Opposing Views," *Los Angeles Times* 20 Apr. 2008: M10.
†Susan Abendroth, letter in *New York Times Book Review* 30 Mar. 2008: 12.

■ DEMONSTRATION: DEVELOPING AN ARGUMENT SYNTHESIS—BALANCING PRIVACY AND SAFETY IN THE WAKE OF VIRGINIA TECH

To demonstrate how to plan and draft an argument synthesis, let's suppose you are taking a course on Law and Society or Political Science or (from the Philosophy Department) Theories of Justice, and you find yourself considering the competing claims of privacy and public safety. The tension between these two highly prized values burst anew into public consciousness in 2007 after a mentally disturbed student at the Virginia Polytechnic Institute shot to death 32 fellow students and faculty members and injured 17 more. Unfortunately, this incident was only the latest in a long history of mass killings at American schools.* It was later revealed that the shooter had a documented history of mental instability, but because of privacy rules this information was not made available to university officials. Many people demanded to know why this information was not shared with campus police or other officials so that Virginia Tech could take measures to protect members of the university community. Didn't the safety of those who were injured and killed outweigh the privacy of the shooter? At what point, if any, *does* the right to privacy outweigh the right to safety? What *should* the university have done before the killing started? Should federal and state laws on privacy be changed or even abandoned in the wake of this and other similar incidents?

Suppose, in preparing to write a paper on balancing privacy and safety, you located (among others) the following sources:

- *Mass Shootings at Virginia Tech, April 16, 2007: Report of the Review Panel Presented to Governor Kaine, Commonwealth of Virginia*, August 2007 (a report)
- "Laws Limit Schools Even After Alarms" (a newspaper article)
- "Perilous Privacy at Virginia Tech" (an editorial)
- "Colleges Are Watching Troubled Students" (a newspaper article)
- "Virginia Tech Massacre Has Altered Campus Mental Health Systems" (a newspaper article)
- *The Family Educational Rights and Privacy Act (FERPA)*, sec.1232g (a federal statute)

Read these sources (which follow) carefully, noting the kinds of information and ideas you could draw on to develop an *argument synthesis*. Some of these passages are excerpts only; in preparing your paper, you would draw on the

---

*In 1966 a student at the University of Texas at Austin, shooting from the campus clock tower, killed 14 people and wounded 31. In 2006 a man shot and killed five girls at an Amish school in Lancaster, Pennsylvania.

entire articles, reports, and book chapters from which these passages were taken. And you would draw on more sources than these in your search for supporting materials (as the writer of the model synthesis has done; see pp. 161–169). But these six sources provide a good introduction to the subject. Our discussion of how these passages can form the basis of an argument synthesis resumes on p. 156.

Mass Shootings at Virginia Tech, April 16, 2007

Report of the Review Panel
Presented to Governor Kaine, Commonwealth of Virginia,
August 2007

The following passage leads off the official report of the Virginia Tech shootings by the panel appointed by Virginia Governor Tim Kaine to investigate the incident. The mission of the panel was "to provide an independent, thorough, and objective incident review of this tragic event, including a review of educational laws, policies and institutions, the public safety and health care procedures and responses, and the mental health delivery system." Panel members included the chair, Colonel Gerald Massenghill, former Virginia State Police Superintendent; Tom Ridge, former Director of Homeland Security and former governor of Pennsylvania; Gordon Davies; Dr. Roger L. Depue; Dr. Aradhana A. "Bela" Sood; Judge Diane Strickland; and Carol L. Ellis. The panel Web site may be found at <http://www.vtreviewpanel.org/panel_info/>.

Summary Of Key Findings

On April 16, 2007, Seung Hui Cho, an angry and disturbed student, shot to death 32 students and faculty of Virginia Tech, wounded 17 more, and then killed himself.

The incident horrified not only Virginians, but people across the United States and throughout the world.

Tim Kaine, Governor of the Commonwealth of Virginia, immediately appointed a panel to review the events leading up to this tragedy; the handling of the incidents by public safety officials, emergency services providers, and the university; and the services subsequently provided to families, survivors, caregivers, and the community.

The Virginia Tech Review Panel reviewed several separate but related issues in assessing events leading to the mass shootings and their aftermath:

- The life and mental health history of Seung Hui Cho, from early childhood until the weeks before April 16.
- Federal and state laws concerning the privacy of health and education records.
- Cho's purchase of guns and related gun control issues.
- The double homicide at West Ambler Johnston (WAJ) residence hall and the mass shootings at Norris Hall, including the responses of Virginia Tech

leadership and the actions of law enforcement officers and emergency responders.

- Emergency medical care immediately following the shootings, both onsite at Virginia Tech and in cooperating hospitals.
- The work of the Office of the Chief Medical Examiner of Virginia.
- The services provided for surviving victims of the shootings and others injured, the families and loved ones of those killed and injured, members of the university community, and caregivers.

5   The panel conducted over 200 interviews and reviewed thousands of pages of records, and reports the following major findings:

1. Cho exhibited signs of mental health problems during his childhood. His middle and high schools responded well to these signs and, with his parents' involvement, provided services to address his issues. He also received private psychiatric treatment and counseling for selective mutism and depression.

    In 1999, after the Columbine shootings, Cho's middle school teachers observed suicidal and homicidal ideations in his writings and recommended psychiatric counseling, which he received. It was at this point that he received medication for a short time. Although Cho's parents were aware that he was troubled at this time, they state they did not specifically know that he thought about homicide shortly after the 1999 Columbine school shootings.

2. During Cho's junior year at Virginia Tech, numerous incidents occurred that were clear warnings of mental instability. Although various individuals and departments within the university knew about each of these incidents, the university did not intervene effectively. No one knew all the information and no one connected all the dots.

3. University officials in the office of Judicial Affairs, Cook Counseling Center, campus police, the Dean of Students, and others explained their failures to communicate with one another or with Cho's parents by noting their belief that such communications are prohibited by the federal laws governing the privacy of health and education records. In reality, federal laws and their state counterparts afford ample leeway to share information in potentially dangerous situations.

4. The Cook Counseling Center and the university's Care Team failed to provide needed support and services to Cho during a period in late 2005 and early 2006. The system failed for lack of resources, incorrect interpretation of privacy laws, and passivity. Records of Cho's minimal treatment at Virginia Tech's Cook Counseling Center are missing.

5. Virginia's mental health laws are flawed and services for mental health users are inadequate. Lack of sufficient resources results in gaps in the mental health system including short term crisis stabilization and comprehensive outpatient services. The involuntary commitment process is challenged by unrealistic time constraints, lack of critical psychiatric data and collateral information, and barriers (perceived or real) to open communications among key professionals.

6. There is widespread confusion about what federal and state privacy laws allow. Also, the federal laws governing records of health care provided in educational settings are not entirely compatible with those governing other health records.

7. Cho purchased two guns in violation of federal law. The fact that in 2005 Cho had been judged to be a danger to himself and ordered to outpatient treatment made him ineligible to purchase a gun under federal law.

8. Virginia is one of only 22 states that report any information about mental health to a federal database used to conduct background checks on would-be gun purchasers. But Virginia law did not clearly require that persons such as Cho—who had been ordered into out-patient treatment but not committed to an institution—be reported to the database. Governor Kaine's executive order to report all persons involuntarily committed for outpatient treatment has temporarily addressed this ambiguity in state law. But a change is needed in the Code of Virginia as well.

9. Some Virginia colleges and universities are uncertain about what they are permitted to do regarding the possession of firearms on campus.

10. On April 16, 2007, the Virginia Tech and Blacksburg police departments responded quickly to the report of shootings at West Ambler Johnston residence hall, as did the Virginia Tech and Blacksburg rescue squads. Their responses were well coordinated.

11. The Virginia Tech police may have erred in prematurely concluding that their initial lead in the double homicide was a good one, or at least in conveying that impression to university officials while continuing their investigation. They did not take sufficient action to deal with what might happen if the initial lead proved erroneous. The police reported to the university emergency Policy Group that the "person of interest" probably was no longer on campus.

12. The VTPD erred in not requesting that the Policy Group issue a campus-wide notification that two persons had been killed and that all students and staff should be cautious and alert.

13. Senior university administrators, acting as the emergency Policy Group, failed to issue an all-campus notification about the WAJ killings until almost 2 hours had elapsed. University practice may have conflicted with written policies.

14. The presence of large numbers of police at WAJ led to a rapid response to the first 9-1-1 call that shooting had begun at Norris Hall.

15. Cho's motives for the WAJ or Norris Hall shootings are unknown to the police or the panel. Cho's writings and videotaped pronouncements do not explain why he struck when and where he did.

16. The police response at Norris Hall was prompt and effective, as was triage and evacuation of the wounded. Evacuation of others in the building could have been implemented with more care.

17. Emergency medical care immediately following the shootings was provided very effectively and timely both onsite and at the hospitals, although providers from different agencies had some difficulty communicating with one another. Communication of accurate information to hospitals standing by to receive the wounded and injured was somewhat deficient early on. An emergency operations center at Virginia Tech could have improved communications.

18. The Office of the Chief Medical Examiner properly discharged the technical aspects of its responsibility (primarily autopsies and identification of the deceased). Communication with families was poorly handled.

19. State systems for rapidly deploying trained professional staff to help families get information, crisis intervention, and referrals to a wide range of resources did not work.

20. The university established a family assistance center at The Inn at Virginia Tech, but it fell short in helping families and others for two reasons: lack of leadership and lack of coordination among service providers. University volunteers stepped in but were not trained or able to answer many questions and guide families to the resources they needed.

21. In order to advance public safety and meet public needs, Virginia's colleges and universities need to work together as a coordinated system of state-supported institutions.

As reflected in the body of the report, the panel has made more than 70 recommendations directed to colleges, universities, mental health providers, law enforcement officials, emergency service providers, lawmakers, and other public officials in Virginia and elsewhere.

LAWS LIMIT SCHOOLS EVEN AFTER ALARMS[1]

Jeff Gammage and Stacey Burling

This article first appeared in the Philadelphia Inquirer *on April 19, 2007, just three days after the Virginia Tech shootings.* Inquirer *staff writer Paul Nussbaum contributed to the article.*

If Cho Seung-Hui had been a warning light, he would have been blinking bright red.

Two female students complained to campus police that he was stalking them. His poetry was so twisted that his writing professor said she would quit if he weren't removed from her room. Some students found him so menacing that they refused to attend class with him.

Yet Virginia Tech, like other colleges trying to help emotionally troubled students, had little power to force Cho off campus and into treatment.

"We can't even pick up the phone and call their family. They're adults. You have to respect their privacy," said Brenda Ingram-Wallace, director of counseling and chair of the psychology department at Albright College in Reading.

---

[1]*Philadelphia Inquirer* 19 Apr. 2007: A01.

5   In the aftermath of the deadliest shooting in U.S. history, counselors, police authorities, and mental-health professionals say privacy laws prevent colleges from taking strong action regarding students who might be dangerous.

Many at Tech saw Cho as a threat—and shared those fears with authorities. In 2005, after the second stalking complaint, the school obtained a temporary detention order that resulted in Cho undergoing a psychiatric evaluation. But the 23-year-old remained enrolled at the university until the moment he shot himself to death.

Federal laws such as the 1974 Family Educational Rights and Privacy Act (FERPA) and the 1996 Health Insurance Portability and Accountability Act (HIPAA) protect students' right to privacy by banning disclosure of any mental-health problems—even to family members—without a signed waiver.

Patient-therapist confidentiality is crucial, privacy advocates say. Students may shy from treatment for fear of exposure.

FERPA does allow colleges to release information without permission in cases of "health and safety emergencies." But the criteria are so vague, and the potential liability so severe, that administrators say they hesitate to act in any but the most dire circumstances.

10   "The law tends to be protective of individual autonomy rather than getting in there and forcing people to get treatment," said Anthony Rostain, associate professor of psychiatry at the University of Pennsylvania School of Medicine.

Lots of students write violent stories, he noted. How do you distinguish between a future Cho Seung-Hui and a future Quentin Tarantino?*

"This kind of problem happens all the time across college campuses," Rostain said.

The law puts colleges in a tough position, said Dana Fleming, a lawyer with the college and university practice group at Nelson, Kinder, Mousseau & Saturley in Manchester, N.H. Schools may face legal trouble if they try to keep ill students out, if they try to send them home, or if they let them stay.

"No matter which decision they make," she said, "they can find liability on the other end."

15   Colleges can't screen students for mental illnesses during the admissions process because that violates the Americans With Disabilities Act. As a result, schools know which students will need tutoring or want to play soccer, but have no idea who is likely to need mental-health care, Fleming said.

Virginia Tech and most other universities cannot summarily suspend a student. Formal disciplinary charges must be filed and hearings held. Students who initiate a complaint often end up dropping the matter.

Nor can schools expect courts to hospitalize a student involuntarily without solid evidence that he poses a danger to himself or others.

That has left many colleges trying to find creative ways to identify and help troubled students.

---

*Director, screenwriter, and producer of frequently violent films such as *Reservoir Dogs* (1992), *Pulp Fiction* (1994), and *Kill Bill* (vol. 1, 2003; vol. 2, 2004).

At Albright College, administrators recently updated a program where anyone concerned about a student's behavior—a work supervisor, a professor or another student—can fill out a "student alert form."

20   Perhaps friends notice a student has become withdrawn or has stopped showing up for class. If multiple forms arrive concerning the same person, counseling director Ingram-Wallace said, the counseling center investigates by contacting housing officials or by reaching the student via phone or e-mail.

But the choice to speak with a psychological counselor stays with the student. The center can't send a therapist to knock on the student's door, she said.

"On the surface, it sounds like a caring thing to do," she said, but "if they haven't been dangerous to themselves or others, there's no reason to mandate them into any kind of services."

Among students who have been referred to the counseling center, "the responses are mixed," she said. "Some people felt imposed upon."

At St. Lawrence University in Canton, N.Y., every student who visits the health center—even for a head cold—is screened for depression and signs of other mental illness. The effort follows a national study that showed depression rising among college students.

25   If a screening shows someone needs help from the health center, "we literally walk them over there," said Patricia Ellis, director of counseling services.

More than a year before Monday's massacre of 32 students and staff members, Cho was twice accused of stalking female students and taken to a mental-health facility amid fears he was suicidal, police said yesterday.

After the first incident, in November 2005, police referred him to the university disciplinary system. Ed Spencer, Tech's assistant vice president of student affairs, said he could not comment on any proceedings against the gunman because federal law protects students' medical privacy even after death.

The university obtained the detention order after the second stalking complaint, in December 2005. "His insight and judgment are normal," an examiner at the psychiatric hospital concluded.

Yet poet Nikki Giovanni, one of his professors, told CNN that students were so unnerved by Cho's behavior, which included taking cell-phone photos of them in class, that most stopped attending the course. She insisted that he be removed.

30   Lucinda Roy, a codirector of the creative writing program, tutored Cho after that, and tried to get him into counseling. He always refused. Roy sent samples of Cho's writing, with its images of people attacking each other with chain saws, to the campus police, student-affairs office, and other agencies.

PERILOUS PRIVACY AT VIRGINIA TECH

This editorial appeared in the Christian Science Monitor *on September 4, 2007.*

Colleges didn't need last week's report on the Virginia Tech shootings to address a key finding: a faster alert during the crisis may have saved lives. Many colleges have already set blast-notice plans. But here's what needs careful study: the report's conclusions about privacy.

Privacy is a huge issue on campuses. Colleges and universities are dealing with young people who have just become legal adults, but who may still require supervision and even intervention.

That was the case with Seung-Hui Cho, the student who killed 32 people and then himself on April 16. According to the report, which was commissioned by Virginia Gov. Timothy Kaine, this troubled student's behavior raised serious questions about his mental stability while he was at VT, yet no one contacted his parents, and communication about his case broke down among school, law-enforcement, and mental-health officials.

A big reason? A "widespread perception" that privacy laws make it difficult to respond to troubled students, according to the report. But this is "only partly correct."

5   Lack of understanding about federal and state laws is a major obstacle to helping such students, according to the report. The legal complexity, as well as concerns about liability, can easily push teachers, administrators, police, and mental-health workers into a "default" position of withholding information, the report found.

There's no evidence that VT officials consciously decided not to inform Mr. Cho's parents. But the university's lawyer told the panel investigating Cho's case that privacy laws prevent sharing information such as that relating to Cho.

That's simply not true. The report listed several steps that could quite legally have been taken:

The Virginia Tech police, for instance, could have shared with Cho's parents that he was temporarily detained, pending a hearing to commit him involuntarily to a mental-health institution, because that information was public.

And teachers and administrators could have called Cho's parents to notify them of his difficulties, because only student records—not personal observations or conversations—are shielded by the federal privacy law that covers most secondary schools.

10   Notifying Cho's parents was intuitively the right course. Indeed, his middle school contacted his parents to get him help, and they cooperated. His high school also made special arrangements. He improved.

The report points out that the main federal privacy laws that apply to a college student's health and campus records recognize exceptions for information sharing in emergencies that affect public health and safety.

Privacy is a bedrock of American law and values. In a mental-health case, it gives a patient the security to express innermost thoughts, and protects that person from discrimination. But the federal law, at least, does recognize a balance between privacy and public safety, even when colleges can't, or won't.

The report is to be commended for pointing out this disconnect, and for calling for greater clarification of privacy laws and school policies.

Perhaps now, common sense can match up with legal obligations so both privacy and public safety can be served.

COLLEGES ARE WATCHING TROUBLED STUDENTS

Jeffrey McMurray

During the year following the Virginia Tech shootings, many colleges and universities took a hard look at their policies on student privacy and their procedures for monitoring and sharing information about troubled students. This article, by the Associated Press, was first published on March 28, 2008. AP writer Sue Lindsay contributed to this report.

On the agenda: A student who got into a shouting match with a faculty member. Another who harassed a female classmate. Someone found sleeping in a car. And a student who posted a threat against a professor on Facebook.

In a practice adopted at one college after another since the massacre at Virginia Tech, a University of Kentucky committee of deans, administrators, campus police and mental health officials has begun meeting regularly to discuss a watch list of troubled students and decide whether they need professional help or should be sent packing.

These "threat assessment groups" are aimed at heading off the kind of bloodshed seen at Virginia Tech a year ago and at Northern Illinois University last month.

"You've got to be way ahead of the game, so to speak, expect what may be coming. If you're able to identify behaviors early on and get these people assistance, it avoids disruptions in the classrooms and potential violence," said Maj. Joe Monroe, interim police chief at Kentucky.

5   The Kentucky panel, called Students of Concern, held its first meeting last week and will convene at least twice a month to talk about students whose strange or disturbing behavior has come to their attention.

Such committees represent a change in thinking among U.S. college officials, who for a long time were reluctant to share information about students' mental health for fear of violating privacy laws.

"If a student is a danger to himself or others, all the privacy concerns go out the window," said Patricia Terrell, vice president of student affairs, who created the panel.

Terrell shared details of the four discussed cases with The Associated Press on the condition that all names and other identifying information be left out.

Among other things, the panel can order a student into counseling or bar him or her from entering a particular building or talking to a certain person. It can also order a judicial hearing that can lead to suspension or expulsion if the student's offense was a violation of the law or school policy.

10   Although the four cases discussed last week were the ones administrators deemed as needing the most urgent attention, a database listing 26 other student cases has been created, providing fodder for future meetings.

Students are encouraged during their freshman orientation to report suspicious behavior to the dean of students, and university employees all the way down to janitors and cafeteria workers are instructed to tell their supervisors if they see anything.

Virtually every corner of campus is represented in the group's closed-door meetings, including dorm life, academics, counseling, mental health and police.

"If you look back at the Virginia Tech situation, the aftermath, there were several people who knew that student had problems, but because of privacy and different issues, they didn't talk to others about it," said Lee Todd, UK president.

High schools have been doing this sort of thing for years because of shootings, but only since Virginia Tech, when a disturbed student gunman killed 32 people and committed suicide, have colleges begun to follow suit, said Mike Dorn, executive director of Safe Havens International, a leading campus safety firm.

15 "They didn't think it was a real threat to them," Dorn said.

Virginia Tech has added a threat assessment team since the massacre there. Boston University, the University of Utah, the University of Illinois–Chicago and numerous others also have such groups, said Gwendolyn Dungy, executive director of the National Association of Student Personnel Administrators.

Bryan Cloyd, a Virginia Tech accounting professor whose daughter Austin was killed in the rampage, welcomed the stepped-up efforts to monitor troubled students but stressed he doesn't want to turn every college campus into a "police state."

"We can't afford to overreact," Cloyd said, but "we also can't afford to underreact."

Seung-Hui Cho, the Virginia Tech gunman, was ruled a danger to himself in a court hearing in 2005 that resulted from a roommate's call to police after Cho mentioned suicide in an e-mail. He was held overnight at a mental health center off campus and was ordered into outpatient treatment, but he received no follow-up services, despite his sullen, withdrawn behavior and his twisted, violence-filled writings.

20 Mary Bolin-Reece, director of counseling and testing at Kentucky, attends the threat assessment group's meetings but cannot share what she knows or, in most cases, even whether a student has been undergoing counseling. But participants can share information on other possible red flags.

"We always look at, 'Is there a change in the baseline?'" Bolin-Reece said. "The student had previously gotten very good grades, and then there was a drop-off. Something has happened. Is there some shift in their ability to function? If a student is coming to the attention of various parties around the university, we begin to be able to connect the dots."

The University of Kentucky has not had a murder on campus since 1984. Still, the threat-assessment effort has the strong backing of Carol Graham of Fort Carson, Colo., whose son Kevin was a Kentucky student when he committed suicide before leaving for an ROTC summer camp in 2003.

"UK is such a huge university," Graham said. "It's important to know there's a safety net—that people are looking out for each other. With Kevin, his professors thought he was perfect. He'd be an A student. But the people around him were noticing differences."

As for the four cases taken up by the committee: The student who got into an argument with a faculty member—and had also seen a major dip in grades and exhibited poor hygiene—was ordered to meet with the dean of students.

25 The one accused of harassment was referred to a judicial hearing, during which he was expelled from university housing. The student who made the Facebook threat was given a warning. In the case of the student sleeping in a car, a committee member was dispatched to check on the person. No further details were released.

VIRGINIA TECH MASSACRE HAS ALTERED CAMPUS MENTAL HEALTH SYSTEMS

This article, prepared by the Associated Press, is representative of numerous reports of how college administrators across the nation responded to the Virginia Tech killings. Many schools reviewed their existing policies on student privacy and communication and instituted new procedures. The article appeared in the Los Angeles Times *on April 14, 2008.*

The rampage carried out nearly a year ago by a Virginia Tech student who slipped through the mental health system has changed how American colleges reach out to troubled students.

Administrators are pushing students harder to get help, looking more aggressively for signs of trouble and urging faculty to speak up when they have concerns. Counselors say the changes are sending even more students their way, which is both welcome and a challenge, given that many still lack the resources to handle their growing workloads.

Behind those changes, colleges have edged away in the last year from decades-old practices that made student privacy paramount. Now, they are more likely to err on the side of sharing information—with the police, for instance, and parents—if there is any possible threat to community safety. But even some who say the changes are appropriate worry it could discourage students from seeking treatment.

Concerns also linger that the response to shooters like Seung-hui Cho at Virginia Tech and Steven Kazmierczak, who killed five others at Northern Illinois University, has focused excessively on boosting the capacity of campus police to respond to rare events. Such reforms may be worthwhile, but they don't address how to prevent such a tragedy in the first place.

5   It was last April 16, just after 7 a.m., that Cho killed two students in a Virginia Tech dormitory, the start of a shooting spree that continued in a classroom building and eventually claimed 33 lives, including his own.

Cho's behavior and writing had alarmed professors and administrators, as well as the campus police, and he had been put through a commitment hearing where he was found to be potentially dangerous. But when an off-campus psychiatrist sent him back to the school for outpatient treatment, there was no follow-up to ensure that he got it.

People who work every day in the campus mental health field—counselors, lawyers, advocates and students at colleges around the country—say they have seen three major types of change since the Cho shootings:

Faculty are speaking up more about students who worry them. That's accelerating a trend of more demand for mental health services that was already under way before the Virginia Tech shootings.

Professors "have a really heightened level of fear and concern from the behavior that goes on around them," said Ben Locke, assistant director of the counseling center at Penn State University.

10   David Wallace, director of counseling at the University of Central Florida, said teachers are paying closer attention to violent material in writing assignments— warning bells that had worried Cho's professors.

"Now people are wondering, 'Is this something that could be more ominous?'" he said. "Are we talking about the Stephen Kings of the future or about somebody who's seriously thinking about doing something harmful?"

The downside is officials may be hypersensitive to any eccentricity. Says Susan Davis, an attorney who works in student affairs at the University of Virginia: "There's no question there's some hysteria and there's some things we don't need to see."

Changes are being made to privacy policies. In Virginia, a measure signed into law Wednesday by Gov. Tim Kaine requires colleges to bring parents into the loop when dependent students may be a danger to themselves or others.

Even before Virginia Tech, Cornell University had begun treating students as dependents of their parents unless told otherwise—an aggressive legal strategy that gives the school more leeway to contact parents with concerns without students' permission.

15   In Washington, meanwhile, federal officials are trying to clarify privacy guidelines so faculty won't hesitate to report potential threats.

"Nobody's throwing privacy out the window, but we are coming out of an era when individual rights were paramount on college campuses," said Brett Sokolow, who advises colleges on risk management. "What colleges are struggling with now is a better balance of those individual rights and community protections."

The big change since the Virginia Tech shootings, legal experts say, is colleges have shed some of their fear of violating the federal Family Educational Rights and Privacy Act.

Many faculty hadn't realized that the law applies only to educational records, not observations of classroom behavior, or that it contains numerous exceptions.

The stigma of mental illness, in some cases, has grown. "In general, the attention to campus mental health was desperately needed," said Alison Malmon, founder of the national Active Minds group. But some of the debate, she added, "has turned in a direction that does not necessarily support students."

20   All the talk of "threat assessments" and better-trained campus SWAT teams, she said, has distracted the public from the fact that the mentally ill rarely commit violence—especially against others.

"I know that, for many students, it made them feel more stigmatized," Malmon said. "It made them more likely to keep their mental health history silent."

Sokolow, the risk consultant for colleges, estimated in the aftermath of the Virginia Tech and NIU shootings, the schools he works with spent $25 on police and communications for every $1 on mental health. Only recently has he seen a shift.

"Campuses come to me, they want me to help them start behavioral intervention systems," Sokolow said. "Then they go to the president to get the money and, oh, well, the money went into the door locks."

Phone messaging systems and security are nice, he said, but "there is nothing about text-messaging that is going to prevent violence."

THE FAMILY EDUCATIONAL RIGHTS AND PRIVACY ACT

United States Code
Title 20. Education
CHAPTER 31. General Provisions Concerning Education
§ 1232g. Family Educational and Privacy Rights

Following are excerpts from the Family Educational and Privacy Act (FERPA), *the federal law enacted in 1974 that governs restrictions on the release of student educational records. FERPA provides for the withholding of federal funds to educational institutions that violate its provisions, and it is the federal guarantor of the privacy rights of post-secondary students.*

(1) (A) No funds shall be made available under any applicable program to any educational agency or institution which has a policy of denying, or which effectively prevents, the parents of students who are or have been in attendance at a school of such agency or at such institution, as the case may be, the right to inspect and review the education records of their children. If any material or document in the education record of a student includes information on more than one student, the parents of one of such students shall have the right to inspect and review only such part of such material or document as relates to such student or to be informed of the specific information contained in such part of such material. Each educational agency or institution shall establish appropriate procedures for the granting of a request by parents for access to the education records of their children within a reasonable period of time, but in no case more than forty-five days after the request has been made. . . .

   (C) The first sentence of subparagraph (A) shall not operate to make available to students in institutions of postsecondary education the following materials:

   (i) financial records of the parents of the student or any information contained therein;

   (ii) confidential letters and statements of recommendation, which were placed in the education records prior to January 1, 1975, if such letters or statements are not used for purposes other than those for which they were specifically intended;

   (iii) if the student has signed a waiver of the student's right of access under this subsection in accordance with subparagraph (D), confidential recommendations—

      (I) respecting admission to any educational agency or institution,

      (II) respecting an application for employment, and

      (III) respecting the receipt of an honor or honorary recognition.

. . . .

(B) The term "education records" does not include—

   (i) records of instructional, supervisory, and administrative personnel and educational personnel ancillary thereto which are in the sole possession of the maker thereof and which are not accessible or revealed to any other person except a substitute;

(ii) records maintained by a law enforcement unit of the educational agency or institution that were created by that law enforcement unit for the purpose of law enforcement;

(iii) in the case of persons who are employed by an educational agency or institution but who are not in attendance at such agency or institution, records made and maintained in the normal course of business which relate exclusively to such person in that person's capacity as an employee and are not available for use for any other purpose; or

(iv) records on a student who is eighteen years of age or older, or is attending an institution of postsecondary education, which are made or maintained by a physician, psychiatrist, psychologist, or other recognized professional or paraprofessional acting in his professional or paraprofessional capacity, or assisting in that capacity, and which are made, maintained, or used only in connection with the provision of treatment to the student, and are not available to anyone other than persons providing such treatment, except that such records can be personally reviewed by a physician or other appropriate professional of the student's choice. . . .

(h) Certain disciplinary action information allowable. Nothing in this section shall prohibit an educational agency or institution from—

(1) including appropriate information in the education record of any student concerning disciplinary action taken against such student for conduct that posed a significant risk to the safety or well-being of that student, other students, or other members of the school community; or

(2) disclosing such information to teachers and school officials, including teachers and school officials in other schools, who have legitimate educational interests in the behavior of the student.

Exercise 4.5

Critical Reading for Synthesis

Having read the selections relating to privacy and safety, pp. 144–156, write a one-sentence summary of each. On the same page, list two or three topics that you think are common to several of the selections. Beneath each topic, list the authors who have something to say and briefly note what they have to say. Finally, for each topic, jot down what *you* have to say. Now regard your effort: With each topic you have created a discussion point suitable for inclusion in a paper. (Of course, until you determine the claim of such a paper, you won't know to what end you would put the discussion.) Write a paragraph or two in which you introduce the topic and then conduct a brief conversation among the interested parties (including yourself).

Consider Your Purpose

Your specific purpose in writing an argument synthesis is crucial. What exactly you want to do will affect your claim and how you organize the evidence. Your purpose may be clear to you before you begin research, or it may not emerge until after you have completed your research. Of course, the sooner your purpose is clear to you, the fewer wasted motions you will make. On the other hand, the more you approach research as an exploratory process, the likelier that your conclusions will emerge from the sources themselves rather than from preconceived ideas. Each new writing project will have its rhythm in this regard. Be flexible in your approach: through some combination of preconceived structures and invigorating discoveries, you will find your way to the source materials that will yield a promising paper.

Let's say that while reading these six (and additional) sources on the debate about campus safety and student privacy you shared the outrage of many who blamed the university (and the federal privacy laws on which it relied) for not using the available information in a way that might have spared the lives of those who died. Perhaps you also blamed the legislators who wrote the privacy laws for being more concerned about the confidentiality of the mental health records of the individual person than with the safety of the larger college population. Perhaps, you concluded, society has gone too far in valuing privacy more than it appears to value safety.

On the other hand, in your own role as a student, perhaps you share the high value placed on the privacy of sensitive information about yourself. After all, one of the functions of higher education is to foster students' independence as they make the transition from adolescence to adulthood. You can understand that many students like yourself might not want parents or others to know details about academic records or disciplinary measures, much less information about therapy sought and undertaken at school. Historically, in the decades since the university officially stood *in loco parentis*—in place of parents—students have struggled hard to win the same civil liberties and rights (including the right to privacy) of their elders.

Further, you may wonder whether federal privacy laws do in fact forbid the sharing of information about potentially dangerous students when the health and safety of others are at stake. A little research may begin to confirm your doubts about whether Virginia Tech officials were as helpless as they claim they were.

Your purpose in writing, then, emerges from these kinds of responses to the source materials you find.

Making a Claim: Formulate a Thesis

As we indicated in the introduction to this chapter, one useful way of approaching an argument is to see it as making a *claim*. A claim is a proposition, a conclusion that you have made, that you are trying to prove or demonstrate. If your purpose is to argue that we should work to ensure campus safety without enacting restrictive laws that overturn the hard-won privacy rights of students, then that claim (generally expressed in one-sentence form as a *thesis*) is at the heart of your argument. You will draw support from your sources as you argue logically for your claim.

Not every piece of information in a source is useful for supporting a claim. You must read with care and select the opinions, facts, and statistics that best advance your position. You may even find yourself drawing support from sources that make claims entirely different from your own. For example, in researching the subject of student privacy and campus safety, you may come across editorials arguing that in the wake of the Virginia Tech shootings student privacy rights should be greatly restricted. Perhaps you will find information in these sources to help support your own contrary arguments.

You might use one source as part of a *counterargument*—an argument opposing your own—so you can demonstrate its weaknesses and, in the process, strengthen your own claim. On the other hand, the author of one of your sources may be so convincing in supporting a claim that you will adopt it yourself, either partially or entirely. The point is that *the argument is in your hands.* You must devise it yourself and use your sources in ways that will support the claim you present in your thesis.

You may not want to divulge your thesis until the end of the paper, thereby drawing the reader along toward your conclusion, allowing that thesis to flow naturally out of the argument and the evidence on which it is based. If you do this, you are working *inductively*. Or you may wish to be more direct and (after an introduction) *begin* with your thesis, following the thesis statement with evidence and reasoning to support it. If you do this, you are working *deductively*. In academic papers, deductive arguments are far more common than inductive ones.

Based on your reactions to reading sources—and perhaps also on your own inclinations as a student—you may find yourself essentially in sympathy with the approach to privacy taken by one of the schools covered in your sources, M.I.T. At the same time, you may feel that M.I.T.'s position does not demonstrate sufficient concern for campus safety and that Cornell's position, on the other hand, restricts student privacy too much. Perhaps most important, you conclude that we don't need to change the law because, if correctly interpreted, the law already incorporates a good balance between privacy and safety. After a few tries, you develop this thesis:

> In responding to the Virginia Tech killings, we should resist rolling back federal rules protecting student privacy; for as long as college officials effectively respond to signs of trouble, these rules already provide a workable balance between privacy and public safety.

Decide How You Will Use Your Source Material

Your claim commits you to (1) arguing that student privacy should remain protected, and (2) demonstrating that federal law already strikes a balance between privacy and public safety. The sources (some provided here, some located elsewhere) offer information and ideas—evidence—that will allow you to support your claim. The excerpt from the official report on the Virginia Tech shootings reveals a finding that school officials failed to correctly interpret federal privacy rules and failed to "intervene effectively." The article "Virginia Tech Massacre Has Altered Campus Mental Health Systems" outlines some of the ways that campuses around the country have instituted policy changes regarding troubled students and privacy in the wake of Virginia Tech. And the excerpt from the Family Educational Rights and Privacy Act (FERPA), the federal law, reveals that restrictions on revealing students' confidential information have a crucial exception for "the safety or well-being of . . . students, or other members of the school community." (These and several other sources not included in this chapter will be cited in the model argument paper.)

Develop an Organizational Plan

Having established your overall purpose and your claim, having developed a thesis (which may change as you write and revise the paper), and having decided how to draw upon your source materials, how do you logically organize your paper? In many cases, a well-written thesis will suggest an organization. Thus, the first part of your paper will deal with the debate over rolling back student privacy. The second part will argue that as long as educational institutions behave proactively—that is, as long as they actively seek to help troubled students and foster campus safety—existing federal rules already preserve a balance between privacy and safety. Sorting through your material and categorizing it by topic and subtopic, you might compose the following outline:

I. Introduction. Recap Va. Tech shooting. College officials, citing privacy rules, did not act on available info about shooter with history of mental problems.

II. Federal rules on privacy. Subsequent debate over balance between privacy and campus safety. Pendulum now moving back toward safety. *Thesis.*

III. Developments in student privacy in recent decades.
   A. Doctrine of *in loco parentis* defines college-student relationship.
   B. Movement away from *in loco parentis* begins in 1960s, in context not only of student rights but also broader civil rights struggles of the period.
   C. FERPA, enacted 1974, establishes new federal rules protecting student privacy.

IV. Arguments *against* student privacy.
   A. In wake of Virginia Tech, many blame FERPA protections and college officials, believing privacy rights have been taken too far, putting campus community at risk.
   B. Cornell rolls back some FERPA privacy rights.

    V. Arguments *for* student privacy.
       A. M.I.T. strongly defends right to privacy.
       B. Problem is not federal law but incorrect interpretation of federal law. FERPA provides health and safety exceptions. Virginia Tech officials erred in citing FERPA for not sharing info about shooter earlier.
       C. Univ. of Kentucky offers good balance between competing claims of privacy and safety.
          1. watch lists of troubled students
          2. threat assessment groups
          3. open communication among university officials
   VI. Conclusion.
       A. Virginia Tech incident was tragic but should not cause us to overturn hard-won privacy rights.
       B. We should support a more pro-active approach to student mental health problems and improve communication between departments.

Formulate an Argument Strategy

The argument that emerges through this outline will build not only on evidence drawn from sources but also on the writer's assumptions. Consider the bare-bones logic of the argument:

Laws protecting student privacy serve a good purpose. (*assumption*)

If properly interpreted and implemented, federal law as currently written is sufficient both to protect student privacy and to ensure campus safety. (*support*)

We should not change federal law to overturn or restrict student privacy rights. (*claim*)

The crucial point about which reasonable people will disagree is the *assumption* that laws protecting student privacy serve a good purpose. Those who wish to restrict the information made available to parents are likely to agree with this assumption. Those who favor a policy that allows college officials to inform parents of problems without their children's permission are likely to disagree.

Writers can accept or partially accept an opposing assumption by making a *concession*, in the process establishing themselves as reasonable and willing to compromise (see p. 177). David Harrison does exactly this in the model synthesis that follows when he summarizes the policies of the University of Kentucky. By raising objections to his own position and conceding some validity to them, he blunts the effectiveness of *counterarguments*. Thus, Harrison concedes the absolute requirement for campus safety, but he argues that this requirement can be satisfied as long as campus officials correctly interpret existing federal law and implement proactive procedures aimed at dealing more effectively with troubled students.

The *claim* of the argument about privacy vs. safety is primarily a claim about *policy*, about actions that should (or should not) be taken. An argument can also concern a claim about *facts* (Does X exist? How can we define X? Does X lead to Y?), a claim about *value* (What is X worth?), or a claim about *cause and effect* (Why did X happen?). The present argument rests to some degree on a dispute about cause and effect. No one disputes that the primary cause of this tragedy was that a disturbed student was not stopped before he killed people. But many have disputed the secondary cause: Did the massacre happen, in part, because federal law prevented officials from sharing crucial information about the disturbed student? Or did it happen, in part, because university officials failed to interpret correctly what they could and could not do under the law? As you read the following paper, observe how these opposing views are woven into the argument.

Draft and Revise Your Synthesis

The final draft of an argument synthesis, based on the outline above, follows. Thesis, transitions, and topic sentences are highlighted; Modern Language Association (MLA) documentation style is used throughout (except in the citing of federal law).

A cautionary note: When writing syntheses, it is all too easy to become careless in properly crediting your sources. Before drafting your paper, always review the section on Avoiding Plagiarism (pp. 53–55).

MODEL ARGUMENT SYNTHESIS

Harrison 1

David Harrison

Professor Shanker

Law and Society I

14 February 2009

Balancing Privacy and Safety

in the Wake of Virginia Tech

(1)   On April 16, 2007, Seung Hui Cho, a mentally ill student at

Virginia Polytechnic Institute, shot to death 32 fellow students and fac-

ulty members, and injured 17 others, before killing himself. It was the

worst mass shooting in U.S. history, and the fact that it took place on a

college campus lent a special horror to the event. In the days after the

tragedy, several facts about Seung Hui Cho came to light. According to the official Virginia State Panel report on the killings, Cho had exhibited signs of mental disturbance, including "suicidal and homicidal ideations" dating back to high school. And during Cho's junior year at Virginia Tech, numerous incidents occurred that provided clear warnings of Cho's mental instability and violent impulses (Virginia Tech Review 1). University administrators, faculty, and officials were aware of these incidents but failed to intervene to prevent the impending tragedy.

(2) In the search for answers, attention quickly focused on federal rules governing student privacy that Virginia Tech officials said prevented them from communicating effectively with each other or with Cho's parents regarding his troubles. These rules, the officials argued, prohibit the sharing of information concerning students' mental health with parents or other students. The publicity about such restrictions revived an ongoing debate over university policies that balance student privacy against campus safety. In the wake of the Virginia Tech tragedy, the pendulum seems to have swung in favor of safety. In April 2008, Virginia Governor Tim Kaine signed into law a measure requiring colleges to alert parents when dependent students may be a danger to themselves or to others ("Virginia Tech Massacre" 1). Peter Lake, an educator at Stetson University College of Law, predicted that in the wake of Virginia Tech, "people will go in a direction of safety over privacy" (qtd. in Bernstein, "Mother").

(3) The shootings at Virginia Tech demonstrate, in the most horrifying way, the need for secure college campuses. Nevertheless, privacy remains a crucial right to most Americans--including college students, many of whom for the first time are exercising their prerogatives as adults. Many students who pose no threat to anyone will, and should, object strenuously to university administrators peering into and making judgments about their private lives. Some might be unwilling to seek professional therapy if they know that the records of their counseling sessions might be released to their parents or to other students. In responding to the Virginia Tech killings, we should resist rolling back federal rules protecting student privacy; for as long

Harrison 3

as college officials effectively respond to signs of trouble, these rules already provide a workable balance between privacy and public safety.

4   In these days of *Facebook* and reality TV, the notion of privacy rights, particularly for young people, may seem quaint. In fact, recently a top lawyer for the search engine *Google* claimed that in the Internet age, young people just don't care about privacy the way they once did (Cohen A17). Whatever the changing views of privacy in a wired world, the issue of student privacy rights is a serious legal matter that must be seen in the context of the student-college relationship, which has its historical roots in the doctrine of *in loco parentis*, Latin for "in the place of the parents." Generally, this doctrine is understood to mean that the college stands in place as the student's parent or guardian. The college therefore has "a duty to protect the safety, morals, and welfare of their students, just as parents are expected to protect their children" (Pollet).

5   Writing of life at the University of Michigan before the 1960s, one historian observes that "*in loco parentis* comprised an elaborate structure of written rules and quiet understandings enforced in the trenches by housemothers [who] governed much of the what, where, when, and whom of students' lives, especially women: what to wear to dinner, what time to be home, where, when, and for how long they might receive visitors" (Tobin).

6   During the 1960s court decisions began to chip away at the doctrine of *in loco parentis*. These rulings illustrate that the students' rights movement during that era was an integral part of a broader contemporary social movement for civil rights and liberties. In *Dixon v. Alabama State Board of Education*, Alabama State College invoked *in loco parentis* to defend its decision to expel six African-American students without due process for participating in a lunchroom counter sit-in. Eventually, a federal appeals court rejected the school's claim to unrestrained power, ruling that students' constitutional rights did not end once they stepped onto campus (Weigel).

(7)   Students were not just fighting for the right to hold hands in dorm rooms; they were also asserting their rights as the vanguard of a social revolution. As Stetson law professor Robert Bickel notes: "The fall of *in loco parentis* in the 1960s correlated exactly with the rise of student economic power and the rise of student civil rights" (qtd. in Weigel).

(8)   The students' rights movement received a further boost with the Family Educational Rights and Privacy Act (FERPA), signed into law by President Ford in 1974. FERPA barred schools from releasing educational records--including mental health records--without the student's permission. The Act provides some important exceptions: educational records *can* be released in the case of health and safety emergencies or if the student is declared a dependent on his or her parents' tax returns (*Federal*).

(9)   In the wake of Virginia Tech, however, many observers pointed the finger of blame at federal restrictions on sharing available mental health information. Also held responsible were the school's officials, who admitted knowing of Cho's mental instability but claimed that FERPA prevented them from doing anything about it. The State of Virginia official report on the killings notes as follows:

> University officials . . . explained their failures to communicate with one another or with Cho's parents by noting their belief that such communications are prohibited by the federal laws governing the privacy of health and education records. (Virginia Tech Review 2)

(10)   Observers were quick to declare the system broken. "Laws Limit Schools Even after Alarms," trumpeted a headline in the *Philadelphia Inquirer* (Gammage and Burling). Commentators attacked federal privacy law, charging that the pendulum had swung too far away from campus safety. Judging from this letter to the editor of the *Wall Street Journal*, many agreed wholeheartedly: "Parents have a right to know if their child has a serious problem, and they need to know the

progress of their child's schoolwork, especially if they are paying the cost of the education. Anything less than this is criminal" (Guerriero).

(11)   As part of this public clamor, some schools have enacted policies that effectively curtail student privacy in favor of campus safety. For example: after Virginia Tech, Cornell University began assuming that students were dependents of their parents. Exploiting what the *Wall Street Journal* termed a "rarely used legal exception" in FERPA allows Cornell to provide parents with confidential information without students' permission (Bernstein, "Bucking" A9).

(12)   Conversely, the Massachusetts Institute of Technology lies at the opposite end of the spectrum from Cornell in its staunch defense of student privacy. M.I.T. has stuck to its position even in the wake of Virginia Tech, recently demanding that the mother of a missing M.I.T. student obtain a subpoena in order to access his dorm room and e-mail records. That student was later found dead, an apparent suicide (Bernstein, "Mother"). Even in the face of lawsuits, M.I.T. remains committed to its stance. Its Chancellor explained the school's position this way:

> Privacy is important. . . . Different students will do different things they absolutely don't want their parents to know about. . . . Students expect this kind of safe place where they can address their difficulties, try out lifestyles, and be independent of their parents (qtd. in Bernstein, "Mother").

(13)   One can easily understand how parents would be outraged by the M.I.T. position. No parent would willingly let his or her child enter an environment where that child's safety cannot be assured. Just as the first priority for any government is to protect its citizens, the first priority of an educational institution must be to keep its students safe. But does this responsibility justify rolling back student privacy rights or returning to a more traditional interpretation of *in loco parentis* in the relationship between a university and its students? No, for the simple reason that the choice is a false one.

(14)   As long as federal privacy laws are properly interpreted and implemented, they do nothing to endanger campus safety. The problem at
Virginia Tech was not the federal government's policy; it was the university's own practices based on a faulty interpretation of that policy. The
breakdown began with the failure of Virginia Tech officials to understand
federal privacy laws. Interpreted correctly, these laws would *not* have
prohibited officials from notifying appropriate authorities of Cho's problems. The Virginia Tech Review Panel report was very clear on this point:
"[F]ederal laws and their state counterparts afford ample leeway to share
information in potentially dangerous situations" (2). FERPA does, in fact,
provide for a "health and safety emergencies" exception; educational
records *can* be released without the student's consent "in connection
with an emergency, [to] appropriate persons if the knowledge of such information is necessary to protect the health or safety of the student or
other person . . ." (232g (b) (1) (g-h)). But Virginia Tech administrators
did not invoke this important exception to FERPA's privacy rules.

(15)   An editorial in the *Christian Science Monitor* suggested several other
steps that the university could legally have taken, including informing
Cho's parents that he had been briefly committed to a mental health facility, a fact that was public information. The editorial concluded, scornfully,
that "federal law, at least, does recognize a balance between privacy and
public safety, even when colleges can't, or won't" ("Perilous").

(16)   To be fair, such confusion about FERPA's contingencies appears
widespread among college officials. For this reason, the U.S. Department of Education's revised privacy regulations, announced in March
2008 and intended to "clarify" when schools may release student
records, are welcome and necessary. But simply reassuring anxious
university officials that they won't lose federal funds for revealing
confidential student records won't be enough to ensure campus safety.
We need far more effective intervention for troubled students than the
kind provided by Virginia Tech, which the Virginia Tech Review Panel
blasted for its "lack of resources" and "passivity" (2).

Harrison 7

(17)   Schools like the University of Kentucky offer a positive example of such intervention, demonstrating that colleges can adopt a robust approach to student mental health without infringing on privacy rights. At Kentucky, "threat assessment groups" meet regularly to discuss a "watch list" of troubled students and decide what to do about them (McMurray). These committees emphasize proactiveness and communication--elements that were sorely missing at Virginia Tech. The approach represents a prudent middle ground between the extreme positions of M.I.T. and Cornell.

(18)   Schools such as Kentucky carry out their policies with a firm eye toward student privacy rights. For example, the University of Kentucky's director of counseling attends the threat assessment group's meetings but draws a clear line at what information she can share--for instance, whether or not a student has been undergoing counseling. Instead, the group looks for other potential red flags, such as a sharp drop-off in grades or difficulty functioning in the campus environment (McMurray). This open communication between university officials will presumably also help with delicate judgments--whether, for example, a student's violent story written for a creative writing class is an indication of mental instability or simply an early work by the next Stephen King ("Virginia Tech Massacre" 1).

(19)   What happened at Virginia Tech was a tragedy. Few of us can appreciate the grief of the parents of the shooting victims at Virginia Tech, parents who trusted that their children would be safe and who were devastated when that faith was betrayed. To these parents, the words of the MIT chancellor quoted earlier--platitudes about students "try[ing] out lifestyles" or "address[ing] their difficulties"--must sound hollow. But we must guard against allowing a few isolated incidents, however tragic, to restrict the rights of millions of students, the vast majority of whom graduate college safely and without incident. Schools must not use Virginia Tech as a pretext to bring back the bad old days of resident assistants snooping on the private lives of students and infringing on their privacy. That step is the first down a slippery slope

of dictating morality. Both the federal courts and Congress have rejected that approach and for good reason have established the importance of privacy rights on campus. These rights must be preserved.

(20)   The Virginia Tech shooting does not demonstrate a failure of current policy, but rather a breakdown in the enforcement of policy. In its wake, universities have undertaken important modifications to their procedures. We should support changes that involve a more proactive approach to student mental health and improvements in communication between departments, such as those at the University of Kentucky. Such measures will not only bring confidential help to the troubled students who need it, they will also improve the safety of the larger college community. At the same time, these measures will preserve hard-won privacy rights on campus.

Works Cited

Bernstein, Elizabeth. "Bucking Privacy Concerns, Cornell Acts as Watchdog."
     Wall Street Journal 27 Dec. 2007: A1+. *LexisNexis.* Web. 10 Feb. 2009.

---. "A Mother Takes On MIT." *Wall Street Journal* 20 Sept. 2007: A1.
     LexisNexis. Web. 10 Feb. 2009.

Cohen, Adam. "One Friend Facebook Hasn't Made Yet: Privacy Rights."
     New York Times 18 Feb. 2008: A1+. *Academic Search Complete.*
     Web. 9 Feb. 2009.

Federal Educational Rights and Privacy Act (FERPA). 20 U.S.C. §1232g
     (b) (1) (g–h) (2006). Print.

Gammage, Jeff, and Stacy Burling. "Laws Limit Schools Even after
     Alarms." *Philadelphia Inquirer* 19 Apr. 2007: A1. *Academic Search
     Complete.* Web. 10 Feb. 2009.

Guerriero, Dom. Letter. *Wall Street Journal* 7 Jan. 2008. *LexisNexis.*
     Web. 11 Feb. 2009.

McMurray, Jeffrey. "Colleges Are Watching Troubled Students." *AP Online.*
     Associated Press, 28 Mar. 2008. Web. 11 Feb. 2009.

Harrison 10

"Perilous Privacy at Virginia Tech." Editorial. *Christian Science Monitor* 4

> Sept. 2007: 8. *Academic Search Complete*. Web. 10 Feb. 2009.

Pollet, Susan J. "Is 'In Loco Parentis' at the College Level a Dead

> Doctrine?" *New York Law Journal* 288 (2002): 4. Print.

Tobin, James. "The Day 'In Loco Parentis' Died." *Michigan Today*. U of

> Michigan, Nov. 2007. Web. 10 Feb. 2009.

"Virginia Tech Massacre Has Altered Campus Mental Health Systems." *Los*

> *Angeles Times* 14 Apr. 2008: A1+. *LexisNexis*. Web. 8 Feb. 2009.

Virginia Tech Review Panel. *Mass Shootings at Virginia Tech, April 16, 2007:*

> *Report of the Virginia Tech Review Panel Presented to Timothy M. Kaine,*

> *Governor, Commonwealth of Virginia*. Arlington, VA: n.p., 2007. Print.

Weigel, David. "Welcome to the Fun-Free University: The Return of *In*

> *Loco Parentis* Is Killing Student Freedom." *Reasononline*. Reason

> Magazine, Oct. 2004. Web. 7 Feb. 2009.

The Strategy of the Argument Synthesis

In his argument synthesis, Harrison attempts to support a *claim*—one that favors laws protecting student privacy while at the same time helping to ensure campus safety—by offering *support* in the form of facts (what campuses such as the University of Kentucky are doing, what Virginia Tech officials did and failed to do) and opinions (testimony of persons on both sides of the issue). However, because Harrison's claim rests on an *assumption* about the value of student privacy laws, its effectiveness depends partially on the extent to which we, as readers, agree with this assumption. (See our discussion of assumptions in Chapter 2, pp. 71–73.) An assumption (sometimes called a warrant) is a generalization or principle about how the world works or should work—a fundamental statement of belief about facts or values. In this case, the underlying assumption is that college students, as emerging adults, and as citizens with civil rights, are entitled to keep their educational records private. Harrison makes this assumption explicit. Though you are under no obligation to do so, stating assumptions explicitly will clarify your arguments to readers.

Assumptions are often deeply rooted in people's psyches, sometimes derived from lifelong experiences and observations and not easily changed, even by the most logical of arguments. People who lost loved ones in incidents such as Virginia Tech, or people who believe that the right to safety of the larger campus community outweighs the right of individual student privacy, are not likely to accept the assumption underlying this paper, nor are they likely to accept the support provided by Harrison. But readers with no firm opinion might well be persuaded and could come to agree with him that existing federal law protecting student privacy is sufficient to protect campus safety, provided that campus officials act responsibly.

A discussion of the model argument's paragraphs, along with the argument strategy for each, follows. Note that the paper devotes one paragraph to developing each section of the outline on pp. 159–160. Note also that Harrison avoids plagiarism by the careful attribution and quotation of sources.

- **Paragraph 1:** Harrison summarizes the key events of the Virginia Tech killings and establishes that Cho's mental instability was previously known to university officials.

    Argument strategy: Opening with the bare facts of the massacre, Harrison proceeds to lay the basis for the reaction against privacy rules that will be described in the paragraphs to follow. To some extent, Harrison encourages the reader to share the outrage by many in the general public that university officials failed to act to prevent the killings before they started.

- **Paragraph 2:** Harrison now explains the federal rules governing student privacy and discusses the public backlash against such rules and the new law signed by the governor of Virginia restricting privacy at colleges within the state.

    Argument strategy: This paragraph highlights the debate over student privacy—and in particular the sometimes conflicting demands of student privacy and campus safety that will be central to the rest of the paper. Harrison cites both fact (the new Virginia law) and opinion (the quotation by Peter Lake) to develop this paragraph.

- **Paragraph 3:** Harrison further clarifies the two sides of the apparent conflict between privacy and safety, maintaining that both represent important social values but concluding with a thesis that argues for not restricting privacy.

    Argument strategy: For the first time, Harrison reveals his own position on the issue. He starts the paragraph by conceding the need for secure campuses but begins to make the case for privacy (for example, without privacy rules students might be reluctant to enter therapy). In his thesis he emphasizes that the demands of both privacy and safety can be satisfied because existing federal rules incorporate the necessary balance.

- **Paragraphs 4–7:** These paragraphs constitute the next section of the paper (see outline, pp. 159–160), covering the developments in student privacy over the past few decades. Paragraphs 4 and 5 treat the doctrine of *in loco parentis*; paragraph 6 discusses how court decisions like *Dixon v. Alabama State Board of Education* began to erode this doctrine.

Argument strategy: This section of the paper establishes the situation that existed on college campuses before the 1960s—and presumably would exist again were privacy laws to be rolled back. By linking the erosion of the *in loco parentis* doctrine to the civil rights struggle, Harrison attempts to bestow upon pre-1960s college students (especially women), who were "parented" by college administrators, something of the ethos of African–Americans fighting for full citizenship during the civil rights era. Essentially, Harrison is making an analogy between the two groups—one that readers may or may not accept.

- **Paragraph 8:** This paragraph on FERPA constitutes the final part of the section of the paper dealing with the evolution of student privacy since before the 1960s. Harrison explains what FERPA is and introduces an exception to its privacy rules that will be more fully developed later in the paper.

    Argument strategy: FERPA is the federal law central to the debate over the balance between privacy and safety, so Harrison introduces it here as the culmination of a series of developments that weakened *in loco parentis* and guaranteed a certain level of student privacy. But since Harrison in his thesis argues that federal law on student privacy already establishes a balance between privacy and safety, he ends the paragraph by referring to the "health and safety" exception, an exception that will become important later in his argument.

- **Paragraphs 9–11:** These paragraphs constitute the section of the paper that covers the arguments **against** student privacy. Paragraph 9 treats public reaction against both FERPA and Virginia Tech officials who were accused of being more concerned with privacy than with safety. Paragraph 10 cites anti-privacy sentiments expressed in newspapers. Paragraph 11 explains how, in the wake of Virginia Tech, schools like Cornell have enacted new policies restricting student privacy.

    Argument strategy: Harrison sufficiently respects the sentiments of those whose position he opposes to deal at some length with the counterarguments to his thesis. He quotes the official report on the mass shootings to establish that Virginia Tech officials believed that they were acting according to the law. He quotes the writer of an angry letter about parents' right to know without attempting to rebut its arguments. In outlining the newly restrictive Cornell policies on privacy, Harrison also establishes what he considers an extreme reaction to the massacres: essentially gutting student privacy rules. He is therefore setting up one position on the debate which will later be contrasted with other positions—those of M.I.T. and the University of Kentucky.

- **Paragraphs 12–18:** These paragraphs constitute the section of the paper devoted to arguments **for** student privacy. Paragraphs 12 and 13 discuss the M.I.T. position on privacy, as expressed by its chancellor. Paragraph 14 refocuses on FERPA and quotes language to demonstrate that existing federal law provides a health and safety exception to the enforcement of privacy rules. Paragraph 15 quotes an editorial supporting this interpretation of FERPA. Paragraph 16 concedes the existence of confusion about federal rules and makes the transition to an argument about the need for more effective action by campus officials to prevent tragedies like this one.

Argument strategy: Because these paragraphs express Harrison's position, as embedded in his thesis, this is the longest segment of the discussion. Paragraphs 12 and 13 discuss the M.I.T. position on student privacy, which (given that school's failure to accommodate even prudent demands for safety) Harrison believes is too extreme. Notice the transition at the end of paragraph 13: conceding that colleges have a responsibility to keep students safe, Harrison poses a question: Does the goal of keeping students safe justify the rolling back of privacy rights? In a pivotal sentence, he responds, "No, for the simple reason that the choice is a false one." Paragraph 14 develops this response and presents the heart of Harrison's argument. Recalling the health and safety exception introduced in paragraph 8, Harrison now explains *why* the choice is false: he quotes the exact language of FERPA to establish that the problem at Virginia Tech was not due to federal law that prevented campus officials from protecting students, but rather to campus officials who *misunderstood* the law. Paragraph 15 amplifies Harrison's argument with a reference to an editorial in the *Christian Science Monitor*. Paragraph 16 marks a transition, within this section, to a position (developed in paragraphs 17 and 18) that Harrison believes represents a sensible stance in the debate over campus safety and student privacy. Harrison bolsters his case by citing here, as elsewhere in the paper, the official report on the Virginia Tech killings. The report, prepared by an expert panel that devoted months to investigating the incident, carries considerable weight as evidence in this argument.

- **Paragraphs 17–18:** These paragraphs continue the arguments in favor of Harrison's position. They focus on new policies in practice at the University of Kentucky that offer a "prudent middle ground" in the debate.

   Argument strategy: Having discussed schools such as Cornell and M.I.T. where the reaction to the Virginia Tech killings was inadequate or unsatisfactory, Harrison now outlines a set of policies and procedures in place at the University of Kentucky since April 2007. Following the transition at the end of paragraph 16 on the need for more effective intervention on the part of campus officials, Harrison explains how Kentucky established a promising form of such intervention: watch lists of troubled students, threat assessment groups, and more open communication among university officials. Thus Harrison positions what is happening at the University of Kentucky—as opposed to rollbacks of federal rules—as the most effective way of preventing future killings like those at Virginia Tech. Kentucky therefore becomes a crucial example for Harrison of how to strike a good balance between the demands of student privacy and campus safety.

- **Paragraphs 19–20:** In his conclusion, Harrison reiterates points made in the body of the paper. In paragraph 19 he agrees that what happened at Virginia Tech was a tragedy but maintains that an isolated incident should not become an excuse for rolling back student privacy rights and bringing back "the bad old days" when campus officials took an active, and intrusive, interest in students' private lives. In paragraph 20, Harrison reiterates the position stated in his thesis: that the problem at Virginia Tech was not a restrictive federal policy that handcuffed administrators but a breakdown in enforcement. He concludes on a hopeful note that new policies established since Virginia Tech will both protect student privacy and improve campus safety.

    Argument strategy: The last two paragraphs provide Harrison with a final opportunity for driving home his points. These two paragraphs to some degree parallel the structure of the thesis itself. In paragraph 19, Harrison makes a final appeal against rolling back student privacy rights. This appeal parallels the first clause of the thesis ("In responding to the Virginia Tech killings, we should resist rolling back federal rules protecting student privacy"). In paragraph 20, Harrison focuses not on federal law itself but rather on the kind of measures adopted by schools like the University of Kentucky that go beyond mere compliance with federal law—and thereby demonstrate the validity of part two of Harrison's thesis ("As long as college officials effectively respond to signs of trouble, these rules already provide a workable balance between privacy and public safety"). Harrison thus ends a paper on a grim subject with a note that provides some measure of optimism and that attempts to reconcile proponents on both sides of this emotional debate.

Another approach to an argument synthesis based on the same and additional sources could argue (along with some of the sources quoted in the model paper) that safety as a social value should never be outweighed by the right to privacy. Such a position could draw support from other practices in contemporary society—searches at airports, for example—illustrating that most people are willing to give up a certain measure of privacy, as well as convenience, in the interest of the safety of the community. Even if such an argument were not to call for a rollback of federal privacy rules, it could recommend modifying the language of the law to make doubly clear that safety trumps privacy. Some have even argued that safety would be improved if students and teachers were permitted to bring guns to campus and were thereby able to defend themselves and others in the event of being confronted by a deranged gunman. In the wake of Virginia Tech and other recent mass killings (such as the shooting deaths of five Amish children at their schoolhouse in 2006), it is difficult to conceive of support for an extreme claim that the rights of the individual are paramount and that privacy should always trump safety. A more reasonable argument might be made, working in counterpoint to the pro–privacy position of the M.I.T. chancellor, specifying more precisely the criteria that would constitute (in the language of FERPA) "significant risk to the safety or well-being" of the campus community. Having met the clearly defined threshold of a grave risk, university officials could then breach student privacy in the interest of the greater good.

Whatever your approach to a subject, in first *critically examining* the various sources and then *synthesizing* them to support a position about which you feel strongly, you are engaging in the kind of critical thinking that is essential to success in a good deal of academic and professional work.

■ DEVELOPING AND ORGANIZING THE SUPPORT FOR YOUR ARGUMENTS

Experienced writers seem to have an intuitive sense of how to develop and present supporting evidence for their claims; this sense is developed through much hard work and practice. Less experienced writers wonder what to say first, and having decided on that, wonder what to say next. There is no single method of presentation. But the techniques of even the most experienced writers often boil down to a few tried and tested arrangements.

As we've seen in the model synthesis in this chapter, the key to devising effective arguments is to find and use those kinds of support that most persuasively strengthen your claim. Some writers categorize support into two broad types: *evidence* and *motivational appeals*. Evidence, in the form of facts, statistics, and expert testimony, helps make the appeal to reason. Motivational appeals—appeals grounded in emotion and upon the authority of the speaker—are employed to get people to change their minds, to agree with the writer or speaker, or to decide upon a plan of activity.

Following are the most common strategies for using and organizing support for your claims.

Summarize, Paraphrase, and Quote Supporting Evidence

In most of the papers and reports you will write in college and in the professional world, evidence and motivational appeals derive from your summarizing, paraphrasing, and quoting of material in sources that either have been provided to you or that you have independently researched. For example, in paragraph 9 of the model argument synthesis, Harrison uses a long quotation from the Virginia Tech Review Panel report to make the point that college officials believed they were prohibited by federal privacy law from communicating with one another about disturbed students like Cho. You will find another long quotation later in the synthesis and a number of brief quotations woven into sentences throughout. In addition, you will find summaries and paraphrases. In each case, Harrison is careful to cite a source.

Provide Various Types of Evidence and Motivational Appeals

Keep in mind that you can use appeals to both reason and emotion. The appeal to reason is based on evidence that consists of a combination of *facts* and *expert testimony*. The sources by Tobin and Weigel, for example, offer facts about the evolution over the past few decades of the *in loco parentis* doctrine. Bernstein and McMurray interview college adminstrators at Cornell, M.I.T., and the University of Kentucky who explain the changing policies at those institutions. The model synthesis makes an appeal to emotion by engaging the reader's self-interest: If campuses are to be made more secure from the acts of mentally disturbed persons, then college officials should take a proactive approach to monitoring and intervention.

Use Climactic Order

Climactic order is the arrangement of examples or evidence in order of anticipated impact on the reader, least to greatest. Organize by climactic order when you plan to offer a number of categories or elements of support for your claim. Recognize that some elements will be more important—and likely more persuasive—than others. The basic principle here is that you should *save the most important evidence for the end* because whatever you say last is what readers are likely to remember best. A secondary principle is that whatever you say first is what they are *next* most likely to remember. Therefore, when you have several reasons to offer in support of your claim, an effective argument strategy is to present the second most important, then one or more additional reasons, and finally the most important reason. Paragraphs 7–11 of the model synthesis do exactly this.

Use Logical or Conventional Order

Using logical or conventional order involves using as a template a pre-established pattern or plan for arguing your case.

- One common pattern is describing or arguing a *problem/solution*. Using this pattern, you begin with an introduction in which you typically define the problem, perhaps explain its origins, then offer one or more solutions, then conclude.
- Another common pattern presents *two sides of a controversy*. Using this pattern, you introduce the controversy and (in an argument synthesis) your own point of view or claim, then you explain the other side's arguments, providing reasons why your point of view should prevail.
- A third common pattern is *comparison-and-contrast*. This pattern is so important that we will discuss it separately in the next section.

The order in which you present elements of an argument is sometimes dictated by the conventions of the discipline in which you are writing. For example, lab reports and experiments in the sciences and social sciences often follow this pattern: *Opening* or *Introduction, Methods and Materials* (of the experiment or study), *Results, Discussion.* Legal arguments often follow the so-called IRAC format: *Issue, Rule, Application, Conclusion.*

Present and Respond to Counterarguments

When developing arguments on a controversial topic, you can effectively use *counterargument* to help support your claims. When you use counterargument, you present an argument *against* your claim and then show that this argument is weak or flawed. The advantage of this technique is that you demonstrate that you are aware of the other side of the argument and that you are prepared to answer it.

Here is how a counterargument is typically developed:

I. Introduction and claim

II. Main opposing argument

III. Refutation of opposing argument

IV. Main positive argument

Use Concession

Concession is a variation of counterargument. As in counterargument, you present an opposing viewpoint, but instead of dismissing that position you *concede* that it has some validity and even some appeal, although your own position is the more reasonable one. This concession bolsters your standing as a fair-minded person who is not blind to the virtues of the other side. In the model synthesis, Harrison acknowledges the grief and sense of betrayal of the parents of the students who were killed. He concedes that parents have a right to expect that "the first priority of an educational institution must be to keep students safe." But he insists that this goal of achieving campus safety can be accomplished without rolling back hard-won privacy rights.

Here is an outline for a typical concession argument:

I. Introduction and claim

II. Important opposing argument

III. Concession that this argument has some validity

IV. Positive argument(s)

Sometimes, when you are developing a counterargument or concession argument, you may become convinced of the validity of the opposing point of view and change your own views. Don't be afraid of this happening. Writing is a tool for learning. To change your mind because of new evidence is a sign of flexibility and maturity, and your writing can only be the better for it.

Developing and Organizing Support for Your Arguments

- *Summarize, paraphrase, and quote supporting evidence.* Draw on the facts, ideas, and language in your sources.
- *Provide various types of evidence and motivational appeal.*
- *Use climactic order.* Save the most important evidence in support of your argument for the *end,* where it will have the most impact. Use the next most important evidence *first.*
- *Use logical or conventional order.* Use a form of organization appropriate to the topic, such as problem/solution; sides of a controversy; comparison/contrast; or a form of organization appropriate to the academic or professional discipline, such as a report of an experiment or a business plan.
- *Present and respond to counterarguments.* Anticipate and evaluate arguments against your position.
- *Use concession.* Concede that one or more arguments against your position have some validity; re-assert, nonetheless, that your argument is the stronger one.

Avoid Common Fallacies in Developing and Using Support

In Chapter 2, in the section on critical reading, we considered criteria that, as a reader, you may use for evaluating informative and persuasive writing (see pp. 60–61, 63–70). We discussed how you can assess the accuracy, the significance, and the author's interpretation of the information presented. We also considered the importance in good argument of clearly defined key terms and the pitfalls of emotionally loaded language. Finally, we saw how to recognize such logical fallacies as either/or reasoning, faulty cause-and-effect reasoning, hasty generalization, and false analogy. As a writer, no less than as a critical reader, you need to be aware of these common problems and to avoid them.

Be aware, also, of your responsibility to cite source materials appropriately. When you quote a source, double- and triple-check that you have done so accurately. When you summarize or paraphrase, take care to use your own language and sentence structures (though you can, of course, also quote within these forms). When you refer to someone else's idea—even if you are not quoting, summarizing, or paraphrasing—give the source credit. By being ethical about the use of sources, you uphold the highest standards of the academic community.

■ THE COMPARISON-AND-CONTRAST SYNTHESIS

A particularly important type of argument synthesis is built on patterns of comparison and contrast. Techniques of comparison and contrast enable you to examine two subjects (or sources) in terms of one another. When you compare, you consider *similarities*. When you contrast, you consider *differences*. By comparing and contrasting, you perform a multifaceted analysis that often suggests subtleties that otherwise might not have come to your (or your reader's) attention.

To organize a comparison-and-contrast argument, you must carefully read sources in order to discover *significant criteria for analysis*. A *criterion* is a specific point to which both of your authors refer and about which they may agree or disagree. (For example, in a comparative report on compact cars, criteria for *comparison and contrast* might be road handling, fuel economy, and comfort of ride.) The best criteria are those that allow you not only to account for obvious similarities and differences—those concerning the main aspects of your sources or subjects—but also to plumb deeper, exploring subtle yet significant comparisons and contrasts among details or subcomponents, which you can then relate to your overall thesis.

Note that comparison-and-contrast is frequently not an end in itself but serves some larger purpose. Thus, a comparison-and-contrast synthesis may be a component of a paper that is essentially a critique, an explanatory synthesis, an argument synthesis, or an analysis.

Organizing Comparison-and-Contrast Syntheses

Two basic approaches to organizing a comparison-and-contrast synthesis are organization by *source* and organization by *criteria*.

Organizing by Source or Subject

You can organize a comparative synthesis by first summarizing each of your sources or subjects and then discussing the significant similarities and differences between them. Having read the summaries and become familiar with the distinguishing features of each source, your readers will most likely be able to appreciate the more obvious similarities and differences. In the discussion, your task is to consider both the obvious and the subtle comparisons and contrasts, focusing on the most significant—that is, on those that most clearly support your thesis.

Organization by source or subject works best with passages that can be briefly summarized. If the summary of your source or subject becomes too long, your readers might have forgotten the points you made in the first summary when they are reading the second. A comparison-and-contrast synthesis organized by source or subject might proceed like this:

I. Introduce the paper; lead to thesis.

II. Summarize source/subject A by discussing its significant features.

III. Summarize source/subject B by discussing its significant features.

IV. Discuss in a paragraph (or two) the significant points of comparison and contrast between sources or subjects A and B. Alternatively, begin the comparison-contrast in Section III as you introduce source/subject B.

V. Conclude with a paragraph in which you summarize your points and, perhaps, raise and respond to pertinent questions.

Organizing by Criteria

Instead of summarizing entire sources one at a time with the intention of comparing them later, you could discuss two sources simultaneously, examining the views of each author point by point (criterion by criterion), comparing and contrasting these views in the process. The criterion approach is best used when you have a number of points to discuss or when passages or subjects are long and/or complex. A comparison-and-contrast synthesis organized by criteria might look like this:

I. Introduce the paper; lead to thesis.

II. Criterion 1

A. Discuss what author #1 says about this point. Or present situation #1 in light of this point.

B. Discuss what author #2 says about this point, comparing and contrasting #2's treatment of the point with #1's. Or present situation #2 in light of this point and explain its differences from situation #1.

III. Criterion 2

A. Discuss what author #1 says about this point. Or present situation #1 in light of this point.

B. Discuss what author #2 says about this point, comparing and contrasting #2's treatment of the point with #1's. Or present situation #2 in light of this point and explain its differences from situation #1.

And so on, proceeding criterion by criterion until you have completed your discussion. Be sure to arrange criteria with a clear method; knowing how the discussion of one criterion leads to the next will ensure smooth transitions throughout your paper. End by summarizing your key points and perhaps raising and responding to pertinent questions.

However you organize your comparison-and-contrast synthesis, keep in mind that comparing and contrasting are not ends in themselves. Your discussion should point to a conclusion, an answer to the question "So what— why bother to compare and contrast in the first place?" If your discussion is part of a larger synthesis, point to and support the larger claim. If you write a stand-alone comparison-and-contrast synthesis, though, you must by the final paragraph answer the "Why bother?" question. The model comparison-and-contrast synthesis that follows does exactly this.

Comparing and Contrasting

Review the model argument synthesis (pp. 161–169) for elements of comparison-and-contrast—specifically those paragraphs concerning how Cornell University, M.I.T. and the University of Kentucky balance student privacy with the parental right to know about the health and welfare of their children.

1.   From these paragraphs in the model paper, extract raw information concerning the positions of the three schools on the issue of student privacy and then craft your own brief comparison-and-contrast synthesis. Identify criteria for comparison and contrast, and discuss the positions of each school in relation to these criteria. *Note:* For this exercise, do not concern yourself with parenthetical citation (that is, with identifying your source materials).

2.   Write a paragraph or two that traces the development of comparison-and-contrast throughout the model paper. Having discussed the *how* and *where* of this development, discuss the *why*. Answer this question: Why has the writer used comparison-and-contrast? (Hint: it is not an end in itself.) To what use is it put?

A Case for Comparison-and-Contrast: World War I and World War II

Let's see how the principles of comparison-and-contrast can be applied to a response to a final examination question in a course on modern history. Imagine that having attended classes involving lecture and discussion, and having read excerpts from John Keegan's *The First World War* and Tony Judt's *Postwar: A History of Europe Since 1945,* you were presented with this examination question:

> Based on your reading to date, compare and contrast the two world wars in light of any four or five criteria you think significant. Once you have called careful attention to both similarities and differences, conclude with an observation. What have you learned? What can your comparative analysis teach us?

Comparison-and-Contrast Organized by Criteria

Here is a plan for a response, essentially a comparison-and-contrast synthesis, organized by *criteria* and beginning with the thesis—and the *claim.*

> *Thesis:* In terms of the impact on cities and civilian populations, the military aspects of the two wars in Europe, and their aftermaths, the differences between World War I and World War II considerably outweigh the similarities.

> I. Introduction. World Wars I and II were the most devastating conflicts in history. *Thesis*

II. Summary of main similarities: causes, countries involved, battlegrounds, global scope.
III. First major difference: Physical impact of war.
    A. WWI was fought mainly in rural battlegrounds.
    B. In WWII cities were destroyed.
IV. Second major difference: Effect on civilians.
    A. WWI fighting primarily involved soldiers.
    B. WWII involved not only military but also massive noncombatant casualties: civilian populations were displaced, forced into slave labor, and exterminated.
 V. Third major difference: Combat operations.
    A. World War I, in its long middle phase, was characterized by trench warfare.
    B. During the middle phase of World War II there was no major military action in Nazi-occupied Western Europe.
VI. Fourth major difference: Aftermath.
    A. Harsh war terms imposed on defeated Germany contributed significantly to the rise of Hitler and World War II.
    B. Victorious allies helped rebuild West Germany after World War II but allowed Soviets to take over Eastern Europe.
VII. Conclusion. Since the end of World War II, wars have been far smaller in scope and destructiveness, and warfare has expanded to involve stateless combatants committed to acts of terror.

The following model exam response, a comparison-and-contrast synthesis organized by criteria, is written according to the preceding plan. (Thesis and topic sentences are highlighted.)

MODEL EXAM RESPONSE

(1)   World War I (1914-18) and World War II (1939-45) were the most catastrophic and destructive conflicts in human history. For those who believed in the steady but inevitable progress of civilization, it was impossible to imagine that two wars in the first half of the twentieth century could reach levels of barbarity and horror that would outstrip those of any previous era. Historians estimate that more than 22 million people, soldiers and civilians, died in World War I; they estimate that between 40 and 50 million died in World War II. In many ways, these two conflicts were similar: they were fought on many of the same European and Russian battlegrounds, with more or less the same countries on opposing sides. Even many of the same people were involved: Winston Churchill and Adolf Hitler figured in both wars. And the main outcome in each case was the same: total defeat for Germany. However, in terms of the impact on cities and civilian populations, the military aspects of the two wars in Europe, and their aftermaths, the differences between World Wars I and II considerably outweigh the similarities.

(2)   The similarities are clear enough. In fact, many historians regard World War II as a continuation--after an intermission of about twenty years--of World War I. One of the main causes of each war was Germany's dissatisfaction and frustration with what it perceived as its diminished place in the world. Hitler launched World War II partly out of revenge for Germany's humiliating defeat in World War I. In each conflict Germany and its allies (the Central Powers in WWI, the Axis in WWII) went to war against France, Great Britain, Russia (the Soviet Union in WWII), and eventually, the United States. Though neither conflict included literally the entire world, the participation of countries not only in Europe but also in the Middle East, the Far East, and the Western hemisphere made both conflicts global in scope. And as indicated earlier, the number of casualties in each war was unprecedented in history, partly because modern technology had enabled the creation of deadlier weapons--including tanks, heavy artillery, and aircraft--than had ever been used in warfare.

③   Despite these similarities, the differences between the two world wars are considerably more significant. One of the most noticeable differences was the physical impact of each war in Europe and in Russia--the western and eastern fronts. The physical destruction of World War I was confined largely to the battlefield. The combat took place almost entirely in the rural areas of Europe and Russia. No major cities were destroyed in the first war; cathedrals, museums, government buildings, urban houses and apartments were left untouched. During the second war, in contrast, almost no city or town of any size emerged unscathed. Rotterdam, Warsaw, London, Minsk, and--when the Allies began their counterattack--almost every major city in Germany and Japan, including Berlin and Tokyo, were flattened. Of course, the physical devastation of the cities created millions of refugees, a phenomenon never experienced in World War I.

④   The fact that World War II was fought in the cities as well as on the battlefields meant that the second war had a much greater impact on civilians than did the first war. With few exceptions, the civilians in Europe during WWI were not driven from their homes, forced into slave labor, starved, tortured, or systematically exterminated. But all of these crimes happened routinely during WWII. The Nazi occupation of Europe meant that the civilian populations of France, Belgium, Norway, the Netherlands, and other conquered lands, along with the industries, railroads, and farms of these countries, were put into the service of the Third Reich. Millions of people from conquered Europe--those who were not sent directly to the death camps--were forcibly transported to Germany and put to work in support of the war effort.

⑤   During both wars, the Germans were fighting on two fronts--the western front in Europe and the eastern front in Russia. But while both wars were characterized by intense military activity during their initial and final phases, the middle and longest phases--at least in Europe--differed considerably. The middle phase of the First World War was characterized by trench warfare, a relatively static form of military activity in which fronts seldom moved, or moved only a few hundred yards at a time, even after major battles. By contrast, in the years between the German conquest of most of Europe by early 1941 and the Allied invasion of Normandy in mid-1944, there was no major fighting in Nazi-occupied Western Europe. (The land battles then shifted to North Africa and the Soviet Union.)

6   And of course, the two world wars differed in their aftermaths. The most significant consequence of World War I was that the humiliating and costly war reparations imposed on the defeated Germany by the terms of the 1919 Treaty of Versailles made possible the rise of Hitler and thus led directly to World War II. In contrast, after the end of the Second World War in 1945, the Allies helped rebuild West Germany (the portion of a divided Germany which it controlled), transformed the new country into a democracy, and helped make it one of the most thriving economies of the world. But perhaps the most significant difference in the aftermath of each war involved Russia. That country, in a considerably weakened state, pulled out of World War I a year before hostilities ended so that it could consolidate its 1917 Revolution. Russia then withdrew into itself and took no significant part in European affairs until the Nazi invasion of the Soviet Union in 1941. In contrast, it was the Red Army in World War II that was most responsible for the crushing defeat of Germany. In recognition of its efforts and of its enormous sacrifices, the Allies allowed the Soviet Union to take control of the countries of Eastern Europe after the war, leading to fifty years of totalitarian rule--and the Cold War.

7   While the two world wars that devastated much of Europe were similar in that, at least according to some historians, they were the same war interrupted by two decades, and similar in that combatants killed more efficiently than armies throughout history ever had, the differences between the wars were significant. In terms of the physical impact of the fighting, the impact on civilians, the action on the battlefield at mid-war, and the aftermaths, World Wars I and II differed in ways that matter to us decades later. Recently, the wars in Iraq, Afghanistan, and Bosnia have involved an alliance of nations pitted against single nations; but we have not seen, since the two world wars, grand alliances moving vast armies across continents. The

> destruction implied by such action is almost unthinkable today. Warfare
> is changing, and "stateless" combatants like Hamas and Al Qaeda wreak
> destruction of their own. But we may never see, one hopes, the
> devastation that follows when multiple nations on opposing sides of a
> conflict throw millions of soldiers--and civilians--into harm's way.

The Strategy of the Exam Response

The general strategy of this argument is an organization by *criteria*. The writer argues that although the two world wars exhibited some similarities, the differences between the two conflicts were more significant. Note that the writer's thesis doesn't merely establish these significant differences; it enumerates them in a way that anticipates both the content and the structure of the response to follow.

In argument terms, the *claim* the writer makes is the conclusion that the two global conflicts were significantly different, if superficially similar. The *assumption* is that careful attention to the impact of the wars upon cities and civilian populations and to the consequences of the Allied victories is the key to understanding the differences between them. The *support* comes in the form of historical facts regarding the levels of casualties, the scope of destruction, the theaters of conflict, the events following the conclusions of the wars, and so on.

- **Paragraph 1:** The writer begins by commenting on the unprecedented level of destruction of World Wars I and II and concludes with the thesis summarizing the key similarities and differences.
- **Paragraph 2:** The writer summarizes the key similarities in the two wars: the wars' causes, their combatants, their global scope, the level of destructiveness made possible by modern weaponry.
- **Paragraph 3:** The writer discusses the first of the key differences: the fact that the battlegrounds of World War I were largely rural, but in World War II cities were targeted and destroyed.
- **Paragraph 4:** The writer discusses the second of the key differences: the impact on civilians. In World War I, civilians were generally spared from the direct effects of combat; in World War II, civilians were targeted by the Nazis for systematic displacement and destruction.
- **Paragraph 5:** The writer discusses the third key difference: Combat operations during the middle phase of World War I were characterized by static trench warfare. During World War II, in contrast, there were no major combat operations in Nazi-occupied Western Europe during the middle phase of the conflict.

- **Paragraph 6:** The writer focuses on the fourth key difference: the aftermath of the two wars. After World War I, the victors imposed harsh conditions on a defeated Germany, leading to the rise of Hitler and the Second World War. After World War II, the Allies helped Germany rebuild and thrive. However, the Soviet victory in 1945 led to its postwar domination of Eastern Europe.

- **Paragraph 7:** In the conclusion, the writer sums up the key similarities and differences just covered and makes additional comments about the course of more recent wars since World War II. In this way, the writer responds to the questions posed at the end of the assignment: "What have you learned? What can your comparative analysis teach us?"

■ SUMMARY OF SYNTHESIS CHAPTERS

In this chapter and in Chapter 3 we've considered three main types of synthesis: the *explanatory synthesis*, the *argument synthesis*, and the *comparison-and-contrast synthesis*. Although for ease of comprehension we've placed them in separate categories, these types are not mutually exclusive. Both explanatory syntheses and argument syntheses often involve elements of one another, and comparison-and-contrast syntheses can fall into either of the other two categories. Which approach you choose will depend on your *purpose* and the method that you decide is best suited to achieve this purpose.

If your main purpose is to help your audience understand a particular subject, and in particular to help them understand the essential elements or significance of this subject, then you will be composing an explanatory synthesis. If your main purpose, on the other hand, is to persuade your audience to agree with your viewpoint on a subject, or to change their minds, or to decide on a particular course of action, then you will be composing an argument synthesis. If one effective technique of making your case is to establish similarities or differences between your subject and another one, then you will compose a comparison-and-contrast synthesis—which may well be just *part* of a larger synthesis.

In planning and drafting these syntheses, you can draw on a variety of strategies: supporting your claims by summarizing, paraphrasing, and quoting from your sources; using appeals to *logos*, *pathos*, and *ethos*; and choosing from among strategies such as climactic or conventional order, counterargument, and concession the approach that will best help you to achieve your purpose.

The strategies of synthesis you've practiced in these two chapters will be dealt with again in Chapter 7, where we'll consider a category of synthesis commonly known as the research paper. The research paper involves all of the skills in summary, critique, and synthesis that we've discussed so far, the main difference being that you won't find the sources you need in this particular text. We'll discuss approaches to locating and critically evaluating sources, selecting material from among them to provide support for your claims, and, finally, documenting your sources in standard professional formats.

We turn, now, to analysis, which is another important strategy for academic thinking and writing. Chapter 5, Analysis, will introduce you to a strategy that, like synthesis, draws upon all the strategies you've been practicing as you move through *A Sequence for Academic Writing*.

 ## WRITING ASSIGNMENT: THE CHANGING LANDSCAPE OF WORK IN THE TWENTY-FIRST CENTURY

Now we'll give you an opportunity to practice your skills in planning and writing an argument synthesis. See Chapter 8, pp. 309–343, where we provide nine sources on the way that work will continue to change over the next few decades. Who will be the "winners" and "losers" among American workers? To what extent will education be a factor in your having the career of your choice? Is your job likely to be exported? What are some of the forces changing the shape of employment in business, technology, law, and medicine? In the synthesis, your task will be to take a stand in response to one or more of these questions and then defend your response to readers.

Note that your instructor may assign related assignments for summary, critique, and explanation to help prepare you for writing a larger argument synthesis.

5 ▪ Analysis

▪ WHAT IS AN ANALYSIS?

An *analysis* is an argument in which you study the parts of something to understand how it works, what it means, or why it might be significant. The writer of an analysis uses an analytical tool: a *principle* or *definition* on the basis of which an object, an event, or a behavior can be divided into parts and examined. Here are excerpts from two analyses of the movie version of L. Frank Baum's *The Wizard of Oz:*

> At the dawn of adolescence, the very time she should start to distance herself from Aunt Em and Uncle Henry, the surrogate parents who raised her on their Kansas farm, Dorothy Gale experiences a hurtful reawakening of her fear that these loved ones will be rudely ripped from her, especially her Aunt (Em—M for Mother!).*

> [*The Wizard of Oz*] was originally written as a political allegory about grassroots protest. It may seem harder to believe than Emerald City, but the Tin Woodsman is the industrial worker, the Scarecrow [is] the struggling farmer, and the Wizard is the president, who is powerful only as long as he succeeds in deceiving the people.†

As these paragraphs suggest, what you discover through an analysis depends entirely on the principle or definition you use to make your insights. Is *The Wizard of Oz* the story of a girl's psychological development, or is it a story about politics? The answer is *both*. In the first example, the psychiatrist Harvey Greenberg applies the principles of his profession and, not surprisingly, sees *The Wizard of Oz* in psychological terms. In the second example, a newspaper reporter applies the political theories of Karl Marx and, again not surprisingly, discovers a story about politics.

Different as they are, these analyses share an important quality: Each is the result of a specific principle or definition used as a tool to divide an object into parts in order to see what it means and how it works. The writer's choice of analytical tool simultaneously creates and limits the possibilities for analysis. Thus, working with the principles of Freud, Harvey Greenberg sees *The Wizard of Oz* in psychological, not political, terms; working with the theories of Karl Marx, Peter Dreier understands the movie in terms of the economic relationships among characters. It's as if the writer of an analysis who adopts one analytical tool puts on a pair of glasses

---

*Harvey Greenberg, *The Movies on Your Mind* (New York: Dutton, 1975).
†Peter Dreier, "Oz Was Almost Reality," *Cleveland Plain Dealer* 3 Sept. 1989.

and sees an object in a specific way. Another writer, using a different tool (and a different pair of glasses), sees the object differently.

You might protest: Are there as many analyses of *The Wizard of Oz* as there are people to read the book or to see the movie? Yes, or at least as many analyses as there are analytical tools. This does not mean that all analyses are equally valid or useful. Each writer must convince the reader. In creating an essay of analysis, the writer must organize a series of related insights, using the analytical tool to examine first one part and then another of the object being studied. To read Harvey Greenberg's essay on *The Wizard of Oz* is to find paragraph after paragraph of related insights—first about Aunt Em, then the Wicked Witch,

Where Do We Find Written Analyses?

Here are just a few of the types of writing that involve analysis:

ACADEMIC WRITING

- **Experimental and lab reports** analyze the meaning or implications of the study results in the Discussion section.
- **Research papers** analyze information in sources or apply theories to material being reported.
- **Process analyses** break down the steps or stages involved in completing a process.
- **Literary analyses** examine characterization, plot, imagery, or other elements in works of literature.
- **Essay exams** demonstrate understanding of course material by analyzing data using course concepts.

WORKPLACE WRITING

- **Grant proposals** analyze the issues you seek funding for in order to address them.
- **Reviews of the arts** employ dramatic or literary analysis to assess artistic works.
- **Business plans** break down and analyze capital outlays, expenditures, profits, materials, and the like.
- **Medical charts** record analytical thinking and writing in relation to patient symptoms and possible options.
- **Legal briefs** break down and analyze facts of cases and elements of legal precedents and apply legal rulings and precedents to new situations.
- **Case studies** describe and analyze the particulars of a specific medical, social service, advertising, or business case.

then Toto, and then the Wizard. All these insights point to Greenberg's single conclusion: that "Dorothy's 'trip' is a marvelous metaphor for the psychological journey every adolescent must make." Without Greenberg's analysis, we would probably not have thought about the movie as a psychological journey. This is precisely the power of an analysis: its ability to reveal objects or events in ways we would not otherwise have considered.

The writer's challenge is to convince readers that (1) the analytical tool being applied is legitimate and well matched to the object being studied; and (2) the analytical tool is being used systematically to divide the object into parts and to make a coherent, meaningful statement about these parts and the object as a whole.

When *Your* Perspective Guides the Analysis

In some cases a writer's analysis of a phenomenon or a work of art may not result from anything as structured as a principle or a definition. It may follow from the writer's cultural or personal outlook, perspective, or interests. Imagine reading a story or observing the lines of a new building and being asked to analyze it—not based on someone else's definition or principle, but on your own. Analyses in this case continue to probe the parts of things to understand how they work and what they mean. And they continue to be carefully structured, examining one part of a phenomenon at a time. The essential purpose of the analysis, to *reveal*, remains unchanged. This goal distinguishes the analysis from the critique, whose main purpose is to *evaluate* and *assess validity*.

Consider this passage from an op-ed article by Terri Martin Hekker, "The Satisfactions of Housewifery and Motherhood in an Age of 'Do Your Own Thing,'" which appeared in the *New York Times* in 1977:

> I come from a long line of women . . . who never knew they were unfulfilled. I can't testify that they were happy, but they *were* cheerful. And if they lacked "meaningful relationships," they cherished relations who meant something. They took pride in a clean, comfortable home and satisfaction in serving a good meal because no one had explained to them that the only work worth doing is that for which you get paid.
>
> They enjoyed rearing their children because no one ever told them that little children belonged in church basements and their mothers belonged somewhere else. They lived, very frugally, on their husbands' paychecks because they didn't realize that it's more important to have a bigger house and a second car than it is to rear your own children. And they were so incredibly ignorant that they died never suspecting they'd been failures.
>
> That won't hold true for me. I don't yet perceive myself as a failure, but it's not for want of being told I am.
>
> The other day, years of condescension prompted me to fib in order to test a theory. At a party where most of the guests were business associates of my husband, a Ms. Putdown asked me who I was. I told

her I was Jack Hekker's wife. That had a galvanizing effect on her. She took my hand and asked if that was all I thought of myself—just someone's wife? I wasn't going to let her in on the five children but when she persisted I mentioned them but told her that they weren't mine, that they belonged to my dead sister. And then I basked in the glow of her warm approval.

It's an absolute truth that whereas you are considered ignorant to stay home to rear *your* children, it is quite heroic to do so for someone else's children. Being a housekeeper is acceptable (even to the Social Security office) as long as it's not *your* house you're keeping. And treating a husband with attentive devotion is altogether correct as long as he's not *your* husband.

Sometimes I feel like Alice in Wonderland. But lately, mostly, I feel like an endangered species.

Hekker's view of the importance of what she calls "housewifery"—the role of the traditional American wife and mother—derives from her own personal standards and ideals, which themselves derive from a cultural perspective that she admits is no longer in fashion in the late 1970s. This cultural and personal perspective places great value on such aspects of marriage and motherhood as having "a clean, comfortable home," the satisfaction of "serving a good meal," and the enjoyment of rearing "your own children," and it places less value on "having a big house and a second car." She refuses to consider herself a failure (as she believes others do) because she takes pride in identifying herself as her husband's wife. Hekker's analysis of her own situation, in contrast to the situation of the more "liberated" working wife, throws a revealing light on the cultural conflicts of that period regarding marriage.

Almost thirty years after she wrote this op-ed article, Hekker's perspective had dramatically shifted. Her shattering experiences in the wake of her unexpected divorce had changed her view—and as a result, her analysis—of the status, value, and prospects of the traditional wife:

> Like most loyal wives of our generation, we'd contemplated eventual widowhood but never thought we'd end up divorced. And "divorced" doesn't begin to describe the pain of this process. "Canceled" is more like it. . . . If I had it to do over again, I'd still marry the man I married and have my children: they are my treasure and a powerful support system for me and for one another. But I would have used the years after my youngest started school to further my education. I could have amassed two doctorates using the time and energy I gave myself to charitable and community causes and been better able to support myself.

Hekker's new analysis of the role of the traditional wife (published in the *New York Times* in 2006) derives from her changed perspective, based on her own experience and the similar experiences of a number of her divorced friends. Notice, again, that the analysis is meant to *reveal*.

If you find yourself writing an analysis guided by your own insights, not by someone else's, then you owe your reader a clear explanation of your guiding principles and the definitions by which you will probe the subject under study. Continue using the Guidelines for Writing Analyses (see pp. 203–204), modifying this advice as you think fit to accommodate your own personal outlook, perspective, or interests. Above all, remember to structure your analysis with care. Proceed systematically and emerge with a clear statement about what the subject means, how it works, or why it might be significant.

■ DEMONSTRATION: ANALYSIS

Two examples of analyses follow. The first was written by a professional writer; the second was written by a student in response to an assignment in his sociology class. Each analysis illustrates the two defining features of analysis just discussed: a statement of an analytical principle or definition, and the use of that principle or definition in closely examining an object, behavior, or event. As you read, try to identify these features. An exercise with questions for discussion follows each example.

THE PLUG-IN DRUG

Marie Winn

This analysis of television viewing as an addictive behavior appeared originally in Marie Winn's book The Plug-In Drug: Television, Computers, and Family Life *(2002). A writer and media critic, Winn has been interested in the effects of television on both individuals and the larger culture. In this passage, she carefully defines the term* addiction *and then applies it systematically to the behavior under study.*

The word "addiction" is often used loosely and wryly in conversation. People will refer to themselves as "mystery-book addicts" or "cookie addicts." E. B. White wrote of his annual surge of interest in gardening: "We are hooked and are making an attempt to kick the habit." Yet nobody really believes that reading mysteries or ordering seeds by catalogue is serious enough to be compared with addictions to heroin or alcohol. In these cases the word "addiction" is used jokingly to denote a tendency to overindulge in some pleasurable activity.

People often refer to being "hooked on TV." Does this, too, fall into the light-hearted category of cookie eating and other pleasures that people pursue with unusual intensity? Or is there a kind of television viewing that falls into the more serious category of destructive addiction?

Not unlike drugs or alcohol, the television experience allows the participant to blot out the real world and enter into a pleasurable and passive mental state. To be sure, other experiences, notably reading, also provide a temporary respite from reality. But it's much easier to stop reading and return to reality than to stop watching television. The entry into another world offered by reading includes an easily accessible return ticket. The entry via television does not. In this way television viewing, for those vulnerable to addiction, is more like drinking or taking drugs—once you start it's hard to stop.

Just as alcoholics are only vaguely aware of their addiction, feeling that they control their drinking more than they really do ("I can cut it out any time I want—I just like to have three or four drinks before dinner"), many people overestimate their control over television watching. Even as they put off other activities to spend hour after hour watching television, they feel they could easily resume living in a different, less passive style. But somehow or other while the television set is present in their homes, it just stays on. With television's easy gratifications available, those other activities seem to take too much effort.

5 A heavy viewer (a college English instructor) observes:

> I find television almost irresistible. When the set is on, I cannot ignore it. I can't turn it off. I feel sapped, will-less, enervated. As I reach out to turn off the set, the strength goes out of my arms. So I sit there for hours and hours.

Self-confessed television addicts often feel they "ought" to do other things—but the fact that they don't read and don't plant their garden or sew or crochet or play games or have conversations means that those activities are no longer as desirable as television viewing. In a way, the lives of heavy viewers are as unbalanced by their television "habit" as drug addicts' or alcoholics' lives. They are living in a holding pattern, as it were, passing up the activities that lead to growth or development or a sense of accomplishment. This is one reason people talk about their television viewing so ruefully, so apologetically. They are aware that it is an unproductive experience, that by any human measure almost any other endeavor is more worthwhile.

It is the adverse effect of television viewing on the lives of so many people that makes it feel like a serious addiction. The television habit distorts the sense of time. It renders other experiences vague and curiously unreal while taking on a greater reality for itself. It weakens relationships by reducing and sometimes eliminating normal opportunities for talking, for communicating.

And yet television does not satisfy, else why would the viewer continue to watch hour after hour, day after day? "The measure of health," wrote the psychiatrist Lawrence Kubie, "is flexibility . . . and especially the freedom to cease when sated." But heavy television viewers can never be sated with their television experiences. These do not provide the true nourishment that satiation requires, and thus they find that they cannot stop watching.

Exercise 5.1

Reading Critically: Winn

In an analysis, an author first presents the analytical principle in full and then systematically applies parts of the principle to the object or phenomenon ˙ der study. In her brief analysis of television viewing, Marie Winn p˙

an alternative, though equally effective, strategy by *distributing* parts of her analytical principle across the essay. Locate where Winn defines key elements of addiction. Locate where she uses each element as an analytical lens to examine television viewing as a form of addiction.

What function does paragraph 4 play in the analysis?

In the first two paragraphs, how does Winn create a funnel-like effect that draws readers into the heart of her analysis?

Recall a few television programs that genuinely moved you, educated you, humored you, or stirred you to worthwhile reflection or action. To what extent does Winn's analysis describe your positive experiences as a television viewer? (Consider how Winn might argue that from within an addicted state, a person may feel "humored, moved or educated" but is in fact—from a sober outsider's point of view—deluded.) If Winn's analysis of television viewing as an addiction does *not* account for your experience, does it follow that her analysis is flawed? Explain.

Edward Peselman wrote the following paper as a first-semester sophomore, in response to this assignment from his sociology professor:

> Read Chapter 3, "The Paradoxes of Power," in Randall Collins's *Sociological Insight: An Introduction to Non-Obvious Sociology* (2nd ed., 1992). Use any of Collins's observations to examine the sociology of power in a group with which you are familiar. Write for readers much like yourself: freshmen or sophomores who have taken one course in sociology. Your object in this paper is to use Collins as a way of learning something "nonobvious" about a group to which you belong or have belonged.

Note: The citations are in APA style. (See pp. 301–308.)

MODEL ANALYSIS

Coming Apart   1

Edward Peselman

Sociology of Everyday Life

Murray State University

23 March 2008

The Coming Apart of a Dorm Society

(1)   During my first year of college, I lived in a dormitory, like most freshmen on campus. We inhabitants of the dorm came from different

cultural and economic backgrounds. Not surprisingly, we brought with us many of the traits found in people outside of college. Like many on the outside, we in the dorm sought personal power at the expense of others. The gaining and maintaining of power can be an ugly business, and I saw people hurt and in turn hurt others all for the sake of securing a place in the dorm's prized social order. Not until one of us challenged that order did I realize how fragile it was.

(2)   Randall Collins, a sociologist at the University of California, Riverside, defines the exercise of power as the attempt "to make something happen in society" (1992, p. 61). A society can be understood as something as large and complex as "American society"; something more sharply defined, such as a corporate or organizational society; or something smaller still—a dorm society like my own, consisting of six 18-year-old men who lived at one end of a dormitory floor in an all-male dorm.

(3)   In my freshman year, my society was a tiny but distinctive social group in which people exercised power. I lived with two roommates, Dozer and Reggie. Dozer was an emotionally unstable, excitable individual who vented his energy through anger. His insecurity and moodiness contributed to his difficulty in making friends. Reggie was a friendly, happy-go-lucky sort who seldom displayed emotions other than contentedness. He was shy when encountering new people, but when placed in a socially comfortable situation he would talk for hours.

(4)   Eric and Marc lived across the hall from us and therefore spent a considerable amount of time in our room. Eric could be cynical and was often blunt: He seldom hesitated when sharing his frank and sometimes unflattering opinions. He commanded a grudging respect in the dorm. Marc could be very moody and, sometimes, was violent. His temper and stubborn streak made him particularly susceptible to conflict. The final member of our miniature society was Benjamin, cheerful yet insecure. Benjamin had certain characteristics which many considered effeminate, and he was often teased about his sexuality—which in turn made him insecure. He was naturally friendly but, because of the abuse he took, he largely kept

to himself. He would join us occasionally for a pizza or late-night television.

(5)   Together, we formed an independent social structure. Going out to parties together, playing cards, watching television, playing ball: These were the activities through which we got to know each other and through which we established the basic pecking order of our community. Much like a colony of baboons, we established a hierarchy based on power relationships. According to Collins, what a powerful person wishes to happen must be achieved by controlling others. Collins's observation can help to define who had how much power in our social group. In the dorm, Marc and Eric clearly had the most power. Everyone feared them and agreed to do pretty much what they wanted. Through violent words or threats of violence, they got their way. I was next in line: I wouldn't dare to manipulate Marc or Eric, but the others I could manage through occasional quips. Reggie, then Dozer, and finally Benjamin.

(6)   Up and down the pecking order, we exercised control through macho taunts and challenges. Collins writes that "individuals who manage to be powerful and get their own way must do so by going along with the laws of social organization, not by contradicting them" (p. 61). Until mid-year, our dorm motto could have read: "You win through rudeness and intimidation." Eric gained power with his frequent and brutal assessments of everyone's be-havior. Marc gained power with his temper—which, when lost, made everyone run for cover. Those who were not rude and intimidating drifted to the bottom of our social world. Reggie was quiet and unemotional, which allowed us to take advantage of him because we knew he would back down if pressed in an argument. Yet Reggie understood that on a "power scale" he stood above Dozer and often shared in the group's tactics to get Dozer's food (his parents were forever sending him care packages). Dozer, in turn, seldom missed op-portunities to take swipes at Benjamin, with references to his sexuality. From the very first week of school, Benjamin could never—and never wanted to—compete against Eric's bluntness or Marc's temper. Still, Benjamin hung out

with us. He lived in our corner of the dorm, and he wanted to be friendly. But everyone, including Benjamin, understood that he occupied the lowest spot in the order.

(7)   That is, until he left mid-year. According to Collins, "any social arrangement works because people avoid questioning it most of the time" (p. 74). The inverse of this principle is as follows: When a social arrangement is questioned, that arrangement can fall apart. The more fragile the arrangement (the flimsier the values on which it is based), the more quickly it will crumble. For the entire first semester, no one questioned our rude, macho rules, and because of them we pigeon-holed Benjamin as a wimp. In our dorm society, gentle men had no power. To say the least, ours was not a compassionate community. From a distance of one year, I am shocked to have been a member of it. Nonetheless, we had created a mini-society that somehow served our needs.

(8)   At the beginning of the second semester, we found Benjamin packing up his room. Marc, who was walking down the hall, stopped by and said something like: "Hey buddy, the kitchen get too hot for you?" I was there, and I saw Benjamin turn around and say: "Do you practice at being such a _____, or does it come naturally? I've never met anybody who felt so good about making other people feel lousy. You'd better get yourself a job in the army or in the prison system, because no one else is going to put up with your _____." Marc said something in a raised voice. I stepped between them, and Benjamin said: "Get out." I was cheering.

(9)   Benjamin moved into an off-campus apartment with his girlfriend. This astonished us, first because of his effeminate manner (we didn't know he had a girlfriend) and second because none of the rest of us had been seeing girls much (though we talked about it constantly). Here was Benjamin, the gentlest among us, and he blew a hole in our macho society. Our social order never really recovered, which suggests its flimsy values. People in the dorm mostly went their own ways during the second semester. I'm not surprised, and I was more than a little grateful. Like most people in the dorm, save for

Eric and Marc, I both got my lumps and I gave them, and I never felt good about either. Like Benjamin, I wanted to fit in with my new social surroundings. Unlike him, I didn't have the courage to challenge the unfairness of what I saw.

⑩   By chance, six of us were thrown together into a dorm and were expected, on the basis of proximity alone, to develop a friendship. What we did was sink to the lowest possible denominator. Lacking any real basis for friendship, we allowed the forceful, macho personalities of Marc and Eric to set the rules, which for one semester we all subscribed to—even those who suffered.

⑪   The macho rudeness couldn't last, and I'm glad it was Benjamin who brought us down. By leaving, he showed a different and a superior kind of power. I doubt he was reading Randall Collins at the time, but he somehow had come to Collins's same insight: As long as he played by the rules of our group, he suffered because those rules placed him far down in the dorm's pecking order. Even by participating in pleasant activities, like going out for pizza, Benjamin supported a social system that ridiculed him. Some systems are so oppressive and small-minded that they can't be changed from the inside. They've got to be torn down. Benjamin had to move, and in moving he made me (at least) question the basis of my dorm friendships.

Reference

Collins, R. (1992). *Sociological insight: An introduction to non-obvious sociology* (2nd ed.). New York: Oxford University Press.

Reading Critically: Peselman

What is the function of paragraph 1? Though Peselman does not use the word *sociology*, what signals does he give that this will be a paper that examines the social interactions of a group? Peselman introduces Collins in paragraph 2. Why? What does Peselman accomplish in paragraphs 3–4? How does his use of Collins in paragraph 5 logically follow the presentation in paragraphs 3–4? The actual analysis in this paper takes place in paragraphs 5–11. Point to where Peselman draws on the work of Randall Collins, and explain how he uses Collins to gain insight into dorm life.

■ HOW TO WRITE ANALYSES

Consider Your Purpose

Whether you are assigned a topic to write on or are left to your own devices, you inevitably face this question: What is my idea? Like every paper, an analysis has at its heart an idea you want to convey. For Edward Peselman, it was the idea that a social order based on flimsy values is not strong enough to sustain a direct challenge to its power and thus will fall apart eventually. From beginning to end, Peselman advances this one idea: first, by introducing readers to the dorm society he will analyze; next, by introducing principles of analysis (from Randall Collins); and finally, by examining his dorm relationships in light of those principles. The entire set of analytical insights coheres as a paper because the insights are *related* and point to Peselman's single idea.

Peselman's paper offers a good example of the personal uses to which analysis can be put. Notice that he gravitates toward events in his life that confuse him and about which he wants some clarity. Such topics can be especially fruitful for analysis because you know the particulars well and can provide readers with details; you view the topic with some puzzlement; and, through the application of your analytical tool, you may come to understand it. When you select topics to analyze from your own experience, you provide yourself with a motivation to write and learn. When you are motivated in this way, you spark the interest of readers.

Using Randall Collins as a guide, Edward Peselman returns again and again to the events of his freshman year in the dormitory. We sense that Peselman himself wants to understand what happened in that dorm. He writes, "I saw people hurt and in turn hurt others all for the sake of securing a place in the dorm's prized social order." Peselman does not approve of what happened, and the analysis he launches is meant to help him understand.

Locate an Analytical Principle

When you are given an assignment that asks for analysis, use two specific reading strategies to identify principles and definitions in source materials.

- **Look for a sentence that makes a general statement about the way something works.** The statement may strike you as a rule or a law. The line that Edward Peselman quotes from Randall Collins has this quality: "[A]ny social arrangement works because people avoid questioning it most of the time." Such statements are generalizations—conclusions to sometimes complicated and extensive arguments. You can use these conclusions to guide your own analyses as long as you are aware that for some audiences you will need to re-create and defend the arguments that resulted in these conclusions.
- **Look for statements that take this form: X can be defined as (or X consists of) A, B, and C.** The specific elements of the definition—A, B, and C—are what you use to identify and analyze parts of the object being studied. You've seen an example of this approach in Marie Winn's multipart definition of addiction, which she uses to analyze television viewing. As a reader looking for definitions suitable for conducting an analysis, you might come across Winn's definition of addiction and then use it for your own purposes, perhaps to analyze the playing of video games as an addiction.

Essential to any analysis is the validity of the principle or definition being applied, the analytical tool. Make yourself aware, as both writer and reader, of a tool's strengths and limitations. Pose these questions of the analytical principles and definitions you use: Are they accurate? Are they well accepted? Do *you* accept them? What are the arguments against them? What are their limitations? Since every principle or definition used in an analysis is the end product of an argument, you are entitled—even obligated—to challenge it. If the analytical tool is flawed, the analysis that follows from it will be flawed.

A page from Randall Collins's *Sociological Insight* follows; Edward Peselman uses a key sentence from this extract as an analytical tool in his essay on power relations in his dorm (see p. 197). Notice that Peselman underlines the sentence he will use in his analysis.

1. Try this experiment some time. When you are talking to someone, make them explain everything they say that isn't completely clear. The result, you will discover, is a series of uninterrupted interruptions:

   A: Hi, how are you doing?
   B: What do you mean when you say "how"?
   A: You know. What's happening with you?
   B: What do you mean, "happening"?
   A: Happening, you know, what's going on.
   B: I'm sorry. Could you explain what you mean by "what"?
   A: What do you mean, what do I mean? Do you want to talk to me or not?

2. It is obvious that this sort of questioning could go on endlessly, at any rate if the listener doesn't get very angry and punch you in the mouth. But it illustrates two important points. First, virtually everything can be called into question. We are able to get along with other people not because everything is clearly spelled out, but because we are willing to take most things people say without explanation. Harold Garfinkel, who actually performed this sort of experiment, points out that there is an infinite regress of assumptions that go into any act of social communication. Moreover, some expressions are simply not explainable in words at all. A word like "you," or "here," or "now" is what Garfinkel calls "indexical." You have to know what it means already; it can't be explained.

3. "What do you mean by 'you'?"

4. "I mean *you, you!*" About all that can be done here is point your finger.

5. The second point is that people get mad when they are pressed to explain things that they ordinarily take for granted. This is because they very quickly see that explanations could go on forever and the questions will never be answered. If you really demanded a full explanation of everything you hear, you could stop the conversation from ever getting past its first sentence. The real significance of this for a sociological understanding of the way the world is put together is not the anger, however. It is the fact that people try to avoid these sorts of situations. They tacitly recognize that we have to avoid these endless lines of questioning. Sometimes small children will start asking an endless series of "whys," but adults discourage this.

6. In sum, <u>any social arrangement works because people avoid questioning it most of the time</u>. That does not mean that people do not get into arguments or disputes about just what ought to be done from time to time. But to have a dispute already implies there is a considerable area of agreement. An office manager may dispute with a clerk over just how to take care of some business letter, but they at any rate know more or less what they are disputing about. They do not get off into a . . . series of questions over just what is meant by everything that is said. You could very quickly dissolve the organization into nothingness if you followed that route: there would be no communication at all, even about what the disagreement is over.

7. Social organization is possible because people maintain a certain level of focus. If they focus on one thing, even if only to disagree about it, they are taking many other things for granted, thereby reinforcing their social reality.*

The statement that Peselman has underlined—"any social arrangement works because people avoid questioning it most of the time"—is the end result

---

*Randall Collins, *Sociological Insight: An Introduction to Non–obvious Sociology,* 2nd ed. (New York: Oxford UP, 1992) 73–74.

of an argument that takes Collins several paragraphs to develop. Peselman agrees with the conclusion and uses it in paragraph 7 of his analysis. Observe that for his own purposes Peselman does *not* reconstruct Collins's argument. He selects *only* Collins's conclusion and then imports that into his analysis, which concerns an entirely different subject. Once he identifies in Collins a principle he can use in his analysis, he converts the principle into questions that he then directs to his topic, life in his freshman dorm. Two questions follow directly from Collins's insight:

1. What was the social arrangement in the dorm?
2. How was this social arrangement questioned?

Peselman clearly defines his dormitory's social arrangement in paragraphs 3–6 (with the help of another principle borrowed from Collins). Beginning with paragraph 7, he explores how one member of his dorm questioned that arrangement:

> That is, until he left mid-year. According to Collins, "any social arrangement works because people avoid questioning it most of the time" (p. 74). The inverse of this principle is as follows: When a social arrangement is questioned, that arrangement can fall apart. The more fragile the arrangement (the flimsier the values on which it is based), the more quickly it will crumble. For the entire first semester, no one questioned our rude, macho rules, and because of them we pigeon-holed Benjamin as a wimp. In our dorm society, gentle men had no power. To say the least, ours was not a compassionate community. From a distance of one year, I am shocked to have been a member of it. Nonetheless, we had created a mini-society that somehow served our needs.

Formulate a Thesis

An analysis is a two-part argument. The first part states and establishes the writer's agreement with a certain principle or definition.

Part One of the Argument

This first part of the argument essentially takes this form:

Claim #1: Principle X (or definition X) is valuable.

Principle X can be a theory as encompassing and abstract as the statement that *myths are the enemy of truth.* Principle X can be as modest as the definition of a term such as *addiction* or *comfort.* As you move from one subject area to another, the principles and definitions you use for analysis will change, as these assignments illustrate:

Sociology: Write a paper in which you place yourself in American society by locating both your absolute position and relative rank on each single criterion of social stratification used by Lenski & Lenski. For each criterion, state whether you have attained your social position by yourself or if you have "inherited" that status from your parents.

Literature: *Apply principles of Jungian psychology to Hawthorne's "Young Goodman Brown." In your reading of the story, apply Jung's principles of the* shadow, persona, *and* anima.

Physics: *Use Newton's second law* (F = ma) *to analyze the acceleration of a fixed pulley, from which two weights hang:* m_1 *(.45 kg) and* m_2 *(.90 kg). Explain in a paragraph the principle of Newton's law and your method of applying it to solve the problem. Assume your reader is not comfortable with mathematical explanations: do not use equations in your paragraph.*

Finance: *Using Guidford C. Babcock's "Concept of Sustainable Growth" [Financial Analysis 26 (May–June 1970): 108–14], analyze the stock price appreciation of the XYZ Corporation, figures for which are attached.*

The analytical tools to be applied in these assignments must be appropriate to the discipline. Writing in response to the sociology assignment, you would use sociological principles developed by Lenski and Lenski. In your literature class, you would use principles of Jungian psychology; in physics, Newton's second law; and in finance, a particular writer's concept of "sustainable growth." But whatever discipline you are working in, the first part of your analysis will clearly state which (and whose) principles and definitions you are applying. For audiences unfamiliar with these principles, you will need to explain them; if you anticipate objections, you will need to argue that they are legitimate principles capable of helping you conduct the analysis.

Guidelines for Writing Analyses

Unless you are asked to follow a specialized format, especially in the sciences or the social sciences, you can present your analysis as a paper by following the guidelines below. As you move from one class to another, from discipline to discipline, the principles and definitions you use as the basis for your analyses will change, but the following basic components of analysis will remain the same.

- *Create a context for your analysis.* Introduce and summarize for readers the object, event, or behavior to be analyzed. Present a strong case about why an analysis is needed: Give yourself a motivation to write, and give readers a motivation to read. Consider setting out a problem, puzzle, or question to be investigated.

- *Introduce and summarize the key definition or principle that will form the basis of your analysis.* Plan to devote an early part of your

---

(continues)

analysis to arguing for the validity of this principle or definition if your audience is not likely to understand it or if they are likely to think that the principle or definition is not valuable.

- *Analyze your topic.* Systematically apply elements of this definition or principle to parts of the activity or object under study. You can do this by posing specific questions, based on your analytic principle or definition, about the object. Discuss what you find part by part (organized perhaps by question), in clearly defined sections of the essay.

- *Conclude by stating clearly what is significant about your analysis.* When considering your analytical paper as a whole, what new or interesting insights have you made concerning the object under study? To what extent has your application of the definition or principle helped you to explain how the object works, what it might mean, or why it is significant?

Part Two of the Argument

In the second part of an analysis, you *apply* specific parts of your principle or definition to the topic at hand. Regardless of how it is worded, this second argument in an analysis can be rephrased to take this form:

> **Claim #2:** By applying principle (or definition) X, we can understand *(topic)* as *(conclusion based on analysis).*

This is your thesis, the main idea of your analytical paper. Fill in the first blank with the specific object, event, or behavior you are examining. Fill in the second blank with your conclusion about the meaning or significance of this object, based on the insights you made during your analysis. Mary Winn completes the second claim of her analysis this way:

> By applying my multipart definition, we can understand *television viewing* as *an addiction.*

Develop an Organizational Plan

You will benefit enormously in the writing of a first draft if you plan out the logic of your analysis. Turn key elements of your analytical principle or definition into questions and then develop the paragraph-by-paragraph logic of the paper.

Turning Key Elements of a Principle or a Definition into Questions

Prepare for an analysis by phrasing questions based on the definition or principle you are going to apply, and then directing those questions to the activity or object to be studied. The method is straightforward: State as clearly as possible the principle or definition to be applied. Divide the principle or definition into its parts and, using each part, form a question. For example, Marie Winn develops a multipart definition of addiction, each part of which is readily turned into a question that she directs at a specific behavior: television viewing. Her analysis of television viewing can be understood as *responses* to each of her analytical questions. Note that in her brief analysis, Winn does not first define addiction and then analyze television viewing. Rather, *as* she defines aspects of addiction, she analyzes television viewing.

Developing the Paragraph-by-Paragraph Logic of Your Paper

The following paragraph from Edward Peselman's essay illustrates the typical logic of a paragraph in an analytical essay:

> Up and down the pecking order, we exercised control through macho taunts and challenges. Collins writes that "individuals who manage to be powerful and get their own way must do so by going along with the laws of social organization, not by contradicting them" (p. 61). Until mid-year, our dorm motto could have read: "You win through rudeness and intimidation." Eric gained power with his frequent and brutal assessments of everyone's behavior. Marc gained power with his temper—which, when lost, made everyone run for cover. Those who were not rude and intimidating drifted to the bottom of our social world. Reggie was quiet and unemotional, which allowed us to take advantage of him because we knew he would back down if pressed in an argument. Yet Reggie understood that on a "power scale" he stood above Dozer and often shared in the group's tactics to get Dozer's food (his parents were forever sending him care packages). Dozer, in turn, seldom missed opportunities to take swipes at Benjamin, with references to his sexuality. From the very first week of school, Benjamin could never—and never wanted to—compete against Eric's bluntness or Marc's temper. Still, Benjamin hung out with us. He lived in our corner of the dorm, and he wanted to be friendly. But everyone, including Benjamin, understood that he occupied the lowest spot in the order.

We see in this paragraph the typical logic of analysis:

- *The writer introduces a specific analytical tool.* Peselman quotes a line from Randall Collins:

  > "[I]ndividuals who manage to be powerful and get their own way must do so by going along with the laws of social organization, not by contradicting them."

- *The writer applies this analytical tool to the object being examined.* Peselman states his dorm's law of social organization:

  > Until mid-year, our dorm motto could have read: "You win through rudeness and intimidation."

- *The writer uses the tool to identify and then examine the meaning of parts of the object.* Peselman shows how each member (the "parts") of his dorm society conforms to the laws of "social organization":

  > Eric gained power with his frequent and brutal assessments of everyone's behavior. Marc gained power with his temper—which, when lost, made everyone run for cover. Those who were not rude and intimidating drifted to the bottom of our social world.

An analytical paper takes shape when a writer creates a series of such paragraphs and then links them with an overall logic. Here is the logical organization of Edward Peselman's paper:

- Paragraph 1: Introduction states a problem—provides a motivation to write and to read.
- Paragraph 2: Randall Collins is introduced—the author whose work will provide principles for analysis.
- Paragraphs 3–4: Background information is provided—the cast of characters in the dorm.
- Paragraphs 5–9: The analysis proceeds—specific parts of dorm life are identified and found significant, using principles from Collins.
- Paragraphs 10–11: Summary and conclusion are provided—the freshman dorm society disintegrates for reasons set out in the analysis. A larger point is made: Some oppressive systems must be torn down.

Draft and Revise Your Analysis

You will usually need at least two drafts to produce a paper that presents your idea clearly. The biggest changes in your paper will typically come between your first and second drafts. No paper that you write, including an analysis, will be complete until you revise and refine your single compelling idea: your analytical conclusion about what the object, event, or behavior being examined means or how it is significant. You revise and refine by evaluating your first draft, bringing to it many of the same questions you pose when evaluating any piece of writing:

- Are the facts accurate?
- Are my opinions supported by evidence?
- Are the opinions of others authoritative?
- Are my assumptions clearly stated?
- Are key terms clearly defined?
- Is the presentation logical?

- Are all parts of the presentation well developed?
- Are significant opposing points of view presented?

Address these same questions to the first draft of your analysis, and you will have solid information to guide your revision.

Write an Analysis, Not a Summary

The most common error made in writing analyses—an error that is *fatal* to the form—is to present readers with a summary only. For analyses to succeed, you must *apply* a principle or definition and reach a conclusion about the object, event, or behavior you are examining. By definition, a summary (see Chapter 1) includes none of your own conclusions. Summary is naturally a part of analysis; you will need to summarize the object or activity being examined and, depending on the audience's needs, summarize the principle or definition being applied. But in an analysis you must take the next step and share insights that suggest the meaning or significance of some object, event, or behavior.

Make Your Analysis Systematic

Analyses should give the reader the sense of a systematic, purposeful examination. Marie Winn's analysis illustrates the point: She sets out specific elements of addictive behavior in separate paragraphs and then uses each, within its paragraph, to analyze television viewing. Winn is systematic in her method, and we are never in doubt about her purpose.

Imagine another analysis in which a writer lays out four elements of a definition and then applies only two, without explaining the logic for omitting the others. Or imagine an analysis in which the writer offers a principle for analysis but directs it to only a half or a third of the object being discussed, without providing a rationale for doing so. In both cases the writer would be failing to deliver on a promise basic to analyses: Once a principle or definition is presented, it should be thoroughly and systematically applied.

Answer the "So What?" Question

An analysis should make readers *want* to read. It should give readers a sense of getting to the heart of the matter, that what is important in the object or activity under analysis is being laid bare and discussed in revealing ways. If when rereading the first draft of your analysis, you cannot imagine readers saying, "I never thought of _____ this way," then something may be seriously wrong. Reread closely to determine why the paper might leave readers flat and exhausted, as opposed to feeling that they have gained new and important insights. Closely reexamine your own motivations for writing. Have *you* learned anything significant through the analysis? If not, neither will readers, and they will turn away. If you have gained important insights through your analysis, communicate them clearly. At some point, pull together your related insights and say, in effect, "Here's how it all adds up."

Attribute Sources Appropriately

In an analysis you work with one or two sources and apply insights from them to some object or phenomenon you want to understand more thoroughly. Because you are not synthesizing a great many sources, and because the strength of an analysis derives mostly from *your* application of a principle or definition, the opportunities for not appropriately citing sources are diminished. Take special care to cite and quote, as necessary, the one or two sources you use throughout the analysis.

Critical Reading for Analysis

- *Read to get a sense of the whole in relation to its parts.* Whether you are clarifying for yourself a principle or a definition to be used in an analysis, or you are reading a text that you will analyze, understand how parts function to create the whole. If a definition or principle consists of parts, use them to organize sections of your analysis. If your goal is to analyze a text, be aware of its structure: Note the title and subtitle; identify the main point and subordinate points and where they are located; break the material into sections.

- *Read to discover relationships within the object being analyzed.* Watch for patterns. When you find them, be alert—for they create an occasion to analyze, to use a principle or definition as a guide in discussing what the patterns may mean.

    In fiction, a pattern might involve responses of characters to events or to each other, the recurrence of certain words or phrasings, images, themes, or turns of plot (to name a few).

    In poetry, a pattern might involve rhyme schemes, rhythm, imagery, figurative or literal language, and more.

The challenge to you as a reader is first to see a pattern (perhaps using a guiding principle or definition to do so) and then to locate other instances of that pattern. Reading carefully in this way prepares you to conduct an analysis.

 WRITING ASSIGNMENT: ANALYSIS

Read the following passage, "A Theory of Human Motivation," by Abraham Maslow. Then write a paper using Maslow's theory as an analytical tool, applying what he says about human motivation to some element of your own reading, knowledge, or personal experience. You may wish to use Edward

Peselman's analysis of Randall Collins's theories as a model for your own paper. (More specific suggestions follow the passage.)

A THEORY OF HUMAN MOTIVATION

Abraham H. Maslow

Abraham Maslow (1908–1970) was one of the most influential humanistic psychologists of the twentieth century. He earned his PhD at the University of Wisconsin and spent most of his academic career at Brandeis University in Waltham, Massachusetts. Maslow's theories have been widely applied in business, the military, and academia. His books include Motivation and Personality *(1954) and* Toward a Psychology of Being *(1962). This selection is excerpted from an article that first appeared in* Psychological Review 50 (1943): 371–96.

The Basic Needs

The "physiological" needs   The needs that are usually taken as the starting point for motivation theory are the so-called physiological drives. . . .

[A]ny of the physiological needs . . . serve as channels for all sorts of other needs as well. That is to say, the person who thinks he is hungry may actually be seeking more for comfort, or dependence, than for vitamins or proteins. Conversely, it is possible to satisfy the hunger need in part by other activities such as drinking water or smoking cigarettes. . . .

Undoubtedly these physiological needs . . . exceed all others in power. What this means specifically is, that in the human being who is missing everything in life in an extreme fashion, it is most likely that the major motivation would be the physiological needs rather than any others. A person who is lacking food, safety, love, and esteem would most probably hunger for food more strongly than for anything else.

Obviously a good way to obscure the "higher" motivations, and to get a lopsided view of human capacities and human nature, is to make the organism extremely and chronically hungry or thirsty. Anyone who attempts to make an emergency picture into a typical one, and who will measure all of man's goals and desires by his behavior during extreme physiological deprivation is certainly being blind to many things. It is quite true that man lives by bread alone—when there is no bread. But what happens to man's desires when there is plenty of bread and when his belly is chronically filled?

5   At once other (and "higher") needs emerge and these, rather than physiological hungers, dominate the organism. And when these in turn are satisfied, again new (and still "higher") needs emerge and so on. This is what we mean by saying that the basic human needs are organized into a hierarchy of relative prepotency.

One main implication of this phrasing is that gratification becomes as important a concept as deprivation in motivation theory, for it releases the organism from the domination of a relatively more physiological need, permitting thereby the emergence of other more social goals. The physiological needs, along with their partial goals, when chronically gratified cease to exist as active determinants or organizers of behavior. They now exist only in a potential fashion in the sense that they may emerge again to dominate the organism if they are thwarted. But a want that is satisfied is no longer a want. The organism is dominated and its behavior organized only by unsatisfied needs. If hunger is satisfied, it becomes unimportant in the current dynamics of the individual.

The safety needs   If the physiological needs are relatively well gratified, there then emerges a new set of needs, which we may categorize roughly as the safety needs. All that has been said of the physiological needs is equally true, although in lesser degree, of these desires. The organism may equally well be wholly dominated by them. They may serve as the almost exclusive organizers of behavior, recruiting all the capacities of the organism in their service, and we may then fairly describe the whole organism as a safety-seeking mechanism. Again we may say of the receptors, the effectors, of the intellect and the other capacities that they are primarily safety-seeking tools. Again, as in the hungry man, we find that the dominating goal [is strongly determinant] not only of his current world-outlook and philosophy but also of his philosophy of the future. Practically everything looks less important than safety (even sometimes the physiological needs which being satisfied, are now underestimated). A man, in this state, if it is extreme enough and chronic enough, may be characterized as living almost for safety alone. . . .

The healthy, normal, fortunate adult in our culture is largely satisfied in his safety needs. The peaceful, smoothly running, 'good' society ordinarily makes its members feel safe enough from wild animals, extremes of temperature, criminals, assault and murder, tyranny, etc. Therefore, in a very real sense, he no longer has any safety needs as active motivators. Just as a sated man no longer feels hungry a safe man no longer feels endangered. If we wish to see these needs directly and clearly we must turn to neurotic or near-neurotic individuals, and to the economic and social underdogs. In between these extremes, we can perceive the expressions of safety needs only in such phenomena as, for instance, the common preference for a job with tenure and protection, the desire for a savings account, and for insurance of various kinds (medical, dental, unemployment, disability, old age).

Other broader aspects of the attempt to seek safety and stability in the world are seen in the very common preference for familiar rather than unfamiliar things, or for the known rather than the unknown. The tendency to have some religion or world-philosophy that organizes the universe and the men in it into some sort of satisfactorily coherent, meaningful whole is also in part motivated by safety-seeking. Here too we may list science and philosophy in general as partially motivated by the safety needs.

10 *The love needs*   If both the physiological and the safety needs are fairly well gratified, then there will emerge the love and affection and belongingness needs, and the whole cycle already described will repeat itself with this new center. Now the person will feel keenly, as never before, the absence of friends, or a sweetheart, or a wife, or children. He will hunger for affectionate relations with people in general, namely, for a place in his group, and he will strive with great intensity to achieve this goal. He will want to attain such a place more than anything else in the world and may even forget that once, when he was hungry he sneered at love. . . .

One thing that must be stressed at this point is that love is not synonymous with sex. Sex may be studied as a purely physiological need. Ordinarily sexual behavior is multi-determined, that is to say, determined not only by sexual but also by other needs, chief among which are the love and affection needs. Also not to be over-looked is the fact that the love needs involve both giving and receiving love.

The esteem needs   All people in our society (with a few pathological excep-tions) have a need or desire for a stable, firmly based, (usually) high evaluation of themselves, for self-respect, or self-esteem, and for the esteem of others. By firmly based self-esteem, we mean that which is soundly based upon . . . achievement and respect from others. These needs may be classified into two subsidiary sets. These are, first, the desire for strength, for achievement, for ade-quacy, for confidence in the face of the world, and for independence and free-dom. Secondly, we have what we may call the desire for reputation or prestige (defining it as respect or esteem from other people), recognition, attention, im-portance or appreciation. . . .

Satisfaction of the self-esteem need leads to feelings of self-confidence, worth, strength, capability and adequacy of being useful and necessary in the world. But thwarting of these needs produces feelings of inferiority, of weakness and of helplessness. These feelings in turn give rise to either basic discourage-ment or else compensatory or neurotic trends. An appreciation of the necessity of basic self-confidence and an understanding of how helpless people are without it, can be easily gained from a study of severe traumatic neurosis.

The need for self-actualization   Even if all these needs are satisfied, we may still often (if not always) expect that a new discontent and restlessness will soon develop, unless the individual is doing what he is fitted for. A musician must make music, an artist must paint, a poet must write, if he is to be ultimately happy. What a man can be, he must be. This need we may call self-actualization.

15   This term . . . refers to the desire for self-fulfillment, namely, to the tendency for him to become actualized in what he is potentially. This tendency might be phrased as the desire to become more and more what one is, to become every-thing that one is capable of becoming.

The specific form that these needs will take will of course vary greatly from person to person. In one individual it may take the form of the desire to be an ideal mother, in another it may be expressed athletically, and in still another it may be expressed in painting pictures or in inventions. It is not necessarily a creative urge although in people who have any capacities for creation it will take this form.*

The clear emergence of these needs rests upon prior satisfaction of the phys-iological, safety, love and esteem needs. We shall call people who are satisfied in these needs, basically satisfied people, and it is from these that we may expect the fullest (and healthiest) creativeness. Since, in our society, basically satisfied people are the exception, we do not know much about self-actualization, either experi-mentally or clinically. It remains a challenging problem for research. . . .

---

*In another section of his article Maslow considers the human "desires to know and to under-stand" as "in part, techniques for the achievement of basic safety in the world" and, in part, "expressions of self-actualization." Maslow also indicates that "freedom of inquiry and expression" are "preconditions of satisfactions of the basic needs." [Eds.]

Further Characteristics of the Basic Needs

The degree of fixity of the hierarchy of basic needs   We have spoken so far as if this hierarchy were a fixed order but actually it is not nearly as rigid as we may have implied. It is true that most of the people with whom we have worked have seemed to have these basic needs in about the order that has been indicated. However, there have been a number of exceptions.

Degrees of relative satisfaction   So far, our theoretical discussion may have given the impression that these five sets of needs are somehow in a step-wise, all-or-none relationship to each other. We have spoken in such terms as the following: "If one need is satisfied, then another emerges." This statement might give the false impression that a need must be satisfied 100 percent before the next need emerges. In actual fact, most members of our society who are normal, are partially satisfied in all their basic needs and partially unsatisfied in all their basic needs at the same time. A more realistic description of the hierarchy would be in terms of decreasing percentages of satisfaction as we go up the hierarchy of pre-potency. For instance, if I may assign arbitrary figures for the sake of illustration, it is as if the average citizen is satisfied perhaps 85 percent in his physiological needs, 70 percent in his safety needs, 50 percent in his love needs, 40 percent in his self-esteem needs, and 10 percent in his self-actualization needs.

20   As for the concept of emergence of a new need after satisfaction of the pre-potent need, this emergence is not a sudden salutatory phenomenon but rather a gradual emergence by slow degrees from nothingness. For instance, if . . . need A is satisfied only 10 percent then need B may not be visible at all. However, as this need A becomes satisfied 25 percent, need B may emerge 5 percent, as need A becomes satisfied 75 percent need B may emerge 90 percent, and so on.

Unconscious character of needs   These needs are neither necessarily conscious nor unconscious. On the whole, however, in the average person, they are more often unconscious rather than conscious. It is not necessary at this point to overhaul the tremendous mass of evidence which indicates the crucial importance of unconscious motivation. It would by now be expected . . . that unconscious motivations would on the whole be rather more important than the conscious motivations. What we have called the basic needs are very often largely unconscious although they may, with suitable techniques, and with sophisticated people, become conscious. . . .

Multiple motivations of behavior   These needs must be understood not to be exclusive or single determiners of certain kinds of behavior. An example may be found in any behavior that seems to be physiologically motivated, such as eating, or sexual play or the like. The clinical psychologists have long since found that any behavior may be a channel through which flow various determinants. Or to say it in another way, most behavior is multi-motivated. Within the sphere of motivational determinants any behavior tends to be determined by several or all of the basic needs simultaneously rather than by only one of them. The latter would be more an exception than the former. Eating may be partially for the sake of filling the stomach, and partially for the sake of comfort and amelioration of other needs. One may make love not only for pure sexual release, but also to convince one's self of one's masculinity: or to make a conquest, to feel powerful, or to win more basic affection. As an illustration, I may point out that it would be possible (theoretically if not practically) to analyze a single act of an individual and see in it the expression of his physiological needs, his safety needs, his love needs, his esteem needs and self-actualization.

References
Cannon, W. B. (1932). *Wisdom of the body.* New York: Norton.
Kardiner, A. (1941). *The traumatic neuroses of war.* New York: Hoeber.
Young, P. (1936). *Motivation of behavior.* New York: Wiley.
Young, P. (1941). The experimental analysis of appetite. *Psychology Bulletin, 38,* 129–164.

In his final sentence, Maslow himself points the way to a potentially productive analysis using his hierarchy of needs: "I may point out that it would be possible (theoretically if not practically) to analyze a single act of an individual and see in it the expression of his physiological needs, his safety needs, his love needs, his esteem needs and self-actualization." One way, then, of conceiving your analysis is to choose a single act—yours or anyone's—and analyze it according to Maslow's system. You might begin by introducing the person and setting a context for the act; introducing Maslow's hierarchy; and proceeding with the analysis itself as you apply one element of the hierarchy at a time. Use each element as a lens through which you examine the act in a new or revealing way. As you conduct your analysis, recall Maslow's caution that single acts will typically have "multiple motivations."

■ ANALYZING VISUAL MEDIA

Some people believe that *visual literacy*—that is, the ability to "read" and understand artifacts such as painting, architecture, film, and graphic arts (including Web design)—will be as important in the twenty-first century as textual literacy was in earlier times. While this may be an extreme view, there's no denying that in this multimedia age, interpreting visual media is a vital skill. And of the various forms of visual media, advertising is perhaps omnipresent.

Scholars in the humanities and social sciences study advertising from a number of angles: In the fields of cultural studies, literary studies, and American studies, scholars interpret the messages of advertisements much as they do the messages and meanings of artifacts from "high culture," such as literature and art. In opposition to high culture, advertisements (along with television shows, films, and the like) are considered "popular culture" (or "pop culture"), and in the past twenty years or so, the study of these highly pervasive and influential works has attracted academic attention. Scholars in the fields of sociology, communications, and anthropology are also interested in studying pop cultural artifacts because they exert such powerful influences on our lives.

Analysis of advertisements has therefore become a fairly common practice in academia. Let's now take the analytical thinking skills we used in analyzing a social situation (the subject of the Peselman paper) and apply them to print advertisements. In this case, rather than lead you through the analytical process, we will show you several advertisements, along with two critical approaches to analyzing advertisements, and then ask you to perform your own analysis of the ads' features, leading to a sense of their overall meaning or significance.

WRITING ASSIGNMENT: ANALYZING VISUAL MEDIA

Three advertisements appear on the following pages. The first was created to promote Fancy Feast cat food; the second was created to promote Ikea products; and the third advertises GE Monogram kitchen appliances. Study the illustrations and the text in the ads. Then read the two selections that follow. The first, Roland Marchand's "The Appeal of the Democracy of Goods," from his 1985 book *Advertising the American Dream*, describes a common theme underlying many advertisements. The second, Dorothy Cohen's "Elements of an Effective Layout," offers a number of guiding principles for assessing the layout of visual elements in print advertising.

Consider these questions as you study each ad:

- What is depicted in the ad's images?
- What is the ad's text?
- How do text and images relate to each other in creating the ad's meaning?
- How are shading and font styles used?
- How are words and images placed in relation to one another, and how do these spatial relationships create meaning?
- What is the mood—that is, the emotional output—of the ad? How does this mood help create the ad's meaning?
- How does the ad allude to images, ideas, events, or trends from our knowledge of the contemporary world?

Choose one of the advertisements and the passage by *either* Cohen *or* Marchand. Use the principles presented in the passage you have selected to analyze the ad of your choice. Apply the principles of analytical reasoning demonstrated in the analysis by Edward Peselman earlier in this chapter. That is, apply one or more of the principles explained in the article to one of the advertisements. Develop your analysis in a well-organized, well-developed paper.

"You know, I don't ask for much. I'll settle for a pair of jeans that fit, a man who can surprise me occasionally with a gift (no, honey, I didn't mean a lawnmower...), kids who don't drink too much soda, friends who don't drink too much wine, a red carpet hairdo... and a new kitchen.

So, how am I supposed to make it happen? Dress up my husband as a handyman? Or dress up myself? Or do you expect me to mortgage the house for a million dollars to get a beautiful kitchen that doesn't make my turkey any tastier than before? That's not happening. Huh? What about IKEA? They don't have kitchens do they?"

Is it possible to get great kitchen at IKEA?

90th FL 10 RMS W VU. NEW YORK AT YOUR FEET.
$17 MILLION.

SO WHAT'S COOKING IN THE KITCHEN ?

In this unoccupied 90th floor penthouse, there's a
GE Monogram kitchen.
Every other apartment in this, the tallest residential
building in the world, has a GE Monogram kitchen, too.
Interested parties, please contact Mr. Trump personally.

GE Monogram
Visit monogram.com

imagination at work

For a more ambitious version of this paper, you might use *two* or even *three* ads as the subject of your paper. Review the principles of comparison-and-contrast in Chapter 4 (pp. 178–179). And for an even more ambitious assignment, you could perform a complex analysis, applying both Marchand's *and* Cohen's principles to one or more ads. That is, show how (a) the graphic elements of the ad and (b) its underlying message work to create a unified effect on readers, influencing them to want to buy the product(s) advertised.

THE APPEAL OF THE DEMOCRACY OF GOODS
Roland Marchand

Roland Marchand is a professor of history at the University of California, Davis. This selection originally appeared in Marchand's 1985 book Advertising the American Dream: Making Way for Modernity, 1920–1940.

As they opened their September 1929 issue, readers of the *Ladies Home Journal* were treated to an account of the care and feeding of young Livingston Ludlow Biddle III, son and heir of the wealthy Biddles of Philadelphia, whose family coat-of-arms graced the upper right-hand corner of the page. Young Master Biddle, mounted on his tricycle, fixed a serious, slightly pouting gaze upon the reader, while the Cream of Wheat Corporation rapturously explained his constant care, his carefully regulated play and exercise, and the diet prescribed for him by "famous specialists." As master of Sunny Ridge Farm, the Biddles' winter estate in North Carolina, young Livingston III had "enjoyed every luxury of social position and wealth, since the day he was born." Yet, by the grace of a . . . modern providence, it happened that Livingston's health was protected by "a simple plan every mother can use." Mrs. Biddle gave Cream of Wheat to the young heir for both breakfast and supper. The world's foremost child experts knew of no better diet; great wealth could procure no finer nourishment. Cream of Wheat summarized the central point of the advertisement by claiming that "every mother can give her youngsters the fun and benefits of a Cream of Wheat breakfast just as do the parents of these boys and girls who have the best that wealth can command."

While enjoying this glimpse of childrearing among the socially distinguished, *Ladies Home Journal* readers found themselves drawn in by one of the most pervasive of all advertising strategies of the 1920's—the concept of the Democracy of Goods. According to this idea, the wonders of modern mass production and distribution enabled everyone to enjoy society's most desirable pleasures, conveniences, or benefits. The particular pleasure, benefit, or convenience varied, of course, with each advertiser who used the formula. But the cumulative effect of the constant reminders that "any woman can . . ." and "every home can afford . . ." was to publicize an image of American society in which concentrated wealth at the top of a hierarchy of social classes restricted no family's opportunity to acquire the most desirable products. By implicitly defining "democracy" in terms of equal access to consumer products, these advertisements offered Americans an inviting vision of their society as one of incontestable equality.

In its most common advertising formula, the concept of the Democracy of Goods asserted that although the rich enjoyed a great variety of luxuries, the acquisition of their *one* most precious luxury would provide anyone with the ultimate in satisfaction. For instance, a Chase and Sanborn's Coffee advertisement, with an elegant butler serving a family in a dining room with a sixteen-foot ceiling, reminded Chicago families that although "compared with the riches of the more fortunate, your way of life may seem modest indeed," yet no one—"king, prince, statesman, or capitalist"—could enjoy better coffee. The Association of Soap and Glycerine Producers proclaimed that the charm of cleanliness was as readily available to the poor as to the rich, and Ivory Soap reassuringly related how one young housewife, who couldn't afford a $780-a-year maid like her neighbor, still maintained "nice hands" by using Ivory. The C. F. Church Manufacturing Company epitomized this feature of the Democracy of Goods technique in an ad entitled "a bathroom luxury everyone can afford": "If you lived in one of those palatial apartments on Park Avenue, in New York City, where you have to pay $2,000 to $7,000 a year rent, you still couldn't have a better toilet seat in your bathroom than they have—the Church Sani-white Toilet Seat, which you can afford to have right now."

Thus, according to the concept of the Democracy of Goods, no differences in wealth could prevent the humblest citizens, provided they chose their purchases wisely, from coming home to a setting in which they could contemplate their essential equality, through possession of a particular product, with the nation's millionaires. In 1929, Howard Dickinson, a contributor to *Printers' Ink,* concisely expressed the social psychology behind Democracy of Goods advertisements: "'With whom do the mass of people think they want to foregather?' asks the psychologist in advertising. 'Why, with the wealthy and socially distinguished, of course!' If we can't get an invitation to tea for our millions of customers, we can at least present the fellowship of using the same brand of merchandise. And it works."

ELEMENTS OF AN EFFECTIVE LAYOUT

Dorothy Cohen

This selection originally appeared in Dorothy Cohen's textbook Advertising *(1988).*

Fundamentally a good layout should attract attention and interest and should provide some control over the manner in which the advertisement is read. The message to be communicated may be sincere, relevant, and important to the consumer, but because of the competitive "noise" in the communication channel, the opportunity to be heard may depend on the effectiveness of the layout. In addition to attracting attention, the most important requisites for an effective layout are balance, proportion, movement, utility, clarity, and emphasis.

Balance

Balance is a fundamental law in nature and its application to layout design formulates one of the basic principles of this process. Balance is a matter of weight distribution; in layout it is keyed to the *optical center* of an advertisement, the point which the reader's eye designates as the center of an area. In an advertisement a vertical line which divides the area into right and left halves contains the center; however the optical center is between one-tenth and one-third the distance above the mathematical horizontal center line. . . .

In order to provide good artistic composition, the elements in the layout must be in equilibrium. Equilibrium can be achieved through balance, and this process may be likened to the balancing of a seesaw. The optical center of the advertisement serves as the fulcrum or balancing point, and the elements may be balanced on both sides of this fulcrum through considerations of their size and tonal quality.

The simplest way to ensure formal balance between the elements to the right and left of the vertical line is to have all masses in the left duplicated on the right in size, weight, and distance from the center. . . . Formal balance imparts feelings of dignity, solidity, refinement, and reserve. It has been used for institutional advertising and suggests conservatism on the part of the advertiser. Its major deficiency is that it may present a static and somewhat unexciting appearance; however, formal balance presents material in an easy-to-follow order and works well for many ads.

5   To understand informal balance, think of children of unequal weight balanced on a seesaw; to ensure equilibrium it is necessary to place the smaller child far from the center and the larger child closer to the fulcrum. In informal balance the elements are balanced, but not evenly, because of different sizes and color contrast. This type of a symmetric balance requires care so that the various elements do not create a lopsided or top-heavy appearance. A knowledge or a sense of the composition can help create the feeling of symmetry in what is essentially asymmetric balance.

Informal balance presents a fresh, untraditional approach. It creates excitement, a sense of originality, forcefulness, and, to some extent, the element of surprise. Whereas formal balance may depend on the high interest value of the illustration to attract the reader, informal balance may attract attention through the design of the layout. . . .

Proportion

Proportion helps develop order and creates a pleasing impression. It is related to balance but is concerned primarily with the division of the space and the emphasis to be accorded each element. Proportion, to the advertising designer, is the relationship between the size of one element in the ad to another, the amount of space between elements, as well as the width of the total ad to its depth. Proportion also involves the tone of the ad: the amount of light area in relation to dark area and the amount of color and noncolor.*

As a general rule unequal dimensions and distances make the most lively design in advertising. The designer also places the elements on the page so that each element is given space and position in proportion to its importance in the total advertisement and does not look like it stands alone.

Movement

If an advertisement is to appear dynamic rather than static, it must contain some movement. *Movement* (also called *sequence*) provides the directional flow for the

---

*Roy Paul Nelson, *The Design of Advertising,* 4th ed. (Dubuque, IA: Brown, 1981) 18.

advertisement, gives it its follow-through, and provides coherence. It guides the reader's eye from one element to another and makes sure he or she does not miss anything.

10   Motion in layout is generally from left to right and from top to bottom—the direction established through the reading habits of speakers of Western language. The directional impetus should not disturb the natural visual flow but should favor the elements to be stressed, while care should be taken not to direct the reader's eye out of the advertisement. This can be done by the following:

- *Gaze motion* directs the reader's attention by directing the looks of the people or animals in an ad. If a subject is gazing at a unit in the layout, the natural tendency is for the reader to follow the direction of that gaze; if someone is looking directly out of the advertisement, the reader may stop to see who's staring.

- *Structural motion* incorporates the lines of direction and patterns of movement by mechanical means. An obvious way is to use an arrow or a pointed finger. . . .

Unity

Another important design principle is the unification of the layout. Although an advertisement is made up of many elements, all of these should be welded into a compact composition. Unity is achieved when the elements tie into one another by using the same basic shapes, sizes, textures, colors, and mood. In addition, the type should have the same character as the art.

A *border* surrounding an ad provides a method of achieving unity. Sets of borders may occur within an ad, and, when they are similar in thickness and tone, they provide a sense of unity.

Effective use of white space can help to establish unity. . . . *White space* is defined as that part of the advertising space which is not occupied by any other elements; in this definition, white space is not always white in color. White space may be used to feature an important element by setting it off, or to imply luxury and prestige by preventing a crowded appearance. It may be used to direct and control the reader's attention by tying elements together. If white space is used incorrectly, it may cause separation of the elements and create difficulty in viewing the advertisement as a whole.

Clarity and Simplicity

The good art director does not permit a layout to become too complicated or tricky. An advertisement should retain its clarity and be easy to read and easy to understand. The reader tends to see the total image of an advertisement; thus it should not appear fussy, contrived, or confusing. Color contrasts, including tones of gray, should be strong enough to be easily deciphered, and the various units should be clear and easy to understand. Type size and design should be selected for ease of reading, and lines of type should be a comfortable reading length. Too many units in an advertisement are distracting; therefore, any elements that can be eliminated without destroying the message should be. One way in which clarity can be achieved is by combining the logo, trademark, tag line, and company name into one compact group.

Emphasis

15 Although varying degrees of emphasis may be given to different elements, one unit should dominate. It is the designer's responsibility to determine how much emphasis is necessary, as well as how it is to be achieved. The important element may be placed in the optical center or removed from the clutter of other elements. Emphasis may also be achieved by contrasts in size, shape, and color, or the use of white space.

■ ANALYSIS: A TOOL FOR UNDERSTANDING

As this chapter has demonstrated, analysis involves applying principles as a way to probe and understand. With incisive principles guiding your analysis, you will be able to pose questions, observe patterns and relationships, and derive meaning. Do not forget that this meaning will be one of several possible meanings. Someone else, or even you, using different analytical tools, could observe the same phenomena and arrive at very different conclusions regarding meaning or significance. We end the chapter, then, as we began it: with the two brief analyses of *The Wizard of Oz*. The conclusions expressed in one look nothing like the conclusions expressed in the other, save for the fact that both seek to interpret the same movie. And yet we can say that both are useful, that both reveal meaning.

> At the dawn of adolescence, the very time she should start to distance herself from Aunt Em and Uncle Henry, the surrogate parents who raised her on their Kansas farm, Dorothy Gale experiences a hurtful reawakening of her fear that these loved ones will be rudely ripped from her, especially her Aunt (Em—M for Mother!).*

> [*The Wizard of Oz*] was originally written as a political allegory about grass-roots protest. It may seem harder to believe than Emerald City, but the Tin Woodsman is the industrial worker, the Scarecrow [is] the struggling farmer, and the Wizard is the president, who is powerful only as long as he succeeds in deceiving the people.†

You have seen in this chapter how it is possible for two writers, analyzing the same object or phenomenon but applying different analytical principles, to reach vastly different conclusions about what the object or phenomenon may mean or why it is significant. *The Wizard of Oz* is both an inquiry into the psychology of adolescence and a political allegory. What else the classic film may be awaits revealing with the systematic application of other analytical tools. The insights you gain as a writer of analyses depend entirely on your choice of tools and the subtlety with which you apply them.

   Note: Additional analysis assignments will be found in Chapter 8, Practicing Academic Writing.

---

*Greenberg, Movies.
†Dreier, "Oz."

Part Two ▪ *Strategies*

Writing as a Process ▪ 6

▪ WRITING AS THINKING

Most of us regard writing as an activity that culminates in a product: a paper, a letter to a friend, study notes, and the like. We tend to focus on the result rather than on the process of getting there. But how *do* we produce that paper or letter? Does the thought that you write down not exist until it appears on the page? Does thought precede writing? If so, is writing merely a translation of prior thought? The relationship between thinking and writing is complex and not entirely understood. But it is worth reflecting on, especially as you embark on your writing-intensive career as a college student. Every time you take up a pen or sit down to a computer to write, you engage in a thinking process—and what and how and when you think both affects and is affected by your writing in a variety of ways. Consider the possibilities as you complete the following brief exercises:

> **A:** You find yourself enrolled in a composition class at a particular school. Why are you attending this school and not another? Write for five minutes on the question.

> **B:** Write for five minutes—no more, no less—on this question: What single moment in your freshman experience thus far has been most (a) humorous, (b) promising, (c) vexing, (d) exasperating? Choose *one* and write.

> **C:** Select one page of notes from the presumably many you have taken in any of your classes. Reread the page and rewrite it, converting your first-pass notes into a well-organized study guide that would help you prepare for an exam. Devote five minutes to the effort.

Reflect on these exercises. Specifically, locate in your response to each one the point at which you believe your thinking took place. (Admittedly, this may be difficult, but give it a try.) Before completing Exercise A, you probably gave considerable thought to *where* you are or would like to be attending college. Examine your writing and reflect on your thinking: Were you in any way rethinking your choice of school as you wrote? Or were you explaining a decision you've already made—that is, reporting on *prior* thinking? Some combination? Now turn to your work for Exercise B, for which you wrote (most likely) on a new topic. Where did thinking occur here? As you wrote? Moments prior to your writing, as you selected the topic and focused your ideas? Last, consider Exercise C. Where did your thinking take place? How did revision change your first-draft notes? What makes your second draft a better study guide than your first draft? Finally, consider the differences in the relationship between writing and thinking *across* Exercises A, B, and C as you wrote on a topic you'd previously thought (but not written) about, on a new topic, and on a topic you've written about and are revising. Note the changing relationship between writing and thinking. Note especially how rewriting is related to rethinking.

In completing and reflecting on these exercises, you have glimpsed something of the marvelous complexity of writing. The job of this chapter is to help you develop some familiarity and comfort with a process that no one fully understands.

■ STAGES OF THE WRITING PROCESS

By breaking the process into stages, writers turn the sometimes overwhelming task of writing a paper into manageable pieces, each requiring different actions that, collectively, build to a final draft. Generally, the stages involve *understanding the task, gathering data, invention, drafting, revision,* and *editing.*

Broadly speaking, the six stages of the writing process occur in the order we've listed. But writing is *recursive;* the process tends to loop back on itself. You will move forward as you write, toward a finished product. But moving forward is seldom a straight-line process.

The Writing Process

- *Understanding the task:* Read—or create—the assignment. Understand its purpose, scope, and audience.
- *Gathering data:* Locate and review information—from sources and from your own experience—and formulate an approach.
- *Invention:* Use various techniques (e.g., listing, outlining, freewriting) to generate a definite approach to the assignment. Gather more data if needed. Aim for a working thesis, a tentative (but well-reasoned and well-informed) statement of the direction you intend to pursue.
- *Drafting:* Sketch the paper you intend to write and then write all sections necessary to support the working thesis. Stop if necessary to gather more data. Typically, you will both follow your plan and revise and invent a new (or slightly new) plan as you write. Expect to discover key parts of your paper as you write.

(continues)

- *Revision:* Rewrite in order to make the draft coherent and unified.

  Revise at the *global* level, reshaping your thesis and adding to, rearranging, or deleting paragraphs in order to support the thesis. Gather more data as needed to flesh out paragraphs in support of the thesis.

  Revise at the *local* level of paragraphs, ensuring that each is well reasoned and supports the thesis.

- *Editing:* Revise at the *sentence* level for style and brevity. Revise for correctness: grammar, punctuation, usage, and spelling.

■ STAGE 1: UNDERSTANDING THE TASK

Papers in the Academic Disciplines

Although most of your experience with academic papers may have been in English classes, you should be prepared for instructors in other academic disciplines to assign papers with significant research components. Here is a sampling of topics that have been assigned recently in a broad range of undergraduate courses:

Art History: *Discuss the main differences between Romanesque and Gothic sculpture, using the sculptures of Jeremiah (St. Pierre Cathedral) and St. Theodore (Chartres Cathedral) as major examples.*

Physics: *Research and write a paper on solar cell technology, covering the following areas: basic physical theory, history and development, structure and materials, types and characteristics, practical uses, state of the art, and future prospects.*

Political Science: *Explain the contours of California's water policy in the past few decades and then, by focusing on one specific controversy, explain and analyze the way in which this policy was adapted and why. Consider such questions as these: Where does the water come from? How much is there? Who uses it? Who pays for it? How much does it cost? Should more water resources be developed?*

Religious Studies: *Select a particular religious group or movement present in the nation for at least 20 years and show how its belief or practice has changed since members of the group have been in America or, if the group began in America, since its first generation.*

Some of these assignments allow students a considerable range of choice (within the general subject); others are highly specific in requiring students to address a particular issue. Most call for some library or online research; a few call for a combination of online, library, and field research; others may be based entirely on field research. As with all academic writing, your first task is to make sure you understand the assignment. Remember to critically read and analyze the specific task(s) required of you in a paper assignment. One useful technique for doing this is to locate the assignment's key verb(s), which will stipulate exactly what is expected of you.

Exercise 6.1

Analyze an Assignment

Reread the instructions for a recent assignment from another course. (1) Identify the key verb(s) in each; (2) list the type of print, interview, or graphical data you should gather to complete the assignment; and (3) reflect on your own experience to find some anecdote that might be appropriately included in a paper (or, absent that, a related experience that would provide a personal motivation for writing the paper).

■ STAGE 2: GATHERING DATA

When you begin a writing task, you will want to pose three questions:

1. What is the task?
2. What do I know about the subject?*
3. What do I need to know in order to begin writing?

These questions prompt you to reflect on the task and define what is expected. Taking stock of class notes, readings, and whatever resources are available, you survey what you already know. Once you identify the gaps between what you know and what you need to know in order to write, you can begin to gather data—most likely in stages. You may gather enough, at first, to formulate initial ideas. You may begin to write, see new gaps, and realize you need more data.

Types of Data

Data is a term used most often to refer to *quantitative* information such as the frequencies or percentages of natural occurrences in the sciences or of social phenomena in the social sciences. But *data* also refers to *qualitative* information—the sort that is textual rather than numerical. For example, interviews or ethnographic field notes recorded by a social scientist, also considered to be *data*, are usually qualitative in nature, comprising in-depth interview

---

Note: The terms *subject* and *topic* are often used interchangeably. In this chapter, we use *subject* to mean a broad area of interest that, once narrowed to a *topic*, becomes the focus of a paper. Within a thesis (the major organizing sentence of the paper), we speak of *topic*, not *subject*.

responses or detailed observations of human behavior. In the humanities, the term *data* can refer to the qualitative observations one makes of a particular art object one is interpreting or evaluating. Generally, quantitative data encompasses issues of "how many" or "how often," whereas qualitative research accounts for such issues as "what kind?" and "why?"

Primary and Secondary Sources

When you collect either or both kinds of data, you are generating *primary* data—data that a researcher gathers directly by using the research methods appropriate to a particular field of study, such as experiments or observations in the sciences, surveys or interviews in the social sciences, and close reading and interpretation of unpublished documents and literary texts or works of art in the humanities. More commonly as an undergraduate, however, you will collect types of data that are *secondary* in nature: information and ideas collected or generated by others who have performed their own primary and/or secondary research. The data gathering for most undergraduate academic writing will consist of library research and, increasingly, research conducted online via Internet databases and other resources; you will rely on secondary data more often than you will generate your own primary data.

Chapter 7 provides an in-depth discussion of locating and using secondary sources. Refer also to the material in Chapters 1 and 2 on summary, critical reading, and critique; the techniques of critical reading and assessment of sources will help you make the best use of your sources. And the material in Chapter 1 on avoiding plagiarism will help you conform to the highest ethical standards in your research and writing.

■ STAGE 3: INVENTION

Given an assignment and the fruits of your preliminary data gathering, you are in a position to frame your writing project: to give it scope, to name your main idea, and to create conditions for productive writing. You must define what you are writing about, after all, and this you achieve—in a preliminary way—in the *invention* stage. This stage might also be termed "brainstorming" or "predrafting." Regardless of the name, invention is an important part of the process that typically overlaps with data gathering. The preliminary data you gather on a topic will inform the choices you make in defining (that is, in "inventing" ideas for) your project. As you invent, you will often return to gather more data.

Writers sometimes skip over the invention stage, preferring to save time by launching directly from gathering data into writing a draft. But time spent narrowing your ideas to a manageable scope at the beginning of a project will pay dividends all through the writing process. Many, *many* efforts go wrong when writers choose too broad a topic, resulting in the superficial treatment of subtopics, or when they choose too narrow a topic and then must "pad" their work to meet a length requirement.

The Myth of Inspiration

Some students believe that good writing comes primarily from a kind of magical—and unpredictable—formation of ideas that occurs as one sits down in front of blank paper or a blank computer screen. According to the myth, a writer must be inspired in order to write, as if given his or her ideas from some mystical source such as a muse. While some element of inspiration may inform your writing, most of the time it is hard work—especially in the invention stage—that gets the job done. The old adage attributed to Thomas Edison, "Invention is one part inspiration and ninety-nine parts perspiration," applies here.

Choosing and Narrowing Your Subject

Suppose you have been assigned an open-ended, ten-page paper in an introductory course on environmental science. Not only do you have to choose a subject, but you also have to narrow it sufficiently and formulate your thesis. Where will you begin?

First, you need to select broad subject matter from the course and become knowledgeable about its general features. What if no broad area of interest occurs to you?

- Work through the syllabus or your textbook(s). Identify topics that sparked your interest.
- Review course notes and pay especially close attention to lectures that held your interest.
- Scan recent headlines for news items that bear on your coursework.

Assume for your course in environmental science that you've settled on the broad subject of energy conservation. At this point, the goal of

The Myth of Talent

Many inexperienced writers believe that either you have writing talent or you don't, and if you don't, you are doomed to go through life as a "bad writer." But again, hard work, rather than talent, is the norm. Yes, some people have more natural verbal ability than others—we all have our areas of strength and weakness. But in any endeavor, talent alone can't ensure success, and with hard work, writers who do not yet have much confidence can achieve great results. Not everyone can be a brilliant writer, but everyone *can* be a competent writer.

your research is to limit this subject to a manageable scope. A subject can be limited in at least two ways. First, you can seek out a general article (perhaps an encyclopedia entry, though it would not typically be accepted as a source in a college-level paper). A general article may do the work for you by breaking the larger topic down into smaller subtopics that you can explore and, perhaps, limit even further. Second, you can limit a subject by asking questions about it:

Who?

Which aspects?

Where?

When?

How?

Why?

These questions will occur to you as you conduct your research and see the ways in which various authors have focused their discussions. Having read several sources on energy conservation and having decided that you'd like to use them, you might limit the subject by asking *which aspects* and deciding to focus on energy conservation as it relates to motor vehicles.

Certainly, "energy-efficient vehicles" offers a more specific focus than does "energy conservation." Still, the revised focus is too broad for a ten-page paper. (One can easily imagine several book-length works on the subject.) So again you try to limit your subject by posing other questions from the same list. You might ask which aspects of energy-efficient vehicles are possible and desirable and how auto manufacturers can be encouraged to develop them. In response to these questions, you may jot down preliminary notes:

- Types of energy-efficient vehicles

    All-electric vehicles

    Hybrid (combination of gasoline and electric) vehicles

    Fuel-cell vehicles

- Government action to encourage development of energy-efficient vehicles

    Mandates to automakers to build minimum quantities of energy-efficient vehicles by certain deadlines

    Additional taxes imposed on high-mileage vehicles

    Subsidies to developers of energy-efficient vehicles

Focusing on any *one* of these aspects as an approach to encouraging the use of energy-efficient vehicles could provide the focus of a ten-page paper.

Practice Narrowing Subjects

In groups of three or four classmates, choose one of the following subjects and collaborate on a paragraph or two that explores the questions we listed for narrowing subjects: Who? Which aspects? Where? When? How? Why? See if you can narrow the subject.

- Downloading music off the Internet
- Internet chat rooms
- College sports
- School violence
- America's public school system

Invention Strategies

You may already be familiar with a variety of strategies for thinking through your ideas. Four of these strategies are described below.

Directed Freewriting

To freewrite is to let your mind go and write spontaneously, often for a set amount of time or a set number of pages. The process of "just writing" can often free up thoughts and ideas about which we aren't even fully conscious, or that we haven't articulated to ourselves. In *directed freewriting*, you focus on a subject and let what you think and know about the subject flow out of you in a focused stream of ideas. As a first step in the invention stage, you might sit down with an assignment and write continuously for 15 minutes. If even one solid idea comes through, you've succeeded in using freewriting to help "free up" your thinking. As a second step, you might take that one idea and freewrite about it, shift to a different invention strategy to explore that one idea, or even begin to draft a thesis and then a rough draft, depending on the extent to which your idea is well formed.

Listing

Some writers find it helpful to make *lists* of their ideas, breaking significant ideas into sublists and seeing where they lead. Approach this strategy as a form of freewriting; let your mind go, and jot down words and phrases that are related. Create lists by pulling related ideas out of your notes or your course readings. *A caution:* The linear nature of lists can lead you to jump prematurely into planning your paper's structure before working out your ideas. Instead, list ideas as a way of brainstorming, then generate another list that works out the best structure for your points in a draft.

Outlining

A more structured version of a list, an *outline* groups ideas in hierarchical order, with main points broken into subordinate points, sometimes indicating evidence in support of these points. Use outlines as a first stage in generating ideas during your invention process, or use outlines as a second step in invention. After freewriting and/or listing, refine and build on your ideas by inserting them into an outline for a workable structure in which you can discuss the ideas you've brainstormed.

Clustering and Branching

These two methods of invention are more visual, nonlinear versions of listing and outlining. With both clustering and branching, you start with an assignment's main topic, or with an idea generated by freewriting or thinking, and you brainstorm related ideas that flow from that main idea. *Clustering* involves writing an idea in the middle of a page and circling it; then you draw lines leading from that circle, or "bubble," to new bubbles in which you write subtopics of the central idea. Picking the subtopics that interest you most, draw lines leading to more bubbles wherein you note important aspects of the subtopics. (See the illustration below.) *Branching* follows the same principle, but instead of placing ideas in bubbles, you write them on lines that branch off to other lines that, in turn, contain the related subtopics of your larger topic.

Clustering and branching are useful first steps in invention, for each helps isolate the topics about which you are most knowledgeable. As you branch off into the subtopics of a main paper topic, the number of ideas you generate in relation to these topics will help show where you have the most knowledge and/or interest.

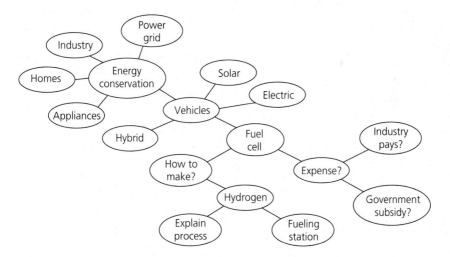

You can modify and combine invention techniques in a number of ways. There is no one right way to generate ideas—or to write a paper—and every writer will want to try different methods to find those that work best. The point to remember is that time spent on invention, regardless of method, creates the conditions for writing a productive first draft.

Exercise 6.3

Practice Invention Strategies

After completing the group exercise (Exercise 6.2, p. 232) in which you narrowed a subject, work individually to brainstorm ideas about the subject your group chose. Use one of the invention strategies listed above—preferably one that you haven't used before. After brainstorming on your own, meet with your group again to compare the ideas you each generated.

■ STAGE 4: DRAFTING

It's usually best to begin drafting a paper after you've settled on at least a working or preliminary thesis. While consulting the fruits of your efforts during invention (notes, lists, outlines, and so on), you face a number of choices about how to proceed with drafting your paper. Let's look at some of them, including the crucial step of drafting the thesis.

Strategies for Writing the Paper

Some writers can sit down very early in the process and put their ideas into an orderly form as they write. This drafting method results in a completed *rough draft*. Good writers rarely, if ever, produce an adequate piece of writing in one draft. Most need to plan the structure of a paper before they can sit down to a first draft. Even if this initial structure proves to be little more than a sketch that changes markedly as the paper develops, some sort of scaffolding usually helps in taking the step from planning to writing a first draft.

Ultimately, *you* will decide how best to proceed. And don't be surprised if you begin different writing projects differently. Whether you jump in without a plan, whether you plan rigorously, or whether you commit yourself to the briefest preliminary sketch, ask yourself:

- On what main point do I intend to focus my paper?
- What subpoints do I need to address in order to develop my main point?
- In what order should my points be arranged? (Do certain subpoints lead naturally to others?)

At Stage 3, as you clarify the direction in which you believe your paper is heading, you ought to be able to formulate at least a *preliminary thesis* (see below). Your thesis can be very rough, but if you don't have some sense of your main point, writing the first draft will not be possible. In this case, you would have to consider what you've written a preliminary or a *discovery draft* (more of an invention strategy than an actual draft), a perfectly sensible way to proceed if you're having difficulty clarifying your thoughts. Even if you begin with what you regard as a clearly stated point, don't be surprised if by the end of the draft—just at the point where you are summing up—you discover that the paper you have in fact written differs from the paper you intended to write. However firm your ideas may be when you begin, the act of writing a draft will usually clarify matters for you.

As you can see, the drafting and invention stages overlap. How much planning you do after working out your ideas and before drafting your paper is a matter of preference. Try different methods to see which work best for you, and keep in mind that different assignments may require new methods for invention and drafting.

Writing a Thesis

A thesis, as we have seen, is a one- or two-sentence summary of a paper's content. Whether it is explanatory, mildly argumentative, or strongly argumentative, the thesis is an assertion about that content—for instance, about what the content is, how it works, what it means, if it is valuable, if action should be taken, and so on. A thesis is similar, actually, to a paper's conclusion, but it lacks the conclusion's concern for broad implications and significance. The thesis is the product of your thinking; it therefore represents *your* conclusion about the topic on which you're writing, and therefore you have to have spent some time thinking (that is, in the invention stage) in order to arrive at the thesis that governs your paper.

For a writer in the drafting stages, the thesis establishes a focus, a basis on which to include or exclude information. For the reader of a finished product, the thesis anticipates the author's discussion. *A thesis, therefore, is an essential tool for both writers and readers of academic papers.*

The Components of a Thesis

Like any other sentence, a thesis includes a subject and a predicate that makes an assertion about the subject. In the sentence "Lee and Grant were different kinds of generals," "Lee and Grant" is the subject and "were different kinds of generals" is the predicate. What distinguishes a thesis from any other sentence with a subject and a predicate is that *the thesis presents the controlling idea of the paper*. The subject of a thesis, and the assertion about it, must present the right balance between the general and the specific to allow for a thorough discussion within the allotted length of the paper. The discussion might include definitions, details, comparisons, contrasts—whatever is needed to illuminate a subject and support the assertion. (If the sentence about Lee and Grant were a thesis, the reader would assume that the rest of the paper contained comparisons and contrasts between the two generals.)

Bear in mind when writing theses that the more general your subject and the more complex your assertion, the longer your paper will be. The broadest theses require book-length treatments, as in this case:

> Meaningful energy conservation requires a shrewd application of political, financial, and scientific will.

One could not write an effective ten-page paper based on this thesis. The topic alone would require pages merely to define carefully what is meant by "energy conservation" and then by "meaningful." Energy can be conserved in homes, vehicles, industries, appliances, and power plants, and each of these areas would need consideration. Having accomplished this task, the writer would then turn his or her attention to the claim, which entails a discussion of how politics, finance, and science individually and collectively influence energy conservation. Moreover, the thesis requires the writer to argue that "shrewd application" of politics, finance, and science is required. The thesis may very well be accurate and compelling. Yet it promises entirely too much for a ten-page paper.

To write an effective thesis and thus a controlled, effective paper, you need to limit your subject and your claims about it. We discussed narrowing your subject during the invention stage (pp. 229–231); this narrowing process should help you arrive at a manageable topic for your paper. You will convert that topic to a thesis when you make an assertion about it—a *claim* that you will explain and support in the paper.

Making an Assertion

Thesis statements constitute an assertion or claim that you wish to make *about* your paper's topic. If you have spent enough time reading and gathering information, and brainstorming ideas about the assignment, you will be knowledgeable enough to have something to say based on a combination of your own thinking and the thinking of your sources.

If you have trouble making an assertion, devote more time to invention strategies: Try writing your subject at the top of a page and then listing everything you now know and feel about it. Often from such a list you will discover an assertion that you can then use to fashion a working thesis. A good way to gauge the reasonableness of your claim is to see what other authors have asserted about the same topic. Your keeping good notes on the views of others will provide you with a useful counterpoint to your own views as you write and think about your claim, and you may want to use those notes in your paper. Next, make several assertions about your topic, in order of increasing complexity, as in the following:

1. Fuel-cell technology has emerged as a promising approach to developing energy-efficient vehicles.
2. To reduce our dependence on nonrenewable fossil fuel, the federal government should encourage the development of fuel-cell vehicles.
3. The federal government should subsidize the development of fuel-cell vehicles as well as the hydrogen infrastructure needed to support them; otherwise, the United States will be increasingly vulnerable to recession and other economic dislocations resulting from our dependence on the continued flow of foreign oil.

Keep in mind that these are *working theses.* Because you haven't begun a paper based on any of them, they remain *hypotheses* to be tested. You might choose one and use it to focus your initial draft. After completing a first draft, you would revise it by comparing the contents of the paper to the thesis and making adjustments as necessary for unity. The working thesis is an excellent tool for planning broad sections of the paper, but—again—don't let it prevent you from pursuing related discussions as they occur to you.

Starting with a Working Thesis

As a student, you are not yet an expert on the subject of your paper and, therefore, won't generally have the luxury of beginning your writing tasks with a definite thesis in mind. But let's assume that you *do* have an area of expertise, that you are in your own right a professional (albeit not in academic matters). We'll assume that you understand some nonacademic subject—say, backpacking—and have been given a clear purpose for writing: to discuss the relative merits of backpack designs. Your job is to write a recommendation for the owner of a sporting-goods chain, suggesting which line of backpacks the chain should carry. Because you already know a good deal about backpacks, you may have some well-developed ideas on the subject before you start doing additional research.

Yet even as an expert in your field, you will find that crafting a thesis is challenging. After all, a thesis is a summary, and it is difficult to summarize a presentation yet to be written—especially if you plan to discover what you want to say during the process of writing. Even if you know your material well, the best you can do at first is to formulate a working thesis—a hypothesis of sorts, a well-informed hunch about your topic and the claim to be made about it. After you have completed a draft, you can evaluate the degree to which your working thesis accurately summarizes the content of your paper. If the match is a good one, the working thesis becomes the thesis. If, however, sections of the paper drift from the focus of the working thesis, you'll need to revise the thesis and the paper itself to ensure that the presentation is unified. (You'll know that the match between content and thesis is a good one when every paragraph directly refers to and develops some element of the thesis.) Later in this chapter we'll discuss revision techniques that will be useful in establishing unity in your work.

This model works whether you are writing about a subject in your area of expertise—backpacking, for example—or one that is more in your professor's territory, such as government or medieval poetry. The difference is that when approaching subjects that are less familiar to you, you will have to spend more time gathering data and brainstorming in order to make assertions about your subject.

Using the Thesis to Plan a Structure

A working thesis will help you sketch the structure of your paper, for the structure flows directly from the thesis. Consider, for example, the third thesis (see p. 236) on fuel-cell technology:

> The federal government should subsidize the development of fuel-cell vehicles as well as the hydrogen infrastructure needed to support them; otherwise, the United States will be increasingly vulnerable to recession and other economic dislocations resulting from our dependence on the continued flow of foreign oil.

This thesis is *strongly argumentative,* or *persuasive.* The economic catastrophes mentioned by the writer indicate a strong degree of urgency in the need for the solution recommended: the federal subsidy of a national hydrogen infrastructure to support fuel-cell vehicles. If a paper based on this thesis is to be well developed, the writer must commit him- or herself to explaining (1) why fuel-cell vehicles are a preferred alternative to gasoline-powered vehicles; (2) why fuel-cell vehicles require a hydrogen infrastructure (i.e., the writer must explain that fuel cells produce power by mixing hydrogen and oxygen, generating both electricity and water in

How Ambitious Should Your Thesis Be?

Writing tasks vary according to the nature of the thesis.

- The *explanatory thesis* is often developed in response to short-answer exam questions that call for information, not analysis (e.g., "How does James Barber categorize the main types of presidential personality?").

- The *mildly argumentative thesis* is appropriate for organizing reports (even lengthy ones), as well as essay questions that call for some analysis (e.g., "Discuss the qualities of a good speech").

- The *strongly argumentative thesis* is used to organize papers and exam questions that call for information, analysis, *and* the writer's forcefully stated point of view (e.g., "Evaluate the proposed reforms of health maintenance organizations").

The strongly argumentative thesis, of course, is the riskiest of the three because you must state your position unequivocally and make it appear reasonable—which requires that you offer evidence and defend against logical objections. But such intellectual risks pay dividends, and if you become involved enough in your work to make challenging assertions, you will provoke challenging responses that enliven classroom discussions and your own learning.

the process); (3) why the government needs to subsidize industry in developing fuel-cell vehicles; and (4) how continued reliance on fossil fuel technology could make the country vulnerable to economic dislocations. This thesis therefore helps the writer plan the paper, which should include a section on each of the four topics. Assuming that the paper follows the organizational plan we've proposed, the working thesis would become the final thesis, on the basis of which a reader could anticipate sections of the paper to come. In a finished product, the thesis becomes an essential tool for guiding readers.

Note, however, that this thesis is still provisional. It may turn out, as you do research or begin drafting, that the paper to which this thesis commits you will be too long and complex. You may therefore decide to drop the second clause of the thesis dealing with the country's vulnerability to economic dislocations and focus on the need for the government to subsidize the development of fuel-cell vehicles and a hydrogen infrastructure, relegating the economic concerns to your conclusion (if at all). If you make this change, your final thesis could read: "The federal government should subsidize the development of fuel-cell vehicles as well as the hydrogen infrastructure needed to support them."

This revised thesis makes an assertive commitment to the subject even though the assertion is not as complex as the original. Still, it is more assertive than the second proposed thesis:

> To reduce our dependence on nonrenewable fossil fuel energy sources, the federal government should encourage the development of fuel-cell vehicles.

Here we have a *mildly argumentative* thesis that enables the writer to express an opinion. We infer from the use of the words "should encourage" that the writer endorses the idea of the government's promoting fuel-cell development. But a government that "encourages" development is making a lesser commitment than one that "subsidizes," which means that it allocates funds for a specific policy. So the writer who argues for mere encouragement takes a milder position than the one who argues for subsidies. Note also the contrast between the second thesis and the first one, in which the writer is committed to no involvement in the debate and suggests no government involvement whatsoever.

> Fuel-cell technology has emerged as a promising approach to developing energy-efficient vehicles.

This, the first of the three thesis statements, is *explanatory,* or *informative.* In developing a paper based on this thesis, the writer is committed only to explaining how fuel-cell technology works and why it is a promising approach to energy-efficient vehicles. Given this thesis, a reader would *not* expect to find the author strongly recommending, for instance, that fuel-cell engines replace internal combustion engines in the near future.

Neither does the thesis require the writer to defend a personal opinion; he or she need only justify the use of the relatively mild term "promising."

As you can see, for any topic you might explore in a paper, you can make any number of assertions—some relatively simple, some complex. It is on the basis of these assertions that you set yourself an agenda for your writing—and readers set for themselves expectations for reading. The more ambitious the thesis, the more complex will be the paper and the greater will be the readers' expectations.

To review: A thesis (a one-sentence summary of your paper) helps you organize your discussion, and it helps your reader anticipate it. Theses are distinguished by their carefully worded subjects and predicates, which should be just broad enough and complex enough to be developed within the length limitations of the assignment. Both novices and experts typically begin the initial draft of a paper with a working thesis—a statement that provides writers with structure enough to get started but with latitude enough to discover what they want to say as they write. Once you have completed a first draft, however, you test the "fit" of your thesis with what you have written. When you have a good fit, every element of the thesis is developed in the paper that follows. Discussions that drift from your thesis should be deleted, or the thesis revised to accommodate the new discussions. These concerns will be addressed more fully when we consider the revision stage of the writing process.

Exercise 6.4

Drafting Thesis Statements

After completing the group exercise in which you narrowed a subject (Exercise 6.2, p. 232) and the individual invention exercise (Exercise 6.3, p. 234), work individually or in small groups to draft three theses in relation to your earlier ideas. Draft one explanatory thesis, one mildly argumentative thesis, and one strongly argumentative thesis.

Writing Introductions and Conclusions

All writers must face the task of writing their paper's introduction and conclusion. How to start? What's the best way to approach your topic? With a serious tone, a light touch, an anecdote? How to end? How best to make the connection from your work back to the reader's world?

Many writers avoid such decisions by putting them off—and productively so. Bypassing careful planning for the introduction and conclusion, they begin writing the body of the piece; only after they've finished the body do they go back to write the opening and closing paragraphs. There's a lot to be said for this approach: Because you have presumably spent more time thinking and writing about the topic itself than about how you're going to introduce or conclude it, you are in a better position to set out your ideas. And often it's not until you've actually seen the piece on paper and read it over once or twice that a natural way of introducing or concluding it becomes apparent. You are generally in better psychological shape to write both the introduction and the conclusion after the major task of writing is behind you and you know exactly what your major points are.

Introductions

The purpose of an introduction is to prepare the reader to enter the world of your paper. The introduction makes the connection between the more familiar world inhabited by the reader and the less familiar world of the writer's topic; it places a discussion in a context that the reader can understand. If you find yourself getting stuck on an introduction at the beginning of a first draft, skip over it for the moment. State your working thesis directly and move on to the body of the paper.

There are many strategies for opening a paper; we'll consider the most common ones.

Quotation   Here are the two introductory paragraphs to an article titled "The Radical Idea of Marrying for Love," from Stephanie Coontz's *Marriage: A History.*

> George Bernard Shaw described marriage as an institution that brings together two people "under the influence of the most violent, most insane, most delusive, and most transient of passions. They are required to swear that they will remain in that excited, abnormal, and exhausting condition continuously until death do them part."
>
> Shaw's comment was amusing when he wrote it at the beginning of the twentieth century, and it still makes us smile today, because it pokes fun at the unrealistic expectations that spring from a dearly held cultural ideal—that marriage should be based on intense, profound love and a couple should maintain their ardor until death do them part. But for thousands of years the joke would have fallen flat.*

The provocative quotation by Shaw is intended by Coontz to puncture our romantic assumptions about the role of love and passion in marriage. She follows the quotation with an explanation of why Shaw's statement "makes us smile" before setting out on her main undertaking in this article—as indicated in the final sentence of the second paragraph—a historical survey demonstrating that for most of the last few thousand years, love and marriage have had little to do with one another. Quoting the words of others offers you many points of departure for your paper: You can agree with the quotation. You can agree and expand. You can sharply disagree. You can use the quotation to set a context or tone.

---

*"The Radical Idea of Marrying for Love," from *Marriage: A History,* by Stephanie Coontz, copyright 2005 by the S.J. Coontz Company. Used by permission of Viking Penguin, a division of Penguin Group (USA), Inc.

Historical Review   In many cases, the reader will be unprepared to follow the issue you discuss unless you provide some historical background. Consider this introduction to a paper on the film-rating system:

> Sex and violence on the screen are not new issues. In the Roaring Twenties there was increasing pressure from civic and religious groups to ban depictions of "immorality" from the screen. Faced with the threat of federal censorship, the film producers decided to clean their own house. In 1930, the Motion Picture Producers and Distributors of America established the Production Code. At first, adherence to the Code was voluntary; but in 1934 Joseph Breen, newly appointed head of the MPPDA, gave the Code teeth. Henceforth all newly produced films had to be submitted for approval to the Production Code Administration, which had the power to award or withhold the Code seal. Without a Code seal, it was virtually impossible for a film to be shown anywhere in the United States, since exhibitors would not accept it. At about the same time, the Catholic Legion of Decency was formed to advise the faithful which films were and were not objectionable. For several decades the Production Code Administration exercised powerful control over what was portrayed in American theatrical films. By the 1960s, however, changing standards of morality had considerably weakened the Code's grip. In 1968, the Production Code was replaced with a rating system designed to keep younger audiences away from films with high levels of sex or violence. Despite its imperfections, this rating system has proved more beneficial to American films than did the old censorship system.

The paper examines the relative benefits of the rating system. By beginning with some historical background on the rating system, the writer helps readers understand his arguments. (Notice the chronological development of details.)

Review of a Controversy   A particular type of historical review provides the background on a controversy or debate. Consider this introduction:

> The *American Heritage Dictionary*'s definition of civil disobedience is rather simple: "the refusal to obey civil laws that are regarded as unjust, usually by employing methods of passive resistance." However, despite such famous (and beloved) examples of civil disobedience as the movements of Mahatma Gandhi in India and the Reverend Martin Luther King, Jr., in the United States, the question of whether or not civil disobedience should be considered an asset to society is hardly clear cut. For instance, Hannah Arendt, in her article "Civil Disobedience," holds that "to think of disobedient minorities as rebels and truants is against the letter and spirit of a constitution whose framers were especially sensitive to the dangers of unbridled majority rule." On the other hand, a noted

lawyer, Lewis Van Dusen, Jr., in his article "Civil Disobedience: Destroyer of Democracy," states that "civil disobedience, whatever the ethical rationalization, is still an assault on our democratic society, an affront to our legal order and an attack on our constitutional government." These two views are clearly incompatible. I believe, though, that Van Dusen's is the more convincing. On balance, civil disobedience is dangerous to society.*

The negative aspects of civil disobedience, rather than Van Dusen's essay, are the topic of this paper. But to introduce this topic, the writer has provided quotations that represent opposing sides of the controversy over civil disobedience, as well as brief references to two controversial practitioners. By focusing at the outset on the particular rather than on the abstract qualities of the topic, the writer hopes to secure the attention of her readers and involve them in the controversy that forms the subject of her paper.

From the General to the Specific   Another way of providing a transition from the reader's world to the less familiar world of the paper is to work from a general subject to a specific one. The following introduction begins a paper on improving our air quality by urging people to trade the use of their cars for public transportation.

> While generalizations are risky, it seems pretty safe to say that most human beings are selfish. Self-interest may be part of our nature, and probably aids the survival of our species, since self-interested pursuits increase the likelihood of individual survival and genetic reproduction. Ironically, however, our selfishness has caused us to abuse the natural environment upon which we depend. We have polluted, deforested, depleted, deformed, and endangered our earth, water, and air to such an extent that now our species' survival is gravely threatened. In America, air pollution is one of our most pressing environmental problems, and it is our selfish use of the automobile that poses the greatest threat to clean air, as well as the greatest challenge to efforts to stop air pollution. Very few of us seem willing to give up our cars, let alone use them less. We are spoiled by the individual freedom afforded us when we can hop into our gas-guzzling vehicles and go where we want, when we want. Somehow, we as a nation will have to wean ourselves from this addiction to the automobile, and we can do this by designing alternative forms of transportation that serve our selfish interests.[†]

---

*Michele Jacques, "Civil Disobedience: Van Dusen vs. Arendt," unpublished paper, 1993, 1. Used by permission.

[†]Travis Knight, "Reducing Air Pollution with Alternative Transportation," unpublished paper, 1998, 1. Used by permission.

Anecdote and Illustration: From the Specific to the General   The following two paragraphs offer an anecdote in order to move from the specific to a general subject:

> The night of March 24, 1989, was cold and calm, the air crystalline, as the giant *Exxon Valdez* oil tanker pulled out of Valdez, Alaska, into the tranquil waters of Prince William Sound. In these clearest of possible conditions the ship made a planned turn out of the shipping channel and didn't turn back in time. The huge tanker ran aground, spilling millions of gallons of crude oil into the sound. The cost of the cleanup effort was over $2 billion. The ultimate cost of continuing environmental damage is incalculable. Furthermore, when the civil trial was finally over in the summer of 1995, the Exxon Corporation was assessed an additional $5 billion in punitive damages. Everyone I query in my travels vividly recalls the accident, and most have the impression that it had something to do with the master's alcohol consumption. No one is aware of the true cause of the tragedy. In its final report, the National Transportation Safety Board (NTSB) found that sleep deprivation and sleep debt were direct causes of the accident. This stunning result got a brief mention in the back pages of the newspapers.
>
> Out of the vast ocean of knowledge about sleep, there are a few facts that are so important that I will try to burn them into your brain forever. None is more important than the topic of sleep debt. If we can learn to understand sleep indebtedness and manage it, we can improve everyday life as well as avoid many injuries, *horribly diminished lives, and premature deaths.**

The previous introduction went from the general (the statement that human beings are selfish) to the specific (how to decrease air pollution). This one goes from the specific (a calamitous oil spill by a giant oil tanker in Alaskan waters) to the general (the enormous financial and human costs of "sleep debt," or not getting enough sleep). The anecdote is one of the most effective means at your disposal for capturing and holding your reader's attention. It is also one of the most commonly used types of introduction in popular articles. For decades, speakers have begun their remarks with a funny, touching, or otherwise appropriate story. (In fact, plenty of books are nothing but collections of such stories, arranged by subject.)

Question   Frequently you can provoke the reader's attention by posing a question or a series of questions:

> **Which of the following people** would you say is the most admirable: Mother Teresa, Bill Gates, or Norman Borlaug? And which do you think is the least admirable? For most people, it's an easy question.

---

*From "The Promise of Sleep," copyright 1999 by William C. Dement. Used by permission of Dell Publishing, a division of Random House, Inc.

Mother Teresa, famous for ministering to the poor in Calcutta, has been beatified by the Vatican, awarded the Nobel Peace Prize and ranked in an American poll as the most admired person of the 20th century. Bill Gates, infamous for giving us the Microsoft dancing paper clip and the blue screen of death, has been decapitated in effigy in "I Hate Gates" Web sites and hit with a pie in the face. As for Norman Borlaug . . . who the heck is Norman Borlaug?

Yet a deeper look might lead you to rethink your answers. Borlaug, father of the "Green Revolution" that used agricultural science to reduce world hunger, has been credited with saving a billion lives, more than anyone else in history. Gates, in deciding what to do with his fortune, crunched the numbers and determined that he could alleviate the most misery by fighting everyday scourges in the developing world like malaria, diarrhea and parasites. Mother Teresa, for her part, extolled the virtue of suffering and ran her well-financed missions accordingly: their sick patrons were offered plenty of prayer but harsh conditions, few analgesics and dangerously primitive medical care.

It's not hard to see why the moral reputations of this trio should be so out of line with the good they have done. . . .*

In this introduction to "The Moral Instinct," Steven Pinker asks a question that appears to be easy; but the answer turns out to be more complex than the average reader would have suspected. Pinker uses the rest of the first paragraph to explain why the question appears to be so easy. (After all, no one was more widely admired than Mother Teresa; and for many people— especially Apple partisans!—former Microsoft CEO Bill Gates was an emblem of capitalist greed.) In the second paragraph, Pinker overturns these assumptions as he begins his exploration of the moral sense. Opening your paper with a question can be provocative because it places the reader in an active role. Put on the spot by the author, he or she must consider answers— in this case, Who *is* the most admirable? What kind of qualities or activities *should* we admire? An opening question, chosen well, will engage readers and launch them into your paper.

Statement of Thesis   Perhaps the most direct method of introduction is to begin immediately with the thesis:

The contemporary American shopping mall is the formal garden of late twentieth-century culture, a commodified version of the great garden styles of Western history with which it shares fundamental characteristics. Set apart from the rest of the world as a place of earthly delight like the medieval walled garden; filled with fountains, statuary, and ingeniously devised machinery like the Italian Renaissance garden; designed on grandiose and symmetrical principles like the seventeenth-century French garden; made up of the fragments of cultural and architectural history like the eighteenth-century irregular

---

*Steven J. Pinker, "The Moral Instinct," *New York Times Magazine* 12 Jan. 2008.

English garden; and set aside for the public like the nineteenth-century American park, the mall is the next phase of this garden history, a synthesis of all these styles that have come before. But it is now joined with the shopping street, or at least a sanitized and standardized version of one, something that never before has been allowed within the garden.*

This selection begins with a general assertion—that the American shopping mall is analogous to the great formal gardens of Western history. This idea is Richard Keller Simon's thesis, for an article titled "The Formal Garden in the Age of Consumer Culture," which he begins to develop in his second sentence with comparisons between the modern shopping mall and various types of gardens throughout history. In the paragraphs following this introduction, Simon draws correspondences between contemporary shopping malls in Houston, Philadelphia, and Palo Alto and such classic formal gardens as Henry VIII's Hampton Court. The "promenades, walls, vistas, mounts, labyrinths, statues, archways" of classic gardens, he writes, all have their analogs in the modern mall. Beginning with a thesis statement (as opposed to a quotation, question, or anecdote) works well when you want to develop an unexpected, or controversial, argument. The mall as a formal garden? Who would think so? We read on.

Or perhaps you open with the provocative assertion that "Reading is dead" in a paper examining the problem of declining literacy in the digital age. The reader sits up and takes notice, perhaps even protesting ("No, it's not—I read all the time!"). This strategy "hooks" a reader, who is likely to want to find out how you will support such an emphatic thesis.

One final note about our model introductions: They may be longer than introductions you have been accustomed to writing. Many writers (and readers) prefer a shorter, snappier introduction. The length of an introduction can depend on the length of the paper it introduces, and it is also largely a matter of personal or corporate style. There is no rule concerning the correct length of an introduction. If you feel that a short introduction is appropriate, use one. Or you may wish to break up what seems like a long introduction into two paragraphs.

Exercise 6.5

Drafting Introductions

Imagine that you are writing a paper using the topic, ideas, and thesis you developed in the exercises in this chapter. Conduct some preliminary research on the topic, using an Internet search engine such as *Google* or an article

---

*Excerpted from "The Formal Garden in the Age of Consumer Culture: A Reading of the Twentieth-Century Shopping Mall," copyright 1992 by Richard Keller Simon. Reprinted from *Mapping the American Culture*, ed. Wayne Franklin and Michael Steiner, by permission of the University of Iowa Press.

database available at your college. Choose one of the seven types of introductions we've discussed—preferably one you have never used before—and draft an introduction that would work to open a paper on your topic. Use our examples as models to help you draft your introduction.

Conclusions

One way to view the conclusion of your paper is to see it as an introduction in reverse, a bridge from the world of your paper back to the world of your reader. A conclusion is the part of your paper in which you restate and (if necessary) expand on your thesis. Essential to many conclusions is the summary, which is not merely a repetition of the thesis but a restatement that takes advantage of the material you've presented. *The simplest conclusion is a summary of the paper, but you should want more than this.* Depending on your needs, you might offer a summary and then build onto it a discussion of the paper's significance or its implications for future study, for choices that individuals might make, for policy, and so on. You might also want to urge readers to change an attitude or modify behavior. Certainly, you are under no obligation to discuss the broader significance of your work (and a summary, alone, will satisfy the formal requirement that your paper have an ending); but the conclusions of better papers often reveal that authors are "thinking large" and want to connect their concerns with the broader concerns of society.

Two words of advice: First, no matter how clever or beautifully executed, a conclusion cannot salvage a poorly written paper. Second, by virtue of its placement, the conclusion carries rhetorical weight; it is the last statement a reader will encounter before turning from your work. Realizing this, writers who expand on the basic summary conclusion often wish to give their final words a dramatic flourish, a heightened level of diction. Soaring rhetoric and drama in a conclusion are fine as long as they do not unbalance the paper and call attention to themselves. Having labored long hours over your paper, you may be inclined at this point to wax eloquent. But keep a sense of proportion and timing; make your points quickly and end crisply.

Statement of the Subject's Significance   One of the more effective ways to conclude a paper is to discuss the larger significance of what you have written, providing readers with one more reason to regard your work as a serious effort. When using this strategy, you move from the specific concern of your paper to the broader concerns of the reader's world. Often, you will need to choose among a range of significances: A paper on the Wright brothers might end with a discussion of air travel as it affects economies, politics, or families; a paper on contraception might end with a discussion of its effect on sexual mores, population, or the church. But don't overwhelm your reader with the importance of your remarks. Keep your discussion well focused.

The following paragraph by June J. Pilcher and Amy S. Walters concludes a paper on how "sleep debt" hurts college students.

> In sum, our findings suggest that college students are not aware of the extent to which sleep deprivation impairs their ability to complete cognitive tasks successfully because they consistently overrate their concentration and effort, as well as their estimated performance. In addition, the current data suggest that 24 hours of sleep deprivation significantly affects only fatigue and confusion and does not have a more general effect on positive or negative mood states. The practical implication of these findings is that many college students are unknowingly sabotaging their own performance by choosing to deprive themselves of sleep [while] they complete complex cognitive tasks.*

The first sentence (as the initial phrase indicates) summarizes the chief finding of the study on which the authors have written. They expand on this conclusion before ending with a statement of the subject's significance ("The practical implication of these findings is that . . ."). Ending the paper in this fashion is another way of saying, "The conclusions of this paper matter." If you have taken the trouble to write a good paper, the conclusions *do* matter. Don't be bashful: State the larger significance of the point(s) you have made. Just don't claim too great a significance for your work, lest by overreaching you pop the balloon and your reader thinks, "No, the paper's not *that* important."

Call for Further Research In the scientific and social scientific communities, papers often end with a review of what has been presented (as, for instance, in an experiment) and the ways in which the subject under consideration needs to be further explored. *A word of caution:* If you raise questions that you call on others to answer, make sure you know that the research you are calling for hasn't already been conducted.

The following conclusion comes from a sociological report on the placement of elderly men and women in nursing homes.

> Thus, our study shows a correlation between the placement of elderly citizens in nursing facilities and the significant decline of their motor and intellectual skills over the ten months following placement. What the research has not made clear is the extent to which this marked decline is due to physical as opposed to emotional causes. The elderly are referred to homes at that point in their lives when they grow less able to care for themselves—which suggests that the drop-off in skills

---

*"How Sleep Deprivation Affects Psychological Variables Related to College Students' Cognitive Performance" by June J. Pilcher and Amy S. Walters, from *Journal of American College Health*, Vol. 46, issue 3, November 1997, pp. 121–126. Reprinted with permission of the Helen Dwight Reid Educational Foundation. Published by Heldref Publications, 1319 Eighteenth St., N.W., Washington, DC 20036-1802. Copyright 1997.

may be due to physical causes. But the emotional stress of being placed in a home, away from family and in an environment that confirms the patient's view of himself as decrepit, may exacerbate—if not itself be a primary cause of—the patient's rapid loss of abilities. Further research is needed to clarify the relationship between depression and particular physical ailments as these affect the skills of the elderly in nursing facilities. There is little doubt that information yielded by such studies can enable health care professionals to deliver more effective services.*

Notice how this call for further study locates the author in a larger community of researchers on whom he depends for assistance in answering the questions that have come out of his own work. The author summarizes his findings (in the first sentence of the paragraph), states what his work has not shown, and then extends his invitation.

Solution/Recommendation   The purpose of your paper might be to review a problem or controversy and to discuss contributing factors. In such a case, it would be appropriate, after summarizing your discussion, to offer a solution based on the knowledge you've gained while conducting research, as the writer of the following conclusion does. If your solution is to be taken seriously, however, your knowledge must be amply demonstrated in the body of the paper.

The major problem in college sports today is not commercialism—it is the exploitation of athletes and the proliferation of illicit practices which dilute educational standards.

Many universities are currently deriving substantial benefits from sports programs that depend on the labor of athletes drawn from the poorest sections of America's population. It is the responsibility of educators, civil rights leaders, and concerned citizens to see that these young people get a fair return for their labor both in terms of direct remuneration and in terms of career preparation for a life outside sports.

Minimally, scholarships in revenue-producing sports should be designed to extend until graduation, rather than covering only four years of athletic eligibility, and should include guarantees of tutoring, counseling, and proper medical care. At institutions where the profits are particularly large (such as Texas A & M, which can afford to pay its football coach $280,000 a year), scholarships should also provide salaries that extend beyond room, board, and tuition. The important thing is that the athlete be remunerated fairly and have the opportunity to gain skills from a university environment without undue competition from a physically and psychologically demanding full-time job. This may well require that scholarships be extended over five or six years, including summers.

---

*Adam Price, "The Crisis in Nursing Home Care," unpublished paper, 2001. Used by permission.

Such a proposal, I suspect, will not be easy to implement. The current amateur system, despite its moral and educational flaws, enables universities to hire their athletic labor at minimal cost. But solving the fiscal crisis of the universities on the backs of America's poor and minorities is not, in the long run, a tenable solution. With the support of concerned educators, parents, and civil rights leaders, and with the help from organized labor, the college athlete, truly a sleeping giant, will someday speak out and demand what is rightly his—and hers—a fair share of the revenue created by their hard work.*

In this conclusion, the author summarizes his article in one sentence: "The major problem in college sports today is not commercialism—it is the exploitation of athletes and the proliferation of illicit practices which dilute educational standards." In paragraph 2, he continues with an analysis of the problem just stated and follows with a general recommendation that "educators, civil rights leaders, and concerned citizens" be responsible for the welfare of college athletes. In paragraph 3, he makes a specific proposal, and in the final paragraph, he anticipates resistance to the proposal. He concludes by discounting this resistance and returning to the general point, that college athletes should receive a fair deal.

Anecdote   As you learned in the context of introductions, an anecdote is a briefly told story or joke, the point of which is to shed light on your subject. The anecdote is more direct than an allusion. With an allusion, you merely refer to a story ("Too many people today live in Plato's cave . . ."); with the anecdote, you retell the story. The anecdote allows readers to discover for themselves the significance of a reference to another source—an effort most readers enjoy because they get to exercise their creativity.

The following anecdote concludes a political-philosophical essay. First, the author sums up her argument in a paragraph, then she follows that with a brief story.

Ironically, our economy is fueled by the very thing that degrades our value system. But when politicians call for a return to "traditional family values," they seldom criticize the business interests that promote and benefit from our coarsened values. Consumer capitalism values things over people; it thrives on discontent and unhappiness since discontented people make excellent consumers, buying vast numbers of things that may somehow "fix" their inadequacies. We buy more than we need, the economy chugs along, but such materialism is the real culprit behind our warped value systems. Anthony de Mello tells the following story:

Socrates believed that the wise person would instinctively lead a frugal life, and he even went so far as to refuse to wear shoes. Yet

---

*Mark Naison, "Scenario for Scandal," *Commonweal* 109.16 (1982).

> he constantly fell under the spell of the marketplace and would go there often to look at the great variety and magnificence of the wares on display.
>
> A friend once asked him why he was so intrigued with the allures of the market. "I love to go there," Socrates replied, "to discover how many things I am perfectly happy without."*

The writer chose to conclude her article with this anecdote. She could have developed an interpretation, but this would have spoiled the dramatic value for the reader. The purpose of using an anecdote is to make your point with subtlety, to resist the temptation to interpret. When selecting an anecdote, keep in mind four guidelines: The anecdote should fit your content, it should be prepared for (readers should have all the information they need to understand it), it should provoke the readers' interest, and it should not be so obscure as to be unintelligible.

Quotation   A favorite concluding device is the quotation—the words of a famous person or an authority in the field on which you are writing. The purpose of quoting another is to link your work to theirs, thereby gaining for your work authority and credibility. The first criterion for selecting a quotation is its suitability to your thesis. But consider carefully what your choice of sources says about you. Suppose you are writing a paper on the American work ethic. If you could use a line by the comedian Jon Stewart or one by the current secretary of labor to make the final point of your conclusion, which would you choose and why? One source may not be inherently more effective than the other, but the choice certainly sets a tone for the paper. The following paragraph concludes an article on single-sex education:

> But schools, inevitably, present many curriculums, some overt and some subtle; and critics argue that with Sax's** model comes a lesson that our gender differences are primary, and this message is at odds with one of the most foundational principles of America's public schools. Given the myriad ways in which our schools are failing, it may be hard to remember that public schools were intended not only to instruct children in reading and math but also to teach them commonality, tolerance and what it means to be American. "When you segregate, by any means, you lose some of that," says Richard Kahlenberg, a senior fellow at the Century Foundation. "Even if one could prove that sending a kid off to his or her own school based on religion or race or ethnicity or gender did a little bit better job of raising the academic skills for workers in the economy, there's also the issue of trying to create tolerant citizens in a democracy."†

---

*Frances Wageneck, "Family Values in the Marketplace," unpublished paper, 2000. Used by permission.

**Leonard Sax is a psychologist and physician who gave up medicine to devote himself to promoting single-sex public education.

†Elizabeth Weil, "Teaching Boys and Girls Separately," *New York Times Magazine* 2 Mar. 2008.

In the article leading up to this conclusion, Elizabeth Weil takes a somewhat skeptical view of the virtues of "teaching boys and girls separately." She concludes with an apt quotation by Richard Kahlenberg who, while conceding some value for single-sex education, supports Weil's own skepticism by suggesting that single-sex education may not create citizens as tolerant as those who have been through classes that include both genders.

Using quotations poses one potential problem: If you end with the words of another, you may leave the impression that someone else can make your case more eloquently than you. The language of the quotation will put your own prose into relief. If your prose suffers by comparison—if the quotations are the best part of your paper—you need to spend time revising. Avoid this kind of problem by making your own presentation a strong one.

Question   Questions are useful for opening papers, and they are just as useful for closing them. Opening and closing questions function in different ways, however. The introductory question promises to be addressed in the article that follows. But the concluding question leaves issues unresolved, calling on the readers to assume an active role by offering their own answers. Consider the following two paragraphs, written to conclude an article on genetically modified (GM) food:

> Are GM foods any more of a risk than other agricultural innovations that have taken place over the years, like selective breeding? Do the existing and potential future benefits of GM foods outweigh any risks that do exist? And what standard should governments use when assessing the safety of transgenic crops? The "frankenfood" frenzy has given life to a policy-making standard known as the "precautionary principle," which has been long advocated by environmental groups. That principle essentially calls for governments to prohibit any activity that raises concerns about human health or the environment, even if some cause-and-effect relationships are not fully established scientifically. As Liberal Democrat MP [Member of Parliament] Norman Baker told the BBC: "We must always apply the precautionary principle. That says that unless you're sure of adequate control, unless you're sure the risk is minimal, unless you're sure nothing horrible can go wrong, you don't do it."
>
> But can any innovation ever meet such a standard of certainty—especially given the proliferation of "experts" that are motivated as much by politics as they are by science? And what about those millions of malnourished people whose lives could be saved by transgenic foods?*

Rather than end with a question, you may choose to *raise* a question in your conclusion and then answer it, based on the material you've provided in the paper. The answered question challenges a reader to agree or disagree

---

*"Frankenfoods Frenzy," *Reason* 13 Jan. 2000.

with you and thus places the reader in an active role. The following brief conclusion ends a student paper titled "Is Feminism Dead?"

> So the answer to the question "Is the feminist movement dead?" is no, it's not. Even if most young women today don't consciously identify themselves as "feminists"—due to the ways in which the term has become loaded with negative associations—the principles of gender equality that lie at feminism's core are enthusiastically embraced by the vast number of young women, and even a large percentage of young men.

Speculation   When you speculate, you ask about and explore what has happened or what might happen. Speculation involves a spinning out of possibilities. It stimulates readers by immersing them in your discussion of the unknown, implicitly challenging them to agree or disagree. The following paragraph concludes a brief article, "The Incandescent Charisma of the Lonely Light Bulb" by Dan Neil. The author laments the passing of the familiar electric light bulb (in favor of lower wattage compact fluorescent lights) as one more indication of the end of the analog age and the triumph of the digital: "The demise of the light bulb marks the final transition from electrics to electronics":

> The passing of any technology provokes nostalgia. I'm sure someone bemoaned the rise of the push-button phone and eulogized the rotary dialer. (*What a beautiful sound, the "shickity-shick" of a well-spun number. . . .*) But the Edisonian light bulb is a more fundamental thing—so much the proverbial better idea that it came to symbolize the eureka moment, the flash of insight, when it appeared over a cartoon character's head. The fact is, how we light the world inevitably affects how we see the world. I predict we're going to miss the soft, forgiving light of the incandescent bulb with its celestial geometry. *I predict a more harshly lighted future.**

The author's concluding speculation may not be entirely serious (though a few people do lament the passing of the manual typewriter and the phonograph record), but it does highlight what is often lost, and subsequently missed, in the relentless journey of technological progress. If you have provided the necessary information prior to a concluding speculation, you will send readers back into their lives (and away from your paper) with an implicit challenge: Do they regard the future as you do? Whether they do or do not, you have set an agenda. You have got them thinking.

---

*Dan Neil, "The Incandescent Charisma of the Lonely Light Bulb," *Los Angeles Times Magazine* 3 Feb. 2008: 70.

Drafting Conclusions

Imagine that you have written a paper using the topic, ideas, and thesis you developed in the earlier exercises in this chapter. Conduct some preliminary research on the topic, using an Internet search engine such as *Google* or an article database available at your college. Choose one of the seven types of conclusions we've discussed—preferably one you have never used before—and draft a conclusion that would work to end your paper. Use our examples as models to help you draft your conclusion.

■ STAGE 5: REVISION

Perhaps it's stating the obvious to say that rough drafts need revision, but we find that too often students skimp on this phase of the writing process. The word *revision* can be used to describe all modifications one makes to a written document. However, it's useful to distinguish among three kinds of revision.

> *Global revisions* focus on the thesis, the type and pattern of evidence employed, the overall organization, the match between thesis and content, and the tone. A global revision may also emerge from a change in purpose.
>
> *Local revisions* focus on paragraphs: topic and transitional sentences; the type of evidence presented within a paragraph; evidence added, modified, or dropped within a paragraph; and logical connections from one sentence (or set of sentences) within a paragraph to another.
>
> *Surface revisions* deal with sentence style and construction as well as word choice. Sentence editing involves correcting errors of grammar, mechanics, spelling, and citation form.

Global and local revisions fall within Stage 5 of the writing process; surface revisions are covered in Stage 6, editing.

We advise separating large-scale (global and local) revision from later (sentence-editing) revision as a way of keeping priorities in order. If you take care of larger, global problems, you may find that in the process you have fixed or simply dropped awkward sentences. Get the large pieces in place first: *content* (your ideas), *structure* (the arrangement of your paragraphs), and *paragraph structure* (the arrangement of ideas within your paragraphs). Then tend to the smaller elements, much as you would in building a house. You wouldn't lay the carpet before setting the floor joists.

Think of revision as re-vision, or "seeing anew." In order to re-see, it's often useful to set your paper aside for a time and come back later to view your rough draft with a fresh eye. Doing so will better allow you to determine whether your work exhibits the characteristics of a good paper.

Characteristics of Good Papers

Apply the principles of *unity, coherence,* and *development* to the revision process. Let's start with unity, which we've already discussed in the context of the thesis.

Unity

A paper is unified when it is focused on a main point. The chief tool for achieving paper unity is the thesis, as we've noted: It's hard to achieve unity in a paper when a central point remains unstated. Unity, however, doesn't stop at the thesis; the body paragraphs that follow must clearly support and explain that thesis. Thus, the steps for determining unity are to examine your introduction and make sure you have a clear, identifiable thesis; to check your paper's interior paragraphs to make sure your points all relate to that thesis; and to ask yourself how your conclusion provides closure to your overall discussion.

Coherence

Coherence means "logical interconnectedness." When things cohere, elements come together and make a whole. As applied to paper writing, coherence is very closely related to unity: Good papers cohere. They hold together logically and stay focused on a main point. All subordinate points addressed in the body of the paper clearly relate to the main point expressed in the thesis. Moreover, all those subpoints, examples, and supporting quotations are presented in a logical order so that connections between them are clear. You could write a highly unified paper, but if your points are discussed in a haphazard order, the reader will have a hard time following your argument or staying focused on your point. Lead readers along with your writing. Show them not only how subpoints relate to the main point, but also how they relate to one another.

Development

Good papers are also well developed, meaning that their points are fully explained and supported. Readers do not live inside your head. They will not fully understand your points unless you adequately explain them. A reader may not be persuaded that your paper's main point is valid unless you provide sufficient support for your arguments by using examples, the opinions of authorities on the subject, and your own sound logic to hold it all together.

Use the three principles of unity, coherence, and development to analyze what you have written, and make necessary revisions. Does your paper stay focused on the main point? Do your paper's points clearly relate to each other? Do you need better transitions between some paragraphs to help the ideas flow more logically and smoothly? Have you fully explained and given adequate support for all your points?

These three principles for good papers also apply to the composition of good paragraphs. Paragraphs are "minipapers": they should stick to a main point (the topic sentence) and fully develop that point in an orderly fashion. Transitional words or phrases such as *however, thus, on the other hand,* and *for example* help make clear to a reader how the sentences within individual paragraphs are related.

The Reverse Outline

The *reverse outline* is a useful technique for refining a working thesis and for establishing unity between your thesis statement and the body of your paper. When you outline a paper you intend to write, you do so *prospectively*—that is, before the fact of writing. In a reverse outline you outline the paper *retrospectively*—after the fact. The reverse outline is useful for spotting gaps in logic or development as well as problems with unity or coherence. Follow these steps to generate a reverse outline:

1. On a fresh sheet of paper (or electronic document), restate your thesis, making certain that the thesis you began with is the thesis that in fact governs the logic of the paper. (Look for a competing thesis in your conclusion. In summing up, you may have clarified for yourself what your *actual* governing idea is, as opposed to the idea you thought would organize the paper.)

2. In the margin of your draft, summarize *each* paragraph in a phrase. If you have trouble writing a summary, place an asterisk by the paragraph as a reminder to clarify it later.

3. Beneath your thesis, write your paragraph-summary phrases, one to a line, in outline format.

4. Review the outline you have just created. Is the paper divided into readily identifiable major points in support of the thesis? Have you supported each major point sufficiently? Do the sections of the outline lead logically from one to the next? Do all sections develop the thesis?

5. Watch especially for uneven development. Add or delete material as needed to ensure a balanced presentation.

■ STAGE 6: EDITING

After revising a paper's large-scale elements—its unity, coherence, and content development; its overall structure; and its paragraph structure—you are ready to polish your paper by editing its sentences for style and correctness. At this stage you may be tired, and the temptation to merely correct the obvious mistake here and there may be strong. Resist that impulse: A paper with excellent ideas and structure can be ruined by mechanical, sentence-level errors. After all your work, you don't want readers to be distracted by sentence or punctuation errors.

Editing for Style

Developing an engaging writing style takes long practice. It's beyond the scope of this book to teach you the nuances of writing style, and you can consult many fine books for help. (See, for example, William Zinsser's *On Writing Well.*) Here we'll focus on just one common stylistic problem: short, choppy sentences.

Perhaps out of fear of making sentence errors such as run-ons or comma splices, some writers avoid varying their sentence types, preferring strings of simple sentences. The result is usually unsatisfying. Compare, for instance, two versions of the same paragraph on a study of the human genome:

> Scientists have finally succeeded in decoding the human genome. This accomplishment opens up a whole new field of study. Researchers now have new ways to understand human biological functioning. We may also be able to learn new perspectives on human behavior. For centuries people have wondered about how much we are shaped by genetics. They have also wondered how much environment shapes us. The age-old questions about nature vs. nurture may now be answered. Each individual's genetic heritage as well as his or her genetic future will be visible to geneticists. All of these discoveries may help us to improve and extend human life. Many diseases will be detectable. New treatments will be developed. These new discoveries open up a new area of ethical debate. Scientists and the public are going to have to decide how far to take this new genetic technology.

This paragraph illustrates the problems with choppy, repetitive sentences. First, the writer hasn't connected ideas, and sentences don't flow smoothly from one to the next. Second, the same sentence structure (the simple sentence) appears monotonously, each following the simple subject-predicate form. The result, while grammatically correct, taxes the reader's patience. Compare the preceding version to this revision (which represents just one way the paragraph could be rewritten):

> Scientists have opened a whole new field of study following their recent decoding of the human genome. Armed with new ways of understanding human biological and behavioral functioning, researchers may someday sort out the extent to which we are shaped by our genes and by our environment. When geneticists can examine an individual's genetic past and future, they may also be able to alter these things, with the goal of improving and extending human life through early disease detection and the development of new treatments. However, such promise is not without its pitfalls: genetic research must be scrutinized from an ethical standpoint, and scientists and the public will have to decide the uses and the limits of this new technology.

Not only is the revised version of this paragraph more pleasant to read, it's also more concise, clear, and coherent. Sentences with related content have been combined. Brief sentences have been converted to clauses or phrases and incorporated into the structure of other sentences to form more complex units of meaning.

Guard against strings of short, choppy sentences in your own writing. Learn strategies for sentence-level revision by learning how different sentence structures work. You can link related ideas with subordinating conjunctions (*because, since, while, although,* etc.), commas and coordinating conjunctions (*for, and, nor, but, or, yet, so*), and semicolons and coordinating adverbs (*however, thus, therefore,* etc.).

Editing for Correctness

On matters of sentence style, there is no "correct" approach. Each writer will have a different idea about what sentence structures, sentence lengths, and word choices sound best and best convey meaning. Often, personal style and taste influence sentence construction. Grammar and punctuation, on the other hand, follow more widely accepted, objective standards. Of these we (and your instructors) can speak in terms of "correctness"—of agreed-upon conventions, or rules, that people working in academic, professional, and business environments adopt as a standard of communication. You will find the rules (for comma placement, say, or the use of "amount" versus "number" and "affect" versus "effect") in up-to-date writing handbooks. Review the list in the Common Sentence-level Errors box, and eliminate such errors from your papers before submitting them.

The Final Draft

When you have worked on a paper for days (or weeks), writing and revising several drafts, you may have trouble knowing when you're finished. Speaking of poetry, the Pulitzer Prize–winning poet Henry Taylor once remarked that a writer is done when revisions begin to move the project laterally instead of vertically. We think the same distinction applies to academic writing. Assuming you have revised at the sentence level for grammar and punctuation, when you get the impression that your changes *do not actively advance* the main point with new facts or arguments or illustrations or supporting quotations, you are probably done. Stop writing and prepare a clean draft. Set it aside for a day or two (if you have that luxury), and read it one last time to catch remaining sentence-level errors.

Most difficult will be deciding when the paper is done stylistically, especially for the papers you care most deeply about. With respect to style,

Common Sentence-level Errors

ERRORS IN GRAMMAR

Sentence fragments—word groups lacking a subject or a predicate

Run-on sentences—two independent clauses joined without the proper conjunction (connecting word) or punctuation

Comma splices—two independent clauses joined by a comma alone when they need stronger linkage such as a coordinating conjunction, a conjunctive adverb, a semicolon, or a period

Subject-verb agreement errors—the verb form doesn't match the plural or singular nature of the subject

Pronoun usage—pronoun reference errors, lack of clarity in pronoun reference, or errors of pronoun-antecedent agreement

ERRORS IN PUNCTUATION

Misplaced commas, missing commas, improper use of semicolons or colons, missing apostrophes, and the like

ERRORS IN SPELLING

Misspelled words

---

one could revise endlessly—and many writers do because there is no one correct way (stylistically speaking) to write a sentence. As long as a sentence is grammatical, you can write it numerous ways. Still, if a given sentence is dull, you will want to improve it, for an excessively dull style will bore the reader and defeat the paper as surely as a flawed argument or a host of grammatical errors. But having devoted time to polishing your sentences, you will at some point need to pronounce yourself finished. When your changes make your work merely different, not better, stop.

Your instructor will (likely) return the paper with comments and suggestions. Read them carefully. If you or the instructor feels that a revision is appropriate, think through the options for recasting the paper. Instructors generally respond well when you go into a conference with an action plan.

At some point, instructor's comments or no, the paper will be done and graded. Read it through one last time, and learn from it. Once you have determined what you did well and what you could improve on for the next effort, it is time to move on.

WRITING ASSIGNMENT: PROCESS

Choose either of the following writing assignments.

1. Write a paper following the process outlined in this chapter. As a guide, you may want to complete Exercises 6.1–6.6, which will serve as prompts. As you write, keep a log in which you record brief observations about each stage of the writing process. Share the log with your classmates and discuss the writing process with them.

2. In this chapter you have learned to approach writing as a task divided into stages that blend together and loop back on one another: data gathering, invention, drafting, revision, and editing. Write a one- or two-page statement in which you compare your writing process *prior* to taking a composition course to the process you've learned from this text and from your instructor. What are the salient differences? similarities? At the end of your statement, you may want to speculate on the ways you might alter this process to better suit you.

Locating, Mining, and Citing Sources

7

■ SOURCE-BASED PAPERS

Summaries, critiques, and analyses are generally based on only one or two sources. Syntheses, by definition, are based on multiple sources. But whatever you call the final product, the quality of your paper will be directly related to your success in locating and using a sufficient number of relevant, significant, reliable, and up-to-date sources.

Research involves many of the skills we have been discussing in this book. It requires you to (1) locate and take notes on relevant sources; (2) organize your findings; (3) summarize, paraphrase, or quote these sources accurately and ethically; (4) critically evaluate them for their value and relevance to your subject; (5) synthesize information and ideas from several sources that best support your own critical viewpoint; and (6) analyze subjects for meaning and significance.

The model argument synthesis in Chapter 4, "Balancing Privacy and Safety in the Wake of Virginia Tech" (pp. 161–169), is an example of a research paper that fulfills these requirements.

Where Do We Find Written Research?

Here are just a few of the types of writing that involve research:

ACADEMIC WRITING

- **Research papers** research an issue and incorporate the results of that research.
- **Literature reviews** research and review relevant studies and approaches to a particular science or social-science topic.
- **Experimental reports** research previous studies in order to refine— or show need for—a new approach; they may also report on primary research.
- **Case studies** conduct and report the results of both primary and secondary research.
- **Position papers** research approaches to an issue in order to formulate a new approach.

(continues)

WORKPLACE WRITING

- **Reports** in business, science, engineering, social services, medicine
- **Market analyses**
- **Business plans**
- **Environmental impact reports**
- **Legal research:** memoranda of points and authorities

Writing the Research Paper

Here is an overview of the main steps involved in writing research papers. Keep in mind that, as with other writing projects, writing such papers is a recursive process. For instance, you will gather data at various stages of your writing, as the list below illustrates.

DEVELOPING THE RESEARCH QUESTION

- *Find a subject.* Decide what subject you are going to research and write about.
- *Develop a research question.* Formulate an important question that you would like to answer through your research.

LOCATING SOURCES

- *Conduct preliminary research.* Consult knowledgeable people, general and specialized encyclopedias, overviews and bibliographies in recent books, the *Bibliographic Index*, and subject heading guides.
- *Refine your research question.* Based on your preliminary research, brainstorm about your topic and ways to answer your research question. Sharpen your focus, refining your question and planning the sources you'll need to consult.
- *Conduct focused research.* Consult books, electronic databases, general and specialized periodicals, biographical indexes, general and specialized dictionaries, government publications, and other appropriate sources. Conduct interviews and surveys, as necessary.

MINING SOURCES

- *Develop a working thesis.* Based on your initial research, formulate a working thesis that attempts to respond to your research question.
- *Develop a working bibliography.* Keep track of your sources, either on paper or electronically, including both bibliographic information and key points about each source. Make this bibliography easy to sort and rearrange.

(continues)

- *Evaluate sources.* Attempt to determine the veracity and reliability of your sources; use your critical reading skills; check *Book Review Digest*; look up biographies of authors.

- *Take notes from sources.* Paraphrase and summarize important information and ideas from your sources. Copy down important quotations. Note page numbers from sources of this quoted and summarized material.

- *Develop a working outline and arrange your notes according to your outline.*

DRAFTING; CITING SOURCES

- *Write your draft.* Write the preliminary draft of your paper, working from your notes, according to your outline.

- *Avoid plagiarism.* Take care to cite all quoted, paraphrased, and summarized source material, making sure that your own wording and sentence structure differ from those of your sources.

- *Cite sources.* Use in-text citations and a Works Cited or References list, according to the conventions of the discipline (e.g., MLA, APA, CSE).

REVISING (GLOBAL AND LOCAL CHANGES)

- *Revise your draft.* Consider global, local, surface revisions. Check that your thesis still fits with your paper's focus. Review topic sentences and paragraph development and logic. Use transitional words and phrases to ensure coherence. Make sure that the research paper reads smoothly and clearly from beginning to end.

EDITING (SURFACE CHANGES)

- *Edit your draft.* Check for style, combining short, choppy sentences and ensuring variety in your sentence structures. Check for grammatical correctness, punctuation, and spelling.

■ THE RESEARCH QUESTION

Research handbooks generally advise students to narrow their subjects as much as possible, as we discussed in Chapter 6. A ten-page paper on the modern feminist movement would be unmanageable. You would have to do an enormous quantity of research (a preliminary computer search of this subject would yield several thousand items), and you couldn't hope to produce anything other than a superficial treatment of such a broad subject. You could, however, write a paper on the contemporary feminist response to a particular social issue, or the relative power of current feminist political organizations. It's difficult to say, however, how narrow is narrow enough. (A literary critic once produced a twenty-page article analyzing the first paragraph of Henry James's *The Ambassadors*.)

Perhaps more helpful as a guideline on focusing your research is to seek to answer a particular question, a *research question*. For example, how did the Bush administration respond to criticisms of its policies on the detention of "enemy combatants"? To what extent is American power perceived by foreign observers to be in decline? What factors led to the collapse of the housing market? How has the debate over genetic engineering evolved during the past decade? To what extent do contemporary cigarette ads perpetuate sexist attitudes? Or how do contemporary cigarette ads differ in message and tone from cigarette ads in the 1950s? Focusing on questions such as these and approaching your research as a way of answering such questions is probably the best way to narrow your subject and ensure focus in your paper. The essential answer to this research question eventually becomes your *thesis*, which we discussed in Chapter 6; in the paper, you present evidence that systematically supports your thesis.

Narrowing the Subject via Research

If you need help narrowing a broad subject, try one or more of the following:

- Search by subject in an electronic database to see how the subject breaks down into components.

- Search the subject heading in an electronic periodical catalog, such as *InfoTrac*®, or in a print catalog such as the *Readers' Guide to Periodical Literature*.

- Search the *Library of Congress Subject Headings* catalog (see Subject-Heading Guides, p. 269, for details).

Exercise 7.1

Constructing Research Questions

Moving from a broad topic or idea to the formulation of precise research questions can be challenging. Practice this skill by working with small groups of your classmates to construct research questions about the following topics (or come up with topics of your own). Write at least one research question for each topic listed, then discuss these topics and questions with the other groups in class.

Racial or gender stereotypes in television shows

Drug addiction in the U.S. adult population

Global environmental policies

Employment trends in high-technology industries

U.S. energy policy

■ LOCATING SOURCES ■

Once you have a research question, you want to see what references are available. You'll begin with what we call "preliminary research," in which you familiarize yourself quickly with the basic issues and generate a preliminary list of sources. This effort will help you refine your research question and conduct efficient research when you move into the stage that we call "focused research."

Types of Research Data *(see also Chapter 6, pp. 228–229)*

PRIMARY SOURCES

- Data gathered using research methods appropriate to a particular field

    sciences: experiments, observations

    social sciences: experiments, surveys, interviews

    humanities: diaries, letters, and other unpublished documents; close reading, observation, and interpretation

SECONDARY SOURCES

- Information and ideas collected or generated by others who have performed their own primary and/or secondary research

    library research: books, periodicals, etc.

    online research

■ PRELIMINARY RESEARCH

You can go about finding preliminary sources in many ways; some of the more effective ones are listed in the box on the next page. We'll consider a few of these suggestions in more detail.

Consulting Knowledgeable People

When you think of research, you may immediately think of libraries and print material. But don't neglect a key reference: other people. Your *instructor* can probably suggest fruitful areas of research and some useful sources. Try to see your instructor during office hours, however, rather than immediately before or after class, so that you'll have enough time for a productive discussion.

Once you get to the library, ask a *reference librarian* which reference sources (e.g., bibliographies, specialized encyclopedias, periodical indexes, statistical

Locating Preliminary Sources

- Ask your instructor to recommend sources on the subject.
- Scan the "Suggestions for Further Reading" sections of your textbooks. Ask your college librarian for useful reference tools in your subject area.
- Read an encyclopedia article on the subject and use the bibliography following the article to identify other sources.
- Read the introduction to a recent book on the subject and review that book's bibliography to identify more sources.
- Consult the annual *Bibliographic Index* (see p. 269 for details).
- Use an Internet search engine to explore your topic. Type in different keyword or search term combinations and browse the sites you find for ideas and references to sources you can look up later (see the box on pp. 271–272 for details).

almanacs) you need for your particular area of research. Librarians won't do your research for you, but they'll be glad to show you how to research efficiently and systematically.

You can also obtain vital primary information from people when you interview them, ask them to fill out questionnaires or surveys, or have them participate in experiments. We'll cover this aspect of research in more detail below.

Encyclopedias

Reading an encyclopedia entry about your subject will give you a basic understanding of the most significant facts and issues. Whether the subject is American politics or the mechanics of genetic engineering, the encyclopedia article—written by a specialist in the field—offers a broad overview that may serve as a launching point to more specialized research in a particular area. The article may illuminate areas or raise questions that motivate you to pursue further. Equally important, the encyclopedia article frequently concludes with an *annotated bibliography* describing important books and articles on the subject.

Encyclopedias have limitations, however. First, most professors don't accept encyclopedia articles as legitimate sources for academic papers. You should use encyclopedias primarily to familiarize yourself with (and to select a particular aspect of) the subject area and as a springboard for further research. Also, because new editions of encyclopedias appear only once every five or ten years, the information they contain—including bibliographies—may not be current. Current editions of the *Encyclopaedia Britannica* and the *Encyclopedia Americana*, for instance, may not include information about the most recent developments in biotechnology. Some encyclopedias are now also available online—*Britannica Online*, for example—and this may mean, but not guarantee, that information is up to date.

Some of the most useful general encyclopedias are:

Academic American Encyclopedia

Encyclopedia Americana

New Encyclopaedia Britannica (or *Britannica Online*)

Wikipedia (online)

Wikipedia: An Online Encyclopedia

One of the Web's most popular sites for general information is *Wikipedia* <http://www.wikipedia.org>. Launched in 2001 by the Internet entrepreneur Jimmy Wales, *Wikipedia* bills itself as "the free encyclopedia that anyone can edit." (The name, originally applied to a type of software, was derived from the Hawaiian phrase *wiki wiki*, meaning "quick.") *Wikipedia* boasts a content of more than 3,200,000 articles in more than 200 languages. This site incorporates some of the most and least appealing characteristics of the Web: It is thoroughly democratic because anyone can not only write an article for *Wikipedia* but can also edit articles that others have written. In this sense, it is a collaborative enterprise (with multiple versions of the same article available to users).

At the same time, and for the same reasons, its articles are frequently of doubtful accuracy and reliability. Authors of *Wikipedia* articles need no qualifications to write on their chosen subject, and their articles are subject to no peer review or fact-checking. On numerous occasions vandals have written or rewritten articles in a defamatory manner, so "the subject of a biographical article must fix blatant lies about his own life" <http://en.wikipedia.org/wiki/Criticism_of_Wikipedia>.

While users may find numerous *Wikipedia* articles informative and useful (particularly in the sciences), there are also—as the site itself admits—"many articles . . . which are amateurish, unauthoritative, and even incorrect, making it difficult for a reader unfamiliar with the subject matter to know which articles are correct and which are not." The bottom line on *Wikipedia?* Caveat emptor: Let the buyer beware.

Note, however, that even if researchers can't always be sure of the reliability or accuracy of *Wikipedia* articles, many of these articles conclude with a section of "External Links." These links often provide access to sources of established reliability, such as government agencies or academic sites.

Keep in mind that the library also contains a variety of more *specialized encyclopedias*. These encyclopedias restrict themselves to a particular disciplinary area, such as chemistry, law, or film, and are considerably more detailed in their treatment of a subject than are general encyclopedias.

Exercise 7.2

Exploring Specialized Encyclopedias

Go to the reference section of your campus library and locate several specialized encyclopedias within your major or area of interest. Look through the encyclopedias, noting their organization, and read entries on topics that interest you. Jot down some notes describing the kinds of information you find. You might also use this opportunity to look around at the other materials available in the reference section, including the *Bibliographic Index* and the *Book Review Digest.*

Overviews and Bibliographies in Recent Books

If your professor or a bibliographic source directs you to an important recent book on your subject, skim the introductory (and possibly the concluding) material to the book, along with the table of contents, for an overview of key issues. Look also for a bibliography, Works Cited, and/or References list. These lists are extremely valuable resources for locating material for research. For example, Robert Dallek's 2003 book, *An Unfinished Life: John Fitzgerald Kennedy, 1917–1963,* includes a seven-page bibliography of reference sources on President Kennedy's life and times.

Keep in mind that authors are not necessarily objective about their subjects, and some have particularly biased viewpoints that you may unwittingly carry over to your paper, treating them as objective truth.* However, you may still be able to get useful information out of such sources. Alert yourself to authorial biases by looking up the reviews of your book in the *Book Review Digest* (described on p. 279). Additionally, look up biographical information on the author (see Biographical Indexes, p. 279), whose previous writings or professional associations may suggest a predictable set of attitudes on the subject of your book.

---

*Bias is not necessarily bad. Authors, like all other people, have their preferences and predilections that influence the way they view the world and the kinds of arguments they make. As long as they inform you of their biases, or as long as you are aware of them and take them into account, you can still use these sources judiciously. (You might gather valuable information from a book about the Watergate scandal, even if it were written by former president Richard Nixon or one of his top aides, as long as you make proper allowance for their understandable biases.) Bias becomes a potential problem only when it masquerades as objective truth or is accepted as such by the reader. For suggestions on identifying and assessing authorial bias, see the material in Chapter 2 on persuasive writing (pp. 63–69) and evaluating assumptions (pp. 71–73).

Bibliographic Index

The *Bibliographic Index* is a series of annual volumes that enables you to locate bibliographies on a particular subject. The bibliographies referred to in the *Index* generally appear at the end of book chapters or periodical articles, or they may themselves be book or pamphlet length. Browsing through the *Bibliographic Index* in a general subject area may give you ideas for further research in particular aspects of the subject, along with particular references.

Subject-Heading Guides

Seeing how a general subject (e.g., education) is broken down in other sources also could stimulate research in a particular area (e.g., bilingual primary education in California). In subject heading guides, general subjects are analyzed into secondary subject headings, as chapter titles in a book's table of contents represent subcomponents of a general subject (indicated in the book title). To locate sets of secondary subject headings, consult:

An electronic database

An electronic or print periodical catalog (e.g., *InfoTrac, Readers' Guide, Social Science Index*)

The *Library of Congress Subject Headings* catalog

The *Propaedia* volume of the *Encyclopaedia Britannica* (2007)

Once you've used these kinds of tools to narrow your scope to a particular subject and research question (or set of research questions), you're ready to undertake more focused research.

■ FOCUSED RESEARCH

Your objective now is to learn as much as you can about your particular subject. Only in this way will you be qualified to make an informed response to your research question. This means you'll have to become something of an expert on the subject—or, if that's not possible, given time constraints, you can at least become someone whose critical viewpoint is based solidly on the available evidence. In the following pages we'll suggest how to find sources for this kind of focused research. In most cases, your research will be *secondary* in nature, based on (1) books; (2) electronic databases; (3) articles; and (4) specialized reference sources. In certain cases, you may gather your own *primary* research, using (5) interviews, surveys, structured observation, diaries, letters, and other unpublished sources, or content/textual analysis of literary or other artistic texts.

Electronic Databases

Much of the information that is available in print—and a good deal that is not—is also available in electronic form. Almost certainly, your library card catalog has been computerized, allowing you to conduct searches much faster and more easily than in the past. Increasingly, researchers access magazine, newspaper, and journal articles and reports, abstracts, and other forms of information through *online databases* (many of them on the Internet) and through databases on *CD-ROMs*. One great advantage of using databases (as opposed to print indexes) is that you can search several years' worth of different periodicals at the same time.

Online databases—that is, those that originate outside your computer—are available through international, national, and local (e.g., campus) networks. The largest such database is DIALOG, which provides access to more than 300 million records in more than 400 databases ranging from sociology to business to chemical engineering. Another large database is LEXIS-NEXIS (like DIALOG, available only through online subscription). *LEXIS-NEXIS Academic* provides access to numerous legal, medical, business, and news sources. In addition to being efficient and comprehensive, online databases are generally far more up-to-date than print sources. If you have an Internet connection from your own computer, you can access many of these databases—including those available through commercial online services such as CompuServe and America Online—without leaving your room.

Access to online databases often requires an account and a password, which you may be able to obtain by virtue of your student status. In some cases, you will have to pay the local provider of the database a fee based on how long you are online. But many databases will be available to you free of charge. For example, your library's computers may offer access to magazine and newspaper databases such as *Academic Search Complete, InfoTrac, EbscoHost,* and *National Newspaper Index,* as well as to the Internet itself.

The *World Wide Web* offers graphics, multimedia, and hyperlinks to related material in numerous sources. To access these sources, you can either browse (i.e., follow your choice of paths or links wherever they lead) or type in a site's address.

To search for Web information on a particular topic, try using one of the more popular search engines:

Google: http://www.google.com

Yahoo: http://www.yahoo.com

Alta Vista: http://altavista.com

WebCrawler: http://webcrawler.com

SearchCom: http://www.search.com

Lycos: http://www.lycos.com

Review the "Help" and "Advanced Search" sections of search engines to achieve the best results. See the box on pp. 271–272 for some general tips on searching online.

Many databases and periodical indexes are available online. Among them: the *Readers' Guide to Periodical Literature* [index only], *The New York Times* [available full-text online], *Film Index International* [index only], *PAIS International* [index only], and *America: History and Life* [index only], as are other standard reference sources such as *Statistical Abstract of the U.S.* [full text], *The Encyclopaedia Britannica* [full text—called *Britannica Online*], *Bibliography of Native North Americans* [index only], *Environment Reporter* [full text], and *National Criminal Justice Reference Service* [index with some links to full text]. Of particular interest is *InfoTrac*, which (if you are in a participating library or have a password) provides access to more than one thousand general interest, business, government, and technological periodicals. In recent years, CD-ROM (compact disk-read only memory) indexes and databases have given way to online versions.

Keep in mind, however, that while electronic sources make it far easier to access information than do their print counterparts, they often do not go back more than 15 years. For earlier information (e.g., the original reactions to the Milgram experiments of the 1960s), therefore, you would have to rely on print indexes.

Using Keywords and Boolean Logic to Refine Online Searches

You will find more—and more relevant—sources on Internet search engines and library databases if you carefully plan your search strategies. *Note:* Some search engines and online databases have their own systems for searching, so review the "Help" section of each search engine, and use "Advanced Search" options where available. The following tips are general guidelines, and their applicability in different search engines may vary somewhat.

1. *Identify multiple keywords:*

   Write down your topic and/or your research question, then brainstorm synonyms and related terms for the words in that topic/question.

   Sample topic: Political activism on college campuses

   Sample research question: What kinds of political activism are college students involved in today?

   Keywords: Political activism; college students

   Synonyms and related terms: politics; voting; political organizations; protests; political issues; universities; colleges; campus politics

2. *Conduct searches using different combinations of synonyms and related terms.*

3. *Find new terms in the sources you locate and search with them.*

4. *Use quotation marks around words you want linked: "political activism"*

(continues)

5. *Use "Boolean operators" to link keywords:*

The words AND, OR, and NOT are used in "Boolean logic" to combine search terms and get more precise results than using keywords alone.

AND: Connecting keywords with AND narrows a search by retrieving only sources that contain *both* keywords:

> political activism AND college students

OR: Connecting keywords with OR broadens a search by retrieving all sources that contain at least one of the search terms. This operator is useful when you have a topic/keyword for which there are a number of synonyms. Linking synonyms with OR will lead you to the widest array of sources:

> political activism OR protests OR political organizing OR voting OR campus politics

> college OR university OR campus OR students

AND and OR: You can use these terms in combination, by putting the OR phrase in parentheses:

> (political activism OR protests) AND (college OR university)

NOT: Connecting keywords with NOT (or, in some cases, AND NOT) narrows a search by excluding certain terms. If you want to focus on a very specific topic, NOT can be used to limit what the search engine retrieves; however, this operator should be used carefully as it can cause you to miss sources that may actually be relevant:

> college students NOT high school

> political activism NOT voting

Exercise 7.3

Exploring Electronic Sources

Use your library's Internet connection (or your home computer if you have Internet access) to access a search engine or academic/professional database. Select a topic/research question of interest to you. Review the box above and try different combinations of keywords and Boolean operators to see what sources you can find for your topic. Jot down notes describing the kinds of sources you find and which terms seem to yield the best results. Effective searching on the Internet takes practice; you'll save time when conducting research if you have a good sense of how to use these search strategies.

The Benefits and Pitfalls of the World Wide Web

In the past few years, the Web has become not just a research tool but a cultural phenomenon. The pop artist Andy Warhol once said that in the future everyone would be famous for 15 minutes. He might have added that everyone would also have a personal Web site. People use the Web not just to look up information but also to shop, to make contact with long-lost friends and relatives, to grind their personal or corporate axes, and to advertise themselves and their accomplishments.

The Web makes it possible for people at home, work, or school to gain access to the resources of large libraries and explore corporate and government databases. In her informative book *The Research Paper and the World Wide Web*, Dawn Rodrigues quotes Bruce Dobler and Harry Bloomberg on the essential role of the Web in modern research:

> It isn't a matter anymore of using computer searches to locate existing documents buried in some far-off library or archive. The Web is providing documents and resources that simply would be too expensive to publish on paper or CD-ROM.
>
> Right now—and not in some distant future—doing research without looking for resources on the Internet is, in most cases, not really looking hard enough. . . . A thorough researcher cannot totally avoid the Internet and the Web.*

Indeed, Web sites are increasingly showing up as sources in both student and professional papers. But like any other rapidly growing and highly visible cultural phenomenon, the Web has created its own backlash. As anyone who has tried it knows, for many subjects, systematic research on the Web is rarely possible. For all the information that is on the Internet, a great deal more is not and never will be converted to digital format. One library director has estimated that only about 4,000 of 150,000 published scholarly journals are available online, and many of these online sources provide only partial texts of relatively recent articles in the paper editions. *The New York Times* is available on the Web, but the online edition includes only a fraction of the content of the print edition, and online versions of the articles generally are abridged and often must be paid for. If you are researching the rise of McCarthyism in America during the early 1950s or trying to determine who else, since Stanley Milgram, has conducted psychological experiments on obedience, you are unlikely to find much useful information for your purpose on the Web.

Moreover, locating what *is* available is not always easy because there's no standardized method—like the Library of Congress subheading and call number system—of cataloging and cross-referencing online information. The tens of thousands of Web sites and millions of Web pages, together with

---

*Dawn Rodrigues, *The Research Paper and the World Wide Web* (Upper Saddle River, NJ: Prentice Hall, 1997).

the relative crudity of search engines such as *Yahoo, Google, AltaVista,* and *WebCrawler,* have made navigating an ever-expanding cyberspace an often daunting and frustrating procedure.

At the same time, it is not a given that people who do research on the Web will produce better papers as a result. David Rothenberg, a professor of philosophy at New Jersey Institute of Technology, believes that "his students' papers had declined in quality since they began using the Web for research."[*] Neil Gabler, a cultural critic, writes:

> The Internet is such a huge receptacle of rumor, half-truth, misinformation and disinformation that the very idea of objective truth perishes in the avalanche. All you need to create a "fact" in the web world is a bulletin board or chat room. Gullible cybernauts do the rest.[†]

Another critic is even blunter: "Much of what purports to be serious information is simply junk—neither current, objective, nor trustworthy. It may be impressive to the uninitiated, but it is clearly not of great use to scholars."[‡] The accuracy and reliability of articles on the popular—and vast—online encyclopedia *Wikipedia* has been called into question because anyone with an Internet connection can write or edit most articles.

Of course, print sources are not necessarily objective or reliable either, and in Chapter 2, Critical Reading and Critique, we discussed criteria by which readers may evaluate the quality and reliability of information and ideas in *any* source (pp. 59–69). Web sources, however—particularly self-published Web pages—present a special problem. In most cases, material destined for print has to go through one or more editors and fact checkers before being published, since most authors don't have the resources to publish and distribute their own writing. But anyone with a computer and a modem can "publish" on the Web; furthermore, those with a good Web authoring program and graphics software can create sites that, outwardly at least, look just as professional and authoritative as those of the top academic, government, and business sites. These personal sites will appear in search-engine listings—generated through keyword matches rather than through independent assessments of quality or relevance—and uncritical researchers who use their information as a factual basis for the claims they make in their papers do so at their peril.

The Internet has also led to increased problems with plagiarism. Many college professors complain about receiving work copied directly from Web sites. Such copying runs the gamut from inadvertent plagiarism of passages—copied and pasted off the Web into notes and then transferred verbatim to papers—to intentional theft of others' work, pasted into

---

[*]Steven R. Knowlton, "Students Lost in Cyberspace," *Chronicle of Higher Education* 2 Nov. 1997: 21.
[†]Neil Gabler, "Why Let Truth Get in the Way of a Good Story?" *Los Angeles Times* 26 Oct. 1997, Opinion sec.: 1.
[‡]William Miller, "Troubling Myths about On-Line Information," *Chronicle of Higher Education* 1 Aug. 1997: A44.

a document and claimed as the student's own. But while cheating is now made easier by the Internet, the converse is also true: Instructors can often track down the sources for material plagiarized from the Internet just as easily as the student found them. One instructor who recently received a student paper characterized by a more professional writing style than usual for that student simply typed a few keywords from the paper into an Internet search engine; one of the first sources retrieved was the professional journal article from which the student had copied whole passages and pasted them together to create a "report." This student received an F in the course and was referred to a university disciplinary committee for further action.

The Internet may seem a very tempting source from which to lift materials. But not only is such activity ethically wrong, it is likely to result in a permanent notation on your academic transcript or expulsion from school. And all students should know that instructors will scan papers into software or Internet programs that search the Web for matching text. For more on plagiarism, see the section devoted to this subject in Chapter 1, pp. 53–55.

We certainly don't mean to discourage Web research. Thousands of excellent sites—and many invaluable databases—exist in cyberspace. The reference department of most college and university libraries will provide lists of such sites, and the most useful sites are also listed in the research sections of many handbooks. Most people locate Web sites, however, by using search engines and by "surfing" the hyperlinks. And for Web sources, more than for print sources, the warning *caveat emptor*—let the buyer beware—applies.

Evaluating Web Sources

In their useful site "Evaluating Web Resources," <http://www3.widener.edu/ Academics/Libraries/Wolfgram_Memorial_Library/Evaluate_Web_Pages/ Original_Web_Evaluation_Materials/6160/>, the reference librarians Jan Alexander and Marsha Tate offer important guidelines for assessing Web sources. First, they point out, it's important to determine what *type* of Web page you are dealing with. Web pages generally fall into one of five types, each with a different purpose: (1) business/marketing, (2) reference/information, (3) news, (4) advocacy of a particular point of view or program, (5) personal page. The purpose of the page—informing, selling, persuading, entertaining— has a direct bearing on the objectivity and reliability of the information presented.

Second, when evaluating a Web page, one should apply the same general criteria as are applied to print sources: (1) accuracy, (2) authority, (3) objectivity, (4) currency, (5) coverage. As we've noted, when assessing the *accuracy* of a Web page, it's important to consider the likelihood that its information has been checked by anyone other than the author. When assessing the *authority* of the page, one considers the author's qualifications to write on the subject and the reputability of the publisher. In many cases on the Web, it's difficult to determine not just the qualifications but the very identity of the author. When assessing the *objectivity* of a Web page, one considers the bias on the part of the author or authors and the extent to which they are trying to sway their reader's opinion. Many Web pages passing themselves off as informational are in fact little more than infomercials. When assessing the *currency* of a Web page, one asks whether the content is up to date and whether the publication date is clearly labeled. Many Web pages lack clearly indicated dates. And even if a date is provided, it may be difficult to tell whether the date indicates when the page was written, when it was placed on the Web, or when it was last revised. Finally, when assessing the *coverage* of a Web page, one considers which topics are included (and not included) in the work and whether the topics are covered in depth. Depth of coverage has generally not been a hallmark of Web information.

Other pitfalls of Web sites: Reliable sites may include links to other sites that are inaccurate or outdated, so users cannot rely on the link as a substitute for evaluating the five criteria just outlined. Web pages are also notoriously unstable, frequently changing and even disappearing without notice.

Perhaps most serious, the ease with which it's possible to surf the Net can encourage intellectual laziness and make researchers too dependent on Web resources. Professors are increasingly seeing papers largely or even entirely based on information from Web sites. While Web sources are indeed an important new source of otherwise unavailable information, there's usually no substitute for library or primary research such as interviews or field study. The vast majority of printed material in even a small college library—much of it essential to informed research—does not appear on the Web, nor is it likely to in the immediate future. Much of the material you will research in the next few years remains bound within covers. You may well learn of its existence in electronic databases, but at some point you'll have to walk over to a library shelf, pull out a book, and turn printed pages.

Above all, you must apply the critical reading skills you've been practicing throughout this textbook to all your sources—no matter what types they are or where you found them (see Chapter 2 for coverage of critical reading).

Exercise 7.4

Practice Evaluating Web Sources

To practice applying the evaluation criteria discussed in the section above on Web sources, go to an Internet search engine and look for sources addressing a topic of interest to you (perhaps following completion of Exercise 7.3, p. 272). Try to locate one source representing each of the five types of Web pages (business/marketing, reference/information, news, advocacy, and personal). Print out the home page of each source and bring the copies to class. In small groups of classmates look over the sites each student found and make notes on each example's (1) accuracy, (2) authority, (3) objectivity, (4) currency, and (5) coverage.

Periodicals: General

Because many more periodical articles than books are published every year, you are likely (depending on the subject) to find more information in periodicals than in books. General periodicals are the magazines and newspapers that are usually found on newsstands, such as *The New York Times, Newsweek,* and *The New Yorker.* By their nature, general periodical articles tend to be more current than books. The best way, for example, to find out about the federal government's current policy on Social Security reform is to look for articles in periodicals and newspapers. However, periodical articles may have less critical distance than books, and like books, they may become dated, to be superseded by more recent articles. Let's look first at the use of magazines from a research perspective.

Magazines

General periodicals (such as *Time, The New Republic,* and *The Nation*) are intended for nonspecialists. Their articles, which tend to be highly readable, may be written by staff writers, freelancers, or specialists. But usually they do not provide citations or other indications of sources, so they are of limited usefulness for scholarly research.

The most well-known general index to this kind of material is the *Readers' Guide to Periodical Literature,* an index of articles that have appeared in several hundred general-interest magazines and a few more specialized magazines such as *Business Week* and *Science Digest.* Articles in the *Readers' Guide* are indexed by author, title, and subject.

Another general reference for articles is the *Essay and General Literature Index,* which indexes essays (sometimes called book articles) contained in anthologies.

Increasingly, texts and abstracts of articles are available on online databases. These texts may be downloaded to your computer or e-mailed to you.

Newspapers

News stories, feature stories, and editorials (even letters to the editor) may be important sources of information. Your library will certainly have *The New York Times* index, and it may have indexes to other important newspapers such as the *Washington Post,* the *Los Angeles Times,* the *Chicago Tribune, The Wall Street Journal,* and the *Christian Science Monitor.* Newspaper holdings will be on microfilm, CD-ROM, or online. You will need a microprinter/viewer to read hard copies if you are using microfilm.

Note: Because of its method of cross-referencing, *The New York Times* index may at first be confusing. Suppose that you want to find stories on bilingual education during a given year. When you locate the "Bilingual education" entry, you won't find citations but rather a *"See also* Education" reference that directs you, say, to seven dates (August 14, 15, and 17; September 11; October 20, 29, and 30) under the heading of "Education." Under this major heading, references to stories on education are arranged in chronological order from January to December. When you look up the dates you were directed to, you'll see brief descriptions of these stories on bilingual education.

Periodicals: Specialized

Many professors will expect at least some of your research to be based on articles in specialized periodicals or scholarly journals. So instead of (or in addition to) relying on an article from *Psychology Today* (considered a general periodical even though its subject is somewhat specialized) for an account of the effects of crack cocaine on mental functioning, you might also rely on an article from the *Journal of Abnormal Psychology*. If you are writing a paper on the satirist Jonathan Swift, in addition to a recent reference that may have appeared in *The New Yorker*, you may need to locate a relevant article in *Eighteenth-Century Studies*. Articles in such journals are normally written by specialists and professionals in the field, rather than by staff writers or freelancers, and the authors will assume that their readers already understand the basic facts and issues concerning the subject. Other characteristics of scholarly journals: They tend to be heavily researched, as indicated by numerous notes and references; they are generally published by university presses; most of the authors represented are university professors; the articles, which have a serious, formal, and scholarly tone, are generally peer reviewed by other scholars in the field.

To find articles in specialized periodicals, you'll use specialized indexes—that is, indexes for particular disciplines, such as the *Anthropological Index* and the *Education Index*. You also may find it helpful to refer to *abstracts*. Like specialized indexes, abstracts list articles published in a particular discipline over a given period, but they also provide summaries of the articles listed. Abstracts tend to be more selective than indexes, since they consume more space (and involve considerably more work to compile); but, because they also describe the contents of the articles covered, they can save you a lot of time in determining which articles you should read and which ones you can safely skip. Don't treat abstracts alone as sources for research; when you find useful material in an abstract, you need to locate the article to which it applies and use that as your source of information.

Exercise 7.5

Exploring Specialized Periodicals

Visit your campus library and locate the specialized periodical indexes for your major or area of interest (ask a reference librarian to help you). Note the call numbers for specialized periodicals (also called academic journals) in your field, and visit the section of the library where recent editions of academic journals are usually housed. Locate the call numbers you've noted and look through the specialized periodicals in your field. The articles you find in these journals represent some of the most recent scholarship in your field—the kind of scholarship many of your professors are busy conducting. Write half a page or so describing the articles you find interesting, and why.

Books

Books are useful in providing both breadth and depth of coverage of a subject. Because they are generally published at least a year or two after the events treated, they also tend to provide the critical distance that is sometimes missing from articles. Conversely, this delay in coverage means that the information you find in books will not be as current as the information you find in journals. Books may also be shallow, inaccurate, outdated, or hopelessly biased; for help in making such determinations, see *Book Review Digest*, discussed below. You can locate relevant books through a library's electronic catalog, which you may search in four ways: (1) by *author*, (2) by *title*, (3) by *subject*, and (4) by *keyword*. Entries include the call number, publication information, and frequently, a summary of the book's contents. Larger libraries use the Library of Congress cataloging system for call numbers (e.g., E111/C6); smaller ones use the Dewey Decimal System (e.g., 970.015/C726).

Book Review Digest

Perhaps the best way to determine the reliability and credibility of a book you may want to use is to look it up in the *Book Review Digest* (also available online and issued monthly and cumulated annually). These volumes list (alphabetically by author) the most significant books published during the year, supply a brief description of each, and, most important, provide excerpts from (and references to) reviews. If a book receives bad reviews, you don't necessarily have to avoid it (the book may still have something useful to offer, and the review itself may be unreliable). But you should take any negative reaction into account when using that book as a source.

Biographical Indexes

To look up information on particular people, you can use not only encyclopedias but an array of biographical sources such as the *Dictionary of American Biography* and *Contemporary Authors*. You can also use these biographical sources to alert yourself to potential biases on the part of your source authors, as such biases may be revealed by other work these authors have done and details of their backgrounds.

Government Publications and Other Sources

For statistical and other basic reference information on a subject, consult a *handbook* (such as *Statistical Abstracts of the United States*). For current information on a subject as of a given year, consult an *almanac* (such as *World Almanac*). For annual updates of information, consult a *yearbook* (such as *The Statesman's Yearbook*). For maps and other geographic information, consult an *atlas* (such as *New York Times Atlas of the World*). Often, simply browsing through the reference shelves for data on your general subject—such as biography, public affairs, psychology—will reveal valuable sources of information. And of course, much reference information is available on government sites on the Web.

In addition, many libraries keep pamphlets in a *vertical file* (i.e., a file cabinet). For example, a pamphlet on global warming might be found in the vertical file rather than in the library stacks. Such material is accessible through the *Vertical File Index* (a monthly subject-and-title index to pamphlet material).

Finally, the U.S. government regularly publishes large quantities of useful information. Among the indexes to government publications are:

American Statistics Index

Congressional Information Service

Interviews and Surveys

Depending on the subject of your paper, some or all of your research may be conducted outside the library. In conducting such primary research, you may perform experiments in science labs or make observations or gather data in courthouses, city government files, shopping malls (if you are observing, say, patterns of consumer behavior), the quad in front of the humanities building, or in front of TV screens (if you are analyzing, say, situation comedies or commercials, or if you are drawing on documentaries or interviews—in which cases you should try to obtain transcripts or recordings of the programs).

You may also want to *interview* your professors, your fellow students, or other individuals knowledgeable about your subject. Additionally, or alternatively, you may wish to conduct *surveys* via *questionnaires* (see box, p. 281). When well prepared and insightfully interpreted, such tools can produce valuable information about the ideas or preferences of a group of people.

Guidelines for Conducting Interviews

- Become knowledgeable about the subject before the interview so that you can ask intelligent questions. Prepare most of your questions beforehand.

- Ask "open-ended" questions designed to elicit meaningful responses, rather than "forced choice" questions that can be answered with a word or two, or "leading questions" that presume a particular answer. For example, instead of asking "Do you think that male managers should be more sensitive to women's concerns for equal pay in the workplace?" ask, "To what extent do you see evidence that male managers are insufficiently sensitive to women's concerns for equal pay in the workplace?"

(continues)

- Ask follow-up questions to elicit additional insights or details.
- If you record the interview (in addition to or instead of taking notes), get your subject's permission, preferably in writing.

Guidelines for Conducting Surveys and Designing Questionnaires

- Determine your *purpose* in conducting the survey: what kind of *information* you seek, and *whom* (i.e., what subgroup of the population) you intend to survey.
- Decide whether you want to collect information on the spot or have people send their responses back to you. (You will get fewer responses if they are sent back to you, but those you do get will likely be more complete than surveys conducted on the spot.)
- Devise and word questions carefully so that they (1) are understandable and (2) don't reflect your own biases. For example, for a survey on attitudes toward capital punishment, if you ask, "Do you believe that the state should endorse legalized murder?" you've loaded the question to influence people to answer in the negative.
- Devise short-answer or multiple-choice questions; open-ended questions encourage responses that are difficult to quantify. (You may want to leave space, however, for "additional comments.") Conversely, yes or no responses or rankings on a 5-point scale are easy to quantify.
- It may be useful to break out the responses by as many meaningful categories as possible—for example, gender, age, ethnicity, religion, education, geographic locality, profession, and income.

■ MINING SOURCES ■

Having located your sources (or at least having begun the process), you'll proceed to "mining" them—that is, extracting from them information and ideas that you can use in your paper. To keep track of these sources, you'll need to compile a working bibliography so that you know what information you have and how it relates to your research question. Of course, you'll need to take notes on your sources and evaluate them for reliability and relevance. And you should develop some kind of *outline*—formal or informal—that allows you to see how you are going to subdivide and organize your discussion and, thus, at what points you'll be drawing on relevant sources. In doing this you are engaging in a process that has identifiable stages. For an extended discussion of this writing process, see Chapter 6.

Critical Reading for Research

- *Use all the critical reading tips we've suggested thus far.* The tips contained in the boxes Critical Reading for Summary on p. 6, Critical Reading for Critique on pp. 82–83, Critical Reading for Synthesis on p. 132, and Critical Reading for Analysis on p. 208 are all useful for the kinds of reading used in conducting research.

- *Read for relationships to your research question.* How does the source help you formulate and clarify your research question?

- *Read for relationships between sources.* How does each source illustrate, support, expand upon, contradict, or offer an alternative perspective to those of your other sources?

- *Consider the relationship between your source's form and content.* How does the form of the source—specialized encyclopedia, book, article in a popular magazine, article in a professional journal—affect its content, the manner in which that content is presented, and its relationship to other sources?

- *Pay special attention to the legitimacy of Internet sources.* Consider how the content and validity of the information on the Web page may be affected by the purpose of the site. Assess Web-based information for its (1) accuracy, (2) authority, (3) objectivity, (4) currency, and (5) coverage (see pp. 275–276).

■ THE WORKING BIBLIOGRAPHY

As you conduct your research, keep a *working bibliography*—that is, a compilation of bibliographic information on all the sources you're likely to use in preparing the paper. Note *full* bibliographic information on each source you consider. If you're meticulous about this during the research process, you'll be spared the frustration of having to go back to retrieve information—such as the publisher or the date—just as you're typing your final draft.

Now that library catalogs and databases are available online, it's easy to copy and paste your sources' (or potential sources') bibliographic information into a document, or to e-mail citations to yourself for cutting and pasting later. A more traditional but still very efficient way to compile bibliographic information is on 3" × 5" cards. (Note, also, that certain software programs allow you to create sortable electronic records.) Using any of these methods, you can easily add, delete, and rearrange individual bibliographic records as your research progresses. Whether you keep bibliographic information on 3" × 5" cards or in a document, be sure to record the following:

- The author or editor (last name first) and, if relevant, the translator
- The title (and subtitle) of the book or article

- The publisher and place of publication (if a book) or the title of the periodical
- The date and/or year of publication; if periodical, volume and issue number
- The edition number (if a book beyond its first edition)
- The inclusive page numbers (if article)
- The specific page number of a quote or other special material you might paraphrase

You may also want to include:

- A brief description of the source (to help you recall it later in the research process)
- The library call number (to help you relocate the source if you haven't checked it out)
- A code number, which you can use as a shorthand reference to the source in your notes (see the sample note records on the next page)

Your final bibliography, known as "Works Cited" in Modern Language Association (MLA) format and "References" in American Psychological Association (APA) format, consists of the sources you summarize, paraphrase, or quote in your paper. When you compile the bibliography, arrange your sources alphabetically by authors' last names. Here is an example of a working bibliography notation:

> Gorham, Eric B. National Service, Political Socialization, and Political Education. Albany: SUNY P, 1992.
>
> Argues that the language government uses to promote national service programs betrays an effort to "reproduce a postindustrial, capitalist economy in the name of good citizenship." Chap. 1 provides a historical survey of national service.

Here is an example of a working bibliography record for an article:

> Gergen, David. "A Time to Heed the Call." U.S. News & World Report 24 Dec. 2001: 60-61.
>
> Argues that in the wake of the surge of patriotism that followed the September 11 terrorist attacks, the government should encourage citizens to participate in community and national service. Supports the McCain-Bayh bill.

Here is an example of a working bibliography record for an online source:

> Bureau of Labor Statistics. Table 1: Volunteers by Selected Characteristics, September 2002 and 2003. 18 Dec. 2003. Accessed 17 Jan. 2004. <http://www.bls.gov/news.release/volun.t01.htm>.
>
> Provides statistical data on volunteerism in the U.S.

Some instructors may ask you to prepare—either in addition to or instead of a research paper—an *annotated bibliography.* This is a list of relevant works on a subject, with the contents of each work briefly described or assessed. The sample bibliography records shown could become the basis for three entries in an annotated bibliography on national service. Annotations differ from *abstracts* in that annotations do not claim to be comprehensive summaries; they indicate, rather, how the items may be useful to the researcher.

Note-Taking

People have their favorite ways of note-taking. Some use legal pads or spiral notebooks; others type notes into a laptop computer, perhaps using a database program. Some prefer 4″ × 6″ cards for note-taking. Such cards have some of the same advantages as 3″ × 5″ cards for working bibliographies: They can easily be added to, subtracted from, and rearranged to accommodate changing organizational plans. Also, discrete pieces of information from the same source can easily be arranged (and rearranged) into subtopics—a difficult task if you have taken three pages of notes on an article without breaking the notes down into subtopics.

Whatever your preferred approach, we recommend including, along with the note itself,

- a topic or subtopic label, corresponding to your outline (see below)
- a code number, corresponding to the number assigned the source in the working bibliography
- a page reference at the end of the note

Here is a sample note record for the table "Volunteers by Selected Characteristics, September 2002 and 2003" from the Bureau of Labor Statistics (bibliographic record above):

Pervasiveness of Volunteerism (I)   7

Shows that 28.8 percent of Americans age 16 and older, 63.8 million in all, devote time to community service.

Here is a note record for the periodical article by Gergen (see bibliography note on the previous page):

Beneficial paid volunteer programs (II)   12

Both the community and the individual benefit from voluntary service programs. Cites Teach for America, Alumni of City Year, Peace Corps as programs in which participants receive small stipends and important benefits (60). "Voluntary service when young often changes people for life. They learn to give their fair share." (60)

Both note records are headed by a topic label followed by the tentative location in the paper outline where the information may be used. The number in the upper right corner corresponds to the bibliography note. The note itself in the first record uses *summary*. The note in the second record uses *summary* (sentence 1), *paraphrase* (sentence 2), and *quotation* (sentence 3). Summary is used to condense important ideas; paraphrase (with relevant page number), for the important detail on specific programs; quotation (again with relevant page number), for particularly incisive language by the source authors. For general hints on when to use each of these three forms, see Chapter 1, p. 51.

At this point we must stress the importance of using quotation marks around quoted language *in your notes.* Making sure to note the difference between your own and quoted language will help you avoid unintentionally using someone else's words or ideas without crediting them properly. Such use, whether intentional or unintentional, constitutes plagiarism—a serious academic offense and something that professors don't take lightly; you don't want to invite suspicion of your work, even unintentionally. See the discussion of plagiarism on pp. 53–55 for more details.

Evaluating Sources

Sifting through what seems a formidable mountain of material, you'll need to work quickly and efficiently; you'll also need to do some selecting. This means, primarily, distinguishing the more important from the less important (and the unimportant) material. Draw on your critical reading skills to help you determine the reliability and relevance of a source. See the box Critical Reading for Research on p. 282, and review Chapter 2, Critical

---

Guidelines for Evaluating Sources

- *Skim the source.* With a book, look over the table of contents, the introduction and conclusion, and the index; zero in on passages that your initial survey suggests are important. With an article, skim the introduction and the headings.
- *Be alert for references* in your sources to other important sources, particularly to sources that several authors treat as important.
- Other things being equal, the more *recent* the source, the better. Recent work usually incorporates or refers to important earlier work.
- If you're considering making multiple references to a book, *look up the reviews* in the *Book Review Digest* or the *Book Review Index*. Also, check the author's credentials in a source such as *Contemporary Authors* or *Current Biography*.

Reading and Critique, particularly the sections Evaluating Informative Writing (pp. 59–60) and Evaluating Persuasive Writing (pp. 60–69). The hints in the box above may also simplify the task.

■ ARRANGING YOUR NOTES: THE OUTLINE

Using your original working thesis (see Chapter 6 on theses)—or a new thesis that you have developed during the course of data-gathering and invention— you can begin constructing a *preliminary outline*. This outline indicates the order in which you plan to support your thesis.

Some people prefer not to develop an outline until they have more or less completed their research. At that point they will look over their note records, consider the relationships among the various pieces of evidence, possibly arrange notes or cards into separate piles, then develop an outline based on their perceptions and insights about the material. Subsequently, they rearrange and code the note records to conform to their outline—an informal outline indicating just the main sections of the paper and possibly one level below that. Thus, the model paper on student privacy and campus safety (see Chapter 4) could be informally outlined as follows:

> Introduction
> > Recap of Virginia Tech shooting
> > Officials did not act on available info re: shooter
> Review federal rules on privacy
> Thesis statement:
> > In responding to the Virginia Tech killings, we should resist rolling back federal rules protecting student privacy; for as long as college officials effectively respond to signs of trouble, these rules already provide a workable balance between privacy and public safety.
> History of privacy on campus
> > *In loco parentis*
> > Court cases and law
> > Recent developments on campus
> Argument *against* student privacy
> > Current responses—federal, university, public opinion
> > Cornell response to Va. Tech: extreme, favoring safety
> Argument *for* student privacy
> > M.I.T. response to Va. Tech: extreme, favoring privacy
> > Va. Tech the result of failed enforcement, not failed policy
> > U of Kentucky a reasonable middle ground
> Conclusion

Such an outline will help you organize your research and should not be unduly restrictive as a guide to writing.

The *formal outline* is a multilevel plan with Roman and Arabic numerals, capital and small lettered subheadings that can provide a useful blueprint for composition as well as a guide to revision.

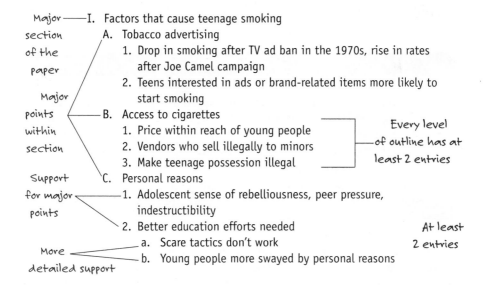

Major section of the paper —— I. Factors that cause teenage smoking

A. Tobacco advertising
1. Drop in smoking after TV ad ban in the 1970s, rise in rates after Joe Camel campaign
2. Teens interested in ads or brand-related items more likely to start smoking

Major points within section ——— B. Access to cigarettes
1. Price within reach of young people
2. Vendors who sell illegally to minors
3. Make teenage possession illegal

Every level of outline has at least 2 entries

Support for major points —— C. Personal reasons
1. Adolescent sense of rebelliousness, peer pressure, indestructibility
2. Better education efforts needed

More detailed support ——
a. Scare tactics don't work
b. Young people more swayed by personal reasons

At least 2 entries

Outlining your draft after you have written it may help you discern structural problems: illogical sequences of material, confusing relationships between ideas, poor unity or coherence, and sections that are too abstract or underdeveloped. (See the discussion of *reverse outlines* in Chapter 6, p. 256.) Many instructors also require that formal outlines accompany the finished research paper.

The formal outline should indicate the logical relationships in the evidence you present. But it may also reflect the general conventions of a particular academic field. Thus, after an *abstract* and an *introduction,* papers in the social sciences often proceed with a description of the *methods* of collecting information, continue with a description of the *results* of the investigation, and end with a *discussion* and a *conclusion.* Papers in the sciences often follow a similar pattern. Papers in the humanities are generally less standardized in form. In devising a logical organization for your paper, ask yourself how your reader might best be introduced to the subject, be guided through a discussion of the main issues, and be persuaded that your viewpoint is a sound one.

Formal outlines are generally of two types: *topic outlines* and *sentence outlines.* In the topic outline, headings and subheadings are words or phrases— as in the informal outline above. In the sentence outline, each heading and subheading is a complete sentence. Both topic and sentence outlines are generally preceded by the thesis.

For the complete formal topic outline of the paper on student privacy and campus safety in Chapter 4, see pp. 159–160.

■ CITING SOURCES ■

When you refer to or quote the work of another, you are obligated to credit or cite your source properly. There are two types of citations—*in-text citations* in the body of a paper and *full citations* at the end of a paper (Works Cited or References)—and they work in tandem.

Types of Citations

- In-text citations indicate the source of quotations, paraphrases, and summarized information and ideas. These citations, generally limited to author's last name, relevant page number, and publication date of source, appear *in the text*, within parentheses.
- Full citations appear in an alphabetical list of "Works Cited" or "References" *at the end of the paper*, always starting on a new page. These citations provide full bibliographical information on the source.

If you are writing a paper in the humanities, you will probably be expected to use the Modern Language Association (MLA) format for citation. This format is fully described in the *MLA Handbook for Writers of Research Papers*, 7th ed. (New York: Modern Language Association of America, 2009). A paper in the social sciences will probably use the American Psychological Association (APA) format. This format is fully described in the *Publication Manual of the American Psychological Association*, 5th ed. (Washington, D.C.: American Psychological Association, 2001) and in the *APA Style Guide to Electronic References* (2007).

In the following section, we will focus on MLA and APA styles, the ones you are most likely to use in your academic work. Keep in mind, however, that instructors often have their own preferences. Check with your instructor for the preferred documentation format if this is not specified in the assignment.[*]

■ DIFFERENCES BETWEEN MLA AND APA STYLES

In-Text Citations

The general rule for in-text citation is to include only enough information to alert the reader to the source of the reference and to the location within that source (Behrens and Rosen 288). For MLA, this information normally includes the author's last name and the page number. For APA, you include last name,

---

[*]Some instructors require the documentation style specified in the *Chicago Manual of Style*, 15th ed. (Chicago: University of Chicago Press, 2003). This style is similar to the American Psychological Association style, except that publication dates are not placed within parentheses. Instructors in the sciences often follow the Council of Science Editors (CSE) formats, one of which is a number format: Each source listed on the bibliography page is assigned a number, and all text references to the source are followed by the appropriate number within parentheses. Some instructors like the old MLA style, which calls for footnotes and endnotes.

year of publication, and page number. With either style, if you have already named the author in the preceding text, do not include the name in the citation.

MLA In-text Citation

> Richard Sennett wonders how "long-term purposes [can] be pursued in a short-term society" (26).

APA In-text Citation

> Randall Collins defines the exercise of power as the attempt "to make something happen in society" (1992, p. 61).

Full Citations

In MLA format, your complete list of sources, with all information necessary for a reader to locate a source, is called "Works Cited" (and should begin on a new page). In APA format, the list of sources is called "References." Entries in both listings should be double-spaced, with second and subsequent lines of each entry indented (a "hanging indent") five spaces or one-half inch. In both styles, a single space follows a period. Here are two sets of sample citations of articles. Both MLA and APA format will differ depending on the medium in which the reader has accessed the source. Citation of books and other sources follow slightly different guidelines.

MLA Full Citations

An article in a magazine or journal (print)

> Packer, George. "The Choice." *New Yorker* 28 Jan. 2008: 28-35. Print.

An article in a magazine or journal (located through a database)

> Packer, George. "The Choice." *New Yorker* 28 Jan. 2008: n. pag. *Academic OneFile.* Web. 8 Nov. 2008.

An article on the Web (*with* a print equivalent)

> Packer, George. "The Choice." *New Yorker* 28 Jan. 2008: n. pag. *NewYorker.com.* Web. 8 Nov. 2008.

An article on the Web (with *no* print equivalent)

> Benjamin, Daniel. "The Mumbai Terrorists' Other Targets." *Slate.* Washington Post.Newsweek Interactive, 1 Dec. 2008. Web. 4 Dec. 2008.

APA Full Citations

An article in a magazine or journal (print)

> Ivanenko, A., & Massie, C. (2006). Assessment and management of sleep disorders in children. *Psychiatric Times, 23*(11), 90–95.

An article in a magazine or journal (located through a database)

Ivanenko, A., & Massie, C. (2006). Assessment and management of sleep disorders in children. *Psychiatric Times, 23*(11), 90–95. Retrieved from http://find.galegroup.com

An article on the Web

Ivanenko, A., & Massie, C. (2006). Assessment and management of sleep disorders in children. *Psychiatric Times, 23*(11), 90–95. Retrieved from http://www.psychiatrictimes.com/display/article/10168/52051?pageNumber=5

The main differences between MLA and APA styles are:

1. In MLA style, the date of the publication follows the name of the publication; in APA style, the date is placed within parentheses following the author's name.

2. In APA style, only the initial of the author's first name is given, and only the first word (and any proper noun) of the book or article title is capitalized. The first letter of the subtitle (after a colon in a title) is also capitalized. In MLA style, the author's full name is given, and all words following the first word of the title (except articles and prepositions) are capitalized.

3. In APA style (unlike MLA style), quotation marks are not used around journal or magazine article titles.

4. APA style (unlike MLA style) requires the use of "p." or "pp." in in-text citations to indicate page numbers of periodical articles.

5. In APA format, the volume number but not the issue number of a periodical is italicized. In MLA, neither the volume number nor the issue number of a periodical is italicized.

6. When citing books, both MLA and APA rules dictate that publishers' names should be shortened; thus, Random House becomes "Random"; William Morrow becomes "Morrow." However, MLA style uses a more extensive system of abbreviations for publishers' names.

Examples of the most commonly used citations in MLA and APA formats are shown below. For a more complete listing, consult the current edition of the MLA *Handbook,* the APA's *Publication Manual* and *Style Guide to Electronic References,* or whatever style guide your instructor has specified. Note that conforming to any citation system requires precision and attention to detail, down to every keystroke and punctuation mark.

■ MLA STYLE: IN-TEXT CITATIONS

Here are sample in-text citations using the MLA system:

> From the beginning, the AIDS antibody test has been "mired in controversy" (Bayer 101).

Notice that in the MLA system no date and no punctuation come between the author's name and the page number in parentheses. Notice also that the parenthetical reference is placed *before* the final punctuation of the sentence because it is considered part of the sentence.

If you have already mentioned the author's name in the text—in a *signal phrase* (e.g., "According to . . . ")—do not repeat it in the citation:

> According to Bayer, from the beginning, the AIDS antibody test has been "mired in controversy" (101).

In MLA format, you must supply page numbers for summaries and paraphrases of print sources as well as for quotations:

> According to Bayer, the AIDS antibody test has been controversial from the outset (101).

Use a block, or indented form, for quotations of five lines or more. Introduce the block quotation with a full sentence followed by a colon. Indent one inch or ten spaces (that is, double the normal paragraph indentation). Place the parenthetical citation *after* the final period:

> Robert Flaherty's refusal to portray primitive people's contact with civilization arose from an inner conflict:
>
> > He had originally plunged with all his heart into the role of explorer and prospector; before Nanook, his own father was his hero. Yet as he entered the Eskimo world, he knew he did so as the advance guard of industrial civilization, the world of United States Steel and Sir William Mackenzie and railroad and mining empires. The mixed feeling this gave him left his mark on all his films. (Barnouw 45)

Again, were Barnouw's name mentioned in the sentence leading into the quotation, the parenthetical reference would be simply (45).

Usually parenthetical citations appear at the end of your sentences; however, if the reference applies only to the first part of the sentence, the parenthetical information is inserted at the appropriate point *within* the sentence:

> While Baumrind argues that "the laboratory is not the place to study degree of obedience" (421), Milgram asserts that such arguments are groundless.

At times, you must modify the basic author and page number reference. Depending on the nature of your source(s), you may need to use one of the following citation formats:

Source Quoted by Another Source

(qtd. in Garber 211)

An Anonymous Work

("Obedience" 32)

Two Authors

(Bernstein and Politi 208)

One of Two or More Works by the Same Author in the List of Works Cited

(Toffler, *Wave* 96-97)

Two or More Sources as the Basis of Your Statement

(Butler 109; Carey 57)

Location of a Passage in a Literary Text

for example, Hardy's *The Return of the Native* (224; ch. 7)

[Page 224 in the edition used by the writer; the chapter number, 7, is provided for the convenience of those referring to another edition.]

A Multivolume Work

(3: 7-12)

[volume number: page numbers; note the space between the colon and the page numbers]

Location of a Passage in a Play

(1.2.308-22) [act.scene.line number(s)]

The Bible

(John 3.16)
(Col. 3.14) [book. chapter.verse]

In-text Citation of Electronic Sources (MLA)

Web sites, CD-ROM data, and e-mail generally do not have numbered pages. Different browsers may display and printers may produce differing numbers of pages for any particular site. You should therefore omit both page numbers and paragraph numbers from in-text citations to electronic sources, unless those page or paragraph numbers are provided within the source itself. For these in-text citations, cite the entire work.

■ MLA STYLE: CITATIONS IN THE WORKS CITED LIST

Electronic Sources (MLA)

Include as much of the following information as you can find when crediting an electronic source. If a model for the citation you are preparing is not listed here, MLA suggests that you combine formats for print books with the nearest electronic format, below. For Web sites that you think may disappear altogether, consider printing a copy of pertinent materials for your records.

1. Name of the author, editor, translator, compiler (as provided)
2. Title, in quotation marks, of a work (such as an article or a story) that is part of a larger work. Italicize the titles of larger works like books or films
3. Name of the Web site, in italics, if different from the title of the work
4. Edition or version used, abbreviated (e.g., 4th ed.)
5. Publisher or sponsor of the site. If none provided, use the abbreviation "N.p."
6. Publication information (day, abbreviation of month, year). If none provided, use the abbreviation "n.d."
7. Publication medium: the word "Web"
8. Access information

   - Day, abbreviation of month, year
   - URL in angle brackets *only* if readers would have difficulty locating the reference using a search engine

Works located on the Web (with no print equivalent)
Entire Web site

> West, Tim, dir. *Southern Historical Collection*. U of North Carolina, 2 July 2008. Web. 14 Sept. 2008.

Part of a site

> McSurely, Alan. "Alan McSurely Papers Inventory." *Southern Historical Collection*. Dir. Tim West. U of North Carolina, Apr. 2000. Web. 14 Sept. 2008.

> McGirt, Ellen. "The Minneapolis Bridge Collapse: Our Crumbling Infrastructure." *Fast Company*. Mansueto Ventures LLC, 2 Aug. 2007. Web. 12 Sept. 2008.

Online newspaper article

>   Jamieson, Robert L., Jr. "Housing Vouchers Help Bring Vets Home."
>
>   *Seattle Post-Intelligencer*. Seattle Post-Intelligencer, 10 Nov. 2008.
>
>   Web. 17 Nov. 2008.

Online magazine article

>   Greenwald, Glenn. "Eric Holder, Jack Quinn and the Rich Pardon."
>
>   *Salon.com*. Salon Media Group, 3 Dec. 2008. Web. 12 Jan. 2009.

Note: Newspaper and magazine articles that exist only on the Web do not typically have page designations, as do articles in print media. Accordingly, the citations for such articles omit page numbers. Articles in Web-based scholarly journals sometimes *do* include page numbers. For this reason, include page numbers (if available) when citing Web-based journals. Use "n. pag." if page numbers are not provided.

Scholarly journal article existing only on the Web

>   Peterson, Karen. "Teens, Literature, and the Web." *The Alan Review* 31.3
>
>   (2004): n. pag. Web. 3 Mar. 2009.

Online reference article

>   Kranzburg, Melvin, and Joseph Gies. "History of the Organization of
>
>   Work." *Encyclopaedia Britannica Online*. Encyclopaedia Britannica,
>
>   2008. Web. 12 Nov. 2008.

Interview

>   Peterson, Paul. Interview by Gary James. *ClassicBands.com*. Classic Bands,
>
>   12 Feb. 2000. Web. 8 Jan. 2008. < http://www.classicbands.com/
>
>   PaulPetersonInterview.html>.

Note: Include a URL in a citation only if readers could not otherwise locate the source through a standard search query or from the home page of the Web site you are referencing. Enclose the URL in angle brackets and position it at the end of the citation. If the URL does not fit on one line, break the address only after a slash. Add no hyphen or other punctuation to the URL.

Review

>   Selegman, Craig. Rev. of *Amsterdam*, by Ian McEwan. *Salon Books*.
>
>   Salon, 9 Dec. 1998. Web. 12 Jan. 2008.

E-mail communication

Mendez, Michael R. "Re: Solar Power." Message to Edgar V. Atamian.

11 Sept. 2008. E-mail.

Morley, Jessica. Message to the author. 14 Dec. 2008. E-mail.

Bibliography

Pfaff, Steve, comp. *Globalization References*. N.p., n.d. Web.

5 May 2008.

Wiki

"Garden Bridge, Shanghai." *CC-Wiki*. Travellerspoint Travel Community,

2008. Web. 15 Nov. 2008.

Blog

O'Toole, Randal. "New Study Questions Cause of Wildfires." *The

Commons: Markets Protecting the Environment*. The Commons Blog,

11 July 2006. Web. 12 Mar. 2008.

Podcast

Reid, Hal, and Joe Francica. "Accurate 3D Geometry for the Automotive

Industry." *Directionsmag.com*. Directions Magazine, 7 Jan. 2007.

Web. 12 Feb. 2009.

Online video

Brown, John. "How to Change a Flat Tire on a Bicycle." *Expert Village*.

YouTube, 19 Nov. 2007. Web. 12 Dec. 2008.

Works located through a database or scholarly project

When citing a work located through a database (such as those available through your college Internet provider) or scholarly project, begin with the citation format for the source as it appeared in print (or another medium). Then (1) give the name of the database, in italics; (2) follow with "Web," the medium of publication; and (3) end with your date of access (day, abbreviation of month, and year). Do *not* include the URL of the database.

Article—magazine

Raghaven, Anita. "Help Wanted." *Forbes* 27 Oct. 2008: 36. *Academic

OneFile*. Web. 3 Nov. 2008.

Article (signed)—newspaper or newswire

Reynolds, Maura, and Andrea Chang. "Retail Slump is a Bad Omen." *Los Angeles Times* 7 Nov. 2008, home ed.: A1+. *LexisNexis*. Web. 12 Nov. 2008.

Article (unsigned)—newspaper or newswire

"Election 2008: Thoughts on Obama's Win." *Atlanta Journal-Constitution* 6 Nov. 2008, main ed.: A1. *LexisNexis*. Web. 12 Nov. 2008.

Article—scholarly journal

Coffey, Warren. "Flannery O'Connor." *Commentary* 40.5 (1965): 93-99. *Contemporary Literary Criticism*. Web. 12 Dec. 2008.

Article—in a scholarly project

Field, Peter S. "Transcendentalist Meditations." *Reviews in American History* 29.1 (2001): 49-61. *Project Muse*. Web. 11 Feb. 2009.

Image

Camel Lights. Advertisement. *Advertising Archives*. Nov. 1992. Web. 28 Nov. 2009.

Book

Dickens, Charles. *Bleak House*. New York, 1853. *Project Gutenberg*. Web. 14 Feb. 2009.

Government document

United States. Extension Service. *4-H and the War.* N.d. *Historic Government Publications from World War II*. Web. 7 May 2008.

Electronic sources also available in another medium

Sources not accessed through a subscription database (such as LexisNexis) may have appeared first in print or in another medium. When citing such works found on the Web, include original publication information if you think this would be useful for your readers. Follow the citation format for the original medium. Instead of ending the citation with "Print," (1) italicize the title of the Web site, (2) indicate "Web" as the medium of publication, and (3) provide your date of access (day, abbreviation of month, and year).

Newspaper

Reynolds, Maura. "Recession Could Last into 2010." *Los Angeles Times* 2 Dec. 2008: A1+. *LATimes.com*. Web. 2 Dec. 2008.

Magazine

Featherstone, Steve. "The Coming Robot Army: Introducing America's Future Fighting Machines." *Harper's Magazine* Feb. 2007: 43-52. *Harpers.org.* Web. 6 Mar. 2009.

Scholarly journal

Macpherson, Alison, Linda Rothman, and Andrew Howard. "Body-Checking Rules and Childhood Injuries in Ice Hockey." *Pediatrics* 117.2 (2006): 143-47. *Pediatrics.aapublications.org.* Web. 19 Nov. 2008.

Translation

Basho, Matsuo. "Climb Mount Fuji." Trans. Robert Hass. *The Essential Haiku.* Ed. Robert Hass. New York: Ecco, 1994. *Dept. of English, U of Illinois at Urbana-Champaign.* Web. 14 Apr. 2009.

Work of art accessed online

Vermeer, Johannes. *View of Delft.* c. 1660-61. Muaritshuis. *The Collection: Top Ten.* Web. 7 Mar. 2009.

Film accessed online

Young Frankenstein. Dir. Mel Brooks. 20th Century Fox, 1974. *Netflix.* Web. 15 Dec. 2008.

Print Sources (MLA)

Periodicals

For all scholarly journals, include both the volume number and the issue number (if available) in the works-cited entry.

Journal: continuous pagination throughout annual cycle

Binder, Sarah. "The Dynamics of Legislative Gridlock, 1947-1996." *American Political Science Review* 93.3 (1999): 519-31. Print.

[Note style of page ranges and use of hyphen.]

Journal: separate pagination each issue

O'Mealy, Joseph H. "Royal Family Values: The Americanization of Alan Bennett's *The Madness of King George III.*" *Literature/Film Quarterly* 27.2 (1999): 90-97. Print.

Magazine article

Davison, Peter. "Girl, Seeming to Disappear." *Atlantic Monthly* May 2000: 108-11. Print.

Newspaper article

Vise, David A. "FBI Report Gauges School Violence Indicators." *Washington Post* 6 Sept. 2000: B1+. Print.

"Strong Opinions in Tough Times." Editorial. *Boston Globe* 2 Dec. 2008: A18. Print.

Unsigned newspaper article

"The World's Meeting Place." *New York Times* 6 Sept. 2000, natl. ed.: A11. Print.

Review

Barber, Benjamin R. "The Crack in the Picture Window." Rev. of *Bowling Alone: The Collapse and Revival of American Community*, by Robert D. Putnam. *Nation* 7 Aug. 2000: 29-34. Print.

Books
One author

Fahs, Alice. *The Imagined Civil War: Popular Literature of the North and South, 1861-1865*. Chapel Hill: U of North Carolina P, 2003. Print.

Note: MLA abbreviates the names of university presses (e.g., Oxford UP for Oxford University Press; as shown above for University of North Carolina Press). Commercial publishers' names are also shortened by dropping such endings as "Co.," and "Inc." The *MLA Handbook* includes a list of abbreviations for publishers' names.

Two or more books by the same author

Gubar, Susan. *Critical Condition: Feminism at the Turn of the Century*. New York: Columbia UP, 2000. Print.

---. *Racechanges: White Skin, Black Face in American Culture*. New York: Oxford UP, 1997. Print.

Note: For MLA style, references to works by the same author are listed in alphabetical order of title.

Two or three authors

Lesmoir-Gordon, Nigel, Will Rood, and Ralph Edney. *Introducing Fractal Geometry*. Cambridge, UK: Icon Books, 2000. Print.

More than three authors

Burawoy, Michael, et al. *Global Ethnography: Forces, Connections, and Imaginations in a Postmodern World*. Berkeley: U of California P, 2000. Print.

Book with an editor and no author

Dean, Bartholomew, and Jerome M. Levi, eds. *At the Risk of Being Heard: Identity, Indigenous Rights, and Postcolonial States*. Ann Arbor: U of Michigan P, 2003. Print.

Second or subsequent edition

Whitten, Phillip. *Anthropology: Contemporary Perspectives*. 8th ed. Boston: Allyn, 2001. Print.

Selection from an anthology

Hardy, Melissa. "The Heifer." *The Best American Short Stories 2002*. Ed. Sue Miller. Boston: Houghton, 2002. 97-115. Print.

Republished book

Dreiser, Theodore. *An American Tragedy*. 1925. Cambridge, UK: Bentley, 1978. Print.

A multivolume work

Slovenko, Ralph. *Psychiatry in Law/Law in Psychiatry*. 2 vols. New York: Brunner-Routledge, 2002. Print.

Translation

Saramago, Jose. *All the Names*. Trans. Margaret Jull Kosta. New York: Harcourt, 1999. Print.

Government publication

National Institute of Child Health and Human Development. *Closing the Gap: A National Blueprint to Improve the Health of Persons with Mental Retardation*. Washington: GPO, 2002. Print.

United States. Cong. House. Committee on Government Reform. *Interim Report of the Activities of the House Committee on Government Reform*. 107th Cong. 1st sess. Washington: GPO, 2001. Print.

The Bible

The New English Bible. New York: Oxford UP, 1972. Print.

Signed encyclopedia article

Kunzle, David M. "Caricature, Cartoon, and Comic Strip." *The New Encyclopaedia Britannica: Macropaedia*. 15th ed. 2002. Print.

Unsigned encyclopedia article

"Tidal Wave." *Encyclopedia Americana*. 2nd ed. 2001. Print.

Other Sources (MLA)

In addition to other pertinent information, record the medium of reception (Radio, Television, Film, CD, DVD, etc.).

Interview conducted by the researcher

Emerson, Robert. Personal interview. 10 Oct. 2002.

Dissertation (abstracted in *Dissertation Abstracts International*)

Sheahan, Mary Theresa. "Living on the Edge: Ecology and Economy in Willa Cather's 'Wild Land': Webster County, Nebraska, 1870–1900." Diss. Northern Illinois U, 1999. *DAI* 60 (1999): 1298A. Print.

Note: If the dissertation is published on microfilm by University Microfilms, give the order number at the conclusion of the reference. Example, in MLA format: Ann Arbor: UMI, 1999. AAT 9316566.

Lecture

Osborne, Michael. "The Great Man Theory: Caesar." History 401. U of California, Santa Barbara. 5 Nov. 2003. Lecture.

Paper delivered at a professional conference

Brodkey, Linda. "The Rhetoric of Race in Practice." Conf. on Coll. Composition and Communication. Palmer House, Chicago. 20 Mar. 2003. Address.

Film

The Pianist. Dir. Roman Polanski. Perf. Adrien Brody. Focus Features and Universal, 2002. Film.

Recording of a TV program or film

Hunting the Hidden Dimension. Narr. Neil Ross. Dir. Michael Schwartz and Bill Jersey. *NOVA*. PBS. WGBH, Boston, 22 Oct. 2008. Television.

Audio recording

Raman, Susheela. "Song to the Siren." *Salt Rain*. Narada, 2001. CD.

> Schumann, Robert. *Symphonies Nos. 1 and 4.* Cond. George Szell. Cleveland
> Orch. Columbia, 1978. CD.

Or, to emphasize the conductor rather than the composer:

> Szell, George, cond. *Symphonies Nos. 1 and 4.* By Robert Schumann. Cleveland
> Orch. Columbia, 1978. CD.

■ APA STYLE: IN-TEXT CITATIONS

In-text citations using the APA system take this form:

> A good deal of research shows that rather than inducing any lasting
> changes in a child's behavior, punishment "promotes only momentary
> compliance" (Berk, 2002, p. 383).

Notice that in the APA system, there is a comma between the author's name and the date, and another comma between the date and the page number, which is preceded by "p." or "pp." Notice also that the parenthetical reference is placed *before* the final punctuation of the sentence.

If you have already mentioned the author's name in the text, do not repeat it in the citation:

> According to Berk (2002), a good deal of research shows that rather than
> inducing any lasting changes in a child's behavior, punishment "promotes
> only momentary compliance" (p. 383).

OR:

> According to Berk, a good deal of research shows that rather than inducing
> any lasting changes in a child's behavior, punishment "promotes only
> momentary compliance" (2002, p. 383).

When using the APA system, provide page numbers only for direct quotations, not for summaries or paraphrases. If you do not refer to a specific page, simply indicate the date:

> Berk (2002) asserted that many research findings view punishment as
> a quick fix rather than a long-term solution to behavior problems in
> children.

For quotations of 40 words or more, use block (indented) quotations. In these cases, place the parenthetical citation *after* the concluding period:

> Various strategies exist for reducing children's tendency to view the
> world in a gender-biased fashion:
>
> > Once children notice the vast array of gender
> > stereotypes in their society, parents and teachers can
> > point out exceptions. For example, they can arrange

> for children to see men and women pursuing nontraditional careers. And they can reason with children, explaining that interests and skills, not sex, should determine a person's occupation and activities. (Berk, 2002, p. 395)

Again, were Berk's name mentioned in the sentence leading into the quotation, the parenthetical reference would be simply (2002, p. 395) for APA style.

If the reference applies only to the first part of a sentence, the parenthetical reference is inserted at the appropriate point *within* the sentence:

> Shapiro (2002) emphasizes the idea that law firms are "continually in flux" (p. 32), while Sikes focuses on their stability as institutions.

At times you must modify the basic author/date/page number reference. Depending on the nature of your source(s), you may need to use one of the following citation formats:

Quoted material appearing in another source

> (as cited in Garber, 2000, p. 211)

An anonymous work

> ("Obedience," 2003, p. 32)

Two authors

> (Striano & Rochat, 2000, p. 257)
>
> [Note use of ampersand.]

Two or more sources (arrange entries in alphabetic order of surname)

> (Ehrenreich, 2001, p. 68; Hitchens, 2001, p. 140)

A multivolume work

> (Brown, 2003, vol. 2, p. 88)

In-text Citation of Electronic Sources (APA)

Web sites, CD-ROM data, and e-mail generally do not have numbered pages (unless they are PDF reproductions of print material). If paragraph numbers are visible in the source, you can use them instead of page numbers for in-text citations. If the document has headings but no page or paragraph numbers, cite the heading and the number of the paragraph following it.

Citation of an electronic source with headings

> (Kishlansky, 2002, Conclusion section, ¶2)

■ APA STYLE: CITATIONS IN THE REFERENCES LIST

Electronic Sources (APA)

The basic information needed to cite electronic sources is:

1. *Name of the author* (if given)
2. *Date of publication* or update; date of retrieval is required only if you think the cited source might change.
3. *Document title, description, and/or source*
4. *URL,* or Internet address

Note: When referring to an online text available only through a subscription service, provide the URL for the home page or menu page of the service. Do the same for online encyclopedias and dictionaries.

The *APA Publication Manual* and the *APA Style Guide to Electronic References* (2007) recommend that writers check URLs regularly while drafting a paper and before submission because the location of documents sometimes changes. Include as much pertinent information as is available to help your reader find the source, such as volume and issue numbers.

The general APA format for online periodical sources is:

> Author, I. (date). Title of article. *Name of Periodical, Volume*(issue number
>
> if available), page numbers. doi: <u>or</u> Retrieved from URL
>
> Rodkin, P.C., & Berger, C. (2008). Who bullies whom? Social status asymmetries
>
> by victim gender. *International Journal of Behavioral Development, 32*(6),
>
> 473–485. doi: 10.1177/0165025408093667

When a Digital Object Identifier (DOI)—a unique digital locator assigned to a source—is available, include it (and *not* the URL) in your citation. If you reference a site where readers can purchase software, articles, or books (as opposed to accessing them directly, for free), use "Available from" instead of "Retrieved from."

Do not add periods or other punctuation immediately following URLs. If you need to continue a URL across lines, break the URL before a slash or before a period. Do not use a hyphen; an extra hyphen or period may prevent a reader from accessing the source.

APA reference format does not require the database name (EBSCO, ProQuest, etc.) in your reference, as long as you provide a URL for the home page or menu page. In no case should you include both the database name and the URL.

An article in a magazine

> Kim, J. (2003, July 16). When cell phones meet camcorders. *Forbes.* Retrieved
>
> from http://www.forbes.com/home/2003/07/16/cx_jk_0716tentech.html

A signed article in a newspaper or on a newswire

> Vartabedian, R. (2003, July 16). Columbia's crew lived after radio calls ended.
>
> > *Chicago Tribune.* Retrieved from http://www.chicagotribune.com/technology
> >
> > /la-na-shuttle16jul16,1,1997210.story?coll=chi-news-hed

An unsigned article in a newspaper or on a newswire

> Verizon to rehire 1,100 laid-off workers. (2003, July 16). *AP Online.* Retrieved
>
> > from http://www.nytimes.com/aponline/technology/AP-Verizon-Jobs.html

An article from a scholarly journal

> Paatz, A. (2004). The socio-cultural function of media in nineteenth-century
>
> > Latin America. *CLCWeb: Comparative Literature and Culture: A WWWeb*
> >
> > *Journal, 3*(2). Retrieved from http://clcwebjournal.lib.purdue.edu
> >
> > /clcweb01-2/paatz01.html

Note: Whether the journal is paginated anew with each issue or is paginated continuously through the annual cycle, provide (if available) the issue number in your citation of the electronic source.

A stand-alone document with author and date

> Winter, M. (2003). *How to talk new age.* Retrieved November 8, 2007, from
>
> > http://www.well.com/user/mick/newagept.html

Note: If no author is identified, begin the reference with the document title. When no date of publication is given, indicate this with n.d. for "no date" in parentheses where the date would usually appear. In this case, provide the date on which you retrieved the information. Present the date in this form:

> Retrieved May 1, 2007, from URL

An abstract

> Eliaphson, N., & Lichterman, P. (2003). Culture in interaction. *American Journal*
>
> > *of Sociology.* Abstract retrieved from http://www.journals.uchicago.edu/AJS
> >
> > /journal/issues/v108n4/040241/brief/040241.abstract.html

Message posting

> Pagdin, F. (2001, July 3). New medium for therapy [Msg 498]. Message posted
>
> > to http://www.groups.yahoo.com/group/cybersociology/message/498

Note: For online postings or synchronous communications, the APA recommends referencing only those sources that are maintained in archived form. However, archived discussions or postings are rarely peer reviewed, are not generally regarded as having scholarly content, and are not archived for very long, so APA advises that you cite them with care in formal works. APA also advises against using nonarchived postings because they are not retrievable by your readers. If you do choose to use sources that are not archived, and this includes e-mail communications between individuals, the APA suggests citing them as personal communications only in the text of your work. Do not include them in the References list. For archived sources, follow this and the following models as appropriate.

Podcast

Academic technology podcasts. (2007, June 1). *Academic Technology Resource Centre, Palomar College.* Podcast retrieved from http://www.palomar.edu/atrc/Pod/podindex.htm

Wiki

Erie canal. (n.d.). Retrieved May 4, 2007, from NY Canals Wiki: http://www.nycanals.com/Erie_Canal

Weblog (blog)

Danielson, S. (2007, June 5). Recognizing the limits of your cultural appropriation. Message posted to http://www.bruchma.com/~acsumama/blog/

Periodicals (APA)

Monthly periodical

Davison, P. (2000, May). Girl, seeming to disappear. *Atlantic Monthly, 285,* 108–111.

Signed article in a weekly periodical

Gladwell, M. (2000, May 29). The new-boy network. *The New Yorker,* 68–86.

Unsigned article in a weekly periodical

Spain and the Basques: Dangerous stalemate. (2003, July 5). *The Economist, 368,* 44–45.

Signed article in a daily newspaper, discontinuous pages

Vise, D. A. (2000, September 6). FBI report gauges school violence indicators. *The Washington Post,* pp. B1, B6.

Unsigned article in a daily newspaper

The world's meeting place. (2000, September 6). *The New York Times,* p. A11.

Review

> Barber, B. R. (2000, August 7). The crack in the picture window. [Review of
> the book *Bowling alone: The collapse and revival of American community*].
> *The Nation*, 29–34.

Note: Some weekly magazines do not have volume numbers, in which case
you include only the date and page numbers in your reference.

Journal: continuous pagination throughout annual cycle

> Tomlins, C. L. (2003). In a wilderness of tigers: Violence, the discourse of
> English colonizing, and the refusals of American history. *Theoretical
> Inquiries in Law, 4*, 505–543.

Journal: separate pagination for each issue

> O'Mealy, J. H. (1999). Royal family values: The Americanization of Alan Bennett's
> *The madness of King George III*. *Literature/Film Quarterly, 27*(2), 90–97.

Books (APA)

One author

> Fahs, Alice. (2003). *The imagined civil war: Popular literature of the north and
> south, 1861–1865*. Chapel Hill: University of North Carolina Press.

Two or more books by the same author

> Gubar, S. (1997). *Racechanges: White skin, black face in American culture*.
> New York: Oxford University Press.
> Gubar, S. (2000). *Critical condition: Feminism at the turn of the century*.
> New York: Columbia University Press.

Note: For APA style, references to works by the same author are listed in chronological order of publication, earliest first. Use the author's name in all entries.

Two authors

> Gerson, A., & Adler, J. (2003). *The price of terror*. New York: Harper.

Three authors

> Booth, W. C., Colomb, G. C., & Williams, J. M. (2003). *The craft of research*
> (2nd ed.). Chicago: University of Chicago Press.

More than three authors

> Burawoy, M., Blum, J. A., George, S., Gille, Z., Gowan, T., Haney, L., et al.
> (2000). *Global ethnography: Forces, connections, and imaginations*

in a postmodern world. Berkeley: University of
California Press.

Note: If more than six, list only the first six, followed by *et al.*

Book with an editor and no author

Dean, B., & Levi, J. M. (Eds.). (2003). *At the risk of being heard: Identity,
indigenous rights, and postcolonial states*. Ann Arbor: University
of Michigan Press.

Second or subsequent edition

Whitten, P. (2001). *Anthropology: Contemporary perspectives* (8th ed.). Boston:
Allyn & Bacon.

Republished book

Dreiser, T. (1978). *An American tragedy*. Cambridge, MA: Bentley.
(Original work published 1925)

A multivolume work

Slovenko, R. (2002). *Psychiatry in law/law in psychiatry* (Vols. 1–2). New York:
Brunner-Routledge.

Translation

Saramago, J. (1999). *All the names*. (M. J. Kosta, Trans.). New York: Harcourt.

Selection from an anthology

Halberstam, D. (2002). Who we are. In S. J. Gould (Ed.), *The best American
essays 2002* (pp. 124–136). New York: Houghton Mifflin.

Government publication

*Caring for children act of 2003: Report of the Senate Committee on Health,
Education, Labor, and Pensions*, S. Rep. No. 108-37 (2003).
National Institute of Child Health and Human Development. (2002). *Closing
the gap: A national blueprint to improve the health of persons with mental
retardation*. Washington, DC: U.S. Government Printing Office.

Signed encyclopedia article

Kunzle, D. M. (2002). Caricature, cartoon, and comic strip. In *The new
encyclopaedia Britannica*. (Vol. 15, pp. 539–552). Chicago:
Encyclopaedia Britannica.

Unsigned encyclopedia article

> Tidal wave. (2001). In *The encyclopedia Americana.* (Vol. 26, p. 730). Danbury, CT: Grolier.

Other Sources (APA)

Dissertation (abstracted in *Dissertation Abstracts International*)

> Sheahan, M. T. (1999). Living on the edge: Ecology and economy in Willa Cather's "Wild Land": Webster County, Nebraska, 1870–1900 (Doctoral dissertation, Northern Illinois University, 1999). *Dissertation Abstracts International, 60,* 1298A.

Note: If the dissertation is obtained from University Microfilms, give the UMI number in parentheses at the conclusion of the reference, after the DAI number: (UMI No. AAD9315947).

Lecture

> Baldwin, J. (1999, January 11). *The self in social interactions.* Sociology 2 lecture, University of California, Santa Barbara.

Paper delivered at a professional conference

> Hollon, S. D. (2003, August). Treatment and prevention of depression with drugs and psychotherapy. Paper presented at the annual convention of the American Psychological Association, Toronto, Ontario.

Film

> Polanski, R. (Director). (2002). *The pianist* [Motion picture]. United States: Focus Features and Universal.

TV series

> Chase, D. (Producer). (2001). *The Sopranos* [Television series]. New York: HBO.

Music recording

> Raman, S. (2001). Song to the siren. On *Salt Rain* [CD]. Milwaukee, WI: Narada.

 ## WRITING ASSIGNMENT: SOURCE-BASED PAPER

Using the methods we have outlined in this chapter—and incorporating the skills covered in this textbook as a whole—conduct your own research on a topic and research question that falls within your major or your area of interest. Your research process should culminate in a 1500- to 1700-word paper in which you use your sources to present an answer to your research question.

Practicing Academic Writing

8

■ THE CHANGING LANDSCAPE OF WORK IN THE TWENTY-FIRST CENTURY

Along with the well-wishes of friends and family, you bring to college many expectations. Some involve your emergence as an independent thinker; others, your emergence as an adult, social being. But perhaps no expectation weighs so heavily as thoughts of future employment and the hope of financial independence. On the far end of this journey you have begun in higher education, you will seek meaningful employment. If you already devote long hours to supporting your family or paying your way through school, then you know *exactly* why so many pursue a degree: the conviction that a diploma will ensure a better, more secure job. Learn, apply yourself, and succeed: This has always been the formula for achieving the American dream.

The times, however (to paraphrase Bob Dylan), are changing.

In the second half of the twentieth century, the labor market rewarded the educated, conferring on those who attended college an "education premium." Even as the forces of globalization reshaped the American economy and workers began losing manufacturing jobs to competitors offshore in China and India, college-educated workers were generally spared severe disruptions. Today, education no longer promises such protection. The relentless search for cheap labor and plentiful raw materials, together with advances in technology, have opened the information-based service economy to foreign competition. According to economists and other analysts, the American, college-educated workforce will increasingly face the same pressures that decades ago so unsettled the automotive and manufacturing sectors. Employers are already offshoring computer coding, certain types of accounting, and medical consultation (the reading of X-rays, MRIs, CT scans, and such)—services that require extensive training.

Experts predict that more American jobs will be lost to foreign competition and fewer will entail a lifelong commitment between employer and employee (pensions, for instance, are fast disappearing). What implications will these developments hold for you and your intended career? Will they affect the courses you take, the major (and minors) you choose, the summer jobs and internships you pursue? Could you conduct an analysis *now* that will help you anticipate and avoid major disruptions to your working life tomorrow?

This chapter provides an opportunity to learn what economists, policy analysts, and educators are thinking about the world of work in the twenty-first century. We open with four selections that set a broad context for the discussion. First, Richard Judy and Carol D'Amico, analysts at the Hudson Institute, offer a "map" of what they think will be a much-changed landscape, with clear winners and losers among American workers. Next, in an excerpt from his best-selling *The Word Is Flat*, the *New York Times* columnist Thomas Friedman urges young people contemplating future work to become "untouchable"—that is, to take on jobs that cannot be easily outsourced. In much the same vein, the Princeton economist and former presidential advisor Alan S. Blinder distinguishes between "personal services" workers and "impersonal services" workers and leaves no room for doubt as to which you want to be. We follow with an article from *The Economist*, "Into the Unknown," which assures us that even as jobs are lost to computerization and automation, and even as overseas competitors siphon off jobs and create concern for the future of the American workforce, the economy will nevertheless grow. Technologies we cannot imagine today will emerge to service the needs and desires of tomorrow, in the process creating jobs for you and your grandchildren.

These selections are followed by five other readings that consider the future of employment in specific career fields: engineering, business, technology/services industries, law, and medicine. These selections provide a glimpse into what experts are saying about the future of work in areas that may touch on your intended career. We introduce this second set of readings with a summary by the Bureau of Labor Statistics of its "Employment Projections: 2006–2016," with links to ten detailed tables on the BLS Web site.

Your main assignment in this practice chapter will be to write an argument that synthesizes your own insights with what various authors have written on the topic. To prepare for this assignment, you will complete several briefer exercises that require you to draw on your sources. During this progression of assignments, you will write a combination of summaries, paraphrases, critiques, and explanations that will prepare you for—and that will produce sections of—your more ambitious argument synthesis. In this respect, the assignments here are typical of other writing you will do in college: While at times you will be called on to write a stand-alone critique or a purely explanatory paper, you will also write papers that blend the basic forms of college writing that you have studied in this text. Both your critiques and your explanations will rely in part on summaries—or partial summaries—of specific articles. Your arguments may rely on summaries, critiques, *and* explanations.

This set of readings on the changing landscape of work in the twenty-first century amounts to controlled research. We have provided the topic; and from a search of books, journals, magazines, and newspapers, we have gathered selections that can provide the basis of an informed discussion that you will present as an academic paper. When an instructor asks you to write a research paper, the end point of your research will be exactly what you will encounter below: a series of readings that await your consideration and synthesis.

■ THE ASSIGNMENTS

Read: Prepare to Write

In this chapter, you will read a variety of sources discussing our topic, "The Changing Landscape of Work in the Twenty-First Century." Preceding the selections, a series of assignments prompts you to write papers based on these sources. We suggest that you read these assignments before reading the selections themselves; knowing what you are expected to write will help prepare you to read.

Your main task in most academic writing is to create and take part in a conversation among source authors—according to your own purpose. As you read the following selections, mark up the texts; write notes to yourself and to the authors in the margins.

To prepare for the most ambitious of the assignments that follow, the explanatory and argumentative syntheses, consider making a topic list of your sources as you read. For each topic about which two or more authors have something to say, jot down notes and page references. Here is a sample entry:

> Who will succeed/Who will fail in twenty-first-century workplace?
>
> Thomas Friedman: untouchables, fungible vs. non-fungible
>   work, pp. 325–326
> Alan Blinder: personal services jobs vs. impersonal services
>   jobs, pp. 10–12
> Victoria Reitz: innovators vs. commodities, p. 334
> Tom Peters: specialists vs. generalists, p. 335

A topic list keyed to your sources will spare you the frustration of reading thirty or more pages and flipping through them later, saying, "Now where did I read that?" In the sample entry, we see that four authors speak to the likely success and failure of different types of work in the coming decades. At this early point, you don't need to know how you might write a paper based on this or any topic. But with your list, you create for yourself the *possibility* of orchestrating a conversation later. A robust list with multiple topics and accurate notes for each puts you in a good position to write a synthesis.

As it happens, the sample entry above should come in handy when you're preparing to write your explanatory and argumentative syntheses on the changing landscape of work in the twenty-first century. Creating a topic list with multiple entries will take you a bit more time as you read, but it will save you even more time as you write.

Group Assignment #1: Make Topic Lists

> Create two topic list entries for the selections in this chapter, making sure to jot down notes and page references for each. Create one topic on your own, based on your own careful reading of the selections. Choose your second topic from the list that follows.

- importance of a global perspective
- effects of globalization, positive and negative
- protecting jobs from outsourcing/offshoring
- effects of (high) technology/automation in general
- disappearance of/changes in traditional jobs/careers/professions
- emergence of new jobs/opportunities, entrepreneurial and otherwise
- thinking "outside the box" of traditional jobs/careers/ways of making money
- "revolution in services" (see Lohr)—implications
- role of education (secondary, postsecondary)
- importance of retraining and continuing education
- effects of aging boomer generation on consumer market/labor market
- effects of changing demographics of workforce, e.g., growing Hispanic population
- role of innovation, technology
- role of telecommunications, telecommuting
- the new business mentality needed for getting ahead, remaining competitive
- changing nature of leadership, teamwork
- "survival of the fittest" economy
- clashes of old and new business models/professional cultures
- personal qualities needed to succeed

Meet in groups of three or four to exchange notes on your topics. As a group, discuss what source authors write about each topic. (Note that not all authors will discuss all topics.) Working together, develop the entries: Create the most comprehensive notes you can for each. As a class, generate a master list of topics and notes. This list should include all topics suggested above and all topics created by individual class members. At the conclusion of this exercise, all class members should have a comprehensive guide to key topics in the source readings. For ease of completing Assignment #2 below, place each topic, with its notes, on a separate sheet of paper.

Group Assignment #2: Create a Topic Web

> **Working in groups of three or four, create a network, or web, of connections among topics. That is, determine which topics relate or "speak" to other topics.**

Articulate these connections. For instance, draw a line from one topic—say, the importance of maintaining a global perspective—to another: say, the role of innovation and technology. How are these topics related? As a group, generate as many connections as possible. At the conclusion of this work, you will have in hand not only the fruits of Assignment #1—potential threads of conversation within topics (multiple authors speaking about specific topics)—you will also have a potential conversation *across* topics. You will have the necessary raw material for writing your syntheses.

Note that one synthesis—a single paper—could not possibly refer to every topic, or every connection among topics, you have found. The craft of preparing and writing a synthesis depends on your ability to *select* closely related topics and then to make and develop a claim that links and is supported by them.

Summary

Summary Assignments #1 and #2: Summarizing Text

#1: Summarize either "Work and Workers in the Twenty-first Century" by Judy and D'Amico or "The Untouchables" by Thomas Friedman. Make careful notes on the selection as you prepare your summary. Follow the guidelines in Chapter 1, particularly the Guidelines for Writing Summaries box on pp. 7–8. Also, consult the advice on note-taking (pp. 13–16). For the selection you are *not* summarizing, read carefully and highlight the text *as if* you were preparing to write a summary.

#2: In preparation for writing a critique, summarize "Into the Unknown," pp. 327–329. As with Summary #1, make careful notes on the selection as you read and then follow the advice for writing summaries in Chapter 1. Before beginning to write, read the assignment for Critique below. The summary that you write will form an important section of that critique.

Summary Assignment #3: Summarizing Tables

#3: Review (online) the ten tables presented by the Bureau of Labor Statistics (see titles and URLs on p. 332). Before selecting a BLS table for this assignment, read the assignments for Argument below. To the extent you are able, decide on the argument you will be writing and choose a table to summarize accordingly. Use your summary of the BLS table to support your argument.

Note: In each table, the BLS presents far too much information for you to summarize in its entirety. Write a *partial* summary, therefore—keeping in mind the argument you expect to write. First, decide which table you think will be most useful to that argument; then decide on a *subset* of information to best advance your argument's claim. For advice on summarizing tables (and parts of tables), see pp. 30–40.

Critique

Write a critique of "Into the Unknown" (pp. 327–329).

You'll find the thesis of the article in the first sentence of paragraph 4: "What the worriers always forget is that the same changes in production technology that destroy jobs also create new ones." This thesis rests on the assumption that the economy will "take care of its own consequences"*—that is, the economy, without any meddling by well-intentioned policymakers, will in the long term create opportunities for workers in new areas even as it eliminates opportunities in other areas. Left alone to operate, market forces will in the end create the best outcomes for the economy as a whole. Individuals may win or lose, but overall the economy remains stable and healthy. In this chapter you'll find this same assumption at work: See, for instance, the footnote on p. 320, explaining the term "creative destruction." See also Alan Blinder's essay, paragraph 8, on p. 10.

To write this critique, you don't need to be an economics major or even to have taken an introductory course in economics. Rather, in developing your critical evaluation of the piece, rely on your own experience. Probe the assumption: Do not feel pressured to agree or disagree with it. Pose questions:

- Have you witnessed the economy treat one group of workers harshly? Have friends or relatives been treated harshly?

- Considering the experience of people you know, do new jobs created by the economy necessarily aid workers who have lost jobs? Would you expect the economy to operate in this way? Think of examples.

- Do you believe that the economy takes care of its own consequences? Think of the winners and losers in our evolving economy. Who provides for the losers? How?

- What happens to the main argument of "Into the Unknown" if this key assumption turns out not to be true—if the economy does *not* take care of its own consequences?

Because the writing you do for this assignment will be incorporated into a larger argument with its own introduction and conclusion, you needn't write an introduction or conclusion to this critique. Instead, write an *abbreviated* critique, consisting of three parts:

1. a summary of the selection (your response to Summary Assignment #2)
2. an evaluation of the presentation for accuracy, clarity, logic, and/or fairness
3. a statement of your agreement and/or disagreement with the author

For parts 2 and 3, be sure to support your evaluation with reasons. Refer to the selection, summarizing or quoting key elements as needed. See Chapter 2 for advice on critical reading. See particularly the Guidelines for Writing Critiques box on pp. 73–74, along with the hints on incorporating quoted material into your own writing, pp. 44–53.

---

*Jonathan Sacks, *Dignity of Difference* (London: Continuum, 2003) 88.

Explanation

Based on the reading selections in this chapter, write three explanations that you might use in a larger argument. The explanations should each consist of two to four well-developed paragraphs on one of the following topics: (1) the developments responsible for the accelerating changes in the American workplace, (2) the jobs that are most—and least—at risk from these changes, and (3) why an American worker has reasons for both optimism and pessimism regarding these changes.

Key requirements for each explanation:

- Consider each explanation to be a paper in miniature with its own thesis: a single statement that will guide the writing of the paragraphs of explanation that follow.

- Each paragraph of explanation that follows the explanatory thesis should begin with a clear topic sentence.

- Each paragraph of explanation should refer to *at least two* different sources. Be sure to set up the reference (which can be a summary, paraphrase, or quotation) with care, using appropriate citation format, most likely MLA (see pp. 290–299).

- To develop your explanation, draw on facts, examples, statistics, and expert opinions from your sources, as needed.

Analysis

Select a principle or definition discussed in one of the readings on "The Changing Landscape of Work in the Twenty-first Century" and apply this principle or definition to (1) a particular situation relating to work of which you have personal knowledge, or (2) a work-related situation involving a particular individual or a group of individuals that you have read about in an article you found through research.

First, review the master list of topics and the notes that you generated for Group Assignment #1 (pp. 311–312) to determine possible analytic principles or definitions. For example, under the topic of technology/automation you may be most interested in Judy and D'Amico's contention that "automation will continue to displace low-skilled or unskilled workers in America's manufacturing firms and offices." In the area of globalization, you may be intrigued by Friedman's concept of making yourself "untouchable" or his distinction between "fungible" and "nonfungible" work. Other possibilities: Blinder's urging young people to prepare for high-end "personal services" jobs; Lohr's quoting the assertion that "We need a revolution in services." Any of these—and numerous other principles or terms introduced in the readings—could serve as a lens through which to study a work-related situation.

In writing your analysis, follow the Guidelines on pp. 203–204. Use the fruits of your earlier assignments involving summary and explanation. Consider using the following structure for your analysis.

- An introductory paragraph that sets a context for the topic you will be analyzing and presents the claim you are going to support. Your claim (your thesis) may appear at the end of this paragraph (or introductory section).

- A paragraph or two explaining the developments responsible for the accelerating changes in the American workplace. See the Explanatory Synthesis assignment and the assignment for your first or second Summary. You may be able to import one or both into this argument. See also the Alan Blinder Summary on pp. 19–22.

- A paragraph or two explaining the jobs that are most—and least—at risk from these changes. See the Explanatory Synthesis assignment and the assignment for your first or second Summary; you may be able to import them into your argument. See also the example topic under "Read: Prepare to Write," p. 311.

- *Claims and support:* (Re)state your analytical claim at the end of a paragraph that sets a work-related experience you know well (or the experience of an individual or group you have researched) in the context of the changing workplace of the twenty-first century.

- A paragraph defining the key term or principle you will be using in your analysis—the term borrowed, with attribution, from one of the source authors in this chapter.

- A systematic inquiry into the work-related experience your analysis seeks to illuminate. *This is the main section of the paper.* It should consist of several paragraphs, each focused on revealing a specific element of the topic.

- A paragraph of supporting data from the Bureau of Labor Statistics.

- A conclusion in which you argue that, based on the insights gained through your analysis, the experience, individual, or group in question can now be understood more deeply. See Chapter 6, pp. 247–253, for advice on concluding your paper.

Argument

Having carefully read the selections in this chapter, develop an argument about the changing landscape of work in the twenty-first century. Adopt *one* of these statements as your claim:

> *Claim #1*
> **Faced with the changing landscape of work, many students will need to adjust their career plans and modify their assumptions about how best to succeed after college.**

Or:

Claim #2
Even though the workplace is likely to undergo profound changes in the coming decades, many students will not need to make significant adjustments in their current plans in order to succeed after college.

In planning your synthesis, review the master list of topics and notes that you and your classmates generated for Group Assignments #1 and #2 (pp. 311–313), and draw on what the authors of the passages have written about these topics in developing your outline. Devise a thesis that summarizes your argument and plan to support it with facts, opinions, and statistics from the passages.

Note that one synthesis—a single paper—could not possibly refer to every topic, or every connection among authors, that you have found. The craft of preparing and writing a synthesis depends on your ability to *select* closely related topics and then to make and develop a claim that links and can be supported by them. You don't have to refer to *all* of the selections in this chapter while developing your paper, but you will likely want to refer to most of them. You may even want to research additional sources.

In writing your argument, follow the Guidelines for Writing Syntheses on pp. 93–95. Use the products of your earlier assignments involving summary and explanation. Consider using the following structure for your argument.

- An introductory paragraph that sets a context for the topic and presents the claim you are going to support in the argument that follows. Your claim (or thesis) may appear at the end of this paragraph (or introductory section).

- A paragraph or two explaining the developments responsible for the accelerating changes in the American workplace. See the Explanatory Synthesis assignment and the assignment for your first or second Summary. You may be able to import one or both into this argument. See also the Alan Blinder Summary on pp. 19–22.

- A paragraph or two explaining the jobs that are most—and least—at risk from these changes. See the Explanatory Synthesis assignment and the assignment for your first or second Summary; you may be able to import them into your argument. See also the example topic under "Read: Prepare to Write," on p. 311.

- An analysis of one job or profession and the importance of considering examples such as this for students preparing to enter the workplace. See the Analysis assignment, paragraphs of which may help you support the claim of this argument.

- Reasons for optimism if students can adapt their thinking—or not, depending on which claim you develop. See the Explanatory

Synthesis assignment and consider importing paragraphs into this argument.

- The dangers if students do not take into account the opinions, facts, and statistics available.

- Counterargument and rebuttal: Consider developing one or both of two counterarguments for Claim #1:

> College years are not only a preparation for the world of work, they are also a safe harbor from it—a time to think broadly, impractically even, and look beyond the narrow needs of the workplace.
>
> Because no one can predict the future with certainty, a college student is best served by training broadly, developing core skills (such as critical thinking, writing, and speaking), and later meeting the challenges of the future workplace as they arise.

Possible counterarguments for Claim #2:

> (1) A favorite uncle or aunt tells you: "You'd better be realistic about your studies. Changes are coming, and you need to be prepared." (2) A college education is expensive. It's unconscionable to spend all that money and not get the training you need for a good job immediately after graduation.

- A paragraph or two of conclusion. See Chapter 6, pp. 247–253, for advice on concluding your papers.

Where you place the individual elements of this argument synthesis will be your decision as a writer. Which sources to use and what logic to present in defense of your claim are also yours to decide. See pp. 156–161 and pp. 177–179 for help in thinking about structuring and supporting your argument.

A Note on Incorporating Quotations and Paraphrases   Identify the sources you intend to use for your synthesis. Working with a phrase, sentence, or brief passage from each, use a variety of the techniques discussed in the section Incorporating Quotations into Your Sentences (pp. 47–53) to advance your argument. Some of these sentences should demonstrate the use of ellipsis marks and brackets. (See pp. 49–52 in Chapter 1.) Paraphrase passages as needed, and incorporate the paraphrases into your papers.

■ THE READINGS

Read the following passages, then complete each writing assignment above. In summarizing, evaluating, analyzing, and synthesizing these sources, you are practicing skills fundamental to all college-level writing.

A cautionary note: When writing source-based papers, it is all too easy to become careless in giving proper credit. Before drafting your paper, review the section on Avoiding Plagiarism (pp. 53–55) and the relevant sections on Citing Sources in Chapter 7.

WORK AND WORKERS IN THE TWENTY-FIRST CENTURY

Richard W. Judy and Carol D'Amico

The selection that follows forms the opening section of the Hudson Institute's Workforce 2020, *which appeared twenty years after its predecessor,* Workforce 2000. *That book challenged policymakers and employers to consider and respond to trends that were revolutionizing the landscape of work at the end of the twentieth century. In this update, Hudson analysts Richard Judy and Carol D'Amico similarly ask us to project current trends into the near future so that we can respond meaningfully. The Hudson Institute describes itself as "a non-partisan policy research organization dedicated to innovative research and analysis that promotes global security, prosperity, and freedom."*

You have before you a map, one that describes the journey America's labor force is now beginning. It lays out the general contours of the employment landscape, not the fine details or the specific landmarks, depicting the many roads to what we call "Workforce 2020." Some will be superhighways and some will be dead ends for American workers. Although immense forces shape the employment landscape, we believe that we know the difference between the superhighways and the dead ends.

Skilled cartographers in the guise of economists, education experts, and policy researchers at Hudson Institute helped prepare this map. It offers our best ideas about what lies ahead and what Americans—collectively and individually, in large and small firms, in federal agencies and in small-town development commissions—should do to prepare for the journey to Workforce 2020.

Our map is needed because American workers at the threshold of the twenty-first century are embarking on mysterious voyages. They seek glittering destinations but travel along roads with numerous pitfalls and unexpected diversions. Many workers—more than at any time in America's history—will reach the glittering destinations. They will enjoy incomes unimaginable to their parents, along with working and living conditions more comfortable than anyone could have dreamed of in centuries past. But many other workers will be stymied by the pitfalls along the road or baffled by the diversions. Their standard of living may stagnate or even decline. Much is already known today about what will divide the hopeful from the anxious along these roads, and we will share that knowledge here.

What makes America's voyage to the workforce of 2020 unique is not merely the heights to which some will climb or the difficulties others will endure. Two qualities give a truly unprecedented character to the roads ahead. First, the gates have lifted before almost every American who wishes to embark on the journey of work. Age, gender, and race barriers to employment opportunity have broken down. What little conscious discrimination remains will be swept away soon—not by government regulation but by the enlightened self-interest of employers. Second, more and more individuals now undertake their own journeys through the labor force, rather than "hitching rides" on the traditional mass transportation provided by unions, large corporations, and government bureaucracies. For most workers, this "free agency" will be immensely liberating. But for others, it will provoke anxiety and anger. For all workers, the premium on education, flexibility, and foresight has never been greater than it will be in the years ahead.

5   What explains the immense satisfactions and dangers ahead? What makes possible the unprecedented expansion of opportunities in the labor force? What forces conspire, for better or worse, to demand that we compete as individuals and contend with ever-changing knowledge and skill requirements? We highlight four forces in particular.

First, the pace of technological change in today's economy has never been greater. It will accelerate still further, in an exponential manner. Innovations in biotechnology, computing, telecommunications, and their confluences will bring new products and services that are at once marvelous and potentially frightening. And the "creative destruction"* wrought by this technology on national economies, firms, and individual workers will be even more powerful in the twenty-first century than when economist Joseph Schumpeter coined the phrase fifty years ago. We cannot know what innovations will transform the global economy by 2020, any more than analysts in the mid-1970s could have foreseen the rise of the personal computer or the proliferation of satellite, fiber-optic, and wireless communications. However, the computer and telecommunications revolutions enable us to speculate in an informed manner on the implications of today's Innovation Age for the American workforce:

- Automation will continue to displace low-skilled or unskilled workers in America's manufacturing firms and offices. Indeed, machines will substitute for increasingly more sophisticated forms of human labor. Even firms that develop advanced technology will be able to replace some of their employees with technology (witness the "CASE tools" that now assist in writing routine computer code) or with lower-paid workers in other countries (witness the rise of India's computer programmers and data processors).

- However, experience suggests that the development, marketing, and servicing of ever more sophisticated products—and the use of those products in an ever richer ensemble of personal and professional services—almost certainly will create more jobs than the underlying technology will destroy. On the whole, the new jobs will also be safer, more stimulating, and better paid than the ones they replace.

- The best jobs created in the Innovation Age will be filled by Americans (and workers in other advanced countries) to the extent that workers possess the skills required to compete for them and carry them out. If jobs go unfilled in the U.S., they will quickly migrate elsewhere in our truly global economy.

---

*In *Capitalism, Socialism and Democracy* (1942), Joseph Schumpeter coined the term "creative destruction" to describe the process by which capitalism, operating through "new consumers, goods, the new methods of production or transportation, the new markets, [and] the new forms of industrial organization, . . . incessantly revolutionizes the economic structure *from within*, incessantly destroying the old one, incessantly creating a new one" (New York, Harper: 1975, pp. 82–85; <http://transcriptions.english.ucsb.edu/archive/courses/liu/english25/materials/schumpeter.html>).

- Because the best new jobs will demand brains rather than brawn, and because physical presence in a particular location at a particular time will become increasingly irrelevant, structural barriers to the employment of women and older Americans will continue to fall away. Americans of all backgrounds will be increasingly able to determine their own working environments and hours.

Second, the rest of the world matters to a degree that it never did in the past. We can no longer say anything sensible about the prospects for American workers if we consider only the U.S. economy or the characteristics of the U.S. labor force. Fast-growing Asian and Latin American economies present us with both opportunities and challenges. Meanwhile, communications and transportation costs have plummeted (declining to almost zero in the case of information exchanged on the Internet), resulting in what some have called "the death of distance." Whereas the costs of shipping an automobile or a heavy machine tool remain consequential, the products of the world's most dynamic industries—such as biological formulas, computers, financial services, microchips, and software—can cross the globe for a pittance. Investment capital is also more abundant and more mobile than ever before, traversing borders with abandon in search of the best ideas, the savviest entrepreneurs, and the most productive economies. The implications of this globalization for U.S. workers are no less complex than the implications of new technology:

- Manufacturing will continue to dominate U.S. exports. Almost 20 percent of U.S. manufacturing workers now have jobs that depend on exports; that figure will continue to escalate. America's growing export dependence in the early twenty-first century will benefit most of America's highly productive workers, because many foreign economies will continue to expand more rapidly than our own, thereby generating massive demand for U.S. goods. Skilled workers whose jobs depend on exports are better paid than other U.S. manufacturing workers as a rule, because the U.S. enjoys a comparative advantage in the specialized manufacturing and service sectors that create their jobs. These workers also tend to earn more than similar workers in other countries.

- But globalization will affect low-skilled or unskilled American workers very differently. They will compete for jobs and wages not just with their counterparts across town or in other parts of the U.S., but also with low-skilled workers around the globe. As labor costs become more important to manufacturers than shipping costs, the U.S. will retain almost no comparative advantage in low-skilled manufacturing. Jobs in that sector will disappear or be available only at depressed wages. Second or third jobs and full-time employment for both spouses—already the norm in households headed by low-skilled workers—will become even more necessary.

- Manufacturing's share of total U.S. employment will continue to decline, due to the combined effects of automation and globalization. But the millions of high-productivity manufacturing jobs that remain will be more highly skilled and therefore better paid than at any other time in U.S. history. Employment growth, meanwhile, will remain concentrated in services, which also will benefit increasingly from export markets and will offer high salaries for skilled workers.

- Globalization and technological change will make most segments of the U.S. economy extremely volatile, as comparative advantages in particular market segments rise and then fall away. Small- and medium-sized firms will be well situated to react to this volatility, and their numbers will grow. Labor unions will cope badly with this rapidly evolving economy of small producers, and their membership and influence will shrink. Individual workers will change jobs frequently over time. For those who maintain and improve their skills, the changes should bring increasing rewards. But the changes may be traumatic for those who fall behind the skills curve and resist retraining.

Third, America is getting older. At some level, all of us are aware of this. Our parents and grandparents are living longer, and we are having fewer children. But U.S. public policy as well as many employers have yet to come to grips with the full implications of America's aging. The oldest among America's so-called baby boomers—the massive cohort born between 1945 and 1965—will begin to reach age 65 in 2010. By 2020, almost 20 percent of the U.S. population will be 65 or older. There will be as many Americans of "retirement age" as there are 20–35-year-olds. America's aging baby boomers will decisively affect the U.S. workforce, through their departure from and continued presence in it, and as recipients of public entitlements and purchasers of services:

- America's taxpayer-funded entitlements for its aging population—Medicare and Social Security—are likely to undergo profound changes in the next two decades. The tax rates necessary to sustain the current "pay-as-you-go" approach to funding these programs as the baby boomers retire will rise, perhaps precipitously, unless the expectations of retirees regarding their benefits become more modest, the economy grows more strongly than expected, or the programs receive fundamental overhauls.

- Depending on how the funding of entitlement programs is resolved and how well individual baby boomers have prepared for retirement, some who reach age 65 will continue to require outside income and will be unable to retire. Many others will not want to retire and will seek flexible work options. As average life expectancies extend past 80 years of age, even many of the well-heeled will conclude that twenty years on golf courses and cruise ships do not present enough of a challenge.

- Whether they continue working or simply enjoy the fruits of past labors, America's aging baby boomers will constitute a large and powerful segment of the consumer market. Their resulting demand for entertainment, travel, and other leisure-time pursuits; specialized health care; long-term care facilities; and accounting, home-repair, and other professional services will fuel strong local labor markets throughout the U.S., but particularly in cities and regions that attract many retirees. The jobs created by this boom in the service sector in local economies may replace many of the low-skilled or unskilled manufacturing jobs the U.S. stands to lose, though not always at comparable wages.

Fourth, the U.S. labor force continues its ethnic diversification, though at a fairly slow pace. Most white non-Hispanics entering America's early twenty-first century workforce simply will replace exiting white workers; minorities will constitute slightly more than half of net new entrants to the U.S. workforce. Minorities will account for only about a third of total new entrants over the next decade. Whites constitute 76 percent of the total labor force today and will account for 68 percent in 2020. The share of African-Americans in the labor force probably will remain constant, at 11 percent, over the next twenty years. The Asian and Hispanic shares will grow to 6 and 14 percent, respectively. Most of this change will be due to the growth of Asian and Hispanic workforce representation in the South and West. The changes will not be dramatic on a national scale. The aging of the U.S. work-force will be far more dramatic than its ethnic shifts.

10   In summary, Hudson Institute's *Workforce 2020* offers a vision of a bifurcated U.S. labor force in the early twenty-first century. As we envision the next twenty-plus years, the skills premium appears even more powerful to us than it did to our predecessors who wrote *Workforce 2000*. Millions of Americans with proficiency in math, science, and the English language will join a global elite whose services will be in intense demand. These workers will command generous and growing compensation. Burgeoning local markets for services in some parts of the U.S. will continue to sustain some decent-paying, low-skill jobs. But other Americans with inadequate education and no technological expertise—how many depends in large part on what we do to improve their training—will face declining real wages or unemployment, particularly in manufacturing.

THE UNTOUCHABLES
Thomas L. Friedman

Thomas Friedman, an investigative reporter and a columnist for the New York Times, *won the National Book Award for* From Beirut to Jerusalem *(1989) and three Pulitzer Prizes for international reporting and commentary. Most recently he has written* Hot, Flat, and Crowded *(2008). The selection that follows appears in his best seller* The World Is Flat: A Brief History of the Twenty-First Century *(2005), in which Friedman explores the opportunities and dangers associated with globalization. Friedman uses the word "flat" to describe "the stunning rise of middle classes all over the world." In this newly flat world, "we are now connecting all the knowledge centers on the planet together into a single global network, which—if politics and terrorism do not get in the way—could usher in an amazing era of prosperity, innovation, and collaboration, by companies, communities, and individuals."*

If the flattening of the world is largely (but not entirely) unstoppable, and if it holds out the potential to be as beneficial to American society in general as past market evolutions have been, how does an individual get the best out of it? What do we tell our kids?

My simple answer is this: There will be plenty of good jobs out there in the flat world for people with the right knowledge, skills, ideas, and self-motivation to seize them. But there is no sugar-coating the new challenge: Every young American today would be wise to think of himself or herself as competing against every young Chinese, Indian, and Brazilian. In Globalization 1.0, countries had to think globally to thrive, or at least survive. In Globalization 2.0, companies had to think globally to thrive, or at least survive. In Globalization 3.0, individuals have to think globally to thrive, or at least survive. This requires not only a new level of technical skills but also a certain mental flexibility, self-motivation, and psychological mobility. I am certain that we Americans can indeed thrive in this world. But I am also certain that it will not be as easy as it was in the last fifty years. Each of us, as an individual, will have to work a little harder and run a little faster to keep our standard of living rising.

"Globalization went from globalizing industries to globalizing individuals," said Vivek Paul, the Wipro president.* "I think today that people working in most jobs can sense how what they are doing integrates globally: 'I am working with someone in India. I am buying from someone in China. I am selling to someone in England.' As a result of the ability to move work around, we have created an amazing awareness on the part of every individual that says: 'Not only does my work have to fit into somebody's global supply chain, but I myself have to understand how I need to compete and have the skill sets required to work at a pace that fits the supply chain. And I had better be able to do that as well or better than anyone else in the world.'" That sense of responsibility for one's own advancement runs deeper than ever today. In many global industries now, you have got to justify your job every day with the value you create and the unique skills you contribute. And if you don't, that job can fly away farther and faster than ever.

In sum, it was never good to be mediocre in your job, but in a world of walls, mediocrity could still earn you a decent wage. You could get by and then some. In a flatter world, you *really* do not want to be mediocre or lack any passion for what you do. You don't want to find yourself in the shoes of Willy Loman in *Death of a Salesman*, when his son Biff dispels his idea that the Loman family is special by declaring, "Pop! I'm a dime a dozen, and so are you!" An angry Willy retorts, "I am not a dime a dozen! I am Willy Loman, and you are Biff Loman!"

5   I don't care to have that conversation with my girls, so my advice to them in this flat world is very brief and very blunt: "Girls, when I was growing up, my parents used to say to me, 'Tom, finish your dinner—people in China and India are starving.' My advice to you is: Girls, finish your homework—people in China and India are starving for your jobs." And in a flat world, they can have them, because in a flat world there is no such thing as an American job. There is just a job, and in more cases than ever before it will go to the best, smartest, most productive, or cheapest worker—wherever he or she resides.

The New Middle

It is going to take more than just doing your homework to thrive in a flat world, though. You are going to have to do the *right kind* of homework as well. Because the companies that are adjusting best to the flat world are not just making minor changes, they are changing the whole model of the work they do and how they do it—in order to take advantage of the flat-world platform and to compete with others who are doing the same. What this means is that students also have to fundamentally reorient what they are learning and educators how they are teaching it. They can't just keep the same old model that worked for the past fifty years, when the world was round. This

---

*Wipro is a global technology company that provides "integrated business, technology, and process solutions" in North and South America, Europe, the Middle East, Asia, and Australia.

set of issues is what I will explore in this and the next chapter: What kind of good middle-class jobs are successful companies and entrepreneurs creating today? How do workers need to prepare themselves for those jobs, and how can educators help them do just that?

Let's start at the beginning. The key to thriving, as an individual, in a flat world is figuring out how to make yourself an "untouchable." That's right. When the world goes flat, the caste system gets turned upside down. In India, untouchables are the lowest social class, but in a flat world everyone should want to be an untouchable. "Untouchables," in my lexicon, are people whose jobs cannot be outsourced, digitized, or automated. And remember, as analyst David Rothkopf notes, most jobs are not lost to outsourcing to India or China—most lost jobs are "outsourced to the past." That is, they get digitized and automated. *The New York Times*'s Washington bureau used to have a telephone operator–receptionist. Now it has a recorded greeting and voice mail. That reception job didn't go to India; it went to the past or it went to a microchip. The flatter the world gets, the more anything that can be digitized, automated, or outsourced will be digitized, automated, or outsourced. As Infosys CEO Nandan Nilekani likes to say, in a flat world there is "fungible and nonfungible work." Work that can be easily digitized, automated, or transferred abroad is fungible. One of the most distinguishing features of the flat world is how many jobs—not just blue-collar manufacturing jobs but now also *white-collar service jobs*—are becoming fungible. Since more of us work in those service jobs than ever before, more of us will be affected.

. . .

[W]ho will the untouchables be? What jobs are not likely to become fungible, easy to automate, digitize, or outsource? I would argue that the untouchables in a flat world will fall into three broad categories. First are people who are really "special or specialized." This label would apply to Michael Jordan, Madonna, Elton John, J. K. Rowling, your brain surgeon, and the top cancer researcher at the National Institutes of Health. These people perform functions in ways that are so special or specialized that they can never be outsourced, automated, or made tradable by electronic transfer. They are untouchables. They have a global market for their goods and services and can command global wages.

Second are people who are really "localized" and "anchored." This category includes many, many people. They are untouchables because their jobs must be done in a specific location, either because they involve some specific local knowledge or because they require face-to-face, personalized contact or interaction with a customer, client, patient, colleague, or audience. All these people are untouchables because they are anchored: my barber, the waitress at lunch, the chefs in the kitchen, the plumber, nurses, my dentist, lounge singers, masseurs, retail sales clerks, repairmen, electricians, nannies, gardeners, cleaning ladies, and divorce lawyers. Note that these people can be working in high-end jobs (divorce lawyer, dentist), vocational jobs (plumber, carpenter), or low-end jobs (garbage collector, maid). Regardless of that worker's level of sophistication, their wages will be set by the local market forces of supply and demand.

10 That then brings me to the third broad category. This category includes people in many formerly middle-class jobs—from assembly line work to data entry to

securities analysis to certain forms of accounting and radiology—that were once deemed nonfungible or nontradable and are now being made quite fungible and tradable thanks to the ten flatteners.* Let's call these the "old middle" jobs. Many of them are now under pressure from the flattening of the world. As Nandan Nilekani puts it: "The problem [for America] is in the middle. Because the days when you could count on being an accounts-payable clerk are gone. And a lot of the middle class are where that [old] middle is. . . . This middle has not yet grasped the competitive intensity of the future. Unless they [do], they will not make the investments in reskilling themselves and you will end up with a lot of people stranded on an island."

That is not something we want. The American economy used to look like a bell curve, with a big bulge in the middle. That bulge of middle-class jobs has been the foundation not only of our economic stability but of our political stability as well. Democracy cannot be stable without a broad and deep middle class. We cannot afford to move from a bell curve economy to a barbell economy—with a big high end and a bigger low end and nothing in the middle. It would be economically unfair and politically unstable. As former Clinton national economic adviser Gene Sperling rightly argues, "We either grow together or we will grow apart."

So if the next new thing is the automation and outsourcing of more and more old middle-class jobs, then the big question for America—and every other developed country—is this: What will be the jobs of the new middle, and what skills will they be based on? In the United States, new middle jobs are coming into being all the time; that is why we don't have large-scale unemployment, despite the flattening of the world. But to get and keep these new middle jobs you need certain skills that are suited to the flat world—skills that can make you, at least temporarily, special, specialized, or anchored, and therefore, at least temporarily, an untouchable. In the new middle, we are all temps now.

WILL YOUR JOB BE EXPORTED?

Alan S. Blinder

Alan S. Blinder is the Gordon S. Rentschler Memorial Professor of Economics at Princeton University. He has served as vice chairman of the Federal Reserve Board and was a member of President Clinton's original Council of Economic Advisers. This article first appeared in The American Prospect *in November 2006. The following summary of "Will Your Job Be Exported?" appears in Chapter 1, in the context of a discussion on how to write summaries. See pp. 8–13 for the complete text of this important article.*

In "Will Your Job Be Exported?" economist Alan S. Blinder argues that the quality and security of future jobs in America's services sector will be determined by how "offshorable" those jobs are. For the past twenty-five years, the greater a worker's

---

*In *The World Is Flat,* Friedman argues that ten forces have "flattened" the world. These forces include the fall of the Berlin Wall (November 1989), the emergence of Internet connectivity, and the outsourcing of work.

skill or level of education, the better and more stable the job. No longer. Advances in technology have brought to the services sector the same pressures that forced so many manufacturing jobs offshore to China and India. The rate of offshoring in the service sector will accelerate, and jobs requiring both relatively little education (like call-center staffing) and extensive education (like software development) will increasingly be lost to workers overseas.

These losses will "eventually exceed" losses in manufacturing, but not all services jobs are equally at risk. While "personal services" workers (like barbers and surgeons) will be relatively safe from offshoring because their work requires close physical proximity to customers, "impersonal services" workers (like call-center operators and radiologists), regardless of their skill or education, will be at risk because their work can be completed remotely without loss of quality and then delivered via phone or computer. "[T]he relative demand for labor in the United States will [probably] shift away from impersonal services and toward personal services."

Blinder recommends three courses of action. He advises young people to plan for "a high-end personal services occupation that is not offshorable." He urges educators to prepare the future workforce by anticipating the needs of a personal services economy and redesigning classroom instruction and vocational training accordingly. Finally, he urges the government to adopt policies that will improve existing personal services jobs by increasing wages for low-wage workers; retraining workers to take on better jobs; and increasing opportunities in high-demand, well-paid areas like nursing and carpentry. Ultimately, Blinder wants America to prepare a new generation to "lead and innovate" in an economy that will continue exporting jobs that require "following and copying."

INTO THE UNKNOWN
The Economist

The following piece first appeared in The Economist *(November 13, 2004).*

Where will the jobs of the future come from?

"Has the machine in its last furious manifestation begun to eliminate workers faster than new tasks can be found for them?" wonders Stuart Chase, an American writer. "Mechanical devices are already ousting skilled clerical workers and replacing them with operators. . . . Opportunity in the white-collar services is being steadily undermined." The anxiety sounds thoroughly contemporary. But Mr. Chase's publisher, MacMillan, "set up and electrotyped" his book, *Men and Machines*, in 1929.

The worry about "exporting" jobs that currently grips America, Germany and Japan is essentially the same as Mr. Chase's worry about mechanization 75 years ago. When companies move manufacturing plants from Japan to China, or call-center workers from America to India, they are changing the way they produce things. This change in production technology has the same effect as automation: some workers in America, Germany and Japan lose their jobs as machines or foreign workers take over. This fans fears of rising unemployment.

What the worriers always forget is that the same changes in production technology that destroy jobs also create new ones. Because machines and foreign workers can perform the same work more cheaply, the cost of production falls.

That means higher profits and lower prices, lifting demand for new goods and services. Entrepreneurs set up new businesses to meet demand for these new necessities of life, creating new jobs.

5   As Alan Greenspan, chairman of America's Federal Reserve Bank, has pointed out, there is always likely to be anxiety about the jobs of the future, because in the long run most of them will involve producing goods and services that have not yet been invented.* William Nordhaus, an economist at Yale University, has calculated that under 30% of the goods and services consumed at the end of the 20th century were variants of the goods and services produced 100 years earlier. "We travel in vehicles that were not yet invented that are powered by fuels not yet produced, communicate through devices not yet manufactured, enjoy cool air on the hottest days, are entertained by electronic wizardry that was not dreamed of and receive medical treatments that were unheard of," writes Mr. Nordhaus. What hardy late 19th-century American pioneer would have guessed that, barely more than a century later, his country would find employment for (by the government's latest count) 139,000 psychologists, 104,000 floral designers and 51,000 manicurists and pedicurists?

Even relatively short-term labor-market predictions can be hazardous. In 1988, government experts at the Bureau of Labor Statistics confidently predicted strong demand in America over the next 12 years for, among others, travel agents and [gas]-station attendants. But by 2000, the number of travel agents had fallen by 6% because more travellers booked online, and the number of pump attendants was down to little more than half because drivers were filling up their cars themselves. Of the 20 occupations that the government predicted would suffer the most job losses between 1988 and 2000, half actually gained jobs. Travel agents have now joined the government's list of endangered occupations for 2012. Maybe they are due for a modest revival. You never know.

The bureau's statisticians are now forecasting a large rise in the number of nurses, teachers, salespeople, "combined food preparation and serving workers, including fast food" (a fancy way of saying burger flippers), waiters, truck drivers and security guards over the next eight years. If that list fails to strike a chord with recent Stanford graduates, the bureau also expects America to create an extra 179,000 software-engineering jobs and 185,000 more places for computer-systems analysts over the same period.

Has the bureau forgotten about Bangalore? Probably not. Catherine Mann of the Institute for International Economics points out that the widely quoted number of half a million for [Information Technology] jobs "lost" to India in the past couple of years takes as its starting point the year 2001, the top of the industry's cycle. Most of the subsequent job losses were due to the recession in the industry rather than to an exodus to India. Measured from 1999 to 2003, the number of IT-related white-collar jobs in America has risen. . . .

Ms. Mann thinks that demand will continue to grow as falling prices help to spread IT more widely through the economy, and as American companies demand more tailored software and services. Azim Premji, the boss of Wipro,† is currently trying to expand his business in America. "IT professionals are in short supply in America," says Mr. Premji. "Within the next few months, we will have a labor shortage."

---

*Alan Greenspan served as chairman of the Federal Reserve Bank from 1987 to 2006.
†See footnote on p. 324.

10   If that seems surprising, it illustrates a larger confusion about jobs and work. Those who worry about the migration of white-collar work abroad like to talk about "lost jobs" or "jobs at risk." Ashok Bardhan, an economist at the University of California at Berkeley, thinks that 14 [million] Americans, a whopping 11% of the workforce, are in jobs "at risk to outsourcing." The list includes computer operators, computer professionals, paralegals and legal assistants. But what Mr. Bardhan is really saying is that some of this work can now also be done elsewhere.

What effect this has on jobs and pay will depend on supply and demand in the labor market and on the opportunity, willingness and ability of workers to retrain. American computer professionals, for instance, have been finding recently that certain skills, such as maintaining standard business-software packages, are no longer in such demand in America, because there are plenty of Indian programmers willing to do this work more cheaply. On the other hand, IT firms in America face a shortage of skills in areas such as tailored business software and services. There is a limited supply of fresh IT graduates to recruit and train in America, so companies such as IBM and Accenture are having to retrain their employees in these sought-after skills.

Moreover, Mr. Bardhan's list of 14 [million] jobs at risk features many that face automation anyway, regardless of whether the work is first shipped abroad. Medical transcriptionists, data-entry clerks and a large category of 8.6 [million] miscellaneous "office support" workers may face the chop as companies find new ways of mechanizing paperwork and capturing information.

Indeed, the definition of the sort of work that Indian outsourcing firms are good at doing remotely—repetitive and bound tightly by rules—sounds just like the sort of work that could also be delegated to machines. If offshoring is to be blamed for this "lost" work, then mechanical diggers should be blamed for usurping the work of men with shovels. In reality, shedding such lower-value tasks enables economies to redeploy the workers concerned to jobs that create more value.

Stuart Chase understood the virtuous economics of technological change, but he still could not stop himself from fretting. "An uneasy suspicion has gathered that the saturation point has at last been reached" he reflected darkly. Could it be that, with the invention of the automobile, central heating, the phonograph and the electric refrigerator, entrepreneurs had at long last emptied the reservoir of human desires? He need not have worried. Today's list of human desires includes instant messaging, online role-playing games and internet dating services, all unknown in the 1920s. And there will be many more tomorrow.

EMPLOYMENT PROJECTIONS: 2006–2016 SUMMARY

Bureau of Labor Statistics

The Bureau of Labor Statistics, a division of the U.S. Department of Labor, releases ten-year employment projections, updated every two years, as part of a "60-year tradition of providing information to individuals who are making education and training choices, entering the job market, or changing careers." What follows is a summary of the data released by the BLS on December 4, 2007. At the end of this selection, you will be referred to ten tables (available online) accompanying this summary.

Over the 2006–2016 decade, total employment is projected to increase by 15.6 million jobs, or 10 percent, slightly less than the 15.9 million jobs, or 12 percent, during the 1996–2006 decade. The labor force filling these jobs, while becoming more racially and ethnically diverse, is projected to grow more slowly than in the past. This slowdown in the growth of the labor force is expected, in part, because of the aging and retiring of baby boomers. As a result, the need to replace workers who retire or leave the labor force for other reasons—called replacement needs—is projected to create a significant number of additional job openings.

Industry Employment

—Employment growth is projected to continue to be concentrated in the service-providing sector of the economy. Service-providing industries will generate almost all of the employment gain from 2006 to 2016 and will provide more than three-quarters of all jobs in 2016. Professional and business services and health care and social assistance, the industry sectors with the largest employment growth, will add 8.1 million jobs, more than half of the projected increase in total employment. (See Table 1.*)

—Within the goods-producing sector, construction is the only sector projected to grow. Employment in manufacturing will decline by 1.5 million jobs. This decline is half of the 3 million manufacturing jobs lost in the previous decade (1996–2006). Employment in goods-producing industries is expected to decrease from 14.9 to 13.1 percent of total employment. (See Table 1.)

—The 10 detailed industries with the largest projected wage and salary employment growth—led by management, scientific, and technical consulting services; employment services; and general medical and surgical hospitals—all are in the service-providing sector. (See Table 2.)

5   —Four of the 10 detailed industries with the largest projected wage and salary employment declines are in the manufacturing sector, including printing and related support activities and motor vehicle parts manufacturing. (See Table 3.)

Occupational Employment

—Professional and related occupations and service occupations—two major occupational groups on opposite ends of the educational and earnings ranges—are projected to grow the fastest and add the most jobs, accounting for more than 6 of 10 new jobs created over the 2006–2016 decade. (See Table 4.)

—A large portion of job gains and losses are projected to be concentrated in a small number of detailed occupations. The 30 occupations with the largest numeric increases will account for more than half of all new jobs. (See Table 5.) The 30 occupations with the largest numeric declines will account for more than two-thirds of all job losses from declining occupations. (See Table 8.)

—Nineteen of the 30 occupations with the largest job growth are in professional and related occupations and service occupations. (See Table 5.)

—Twenty-eight of the 30 fastest-growing occupations are in professional and related occupations and service occupations. (See Table 6.)

*The URLs for Tables 1–10 can be found on p. 332.

10   —Job openings generally are more numerous in large occupations. Of the 30 occupations with the largest number of total job openings due to growth and net replacements, 29 are projected to have more than 1 million jobs in 2016. (See Table 7.)

—Production occupations and farming, fishing, and forestry occupations are the two major occupational groups projected to lose employment over the decade. (See Table 4.)

Education and Training Categories

—For 19 of the 30 occupations with the largest job growth, short- or moderate-term on-the-job training is the most significant source of postsecondary education or training. (See Table 5.)

—For 15 of the 30 fastest-growing occupations, a bachelor's or higher degree is the most significant source of postsecondary education or training. (See Table 6.)

—On-the-job training and work experience are the most significant sources of post-secondary education or training for 24 of the 30 occupations projected to have the most total job openings due to growth and net replacements. (See Table 7.)

15   —For 28 of the 30 occupations projected to have the largest employment declines, on-the-job training and work experience are the most significant sources of postsecondary education or training. (See Table 8.)

—The proportion of jobs in occupations that typically require a college degree will increase slightly between 2006 and 2016. (See Table 9.)

Labor Force

—The civilian labor force is projected to increase by 12.8 million over the 2006–2016 decade, reaching 164.2 million by 2016. This 8.5 percent increase is less than the 13.1 percent increase over the previous decade—1996 to 2006—when the labor force grew by 17.5 million. (See Table 10.)

—The number of workers in the 55-and-older group is projected to grow by 46.7 percent, nearly 5.5 times the 8.5 percent growth projected for the labor force overall. (See Table 10.)

—Youths—those between the ages of 16 and 24—will decline in numbers and will see their share of the labor force fall from 14.8 to 12.7 percent. The number of prime-age workers—those between the ages of 25 and 54—will increase by 2.4 percent, but their share of the labor force will decline from 68.4 to 64.6 percent. (See Table 10.)

20   —The Hispanic labor force is expected to grow by 29.9 percent, reaching 26.9 million by 2016, while the non-Hispanic labor force is projected to grow by only 5.1 percent. (See Table 10.)

—Increases in the labor force will vary by race. Whites will remain the largest race group despite relatively slow growth of 5.5 percent, composing 79.6 percent of the labor force by 2016. The number of blacks will grow by 16.2 percent and will constitute 12.3 percent of the labor force. Asians will continue to be the fastest-growing race group, increasing by 29.9 percent and will make up 5.3 percent of the labor force by 2016. (See Table 10.)

- Table 1. Employment by major industry sector, 1996, 2006, and projected 2016

  [http://www.bls.gov/news.release/ecopro.t01.htm]

- Table 2. The 10 industries with the largest wage and salary employment growth, 2006–2016 (1)

  [http://www.bls.gov/news.release/ecopro.t02.htm]

- Table 3. The 10 industries with the largest wage and salary employment declines, 2006–2016 (1)

  [http://www.bls.gov/news.release/ecopro.t03.htm]

- Table 4. Employment by major occupational group, 2006 and projected 2016

  [http://www.bls.gov/news.release/ecopro.t04.htm]

- Table 5. The 30 occupations with the largest employment growth, 2006–2016

  [http://www.bls.gov/news.release/ecopro.t05.htm]

- Table 6. The 30 fastest-growing occupations, 2006–2016

  [http://www.bls.gov/news.release/ecopro.t06.htm]

- Table 7. The 30 occupations with the largest number of total job openings due to growth and net replacements, 2006–2016

  [http://www.bls.gov/news.release/ecopro.t07.htm]

- Table 8. The 30 occupations with the largest employment declines, 2006–2016

  [http://www.bls.gov/news.release/ecopro.t08.htm]

- Table 9. Employment and total job openings by postsecondary education and training category

  [http://www.bls.gov/news.release/ecopro.t09.htm]

- Table 10. Civilian labor force by age, sex, race, and Hispanic origin, 1996, 2006, and projected 2016

  [http://www.bls.gov/news.release/ecopro.t10.htm]

■ Looking Forward: Five Professions ■

The selections that follow explore the contours of future work in engineering, business, technology, law, and medicine. As you read, apply the observations of writers from the previous selections to the particulars of these five professions. Questions to consider:

- To what extent do the observations of Judy and D'Amico, Friedman, Blinder, and *The Economist* ring true?
- What features do you find most striking about future employment in each profession?
- What features generalize across professions?

- To what extent do you find yourself encouraged or discouraged by what you read?

- To what extent does the Bureau of Labor Statistics data confirm what the authors report (or project) about each profession?

Read actively. For each selection, make marginal notes that both summarize and evaluate. Also, create conversations across sources: List topics and assign authors and page references to each, as appropriate.

ENGINEERING

Victoria Reitz

The selection that follows, originally titled "Want to Outsourceproof Your Career? Don't Become a Commodity," first appeared in Machine Design *(April 26, 2007).*

We asked over 1,500 engineers what they thought about their careers, what keeps them in their jobs, and what the future of engineering will look like. Sixty-four percent of them feel secure or very secure in their current positions, and 24% say engineers have been laid off from their companies in the last year. And best of all, salaries are up. The average annual wage is $76,900, up from $73,300 last year. For 65% of survey takers this was an increase of 1 to 5% over last year.

Sixty-two percent received a bonus, overtime, or special incentive compensation, based mainly on company profit sharing and personal performance. About 40% received 1 to 5% of their annual pay as bonus.

Most respondents, 78%, would recommend engineering as a career to friends and family, and 61% believe the job has gotten better during their careers. Of the 71% whose companies outsource, 78% farm out manufacturing, 44% outsource mechanical design, and 30% contract CAD work.

Is There a Future for Engineers?

Many survey takers expressed concern about the future of technology and innovation in the U.S., feeling that as more manufacturing jobs head overseas, there will be less demand for technical skills. But experts say just the opposite. "There is a high, unmet demand for engineering talent," says Scott Kingdom, a senior client partner and global managing director at Korn/Ferry International. Kingdom oversees recruiting at the executive search firm. "Employers I talk to say they would hire more engineers if they could find them." He also adds, "Because engineering skills are in such demand, other countries are busy training citizens to fill these roles."

5   Why the shortage of talent? "One reason might be that our educational system doesn't foster and promote science and engineering," Kingdom adds. "Another is that the economy is moving more and more into the service sector. Some of our best minds get pulled into service-related organizations such as banking and consulting, that might otherwise have gone into engineering."

Make Yourself Valuable

What can you do to ensure a successful career? "Sharp, intelligent engineers with leadership and business skills can just about write their own career path," says Kingdom. "Make sure your technical skills are cutting edge and develop management skills. Get involved in jobs that put you in leadership roles," he adds. Also, consider accepting projects and responsibilities outside the U.S.

Innovation is the key to keeping technical jobs in the U.S., according to Kingdom. Businesses that manufacture commodities will likely go offshore, "and probably should go offshore. But where there is real innovation, there is real demand for engineering services and skills."

The same can be said of your career. If your skills and talent are a commodity, you're easily replaced. Make sure you add value and innovation. "There's no one in this economy that can sit still and decide they don't want to change. The world is evolving around us so fast, you'll be irrelevant quickly."

BUSINESS

Tom Peters

The selection that follows, originally titled "The New Wired World of Work: A More Transparent Workplace Will Mean More White-collar Accountability and Less Tolerance for Hangers-on," first appeared in Business Week *(April 9, 2008).*

You're hiking along near the Grand Canyon in August, 2000, but fretting about the progress your virtual partner in Kuala Lumpur has made in the past 24 hours? No problem! Your local Kampgrounds of America campsite now has Internet access.

Call it the new wired world of work. Depending on how you view it, it's intrusive, pervasive, or merely ubiquitous. But it's definitely not your dad's office. And this perpetually plugged-in existence is just the beginning of the changes we'll see in the 21st century white-collar workplace.

Work in the '50s and '60s meant trudging to the same office for decades. Same colleagues. Same processes, mostly rote. Former MCI Communications Chief Bill McGowan called yesterday's middle managers "human message switches." And the information was laughably dated. Closing the account books at month's end could drag on for weeks. Customer data were nonexistent, or hopelessly unreliable.

But in the next few years, whether at a tiny company or behemoth, we will be working with an eclectic mix of contract teammates from around the globe, many of whom we'll never meet face-to-face. Every project will call for a new team, composed of specially tailored skills. Info that's more than hours old will be viewed with concern.

5   Every player on this team will be evaluated—pass by pass, at-bat by at-bat—for the quality and uniqueness and timeliness and passion of her or his contribution. And therein lies the peril, and the remarkable opportunity, of this weird, wired, wild new age of work. White-collar accountability has until now been mostly an oxymoron. Show up, suck up, process your paper flow with a modicum of efficiency, and you could count on a pretty decent end-of-year evaluation, a cost-of-living-plus raise, and a sure-as-death-and-taxes 40-year tenure at Desk No. 263.

Now you are like a New York Yankees or Los Angeles Dodgers closer. A couple of blown saves following a night on the town and your pressured and performance-driven teammates, more than your manager, are ready to show you the exit. This will hold for the freshly minted University of Wisconsin grad as well as the 56-year-old who had envisioned himself on a pain-free coast toward retirement. There may be a tight labor market for stellar performers, but the flip side is much less tolerance for hangers-on.

As enterprise resource-planning software and other such systems wreak havoc on the vast majority of staff jobs in the next decade, what will it take for you and me to navigate and win? Here's a list of minimal survival skills for the 21st century office worker:

- Mastery: To thrive in tomorrow's transparent team environment, the typical white-collar worker will have to be noticeably good at something the world values. "HR guy" doesn't cut it. Nor does "CPA." What subset of, say, techie recruiting skills or international accountancy excellence makes you a clearly valued contributor? I firmly believe that if you can't describe your distinction in the space of a one-sixteenth-page Yellow Pages ad, you will be doomed.

- Who Do You Know?: The new Rolodex will deemphasize bosses and traditional power figures, focusing more on peers (future project mates!) who appreciate your clear-cut contributions. I consider my own electronic Rolodex to be my Extended Global University, colleagues I can call upon (and who can call upon me) to further my current and future projects.

- Entrepreneurial Instinct: You do not have to start your own business. But as I see it, all these projects are entrepreneurial. So you must act as if you were running your own business. Think of yourself as Maggie Inc., who happens to be at General Electric Capital Services Inc. at the moment. And speaking of which, I fully expect women to dominate managerial roles. I think they tend to handle ambiguity better than we guys do. The new world is a floating crap game, with new projects, new teammates, and a constant need to adjust. Those who can operate in the absence of laid-out bounds will be the leaders.

- Love of Technology: Technology is changing everything. Believe the hype—if anything, it's understated. You need not be a technologist per se, but you must embrace technology. "Coping" with it is not enough.

- Marketing: You do not have to become a shameless self-promoter, a la Martha Stewart. But you must get your story out on the airwaves. Do it via your personal Web site. Do it by telling your project's story at a trade show.

- Passion for Renewal: You've got to constantly improve and, on occasion, reinvent yourself. My bread and butter—at age 57—are my lectures. But I imagine that the Internet will devour many conventional meetings in a few years. Hence I am madly working with several groups that will deliver my message via the new technologies.

I love to read Dilbert and usually choke with laughter. But I have a problem with the subtext: My company stinks, my boss stinks, my job stinks. If that's your take— at this moment of monumental change and gargantuan opportunity—then I can only feel sad for you. We get to reinvent the world. I feel so damn lucky!

TECHNOLOGY AND SERVICES

Steve Lohr

The selection that follows, originally titled "Creating the Jobs of the Future: Universities Develop 'Services Science,'" first appeared in the International Herald Tribune *(April 18, 2006).*

On his Asian trip last month, President George W. Bush urged Americans to not fear the rise toward prosperity of emerging economies like India. Education, Bush said, was the best response to globalization, climbing further up the ladder of skills to "fill the jobs of the 21st century."

But a ladder to where? That is, where are educated young Americans likely to find good jobs that will not be shipped off to India or China?

The answer, according to a growing number of universities, corporations and government agencies, is in what is being called services science. The hybrid field seeks to use technology, management, mathematics and engineering expertise to improve the performance of service businesses like transportation, retailing and health care—as well as service functions like marketing, design or customer service that are also crucial in manufacturing industries.

A couple of dozen universities—including the University of California at Berkeley, Arizona State, Stanford, North Carolina State, Rensselaer Polytechnic Institute and Georgia Tech—are experimenting with courses or research programs in the field.

5   The push for services science is partly a game of catch-up, a belated recognition that services now account for 70 percent of the U.S. economy, so education, research and policy should reflect the shift. "Services is a drastically understudied field," said Matthew Realff, director of a new program at the National Science Foundation to finance university research in the field. "We need a revolution in services."

Kurt Koester, a 24-year-old graduate student in engineering at Berkeley, is eager to take part. Yet engineering alone, he observes, can often be outsourced to lower-cost economies overseas.

Koester's special interest is in biomedical engineering, which combines engineering and biology. And he is also taking the services science course at the Haas School of Business at Berkeley. He figures it should help him someday better manage teams of technologists, spot innovations and new markets, and blend products and services.

"I love engineering, but I want a much broader and more diverse background," he said. "Hopefully, that will be my competitive advantage."

His personal strategy, according to economists, is the best way to prepare for an increasingly global labor market.

10   "This is how you address the global challenge," said Jerry Sheehan, a senior economist at the Organization for Economic Cooperation and Development. "You have to move up to do more complex, higher-value work."

Representatives from technology companies including International Business Machines, Accenture, Electronic Data Systems and Hewlett-Packard, a few universities and government agencies met in Washington in December to discuss how to raise interest in services science. A further step is a conference on education in services science being held Tuesday at the National Academy of Sciences.

IBM is a leading corporate proponent of services science, sponsoring workshops, awarding research grants and helping develop course materials.

IBM itself is a striking example of the shift toward services over the past decade or two. Once known as a computer maker, the company now gets half its revenue from services. And increasingly, IBM is moving into sophisticated technology services, by working with corporate customers to automate and streamline business tasks like purchasing, human relations and customer relations programs.

In recent years, IBM has shopped the global labor market, expanding significantly in India, especially for software programming work. But it has also reoriented and retrained its existing work force to support the swing to services.

15   The researchers in its laboratories were dubious at first. "The response here was there is no science in services," recalled Paul Horn, the senior vice president in charge of the IBM labs. "But as people got into it, they got excited by working on the fascinating problems in services."

Baruch Schieber, 48, is one of the converts. After joining IBM in 1987, Schieber did basic research and published articles in scholarly journals mostly on algorithms that optimize computing calculations. Yet the math techniques used to make work flow efficiently through a computer—a complex system—can be applied to other complex systems in business. That is what Schieber did, first in manufacturing and later in services.

One recent assignment had Schieber studying drivers and dispatchers at Boston Coach, a limousine service that operates in 10 cities. His job was to create a computerized optimization system to improve the utilization of vehicles and drivers in Boston and New York, where the company handles more than 1,000 rides a day.

The system gathered real-time data on car locations, reservations, travel times, traffic patterns, airport conditions and flight times. The system generated recommendations to the dispatchers about which car and driver to send for each ride. The car utilization rate rose 20 percent, and revenue increased 10 percent.

An accumulation of technological advances is behind the growing interest in services science. The spread of high-speed Internet access, low-cost computing, wireless networks, electronic sensors and ever-smarter software are the tools for building a "globalized services economy," said Anatole Gershman, director of research at Accenture Technology Labs. "That's what is new here."

20   The current wave of technology, according to Gershman, is the digital equivalent of national railways and electric motors in the 19th century. They paved the way for new companies and new kinds of industrial organization, from national retailers like Sears to assembly-line mass production.

He points to projects his company is doing as examples of services made possible by new technology. In transportation, networked sensors and analytic software are being used to diagnose the condition of engines. The goal is to make the mechanical upkeep of everything from jets to municipal buses more intelligent, shifting from regimented maintenance schedules to as-needed maintenance, which can reduce repair and maintenance costs by 50 percent, he said.

In health care, Gershman said, it should be possible to use tiny implants to monitor a person's biological functions, whisk reports wirelessly to personalized databases, automatically analyze the results, and send alerts and updates to patients and doctors.

"Just what will be done with this technology we don't know," Gershman said. "But the significant thing is that we now have the underpinnings for the construction of new services."

Even in manufacturing, the competitive edge of many American companies lies in the intangible realm of service work. Look at the iPod. Apple Computer farms out the manufacturing of its popular music player to Asian subcontractors. But Apple designed the iPod and wrote the software for easily finding, storing and playing music. It built the iPod brand, and guided its advertising and marketing. In short, Apple keeps for itself the most intellectually challenging, creative work, which adds the most value and pays the highest wages.

25   The high-end work, experts say, typically taps several disciplines, requires conceptual thinking and pattern recognition. Such work cannot be easily reduced to a simple step-by-step recipe. "Those are the jobs that are very hard to automate or ship to India," said Frank Levy, a labor economist at the Massachusetts Institute of Technology.

LAW

Tom McGrath

The selection that follows, originally titled "The Last Days of the Philadelphia Lawyer," first appeared in Philadelphia *magazine (April 2008). While nominally the writer investigates changes in the legal profession in Philadelphia, the changes he observes are occurring nationwide, throughout the profession.*

Lawyers, it probably goes without saying, like to argue, but the one thing they all agree on is that over the past two decades, their once high-minded profession has been transformed into a high-stakes business. "A revolution has occurred," says Michael Coleman, one of the city's preeminent legal recruiters. That revolution may only be a prologue to an even bigger transformation now taking place: the high-stakes business slamming head-on into the fast-moving, and generally unforgiving, 21st-century global economy.

"The world is flat," Alderman tells his Penn Law students one day, as they're seated around a seminar table. Alderman's course is called "The Law of Law Firms," and in contrast to the legal-reasoning courses that make up the bulk of a law student's education, this class attempts to give the next generation of lawyers a realistic view of the business they're getting themselves into.

. . . [T]he technological and economic changes affecting all of us are certainly making an impact on lawyers—particularly on the dozen or so largest, most prestigious firms in Philadelphia. For starters, the pressure is on firms to be bigger and broader—to open offices in all the places around the world where their clients are doing business. . . .

Even more important, though, is that the market for legal services has been, if not globalized, at least nationalized—which means that Philly firms are now competing for clients with firms in New York and Chicago and Charlotte and anywhere else easily reachable with a BlackBerry and some frequent-flier miles.

5   The heightened competition—combined with the bottom-line mentality that began taking hold at least 15 years ago—has spun off its own consequences. While lawyers at big firms make more money than ever, there's a certain sense of ennui among many in the profession. Previous generations of attorneys had the sense that in practicing law, they were serving the public good. A fair number of lawyers today fret that what they do has no more value than selling used cars. "It can suck the soul out of you," one lawyer complains of the constant focus on billable hours and client development and all the other things lawyers now do that aren't actually practicing law. Says another, of the pressure to make more and more profits, "How much is enough?"

The answer to . . . the broader question of why the legal profession in America currently operates the way it does—can be traced back to changes that started in the 1980s. . . .

The impact of the *American Lawyer* rankings [of law firms according to how much money they earned] over the past two decades is tough to overestimate. For starters, they've transformed the mind-sets of many lawyers—or at least those who run large law firms. Twenty years ago, a partner at a Philadelphia firm might have been very happy making $150,000 per year—until he saw that lawyers at a firm in, say, Boston were making $250,000 per year. Telling competitive people like lawyers how much their peers were making was like giving someone with an addictive personality his first hit on a crack pipe.

Just as important, though, is that over the years, large firms have come to realize that the Am Law rankings are their best marketing tool when it comes to attracting the best law-school graduates and, now, the best partners from other firms—partners who bring with them books of clients that contribute handsomely to the bottom line. After all, why stay at a firm with profits per partner of only $400,000 per year when folks at the firm down the road are making 20 percent more?

. . . [T]he Am Law rankings—both literally, in the sense that firms care enormously about where they fall on them, and figuratively, in the sense that they represent a legal world all about the Benjamins—have become the dominant measuring stick in the legal industry.

10   If there's an irony in law having become a business, it's that law, it turns out, isn't a very *good* business—or at least doesn't have a very efficient business model. While manufacturers typically make money through economies of scale, and other service professionals, like investment bankers or architects, make money by taking a percentage of a deal or the cost of a project, lawyers for the most part still work for an hourly wage. In short, they're in the business of selling their time.

The problem, of course, is that time is finite, so even if you're selling those hours for an exorbitantly high rate—a handful of lawyers in Philadelphia can charge up to $1,000 an hour—it can be tough to build a successful, globally competitive business.

To compensate for that labor-intensive business model, firms have adopted various strategies. Strategy number one: Make young lawyers—associates—bill as many hours as humanly possible. In the 1960s and '70s, associates at big firms were expected to bill between 1,600 and 1,800 per year; today, the expectation is generally around 2,200 hours per year. And since not every hour you spend at the office can be billed to a client, associates typically end up putting in 80-to-90-hour weeks. With starting associate salaries approaching $150,000 at Philly's biggest firms, this might not be so bad—if the work was consistently challenging intellectually, and if the path to becoming a partner was as fast as it used to be. But some associates complain that they spend their days locked in the office, pushing through paper. As for partnership, it's a reward that takes longer and longer to realize these days.

But associates aren't the only ones for whom the rules of the game have changed. While once it was enough for a partner at a firm simply to be a smart practitioner who understood the law and served his clients well, today the focus is less on what you do in the courtroom or boardroom than on what kind of business you bring in the door. In the past, becoming a partner at a big firm was pretty much like becoming a tenured college professor—you were there for as long as you wanted to be. Today, it's not unheard-of for a partner to be de-equitized—essentially, pushed back to being a salaried employee—or driven out completely. "I know some lawyers in their 50s who have been asked to leave their firms because they don't have a book of business," says Steve Cozen, of Cozen O'Connor. "The problem is, they were never told they *had* to have a book of business. It used to be enough for them just to be good lawyers."

In some firms, it's no longer enough even to have clients—they must be clients who can pay hourly rates hefty enough to support an insatiable appetite for profits. Over the past few years, Dechert [Philadelphia's most profitable law firm] has rid itself of several practice areas that simply didn't command high enough rates from clients, including media law, which was led by respected First Amendment attorney Amy Ginensky, who last year moved to Pepper Hamilton after 28 years at Dechert. Ginensky says she could have stayed, but she didn't like the constraints the firm's economic strategy placed on her. "I didn't want to decide what cases to take based solely on how much money they would make," she says. Dechert's strategy is one any businessman would understand instantly—if a product line isn't profitable enough, you discontinue it and move on to something else. But for the lawyers involved, who were asked to practice a different type of law or simply to leave, it's a tough adjustment to make. "We're dealing with human capital, not widgets," says legal recruiter Michael Coleman. "I don't know if when you're 45, you want to be retooled."

MEDICINE

Matt Richtel

The selection that follows, originally titled "Young Doctors and Wish Lists: No Weekend Calls, No Beepers," first appeared in the New York Times *(January 7, 2004).*

Jennifer C. Boldrick lights up when the topic turns to blisters, eczema and skin cancer. She is also a big fan of getting a full night of sleep. And the combination of these interests has led Dr. Boldrick to become part of a marked shift in the medical profession.

Dr. Boldrick, 31, a graduate of Stanford University Medical School, is training to become a dermatologist. Dermatology has become one of the most competitive fields for new doctors, with a 40 percent increase in students pursuing the profession over the last five years, compared with a 40 percent drop in those interested in family practice.

The field may have acquired its newfound chic from television shows like "Nip/Tuck" and the vogue for cosmetic treatments like Botox, but for young doctors it satisfies another longing. Today's medical residents, half of them women, are choosing specialties with what experts call a "controllable lifestyle." Dermatologists typically do not work nights or weekends, have decent control over their time and are often paid out of pocket, rather than dealing with the inconveniences of insurance.

"The surgery lifestyle is so much worse," said Dr. Boldrick, who rejected a career in plastic surgery. "I want to have a family. And when you work 80 or 90 hours a week, you can't even take care of yourself."

5   Other specialties also enjoying a surge in popularity are radiology, anesthesiology and even emergency-room medicine, which despite their differences all allow doctors to put work behind them when their shifts end, and make medicine less all-encompassing, more like a 9-to-5 job.

What young doctors say they want is that "when they finish their shift, they don't carry a beeper; they're done," said Dr. Gregory W. Rutecki, chairman of medical education at Evanston Northwestern Healthcare, a community hospital affiliated with the Feinberg School of Medicine at Northwestern University.

Lifestyle considerations accounted for 55 percent of a doctor's choice of specialty in 2002, according to a paper in the *Journal of the American Medical Association* in September by Dr. Rutecki and two co-authors. That factor far outweighs income, which accounted for only 9 percent of the weight prospective residents gave in selecting a specialty.

Many of the brightest students vie for several hundred dermatology residency spots. The National Residency Matching Program, which matches medical school graduates to residency openings, reported that in 2002, 338 medical school seniors were interested in dermatology, up from 244 in 1997—though the 2002 figure still represented only 2.3 percent of the potential doctor pool.

In 2002, 944 seniors wanted to pursue anesthesiology, compared with 243 five years earlier—while the interest in radiology almost doubled, to 903 from 463, according to the matching program's figures.

10   Numerous medical educators noted that the growth of interest in these fields coincided with a drop in students drawn to more traditional—and all-consuming—fields. In 2002, the number of students interested in general surgery dropped to 1,123 from 1,437, for example.

And that has many doctors and educators concerned. "There's a brain drain to dermatology, radiology and anesthesia," Dr. Rutecki said. He said that students who are not selected for residencies in these lifestyle-friendly specialties are choosing internal medicine by default.

"Not only are we getting interest from people lower in the class, but we're getting a number of them because they have nowhere else to go," Dr. Rutecki said.

This notion of a "brain drain" to subspecialties from the bread and butter fields of medicine is not new. But in recent years it has come to be associated with a flight to more lucrative fields. What is new, say medical educators, is an emphasis on way of life. In some cases, it even means doctors are willing to take lower-paying jobs—say, in emergency room medicine—or work part time. In other fields, like dermatology and radiology, doctors can enjoy both more control over their time and a relatively hefty paycheck.

According to the American Medical Association, a dermatologist averages $221,000 annually for 45.5 hours of work per week. That's more lucrative—and less time-consuming—than internal medicine or pediatrics, where doctors earn around $135,000 and spend more than 50 hours a week at work. A general surgeon averages $238,000 for a 60-hour week, while an orthopedist makes $323,000 for a 58-hour week. The number of dermatology residencies has been steadily growing. The American Academy of Dermatology says there are 343 dermatology residents in their third year, 377 in their second year, and 392 in their first.

15   The trend comes as the medical profession is already struggling to balance the demands of patient care with the strain put on doctors from overwork. Since last year, new rules have limited a resident's hours to 80 hours a week.

Some medical careers, like radiology, entail working long hours but not responding to patient emergencies on nights and weekends.

Educators point to a number of factors to explain the newfound emphasis on lifestyle. Dr. Elliott Wolfe, director of professional development for medical students at Stanford, cites the growing proportion of medical students who are women; in the 2002–3 year they made up 49.1 percent of entering students, according to the American Medical Association. Dermatology offers more control and income than, say, pediatrics and family medicine, which have traditionally drawn women.

Lee Ann Michelson, director of premedical and health care advising at Harvard University, said undergraduates considering a future in medicine are extremely concerned about whether they can have a life outside of medicine. She said she talks to numerous children of physicians who are concerned they will be as absent in the lives of their children, as their parents were.

The symbol for "controllable lifestyle" is dermatology. And when residents graduate they can count on plenty of faces and bodies to heal and reconstruct, thanks to an aging, and affluent, population. One-stop dermatology spas seem to open weekly in Manhattan, offering lunchtime visitors quick-fix lip fillers, laser procedures and face peels. It's not fast food, it's fast facial.

20   "You make your own hours. You can see 15 patients a day, or 10 patients a day. There are very few emergencies. It's not an acute situation, ever," said Dr. Dennis Gross, a Manhattan dermatologist. Plus, he said the procedures dermatologists perform can be lucrative; a 12-minute Botox treatment can cost a patient $400, with the doctor keeping half, for instance.

And the procedures often are elective, meaning that patients pay out of their own pockets. "It's cash, check or credit card," said Dr. Wolfe of Stanford.

The difference in lives is well illustrated by the experience of Z. Paul Lorenc and Marek M. Lorenc, 48-year-old twin brothers who chose careers on different ends of the spectrum.

Marek is a dermatologist in Santa Rosa, Calif., north of San Francisco. He gets into work at 8 a.m., leaves at 6 p.m., and is rarely called to the hospital at night, giving him ample time to spend with his wife and two children. "When I'm done," he said, "I'm a husband and a father. I go to soccer games. I coach soccer games."

His brother is a plastic surgeon in Manhattan. He arrives at work before 7, kissing his two sleeping children before he leaves the house. He performs face lifts, breast augmentations, brow lifts and liposuction, intensive surgical procedures that demand round-the-clock availability at the hospital. He often does not get home until after 9 p.m., and he goes into the office on Saturday. He doesn't see his children nearly as much as he would like, but he said that is what the pursuit of excellence in his specialty requires.

25   He is bothered by what he sees as a lack of devotion by today's medical students. A faculty member at New York University's medical school, he said the interest in way of life is across the board.

"When residents come looking for jobs, they ask, 'How often do I have to take night calls,'" he said. "There's less intensity, less determination and less devotion."

But Dr. Boldrick said she is not trying to avoid hard work. While she intends to have two children, she still plans to work full time.

What she wants to avoid is chaos and uncertainty and the lack of control that comes with other specialties. "I see people around me who like to do those things, and I think, 'Thank God,'" said Dr. Boldrick, who added that she feels she can make a contribution without taking on the meat and potatoes of say, internal medicine. "If I force myself to do something that didn't make me happy in order to pay a debt to society, that wouldn't do anyone any good," she said.

The reasoning resonates with Dr. Clara Choi, 32, a resident in radiation oncology at Stanford. Dr. Choi finds her field fascinating but pointed out that it also demands few unexpected calls to the hospital.

30   Married, she plans to have a family. "I'd have to get someone to take care of the baby if I spent every third or fourth night in the hospital," Dr. Choi said.

Dr. Rutecki says he completely understands, having missed out on a lot in the lives of his own two children.

"I missed a lot because I was on call three to five days a week," he said. "Rather than take this data as an opportunity to criticize, I think we recognize that this is the way medicine is moving."

CREDITS

Used by permission and protected by the Copyright Laws of the United States. The printing, copying, redistribution, or retransmission of the Material without express written permission is prohibited.

Rifkin: "Using Fossil Fuels in Energy Process Gets Us Nowhere" by Jeremy Rifkin. Los Angeles Times, Nov. 9, 2003, p. M5. Used by permission of Jeremy Rifkin.

Romm: "Lots of Hot Air About Hydrogen" by Joseph Romm, Los Angeles Times, Mar 28, 2004. Used by permission of the author.

Hunte: "The Hydrogen Fuel Cell Car" and "The Car of the Future?" by Janice Hunte. Reprinted by permission. Ministry of Economic Development: Diagram from Ministry of Economic Development, New Zealand, "Sustainable Energy: Fuel Cells," from Creating a Sustainable Energy System for New Zealand, Oct. 2004.

CHAPTER 4

Review Panel: *Mass Shootings at Virginia Tech, April 16, 2007.* Report of the Review Panel: Summary of Key Findings.

Gammage and Burling: "Laws Limit Schools Even After Alarms" by Jeff Gammage and Stacey Burling. Philadelphia Inquirer, Apr 19, 2007, A01. Used by permission.

Christian Science Monitor: "Perilous Privacy at Virginia Tech" Reproduced with permission from the September 4, 2007, issue of The Christian Science Monitor (www.csmonitor.com). © 2007 The Christian Science Monitor. All rights reserved.

McMurray: From "Colleges Are Watching Troubled Students" by Jeffrey McMurray. Associated Press. 28 Mar. 2008. Used with permission.

"Virginia Tech Massacre Has Altered Campus Mental Health Systems." Attributed to the Associated Press; appeared in the Los Angeles Times, 14 Apr. 2008. Used by permission.

The Family Educational Rights and Privacy Act [FERPA]: U.S. Code, Ch.31, sec. 1232g.

CHAPTER 5

Hekker: "The Satisfactions of Housewifery in an Age of 'Do Your Own Thing'" by Terri Martin Hekker. From The New York Times, December 20 © 1977. The New York Times. All rights reserved. Used by permission and protected by the Copyright Laws of the United States. The printing, copying, redistribution, or retransmission of the Material without express written permission is prohibited.

CHAPTER 8

PHOTO CREDITS

INDEX

Abstracts
  citation of
    APA, 304
  research with, 278
Academic writing
  analysis in, 189
  assignments in, 227
  critiques in, 59
  summaries required in, 4–5
  syntheses in, 88
Ad hominem attack, as logical
    fallacy, 65–66
Addiction
  to alcohol, 193
  to television, 192–193
Advertisements
  analysis of, 214
  balance in, 219–220
  clarity and simplicity in, 221
  emphasis in, 222
  movement in, 220–221
  as popular culture, 213
  proportion in, 220
  unity in, 221
Advertising (Cohen), 218–222
Advertising the American Dream
    (Marchand), 214, 218–219
Age, of American workers, 322
The Age of American Unreason
    (Jacoby), 142
Agreement, in critical reading, 70–71
Alcohol, addiction to, 193
All the King's Men (Warren), 89
Alternative energy, appeal of,
    124–125
The Ambassadors (James), 263
America: History and Life, 271
American Heritage Dictionary, 242
American Lawyer, 339
The American Prospect, 8
American Psychological Association
    (APA) citation style
  books in, 306–307
  electronic sources in, 302–305
  guide to, 288

in-text, 301–302
periodicals in, 305–306
American Statistics Index, 280
Americans With Disabilities Act, 148
Analogy
  in argument synthesis, 171
  false, 68
Analysis
  in academic writing, 189
  argument components in, 202–204
  assignments on
    motivation, 208–209
    thesis, 202–203
    visual media, 214
    work landscape, 315–316
  conclusion of, 204
  context for, 203
  critical reading for, 208
  critique *vs.*, 190
  definition in, 188–190, 200
  examples of, 192–198
  exercises on, 193–194
  literary, 189
  organization of, 204–206
  papers with
    summaries in, 4
    syntheses in, 88
  personal use of, 199
  process, 189
  in professional writing, 189
  revealing with, 190–191
  summary *vs.*, 207
  as systematic examination, 207
  of visual media, 213–214
  writing
    guidelines for, 203–204
    logic in, paragraph-by-
      paragraph, 205–206
    principle in, 200–202
    purpose in, considering, 199
    question phrasing in, 204–205
    reading strategies for, 200
    revision of, 206–208
    source attribution in, 208
    thesis formulation in, 202–204

348